ROMANTICISM

AGAINST THE TIDE OF MODERNITY

POST-CONTEMPORARY INTERVENTIONS

SERIES EDITORS

STANLEY FISH AND FREDRIC JAMESON

Romanticism Against the Tide of Modernity

MICHAEL LÖWY AND ROBERT SAYRE

Translated by Catherine Porter

DUKE UNIVERSITY PRESS

DURHAM / LONDON

2001

©2001 Duke University Press
All rights reserved
Printed in the United States of America on acid-free paper ∞
Typeset in Carter and Cone Galliard by Keystone Typesetting, Inc.
Library of Congress Cataloging-in-Publication Data appear
on the last printed page of this book.

015803

Contents

∞

ROMANTICISM

AGAINST THE TIDE OF MODERNITY

1

Redefining Romanticism

∞

What is Romanticism? Apparently an undecipherable enigma, the Romantic phenomenon seems to defy analysis, not only because its exuberant diversity resists any attempt to reduce it to a common denominator but also and especially because of its fabulously contradictory character, its nature as *coincidentia oppositorum:* simultaneously (or alternately) revolutionary and counterrevolutionary, individualistic and communitarian, cosmopolitan and nationalistic, realist and fantastic, retrograde and utopian, rebellious and melancholic, democratic and aristocratic, activist and contemplative, republican and monarchist, red and white, mystical and sensual. These contradictions permeate not only the Romantic phenomenon as a whole but also the life and work of individual authors, and sometimes even individual texts. Some critics seem inclined to see contradiction, dissonance, and internal conflict as the only unifying element of Romanticism.[1] However, it is difficult to take that thesis as anything but an avowal of confusion.

All these complications are compounded because since the nineteenth century we have been in the habit of using the term "Romantic" to designate not only novelists, poets, and artists but also political ideologues (political Romanticism has been the object of numerous studies), philosophers, theologians, historians, economists, and others. In what sense do such diverse phenomena, located in such disparate spheres of cultural life, derive from a single concept?

The easiest solution seems to be to eliminate the term itself. The best-known representative of this approach (which goes back to the nineteenth century) is the American critic Arthur O. Lovejoy, who proposed in a well-known article that literary critics should refrain from using a term that lends itself to such confusion: "The word 'romantic' has come to mean so many things that, by itself, it means nothing. It has ceased to perform the function of a verbal sign. . . . The one really radical remedy — namely, that we should all cease talking about Romanticism — is, I fear, certain not to be adopted." This approach may appear to be effective, but it strikes us as sterile. Indeed, it could be applied to almost any term in literature ("realism"), politics ("left"), or economics ("capitalism"), without increasing our knowledge in the least. Once purged of all its ambiguous terms, language would perhaps be more rigorous, but it would also be quite impoverished. The task of literary criticism — or of cultural sociology — is not to purify language but rather to try to understand and explain it. One of Lovejoy's arguments is the national and cultural multiplicity of the phenomenon. At the very most, one might speak of "Romanticisms," in his view, but not of a universal "Romanticism." Still, as one of Lovejoy's recent critics, Stefanos Rozanis, has observed, the multiplicity of Romanticism's literary expressions in various countries — as a manifestation of national and individual particularities — poses no more than a limited philological problem that in no way calls into question the essential unity of the phenomenon.[2]

As Lovejoy himself predicted, the attempt to cure the Romantic fever simply by abolishing the term has not won support. Most scholars start from the more reasonable hypothesis that there is no smoke without fire. If Romanticism has been a topic of discussion for two centuries, if the term has been used to designate a variety of phenomena, then it must correspond to some reality. Once that point has been acknowledged, the real questions arise. What fire are we talking about? What feeds it? And why does it spread in all directions?

Another expeditious method for getting rid of the irritating contradictions of Romanticism is to dismiss them by attributing them to the inconsistency and frivolity of the Romantic writers and ideologues themselves. The most eminent representative of this school of interpretation is Carl Schmitt, the author of a well-known book on political Romanticism. According to Schmitt,

> the riotous disorder [*tumultuarische Buntheit,* "tumultuous colors"] of
> the romantic is reduced to its simple principle of a subjectivized occa-

sionalism, and the mysterious contradiction of the diverse political tendencies of so-called political romanticism is explained as a consequence of the moral deficiency of a lyricism that can take any content at all as the occasion for aesthetic interest. For the question of whether monarchist or democratic, conservative or revolutionary ideas are romanticized is irrelevant to the nature of the romantic. They signify only occasional points of departure for the romantic productivity of the creative ego.[3]

It is difficult to believe that one can account for the political writings of such authors as Jean-Jacques Rousseau, Edmund Burke, Franz von Baader, or Friedrich Schleiermacher through their "aesthetic interest" or their "occasionalism"—not to mention a so-called moral deficiency. Schmitt emphasizes the "passivity," the "lack of virility," and the "feminine exaltation" (*feminine Schwärmerei*) of authors such as Novalis, Friedrich Schlegel, or Adam Müller, but the argument reveals more about the prejudices of its author than about the nature of Romanticism.

Other writers, too, refer to the femininity of Romanticism—always pejoratively. This is the case, for example, with Benedetto Croce, who tries to account for some of the contradictions by highlighting the "feminine . . . , impressionable, sentimental, incoherent, and voluble" nature of the Romantic soul. The same note is struck by the anti-Romantic (and antifeminist) author Pierre Lasserre, for whom "Romantic idiosyncrasy is inherently feminine." Romanticism everywhere manifests "the instincts and work of woman left to her own devices": that is why it "systematizes, glorifies, and divinizes submission to pure subjectivism."[4] There is no point in dwelling on the superficiality and sexism of such remarks, which make "feminine" synonymous with moral degradation or intellectual inferiority and which claim to make consistency an exclusively masculine attribute.

In reality, for a great many students of Romanticism, the problem of contradictions (political ones in particular) does not even come up, because they strip the phenomenon of all its political and philosophical dimensions and reduce it to a mere literary school whose most visible features they then describe in greater or lesser detail. In its most trivial form, this approach contrasts Romanticism with "classicism." According to the *Larousse du XXᵉ Siècle*, for example, "the term *romantic* is used for writers at the beginning of the 19th century who freed themselves from the classical rules of composition and style. In France, Romanticism embodied a profound reaction against the classic national literature, whereas in England and Germany it constituted the primitive background for the indigenous genius."[5] The second hypothesis is also entertained favorably by several authors; for example, for Fritz Strich, Romanticism is the expression of the deepest innate tendencies of the German soul.[6]

Other critics, without going beyond the strictly literary view of Romanticism, acknowledge the inadequacy of defining the movement by way of nonclassical rules of composition or through the national soul, and they attempt to find more substantial common denominators. This is the approach adopted by the three most famous North American specialists in the history of Romanticism: M. H. Abrams, René Wellek, and Morse Peckham. For Abrams, their diversity notwithstanding, the Romantics share certain values, such as life, love, liberty, hope, and joy. They also have in common a new conception of the mind, one that emphasizes creative activity rather than the reception of external impressions: the mind is a lamp giving off its own light, not a mirror reflecting the world.[7] Wellek, polemicizing against Lovejoy's nominalism, asserts that the Romantic movements form a unified whole and possess a coherent set of ideas, each of which implies the others: imagination, nature, symbol, and myth.[8] Peckham, attempting to reconcile the theses propounded by Lovejoy and Wellek, proposes to define Romanticism as a revolution of the European mind against static, mechanistic thought and in favor of dynamic organicism. Its common values are change, growth, diversity, the creative imagination, and the unconscious.[9]

These attempts at definition — like numerous other, similar attempts — no doubt designate significant features that are present in the work of many Romantic writers, but they fail to deliver the essence of the phenomenon. In the first place, they appear completely arbitrary: why are certain features selected and not others? Authors make their own choices and sometimes revise their earlier decisions in favor of a new, equally arbitrary list. Peckham, for example, reconsidering his 1951 theory ten years later, notes that organicism was really a product of Enlightenment philosophy. It was simply a metaphysical episode of Romanticism, destined to be abandoned, because all the Romantic hypotheses are eventually rejected as inadequate. Romanticism is, in fact, a "pure assertion of identity" that cannot be given any specific and definitive orientation. As the self is the only source of order and value, Romanticism is fundamentally antimetaphysical.[10] Unable to assign any content whatsoever to this self, Peckham's new attempt leads to a conceptual void and takes us back to the starting point — the tumultuous multiplicity of colors in the service of the creative ego cherished by Carl Schmitt.

Given the arbitrary nature of the choice of certain features, several critics try to sidestep the difficulty by creating longer and longer lists of common denominators of Romantic literature. The most extensive of these lists to date is one Henry Remak proposed in an article on European Romanticism in which he establishes a systematic tabulation of twenty-three common factors: medievalism; imagination; the cult of strong emotions; subjectivism; interest in nature, mythology, and folklore; *Weltschmerz;* symbolism; exoticism; realism; rhetoric; and so on.[11] Once again, while acknowledging that these features are found in the work of many, or even most, Romantic writers, we still do not really know what Romanticism is. One could lengthen the lists indefinitely, adding more and more common factors, without coming close to solving the problem.

The chief methodological weakness of this sort of approach, based on an inventory of features, is its empiricism: it does not go below the surface of the phenomenon. As a descriptive glance at the Romantic cultural universe, it can be useful, but its cognitive value is limited. Composite lists of elements leave the principal questions unanswered. What holds everything together? Why are these particular elements associated? What is the unifying force behind them? What gives internal coherence to all these *membra disiecta?* In other words, what is the concept, the *Begriff* (in the Hegelian-Marxist sense of the term) of Romanticism that can explain the innumerable forms in which it appears, its various empirical features, its multiple and tumultuous colors?

One of the most serious limitations of most literary studies is that they ignore the other dimensions of Romanticism, its political forms in particular. In a perfectly complementary fashion — and following the rigorous logic of academic disciplines — political scientists often have a regrettable tendency to neglect the properly literary aspects of Romanticism. How do they approach the movement's contradictions? Historiographers of Romanticism often sidestep the difficulty by focusing exclusively on its conservative, reactionary, and counterrevolutionary aspect while simply ignoring the revolutionary Romantic trends and thinkers.

In their most extreme form, which appeared above all during the Second

World War era (understandably enough), these interpretations see the Romantic political ideologies specifically as a preparation for Nazism. However, while the Nazi ideologues were unquestionably inspired by certain Romantic themes, this influence does not justify rewriting the entire history of political Romanticism as a simple historical preface to the Third Reich. In a book significantly titled *From Luther to Hitler,* William McGovern explains that Thomas Carlyle's writings "appear to be little more than a prelude to Nazism and Hitler." How can Rousseau be included in this theoretical framework? According to McGovern, the absolutist doctrine of fascism "is little more than an expansion of the ideas first laid down by Rousseau."[12] Other, similar works, like Peter Viereck's *Metapolitics: From the Romantics to Hitler,* stress the Germanness of Romanticism: it was a matter of a "cultural and political reaction against the Roman-French-Mediterranean spirit of clarity, rationalism, form, and universal standards. Thereby romanticism is really the nineteenth century's version of the perennial German revolt against the western heritage"[13] — a revolt that led "step by step" toward Nazism, during a complex century-long evolution. Obviously, for this type of analysis, the English and French (Western) Romantics cannot be considered "true" Romantics. And what can we say about the Jacobin and revolutionary German Romantics (Friedrich Hölderlin, Georg Büchner, and so on)? Their texts have to be viewed in their historical context (1939–1945), which was favorable to a unilateral perception of Romanticism in general and of its German version in particular.

Even more serious works, which do not try to explain everything in terms of the universal tendencies of the German soul, have a hard time resisting the temptation to assimilate Romanticism to prefascism. In a very interesting work devoted to the actual immediate precursors of Nazism in Germany (Paul de Lagarde, Julius Langbehn, and Moeller van den Bruck), Fritz Stern connects these authors to what he calls "a formidable tradition": that of Rousseau and his disciples, who had criticized the Enlightenment as a naively rationalist and mechanical form of thought. In this context, he mentions pell-mell Carlyle, Jacob Burckhardt, Friedrich Nietzsche, and Fyodor Dostoevsky.[14]

Many other historians, without going so far as to make Romanticism — especially German Romanticism — the breeding ground for fascism, present it only as a retrograde tendency. In France, this approach is represented in particular by Jacques Droz. His remarkable works on German political

Romanticism locate quite precisely the global character of the phenomenon (its nature as a weltanschauung) and its critique of the capitalist economy, but he sees the movement in the last analysis as a reaction to the "principles of the French Revolution and the Napoleonic conquest," a reaction that aspires to restore medieval civilization, and that is unquestionably inscribed "in the counter-revolutionary camp"; in short, a movement that "expresses the old ruling classes' awareness of the peril that awaited them." This position leads logically to excluding Hölderlin, Büchner, and the other Romantics favorably inclined toward the French Revolution from the analysis; the Jacobin and prorevolutionary phase that many Romantic writers and poets went through remains an inexplicable accident. Referring to Schlegel, for example, Droz recognizes that his passage from republicanism to conservatism is "difficult to explain," and (adopting Carl Schmitt's thesis — which he himself criticizes as erroneous) he ends up attributing this to the poet's "occasionalist dilettantism."[15]

While one interpretive school summarily identifies Romanticism with the counterrevolution, another school (Irving Babbitt, Thomas E. Hulme, Ernest Seillière, Maurice Souriau) does just the opposite. For this group, Romanticism is synonymous with revolution, social dissolution, and anarchy. For the conservative historian Babbitt, for instance, Rousseauist Romanticism transforms the Arcadian dreamer into a utopian and is thus "a veritable menace to civilization": refusing all constraints and all external control, this ideology advocates an absolute freedom that leads to "the most dangerous form of anarchy — anarchy of the imagination." It seems obvious that these two schools, equally one-sided and equally limited, are incapable of accounting for the contradictions of Romanticism and end up neutralizing each other. A more prudent historian of political doctrines, John Bowle, limits himself to noting the paradoxical fact that the "Romantic reaction" was born simultaneously under the sign of revolution (Rousseau) and counterrevolution (Burke), but he is unable to identify what these two antinomic poles of the Romantic spectrum have in common, except for a vague sense of "the will of the community" and a talent for phrasemaking.[16]

In addition to literary and political studies, there is a third type: works that have the virtue of recognizing the cultural multiplicity of Romanticism and that therefore see it as a worldview, a weltanschauung manifested in the most varied forms. This approach represents a major step forward in relation to the narrow outlook that typifies the various academic disciplines. It makes it possible to take in the vast cultural landscape called Romanticism as a whole and to see that the tumultuous variety of its colors is illuminated from a common source.

Trying to describe the spiritual essence common to such diverse manifestations, most of these authors define the Romantic view of the world by its opposition to the Aufklärung, that is, by its rejection of the abstract rationalism of Enlightenment philosophy.[17] Thus in a brilliant essay the intellectual historian Isaiah Berlin presents Romanticism as a manifestation of counter-Enlightenment: rejecting the central principles of Enlightenment philosophy (universality, objectivity, rationality), Johann Georg Hamann, Johann Gottfried Herder, and their Romantic disciples from Burke to Henri Bergson proclaimed their faith in the intuitive spiritual faculties and in the organic forms of social life.[18] This line of interpretation unquestionably reveals an aspect that can be found in the work of many Romantics, but the simple opposition between Romanticism and the Enlightenment is not convincing. To highlight the ambiguity of the relation between these two worldviews, which are far from being as mutually exclusive as some have claimed, we need only recall that, for Berlin, Rousseau offers the prime example of the Enlightenment philosophy that the Romantics want to destroy. The rejection of Enlightenment thought cannot stand as a spiritual category that would unify the field of Romanticism.

One interpretive path that has not been much explored by critics and historians (other than Marxists) is the relation between Romanticism and social and economic realities. Henri Peyre, an eminent specialist and the author of several books on Romantic literature, sums up the issue in his article "Romanticism" in the *Encyclopaedia Universalis*:

> It would be risky to link creations of the mind—the freest human activity there is—too closely to historical events and economic life. . . . The relations between literature and society are in fact virtually impossible to define. . . . To tie Romanticism to the coming of the Industrial Revolution, as some have been tempted to do, is riskier still. . . . If Romanticism then expressed, better than many historians, the upheavals caused by the surge of populations toward industry and cities, the wretchedness of the working classes viewed also as dangerous classes . . . it was because Balzac, the Hugo of *Les Misérables,* even Eugène Sue, and later Dickens and Disraeli in Great Britain, were keen observers of society, and great-hearted men.[19]

The explanation by way of great heartedness is somewhat minimal, and it can hardly fill the analytic void that results from refusing to examine the relation between literature and society.

Most of the authors are simply unaware of the prevailing social conditions and look only at the abstract sequence of literary styles (Classicism-Romanticism) or philosophical ideas (rationalism-irrationalism). Others relate Romanticism in a superficial and external way to some particular historical, political, or economic event: the French Revolution, the Restoration, the Industrial Revolution. In a typical example, Albert Joseph George, the author of a book with the promising title, *The Development of French Romanticism: The Impact of the Industrial Revolution on Literature,* presents Romanticism as a way of "adjusting to the effects of the Industrial Revolution." According to George, the Industrial Revolution simply "functioned as one of the prime sources of romanticism" by providing it with "an imagery closer to reality and presentational forms tailored for modern conditions"; it also "helped focus attention on prose, thereby aiding the shift from the romance to the novel. . . . to both prose and poetry it gave new and striking images. In short, it was a major factor in the development of French romanticism."[20] Far from grasping the deeply antagonistic relations between Romanticism and industrial society, this narrow analysis conceives of their relation only in terms of the modernization of literature and the renewal of its images.

Works on Romanticism by Marxists (or works influenced by Marxism) have the considerable advantage of situating the phenomenon in a social and historical context. In our view, this is an absolutely necessary — but alas! quite insufficient — condition for explaining Romanticism and its antinomies. Among these works, accordingly, we find the best and the worst.

The worst is Stalinist historiography, capable of producing quite remarkable incongruities. One example, among many others: the English literary critic Christopher Caudwell, a tragic figure (he died during the Spanish Civil War) who was a Communist in England between the two world wars. According to Caudwell, Romanticism represents one form of "capitalist poetry" and the English Romantic poets are basically only "bourgeois poets" whose revolt against sterile formalism and the tyranny of the past has its social equivalent in the bourgeoisie's struggle against the Corn Laws and in favor of free trade. To the objection that so eminent a Romantic as George Gordon Byron was an aristocrat, Caudwell replies that that aristocrat in reality deserted his class and went over to the side of the bourgeoisie. He hastens to add, moreover, that deserters of that sort are dangerous allies for a revolutionary movement: "They are always individualist, romantic figures with a strong element of the *poseur*. . . . They become counter-revolutionaries. Danton and Trotsky are examples of this type."[21] This interpretation — an extreme view, to be sure — shows how far a certain type of popular socialism can go. The idea that Romanticism is a bourgeois cultural form often appears — in more nuanced forms — in Marxist literature, even in much more astute authors than Caudwell. We shall come back to this question: in our judgment, approaches like Caudwell's entail a radical lack of understanding that quite simply misses the essential point.

A certain number of Marxist analyses, or analyses influenced by Marxism, get at the heart of the matter. Here the common axis, the unifying element of the Romantic movement in most if not all its manifestations across its principal centers in Europe (Germany, England, France), is opposition to the modern bourgeois world. This hypothesis strikes us as by far the most interesting and productive. However, the bulk of the work that occupies this terrain suffers from a serious disadvantage: like many of the non-Marxist writings mentioned above, they perceive in Romanticism's anti-bourgeois critique only its reactionary, conservative, retrograde aspect.

This is the case in particular with Karl Mannheim, one of the first to develop a systematic analysis of Romantic political philosophy as a manifestation of conservative opposition to "the bourgeois-capitalist mode of experiencing things," that is, as a movement of "ideological hostility to the forces giving rise to the modern world." This text, written in 1927 when its author was fairly close to Marxism and under György Lukács's influence, suggests quite significant parallels between the Romantic critique of the abstract nature of human relations in the capitalist universe — from Adam Müller to the *Lebensphilosophie* of the late nineteenth century — and certain themes developed by Karl Marx and his disciples (Lukács in particular). However, Mannheim construes and analyzes German political and philosophical Romanticism (he does not deal here with literature) exclusively from the standpoint of conservatism.[22]

György Lukács is another Marxist thinker who views Romanticism as a reactionary tendency inclined toward the right and fascism. Still, he deserves credit for inventing the concept of Romantic anticapitalism to designate the set of forms of thought in which the critique of bourgeois society is inspired by nostalgia for the past — a concept that he goes on to use very astutely to study Honoré de Balzac's cultural universe.[23]

Balzac is in fact at the heart of the debate among Marxists on the problem of Romanticism. In his famous letter to Miss Harkness, Friedrich Engels had lauded the "triumphs of realism" in Balzac over the author's own legitimist political prejudices.[24] A vast critical literature took up this brief remark and followed it faithfully, indeed dogmatically, and the mysterious "triumph of realism" became the "tarte à la crème" of many Marxist works on Balzac. Other authors challenged this rather hasty hypothesis, attempting to show that the writer's critical realism was not in contradiction with his worldview; unfortunately, their solution consisted in seeking to demonstrate the progressive, democratic, or leftist character of Balzac's political ideology. Thus the Czech scholar Jan O. Fischer, the author of an excellent book on Romantic realism (he offers a penetrating description of the dual nature of Romanticism, oriented sometimes toward the past, sometimes toward the future), tries in vain to demonstrate that Balzac's legitimism was "objectively democratic" because the "real context" of his royalism was democracy. His arguments are hardly convincing: he claims that Balzac's goal was "the welfare of the people" and the nation, and that the author sympathized with "simple people" and their social needs.[25] However, these are all philanthropic traits characteristic of a certain monarchist paternalism; they have nothing to do with democracy. We encounter a similar approach in Pierre Barbéris, who suggests in some of his writings that one can find in Balzac (especially the youthful Balzac) a "left-wing Romanticism" that is "Promethean" and inspired by the "cult of progress."[26]

We propose to start from a different hypothesis in order to understand Balzac's work and that of many other conservative Romantic authors: their realism and their critical vision are by no means in contradiction with their reactionary past-oriented, legitimist, or Tory ideology. It is fruitless to credit them with nonexistent democratic or progressive virtues: it is because they look toward the past that they criticize the present with so much acuity and realism. Clearly, this critique can also be carried out — and done better — from the viewpoint of the future, as is the case with the utopians and the revolutionaries, whether they are Romantic or not; but conceiving of the critique of social reality exclusively from a progressive perspective betrays a prejudice inherited from the Enlightenment.

Moreover, it seems to us that the category of realism, used as an exclusive criterion, is an obstacle to accounting for the richness and the liberating critical contribution of Romanticism. Too many Marxist texts have as their sole axis the definition of the realist or nonrealist character of a literary work, around which revolve more or less Byzantine discussions that oppose "socialist realism" to "critical realism" or "realism without borders." This was one of the principal reasons for the Marxists' often negative attitude toward Romanticism. In fact, many Romantic or neo-Romantic works are intentionally nonrealist: they are fantastic, symbolist, or, later on, surrealist. Yet this does not lessen their interest, both as critique of social reality and dream of an other world, radically distinct from the existing one: quite the contrary. One would have to introduce a new concept that might be called "critical irrealism" to designate the opposition between a marvelous, imaginary, ideal, utopian world and the gray, prosaic, inhuman reality of the modern world. Even when it takes the superficial form of a flight from reality, this critical irrealism can contain a powerful implicit or explicit negative charge challenging the philistine bourgeois order. It is owing to their character of critical irrealism that not only writers such as Novalis and E. T. A. Hoffmann but also utopians and revolutionaries such as Charles Fourier, Moses Hess, and William Morris contributed an essential dimension to Romanticism, as worthy of attention from an emancipatory standpoint as the implacably realist lucidity of a Balzac or a Charles Dickens.

Unlike the many texts — both Marxist and non-Marxist — that define Romanticism as a cultural avatar of counterrevolution, some Marxist works account in a dialectical fashion for both the contradictions and the essential unity of Marxism — without excluding its revolutionary variant. The Marxist Austrian Jew Ernst Fischer, for example, in his celebrated work *The Necessity of Art,* describes Romanticism as

> a movement of protest — of passionate and contradictory protest against the bourgeois capitalist world, the world of "lost illusions," against the harsh prose of business and profit. . . . at each turning point of events, the movement split up into progressive and reactionary trends. . . . What all the Romantics had in common was an antipathy to capitalism (some viewing it from an aristocratic angle, others from a plebeian), a Faustian or Byronic belief in the insatiability of the individual, and the acceptance of "passion in its own right" (Stendhal).

However, Fischer seems to consider this antipathy with respect to the bourgeois universe as just one aspect of Romanticism among others, and he does not try to establish interrelationships among the three common denominators that he mentions. Furthermore, he relativizes the scope of his analysis to a considerable extent by affirming in the same text — more or less contradicting what he has said earlier — that "despite its invocation of the Middle Ages, Romanticism was an eminently bourgeois movement."[27]

We find interesting intuitions scattered among the texts of some of Lukács's disciples (Ferenc Fehér, György Markus, Paul Breines, Andrew Arato, Norman Rudich, Adolfo Sanchez Vazquez) and also in the writings of Herbert Marcuse, Ernst Bloch, and their disciples. Apart from this tradition, which has German cultural origins, the most penetrating studies of Romanticism as a critique of modernity can be found among the English Marxists: E. P. Thompson and Raymond Williams, for the Anglo-Saxon Romantic universe, and Eric Hobsbawm for the Romantic movement in the first half of the nineteenth century.

Williams's contribution is particularly significant. His remarkable work *Culture and Society* (1958) is the first critical overview, from a socialist perspective, of the entire English tradition of cultural critiques of bourgeois society, from Burke and William Cobbett to Carlyle, from William Blake and Percy Bysshe Shelley to Dickens, and from John Ruskin to Morris. Even while acknowledging the limitations of the attitude manifested by this tradition toward the modern world, Williams argues for the legitimacy of their defense of art and culture as the embodiment of "certain human values, capacities, energies, which the development of society towards an industrial civilization was felt to be threatening and even destroying," as well as the struggle to save "a mode of human experience and activity which progress of society seemed increasingly to deny." The possibility of mobilizing that tradition for socialism is illustrated by Morris, who relates the values of the cultural critique to the organized working-class movement. Unfortunately, Williams uses the concept of Romanticism only in connection with poets (Blake, William Wordsworth, and John Keats), and he does not attempt to define the worldview and history common to these authors; he analyzes their work simply as examples of a cultural critique of industrial society.[28]

Most of these studies are limited and partial. They focus on a single author or a single country or a single period (especially the early nineteenth century); they generally consider only the artistic and literary aspect of the phenomenon. And most important, they develop neither a precise definition nor a global vision of Romanticism: they offer suggestions and interesting insights rather than any overarching theory.

Thus we note an important gap: we find no overarching analysis of the phenomenon that takes its full extent and full multiplicity into account. In what follows, we try to fill that gap, starting from a definition of Romanticism as weltanschauung or worldview, that is, a collective mental structure. Such a structure may be expressed in quite diverse cultural realms: not only in literature and the other arts but also in philosophy and theology; political, economic, and legal thought; sociology and history; and so forth. Thus our definition is by no means limited either to literature and art or to the historical period in which the so-called Romantic artistic movements developed. We include as Romantics — or as having a Romantic aspect — J.-C. S. de Sismondi in economic theory, Ferdinand Tönnies in sociology, and Marcuse in political philosophy, right alongside Alfred de Vigny and Novalis in literature, Dante Gabriel Rossetti and Odilon Redon in painting, Igor Stravinski in music, and so on.[29]

The modern notion of worldview was developed in particular by the French cultural sociologist Lucien Goldmann, who expanded on a long tradition in German thought, especially that of Wilhelm Dilthey, and carried it to a higher level. Our approach to treating the concept of Romanticism falls within that tradition, and Goldmann's work is its point of departure, although we reformulate Goldmann's arguments to a considerable extent. For while he focused especially on worldviews of modern times and explored some of the most important ones in detail, he said little about Romanticism, and what he did say was often negative and somewhat reductive.

It is true that in one text Goldmann refers to Romanticism as being, along with the Enlightenment and the tragic and dialectical worldviews, "one of the four principal forms of modern philosophical thought," adding that the critique of the Enlightenment, as formulated by dialectics, "or even by Romantic thought, . . . is justified to a very considerable extent."[30] But Goldmann's term "even" betrays his rather suspicious attitude toward Romanticism, which he seems to take to be essentially individualist.[31]

However, if Goldmann's reflection on Romanticism as such represents a gap to be filled rather than a productive source to tap, it is paradoxically in quite a different realm of his theorizing that we find our own foothold. In *Towards a Sociology of the Novel,* Goldmann conceives of the novel as staging the conflict between bourgeois society and certain human values; for Goldmann, the novel as a genre thus expresses the aspirations of problematic individuals motivated by qualitative values that are opposed to the reign of exchange value alone: artists, writers, philosophers, theologians, and others. Leaving aside the highly contested notion of "homology" between the structure of the novel and the structure of modern society, this way of seeing the novel can be usefully transferred to the level of worldviews, for it reveals *in nuce* the problematics specific to Romanticism.

Our overall explanatory framework remains primarily the theory of the weltanschauung as found in Goldmann; beyond this, our way of conceptualizing Romanticism is particularly indebted to the analyses of György Lukács, the first to associate Romanticism explicitly with opposition to capitalism (in his formula *"romantischer Antikapitalismus"*). But a considerable evolution has taken place between the Lukácsian conception and the analysis we offer here. For the Hungarian philosopher, "Romantic" is only an adjective characterizing a particular type of anticapitalism. Lukács never raises the question of the nature of Romanticism itself, whereas that is precisely what we are attempting to do by relying on his linking of terms and to a certain extent on his analyses of the phenomenon. In a first stage, we simply sought to invert the terms: in a long essay published several years ago we sketched a portrait of "anticapitalist Romanticism," turning the adjective into a noun.[32] But we came to see that from our own perspective this expression constitutes a pleonasm, since for us Romanticism is anticapitalist by its very nature; thus in this book we shall speak simply of "Romanticism."

We attempt to formulate our concept, then, on the basis of the theory of weltanschauungen and Lukács's and Goldmann's analyses. We shall be trying not to construct a Weberian "ideal type" (necessarily based on a partial selection) but rather to seek the *concept* — in the strong sense of the dialectical Begriff of the Hegelian-Marxist tradition — that can account for the contradictions of the phenomenon and for its diversity.[33] That said, the two approaches strike us as complementary rather than contradictory, and we shall have occasion later on — in the construction of a typology of the forms of Romanticism — to use the Weberian method.

One more preliminary remark about the genesis of our conception may be useful here. It is obvious that we use the term "Romanticism" in a very broad sense; some readers, especially those who are accustomed to associating Romanticism exclusively with artistic movements, may find its extension excessive. But in fact we are far from the first to have expanded the use of the word beyond its earliest literary and artistic manifestations. People have been speaking for a long time about political Romanticism, Romantic economics, and Romantic politics, and even about "neo-Romanticism," with reference to late-nineteenth-century and even sometimes twentieth-century authors.

At the outset, we took the broad span of uses of the terms "Romantic" and "Romanticism" as a given that required explanation. Our working hypothesis was the idea that some real unity underlay the various uses of these terms; we assumed that people had more or less intuitively felt some common sensibility behind them, without knowing exactly in what it consisted. Thus we began with the term "Romanticism" as it is used and in all the ways it has been used, hoping to find the principle that could unite its diversity and define its commonality. Once we had formulated the definition, however, we observed that it could be applied not only to the phenomena that have been designated as Romantic, either by the concerned parties themselves or by others, but also to authors, trends, and periods that are usually not viewed as Romantic or that themselves reject the label.

We do not mean to extend the concept so broadly that it loses its specificity and becomes synonymous with modern culture as a whole. For one thing, the formulation of a coherent concept of Romanticism ought to make it possible to make distinctions — in a move that is the inverse of extending the field — among authors who have ordinarily been called Romantic, and in some instances to discern non-Romantic dimensions in their work. Thus our approach should make it possible to look at the already-constituted corpus of Romanticism — the nominal corpus — and see that certain authors express the fundamental worldview less completely and purely than others. But beyond that, Romanticism is only one tendency in modern culture; there are many others that are non-Romantic or even anti-Romantic (not merely in the way they view Romanticism but also in their own intellectual structures).

Before trying to define the phenomenon of Romanticism more specifically, it is important to establish the chronological framework within which it belongs. As far as its origins are concerned, we must reject as too limited the idea according to which Romanticism is "the fruit of disappointment at the unkept promises of the bourgeois revolution of 1789," or "a set of questions and answers that arose in post-revolutionary society."[34] From this perspective, which is especially prevalent in France, Romanticism as an overall structure did not exist in advance of the French Revolution; it came into being as an effect of the disillusionment that followed the bourgeoisie's seizure of power. A transformation of the political order thus became the catalyst for Romanticism. However, this approach provides no way to account for the prior existence of Romantic tendencies in the eighteenth century. In our own view, the phenomenon has to be understood rather as a response to a slower and more profound economic and social transformation: the advent of capitalism, which was under way well before the Revolution. In fact, important manifestations of an authentic Romanticism can be found beginning in the mid-eighteenth century; in the context our approach creates, the distinction between Romanticism and pre-Romanticism loses its meaning.

Furthermore, none of the ending dates that have been proposed is acceptable from our standpoint. Neither 1848 nor the end of the nineteenth century marks Romanticism's disappearance or even its marginalization. Artistic movements in the twentieth century may have ceased to be described as Romantic, but trends as important as expressionism and surrealism and authors as important as Thomas Mann, William Butler Yeats, Charles Péguy, and Georges Bernanos were very deeply marked by the Romantic vision. Similarly, certain recent sociocultural movements — particularly the revolts of the 1960s, ecology, and pacifism — are hard to explain without referring to that same worldview.[35]

Indeed, if our hypothesis — namely, that Romanticism is essentially a reaction against the way of life in capitalist societies — is justified, this worldview is coextensive with capitalism itself. Now we cannot fail to note that, significant modifications notwithstanding, the fundamental characteristics of capitalism have remained unchanged up to our own day. As Max Milner has pointed out, early Romanticism (from the beginning of the nineteenth century) continues to speak to us because "the crisis of civilization connected with the birth and development of industrial capitalism is far from being resolved."[36] The Romantic worldview was thus established during the second half of the eighteenth century, and it has not yet disappeared.

Let us note right away, very briefly, the crux of our conception of the Romantic movement: Romanticism represents a critique of modernity, that is, of modern capitalist civilization, in the name of values and ideals drawn from the past (the precapitalist, premodern past). From its inception, Romanticism can be said to be illuminated by the dual light of the star of revolt and what Gérard de Nerval called the "black sun of melancholy."

In the analytic definition that follows, we present this worldview as a set of elements articulated according to a specific logic. In other words, we construe it as a signifying structure (though not necessarily a conscious one, and even often a nonconscious one) — underlying a very great diversity of contents and forms of expression (literary, religious, philosophical, political, and so on). By signifying structure, following Goldmann's lead, we do not mean to designate a vague list of ideological themes but rather a coherent totality organized around an axis or frame.[37] The central element of this structure, the one on which all the others depend, is a contradiction, or an opposition, between two systems of values: Romantic values and those of the social reality known as "modern." Romanticism as a worldview is constituted as a specific form of criticism of "modernity."

By the latter term we do not mean "modernism" (theorists of postmodernism or the postmodern sometimes use "modernism" and "modernity" interchangeably), that is, the avant-garde literary and artistic movement that began toward the end of the nineteenth century. Our use of "modernity" includes, but does not coincide with, the meaning Jean Chesneaux gives the term in two recent books, namely, the last stage of the "advanced" societies (for France, this stage began with the Fifth Republic).[38]

In this book, "modernity" will refer to a more fundamental and more encompassing phenomenon than the two evoked above: modern civilization, which was engendered by the Industrial Revolution and in which the market economy prevails. As Max Weber observed, the principal characteristics of modernity — the calculating spirit (*Rechnenhaftigkeit*), the disenchantment of the world (*Entzauberung der Welt*), instrumental rationality (*Zweckrationalität*), and bureaucratic domination — are inseparable from the advent of the "spirit of capitalism." The origins of modernity and capitalism go back of course to the Renaissance and the Reformation (thus the term "modern period" used in history textbooks to designate the period that begins at the end of the fifteenth century); however, these phenomena began to become hegemonic in the West only in the second half of the eighteenth century, when the "primitive accumulation" was completed (Marx), when large-scale industry started to take off and the market broke free of social controls (Karl Polanyi).

We can of course identify instances of noncapitalist modernity in the twentieth century — the Soviet Union and the states inspired by the Soviet model — but their break with industrial bourgeois civilization was only very partial (and ephemeral, in the light of recent developments). In any case, industrial capitalism was the dominant reality of the twentieth century, not only for the major Western countries — those that witnessed the rise of Romantic culture firsthand — but also on a planetary scale. We shall return to this issue in chapter 5.

From our perspective, capitalism has to be viewed as a *Gesamtkomplex,* a complex whole with multiple facets. As a socioeconomic system, capitalism has various aspects: industrialization, the rapid and correlated development of science and technology (a defining feature of modernity, according to the *Petit Robert* dictionary), the hegemony of the market, the private ownership of means of production, the enlarged reproduction of capital, "free" labor, and an intensified division of labor. Around it have emerged integrally related aspects of modern civilization: rationalization, bureaucratization, the predominance of what Charles Cooley calls "secondary relations" in social life, urbanization, secularization, reification, and so on. As mode and relations of production, capitalism is the principle that generates and unifies the overall phenomenon, rich in ramifications, that we know as "modernity."

Romanticism arose out of opposition to this modern, capitalist realism — which is sometimes designated in Romantic terms simply as "reality." In the Grimm brothers' dictionary, *romantisch* is defined, in part, as "belonging to the world of poetry . . . as opposed to prosaic reality," and for François-René de Chateaubriand and Alfred de Musset the overfull heart contrasts with the devastating void of the real.[39] According to the formula of the young Lukács in *The Theory of the Novel,* the "Romanticism of disillusion" is characterized by an incommensurability between the soul and reality, in which "the soul [is] larger and wider than the destinies which life has to offer it."[40]

Balzac characterized a number of texts published in 1830, among them *Le Rouge et le Noir,* as belonging to the "school of disenchantment," and the term could be applied to the Romantic worldview as a whole. In France modern reality was called *le siècle,* source of *le mal du siècle;* in England and Germany, it was labeled "civilization" in opposition to "culture"; everywhere, this modern reality disenchanted. It is often quite clear that the disenchantment arose from what was new in that social reality; thus in signing some of his essays with the name "Neophobus" Charles Nodier betrays a characteristic Romantic attitude.

Understandably, since it represents a revolt against the civilization created by capitalism, Romantic sensibility bears an anticapitalist impulse. Still, its anticapitalism may be more or less conscious, implicit, or mediated. It may entail awareness of the exploitation of one class by another: the harangue John Bell addresses to his workers in Vigny's *Chatterton* is a well-known example. Félicité Robert de Lamennais's *Words of a Believer* also include a passage that analyzes and denounces the oppression of those who sell their capacity to work in terms that prefigure Marx himself.[41] However, this awareness is by no means always present.

Criticism is brought to bear most often on the characteristics of capitalism whose negative effects cut across all social classes, effects experienced as destitution at all levels of society. Many critics denounce a key overall phenomenon known as "reification": the dehumanization of human life, the transforming of human relations into relations among things, inert objects. According to Lukács's analysis in *History and Class Consciousness*,[42] whereas a generalization of exchange value lies at the heart of the concept of reification, other, related aspects of capitalist civilization (especially the ones pointed out by Max Weber that we noted above) may be targeted by a critique of the Romantic type.

Such a critique may focus on any of several major facets of the system: first of all, anything having to do with relations of production (relations centered, in a capitalist regime, on exchange value, quantitative monetary relations); next, the means of production (technological means) with scientific underpinnings; finally the state and the modern political apparatus that governs (and is governed by) the social system. Although some Romantic critics concentrate on a single one of these facets (or even on less secondary or superficial aspects), it must be said that those who display the Romantic worldview most fully bring their critique to bear on the key features of several or all of them.

The most complete and coherent expressions of the Romantic vision also perceive modernity as a whole whose multiple aspects are interrelated and interlocking: an all-encompassing civilization, a world in which everything holds together. Let us recall that, according to Lucien Goldmann, only the greatest cultural works succeed in expressing a worldview that is maximally coherent and that is also infused to the greatest possible extent with the multiplicity and richness of the phenomenal world. If we apply this principle to the Romantic worldview, we are saying in effect that while many works stem from Romanticism in one way or another, to a greater or lesser degree, the ones that protest against modernity as a complex whole and that integrate into their critique the largest possible number of facets of that whole most adequately embody Romanticism as a worldview.

Need we add that the Romantic critique takes very different forms depending on the authors' modes of expression and their individual temperaments? In particular, in works of art, criticism is carried out by properly aesthetic means that are fundamentally different from those used in an essay or treatise. Authors of literary works rarely offer a direct and unequivocal denunciation of the evils of contemporary society. Instead, they rely on a whole arsenal of literary techniques to transmit a particular point of view, ranging from suggestions and irony to the way a narrative is organized.

We must also note that, whether we like it or not, Romanticism is a modern critique of modernity. This means that, even as the Romantics rebel against modernity, they cannot fail to be profoundly shaped by their time. Thus by reacting emotionally, by reflecting, by writing against modernity, they are reacting, reflecting, and writing in modern terms. Far from conveying an outsiders' view, far from being a critique rooted in some elsewhere, the Romantic view constitutes modernity's self-criticism.[43]

Having posited a rejection of capitalist modernity as the foundation and first phase of Romanticism, we need to specify our concept further, since Romanticism represents just one modality, a particular tonality in which critiques of the modern world may be couched. The Romantic critique is bound up with an experience of loss. The Romantic vision is characterized by the painful and melancholic conviction that in modern reality something precious has been lost, at the level of both individuals and humanity at large; certain essential human values have been alienated. This alienation, keenly sensed, is often experienced as exile: in defining the Romantic sensibility, Friedrich Schlegel speaks of the soul "under the willows of exile" (*unter den Trauerweiden der Verbannung*);[44] the soul, the seat of humanness, now lives far removed from its true hearth or homeland (*Heimat*); thus according to Arnold Hauser "the feeling of homelessness (*Heimatlosigkeit*) and loneliness became the fundamental experience" of the Romantics at the beginning of the nineteenth century.[45] And Walter Benjamin, himself deeply imbued with this worldview, sees in the German Romantics' appeal to dream life an indication of the obstacles raised by real life on the "path of the soul's homeward journey to the motherland" (*der Heimweg der Seele ins Mutterland*).[46]

The soul ardently desires to go home again, to return to its homeland, in the spiritual sense, and this nostalgia is at the heart of the Romantic attitude. What is lacking in the present existed once upon a time, in a more or less distant past. The defining characteristic of that past is its difference from the present: the past is the period in which the various modern alienations did not yet exist. Romantic nostalgia looks to a precapitalist past, or at least to a past in which the modern socioeconomic system was not yet fully developed. Thus nostalgia for the past is — to borrow a term from Marx and Engels, who noted this feature among the English capitalists — "closely linked" to the critique of the capitalist world.[47]

The past that is the object of nostalgia may be entirely mythological or legendary, as in the reference to Eden, to the Golden Age, or to the lost Atlantis. It may also constitute a personal myth, like the "mysterious City" in Nerval's *Aurélia*.[48] But even in the many instances in which a real historical past is invoked, the past is always idealized. The Romantic vision selects a moment from the actual past in which the harmful characteristics of modernity did not yet exist and in which the human values that have been since stifled by modernity were still operative; that moment is then transformed into a utopia, shaped as the embodiment of Romantic aspirations. This is one way to explain the seeming paradox according to which the Romantic orientation toward the past can also involve looking ahead; the image of a dreamed-of future beyond the contemporary world is inscribed within the evocation of a precapitalist era.

The term "Romantic" as it was understood at the beginning of the movement that bears the name — early German Romanticism — includes a reference to a specific past era: the Middle Ages. For Friedrich Schlegel, what is involved is "the age of chivalry, love, and fable, from which the phenomenon and the word itself are derived";[49] indeed, one of the principal sources of the word "Romanticism" is the medieval chivalric novel (*le roman courtois*). But the Romantics turned to many other past eras as well. Primitive societies, the Hebrew people of the biblical era, Greek and Roman antiquity, the English Renaissance, the Old Regime in France — all these served as vehicles for the Romantic vision. The choice — and especially the interpretation — of a particular period in the past depended on the specific orientation of the form of Romanticism in question.

Nostalgia for a lost paradise is generally accompanied by a quest for what has been lost. An active principle at the heart of Romanticism has often been noted in various forms: anxiety, a state of perpetual becoming, interrogation, quest, struggle. In general, then, a third moment is constituted by an active response, an attempt to find or to re-create the ideal past state; there is such a thing, nevertheless, as a resigned Romanticism.

Now this quest can be undertaken in a variety of ways. It can be situated on the level of the imaginary or the real, and it can hold out the prospect of realization in the present or the future. One major tendency attempts to re-create paradise in the here and now on the imaginary level, through the poeticization or aestheticization of the present. In *Über die ästhetische Erziehung des Menschen in einer Reihe von Briefen* (Letters on the aesthetic education of man), Friedrich von Schiller advocates the creation of an "aesthetic state" to counter the fragmentation and alienation of modern men and women, and according to Novalis "the world must be romanticised" by a "heightening" (*Potenzierung*) of ordinary and familiary reality.[50]

This impulse can be manifested by the emergence of the supernatural, the fantastic, the oniric, or, in certain works of art, by the tonality of the sublime. But in a different sense, every Romantic artistic creation is a utopian projection — a world of beauty — created by the imagination in the present. That the Romantics were often conscious of what was at stake in this undertaking, and of its subversive character, is illustrated by a remark Dorothea Schlegel makes in a letter: "Since it is altogether contrary to bourgeois order and absolutely forbidden to introduce romantic poetry into life, then let life be brought into romantic poetry; no police force and no educational institution can prevent this."[51]

A second tendency seeks to rediscover paradise in present reality. One way to do this involves transforming one's immediate environment and one's own life while remaining within bourgeois society; this can take the form of dandyism or aestheticism (the literary model being Joris-Karl Huysmans's des Esseintes), the creation of a community of like-minded individuals ("cenacles" or literary circles), a utopian experiment (the Saint-Simonians), or simply falling in love. This last element brings us to the popular meaning that is commonly given to Romanticism today ("romantic" love) — the love about which Max Weber said: "This boundless giving of oneself is as radical as possible in its opposition to all functionality, rationality, and generality."[52] Finally, the ideal can also be sought in the sphere of childhood, in the belief that the values that governed all adult society in a more primitive state of humanity — its "childhood," as it were — can still be found among children.

But one may also choose to flee bourgeois society, leaving cities behind for the country, trading modern countries for exotic ones, abandoning the centers of capitalist development for some "elsewhere" that keeps a more primitive past alive in the present. The approach of exoticism is a search for a past in the present by a mere displacement in space. Nodier brings the fundamental principle of exoticism to light when he explains that his tales *Smarra* and *Trilby* are set in a wild Scottish landscape because it is only by leaving Europe behind that one can find remnants of humanity's springtime, an idyllic period in which the sources of the imagination and sensitivity had not yet dried up.[53]

A third tendency holds the preceding solutions to be illusory, or in any event merely partial; it embarks on the path of authentic future realization. The idea that one can see a premonition of what will be in what was is splendidly illustrated by a story that Jules Michelet borrowed from Herodotus and used in his inaugural lecture at the Sorbonne (1834): in the distant past, when the crown of a kingdom in Asia was promised to the first person to see the dawn, "everyone looked toward the East; just one person, more astute, looked in the opposite direction; and indeed, while the East was still shrouded in darkness, he spotted, looking westward, the glimmers of dawn that were already whitening the top of a tower!"[54]

From the standpoint that is oriented toward future accomplishments, that of Percy Bysshe Shelley, Pierre-Joseph Proudhon, William Morris, or Walter Benjamin, for example, the recollection of the past serves as a weapon in the struggle for the future. A well-known poem by Blake gives remarkable expression to this view. In a short text that is part of the preface to *Milton,* the poet wonders whether the divine presence manifested itself in England "in ancient time," before its hills were covered by "these dark Satanic mills." In conclusion, he commits himself to a "spiritual struggle" that will end only when "we have built Jerusalem / in Englands green & pleasant land."[55] In this form of Romanticism, the quest aims at the creation of a new Jerusalem.

A rejection of contemporary society, an experience of loss, a melancholic nostalgia, and a quest for the lost object: such are the chief components of the Romantic vision. But precisely what has been lost? We still have to address the question of the content of alienation; or, turning the question around, we have to ask about the positive values of Romanticism. Here we find a set of qualitative values, as opposed to exchange value. These are concentrated around two opposite though not contradictory poles. The first is often experienced as loss, but it actually represents a new acquisition, or at least it is a value that can develop fully only in the modern world: the subjectivity of the individual, the development of the richness of the human personality, in its full affective depth and complexity, but also in the full freedom of its imaginary.

The development of the individual subject is directly linked to the history and prehistory of capitalism: the isolated individual emerges along with and because of capitalism. However, this is the source of a major contradiction in modern society, for the individual whom society has created cannot help being frustrated in the attempt to live in that same society and ends up revolting against it. The Romantic exaltation of subjectivity — wrongly considered as the essential feature of Romanticism — is just one of the forms taken by the resistance to reification. Capitalism gives rise to independent individuals who can carry out socioeconomic functions; but when these individuals evolve into subjective individualities, exploring and developing their inner worlds and personal feelings, they enter into contradiction with a universe based on standardization and reification. And when they demand that their imagination be given free play, they collide with the extreme mercantile platitude of the world produced by capitalist relations. In this respect, Romanticism represents the revolt of repressed, channeled, and deformed subjectivity and affectivity.

It follows that the Romantics' "individualism" is fundamentally different from that of modern liberalism. This difference has been analyzed with a good deal of subtlety by Georg Simmel: he calls individualism of the Romantic type "subjective individualism," to distinguish it from eighteenth-century "numeric individualism" and from French and English liberalism. Romantic individualism stresses the unique and incomparable character of each personality — which leads logically, according to Simmel, to the complementarity of individuals in an organic whole.[56]

The other major value of Romanticism, at the dialectically opposite pole from the first one, is unity or totality. Romanticism posits the unity of the self with two all-encompassing totalities: the entire universe, or nature, on the one hand, and the human universe, the human collectivity, on the other. If Romanticism's first value constitutes its individual or individualistic dimension, the second reveals a transindividual dimension. And if the first is modern even while conceiving of itself as nostalgic, the second entails a genuine turning back to the past.

In this connection it is important to emphasize — countering a trend of thought that claims to see in the Romantic phenomenon especially or exclusively an affirmation of exacerbated individualism — that the demand for community is just as essential to the definition of the Romantic vision as its subjective and individualistic aspect. Indeed, this requirement is even more fundamental, for the lost paradise always consists in the plenitude of the whole, both human and natural.

To be sure, some Romantics, and above all certain neo-Romantics, have glorified their own isolation and the "self" of the artist or the privileged individual — the individual as hero. Cut off from the actual surrounding community both through their own inability to integrate themselves into an "alienated" community and by the ostracism practiced by this collectivity with respect to those who do not comply with its ethos, ill-adapted individuals sometimes make "a virtue of necessity" and celebrate their lofty independence, their lack of human connections. But among the Romantics this separation becomes a way of communicating better with nature and with human communities that are remote in time or space, through reading, thought, or spirituality.

The hero of Paul Valéry's *Monsieur Teste* seeks to make individual will and consciousness absolute, as does the young Hegelian Max Stirner with "the self and its propriety" (*Das Ich und sein Eigentum*). In these instances, the individual in the pure state carries the logic of the modern world to extremes; he becomes the embodiment of the capitalist spirit. The Romantic individual, on the contrary, is an unhappy consciousness. Being cut off from others makes him ill; he seeks to restore effective bonds, for nothing else will allow him to achieve self-realization. While it is important to recognize that a Romantic sensibility so constituted may also produce quite forceful expressions of individualist self-affirmation, the true kernel of value among Romantics is oneness with humanity and the natural universe.

Now it is appropriate to note that this dual requirement is defined specifically in opposition to the status quo instituted by capitalism. The capitalist principle of exploitation of nature is in contradiction with the Romantic aspiration to life lived harmoniously in the bosom of nature. And the desire to re-create the human community — envisaged in many forms: in authentic communication with others, in participation in the organic whole of a people (*Volk*) and its collective imaginary as expressed in mythology and folklore, in social harmony, or in a classless society — corresponds to Romanticism's rejection of the modern fragmentation of the collectivity. The critique of modernity and positive Romantic values are thus simply two sides of the same coin.

As for Romantic art, its themes, positive and negative, and its styles or forms may also be construed as two sides of the same coin. It is obvious that no single set of specific formal attributes characterizes Romantic creations over the span of two centuries. The structure of the Romantic sensibility can be expressed through a multiplicity of artistic forms. However, this does not mean that there is no significant link between form and content in Romanticism. On the contrary, we would do well to go back to Romanticism's worldview to account for many of the formal strategies of the Romantic texts, to demonstrate how form embodies a Romantic vision. This move does not contradict our recognition of the diversity of forms, since a given problematic or overall intellectual structure can find adequate representation in different and even contradictory forms. Thus while the prominent lyricism of a great part of early Romanticism is understood as a stylistic negation of the platitude and coldness of the bourgeois world, the "impassibility" of the Parnassus poets or Gustave Flaubert in his later years — fully Romantic figures within our conceptual framework — can be understood as a strategy of self-defense against that same world.

All the articulations of the Romantic worldview are apt to have repercussions at the level of form. Nostalgia for the Middle Ages or antiquity may inflect style in one direction, the attraction of the exotic or of the rural world in another, and so on. No doubt we cannot explain all the formal aspects of a Romantic work directly through reference to the worldview; it is nonetheless true that the Romantic artist wages a battle against modernity on many levels, including the level of form.

The worldview that we have just posited in its broad outlines represents, to our way of thinking, a veritable lost continent that has escaped the usual grids of the human sciences. Literary and artistic studies give it a much more limited extension and do not link it to capitalism. As for the other social sciences (history, sociology, political science, economics, and so forth), Romanticism is not generally recognized as a perspective that can determine mental structures in their realms. Since it does not correspond to the usual categories (in philosophy, rationalism, empiricism, idealism; in history and politics, left-right, conservatives-liberals, progressives-reactionaries), it slips through the social scientists' nets and generally remains invisible in their analyses.[57]

But if this largely hidden phenomenon constitutes in our eyes one of the most important mental structures of the last two centuries, it represents only one of the trends in modern culture. The modern civilization rejected by the Romantics has always had its defenders as well, for instance utilitarians and positivists, classical political economists and theoreticians of liberalism; many others, of course, accept it implicitly without defending it directly. Generally speaking, non-Romantic tendencies may be said to predominate in economic and political thought as well as in the human sciences. This is also true of modern architecture, especially after the Bauhaus and the triumph of functionalism, and it is true of modern painting, from the impressionists to contemporary abstractionism.

As for literature, the currents foreign to Romanticism — those that do not reject modernity — are numerous: naturalism (Emile Zola), the novel of scientific anticipation (Jules Verne), futurism (Emilio Marinetti), certain works of North American literature (Mark Twain's *A Connecticut Yankee in King Arthur's Court,* to mention just one example). We might add that in the literary realm, and especially in modern literature in the United States, the situation is often complicated and more or less contradictory: a modernizing dimension blends with a dimension of nostalgic rejection in a single author or even a single work (this is the case with Ernest Hemingway and John Dos Passos, for example).

We need to emphasize, too, that the Romantic vision represents only one modality of the critique of the modern world governed by capitalism; the specificity of Romanticism is that it develops this critique from the standpoint of a value system — with reference to an ideal — drawn from the past. Romanticism must thus also be distinguished from a modernizing anticapitalism, that is, an approach that criticizes the present in the name of certain modern values — utilitarian rationalism, efficiency, scientific and technological progress — while calling on modernity to surpass itself, to accomplish its own evolution, instead of returning to the sources, reimmersing itself in lost values. This type of critique is found for example in Godwinian rationalism, in democratic socialism, and also in the socialist utopia of *Looking Backward* (1888), a novel by the American Edward Bellamy in which the principal features of an ideal future society are the efficient organization of the production and distribution of industrial goods and the advanced state of technology.

Modernizing anticapitalism is also found in the predominant current of Marxism and Communism. The case of Lenin himself—someone who could define socialism as "the Soviets plus electrification"—is exemplary in this respect. It is more or less beyond dispute that Lenin was a determined enemy of the reign of exchange value, on the one hand, and that he was in no way Romantic, on the other hand. The modernizing tendency of Communism or socialism finds its literary expression in numerous works of progressive realism and "socialist realism" (those of Upton Sinclair, Maksim Gorki, and others).

Finally, we need to distinguish Romanticism from a tendency that might be called "reactionary modernism,"[58] which combines certain backward-looking aspects with an adherence to industrial and/or capitalist modernity: examples include the principal strains of fascism (although some Romantic intellectuals joined forces with fascism), military authoritarianism, and contemporary American televangelism.

Romanticism is thus only one of the multiple tendencies and worldviews that constitute modern culture. While Romanticism as we understand it today exercised a diffuse and tendentially dominating influence over nineteenth-century literature, this dominance does not hold sway in the twentieth century. However, although it may have lost its hegemony over twentieth-century literary creation, the Romantic worldview has continued to play a major role in that arena.

THE ROMANTIC CRITIQUE OF MODERNITY

The Romantic opposition to capitalist-industrialist modernity does not always challenge the system as a whole, far from it: as we have already seen, it reacts to a certain number of features of modernity that it finds unbearable. We offer several examples of those that surface frequently in Romantic works.

The Disenchantment of the World

Here it is less a question of a feature than of an essential lack. In a famous passage of the *Communist Manifesto,* Marx observed that "the most heavenly ecstasies of religious fervor, of chivalrous enthusiasm, of philistine sentimentalism" of the past had been submerged by the bourgeoisie, "drowned . . . in the icy water of egotistical calculation." Seventy years later,

Max Weber noted in a celebrated talk, "Science as a Vocation" (1919): "The fate of our times is characterized by rationalization and intellectualization and, above all, by the 'disenchantment of the world.' Precisely the ultimate and most sublime values have retreated from public life either into the transcendent realm of mystic life or into the brotherliness of direct and personal human relations."[59] Romanticism may be viewed as being to a large extent a reaction on the part of "chivalrous enthusiasm" against the "icy water" of rational calculation and against the Entzauberung der Welt — leading to an often desperate attempt to reenchant the world. From this standpoint, Ludwig Tieck's well-known line, *"die mondbeglanzte Zaubernacht"* (night with its moonlit enchantments) can be read almost as a philosophical and spiritual program.

One of the principal Romantic modalities for reenchanting the world is the return to religious traditions, sometimes with mystical elements, as Weber notes. This is true to such an extent that many critics take religion to be the defining feature of the Romantic spirit. According to Hoxie N. Fairchild, Romanticism, in its deepest and most intense aspects, is essentially a religious experience. For Hulme, an unyielding adversary, Romanticism is really only "spilt religion," that is, a form of culture in which religious concepts have left their proper sphere to spread out everywhere and thus to "mess up, falsify, and blur the clear outlines of human experience."[60] These remarks contain some truth, but they are too one-sided: on the one hand because Romanticism has areligious manifestations (Hoffmann) and even antireligious ones (Proudhon, Friedrich Nietzsche, Oskar Panizza), and on the other hand because they do not make it possible to distinguish the Romantic forms from other forms of religiosity — for example, certain types of Protestantism that are perfectly adapted, as Max Weber observed, to the "spirit of capitalism." In any event, it is true that the great majority of Romantics — especially in the early nineteenth century — sought passionately to restore the religions of the past, and in particular medieval Catholicism. Novalis's lovely political-literary text, *Die Christenheit oder Europa* (Christianity or Europe), is a characteristic example of this Romantic religiosity permeated with nostalgia, which, by its aesthetic sensibility and its mystical poetry, remains in spite of everything rather different from the institutionalized dogmas of the church.

But religion — in its traditional forms or in its mystical and/or heretical manifestations — is not the only means of reenchantment chosen by the Romantics. They also turned to magic, the esoteric arts, sorcery, alchemy, and astrology; they rediscovered Christian and pagan myths, legends, fairy tales, Gothic narratives; they explored the hidden realms of dreams and the fantastic — not only in literature and poetry but also in painting, from Johann Heinrich Füssli (Henry Fuseli) and Blake to Max Klinger and Max Ernst.

Romantic irony is also practiced as a form of resistance to entzauberung. This is the case, for example, with Hoffmann's "Little Zaches," a malicious and captivating satire directed at the prosaic and philistine Prussian "official rationalism." In a small principality with a mild climate there lived many fairies, "for whom warmth and freedom, as is well known, count above everything else." It is probably owing to the fairies that in the villages and forests "the most delightful marvels often occurred, and that everyone, completely surrounded thus by the charm and the bliss of these wonders, fully believed in the marvelous. . . ." One fine day, the new sovereign, Prince Paphnutius, decided to issue an edict instituting the Enlightenment (Auf-klärung); he issued orders to "cut down the forests, make the river passable for ships, raise potatoes . . . lay out highways, and give cowpox vaccina-tions." But before all these good and useful initiatives, he listened to the advice of the prime minister: "It is necessary to banish from the state all persons of dangerous opinions, who lend no ear to Reason, and who mis-lead the common people by downright absurdities." The fairies were the particular target, those "enemies of the Enlightenment" who "ply a dan-gerous trade in the marvelous and do not shrink from preparing, under the name of poetry, a secret poison which makes people completely unfit for service in the Enlightenment. Then they have habits that are so intolerably repugnant to the police (*unleidliche polizeiwidrige Gewohnheiten*) that, on that account alone, they ought to be put up with in no cultivated state." Following this good and wise advice, the prince gave his orders and soon "the edict about the proclaimed Enlightenment shone in splendor at every corner, and at the same time the police broke into the fairies' palaces, seized their total property, and took them away prisoners." It was also decided to roast the fairies' doves and swans in the royal kitchen and to transform their winged horses into useful animals — by cutting off their wings... We hardly need to add that, despite all these precautions by the administration and the police, the fairies continued to haunt the principality and to spread their "secret poison."[61] This *Märchen,* a little masterpiece of irony, stages the final combat of the marvelous and enchantment against the heavy, somber ma-chinery of state rationalism.

The Romantic fascination with night must be interpreted in the same context as a place of spells, mystery, and magic, opposed by writers and poets to light, the classic emblem of rationalism. In one of his *Hymns to the Night,* Novalis poses a strange and paradoxically plaintive question: "Must ever the morning return? / Endeth never the thraldom of Earth? / Unhallowed affairs swallow up / The heavenly coming of Night?"[62]

Finally, facing a science of nature that, starting with Isaac Newton and Antoine-Laurent Lavoisier, seems to have deciphered the mysteries of the universe, and facing a modern technology that is developing a strictly rational (instrumental) and utilitarian approach to the environment (the "raw materials" of industry), Romanticism aspires to reenchant nature. This is the role of the religious philosophy of nature of authors such as Schelling, Ritter, or Baader, but it is also an inexhaustible theme of Romantic painting and poetry, which never cease to seek mysterious analogies and correspondences in the sense that Charles Baudelaire gives the term, after Emanuel Swedenborg, between the human soul and nature, spirit and landscape, inner tempests and outer storms.

Among the Romantics' strategies for reenchanting the world, the recourse to myth holds a special place. At the magic intersection between religion, history, poetry, language, and philosophy, it offers an inexhaustible reservoir of symbols and allegories, phantasms and demons, gods and vipers. There are several ways to delve into this dangerous treasure: poetic or literary reference to ancient, Oriental, or popular myths; the scholarly (i.e., historical, theological, philosophical) study of mythology; and attempts to create new myths. In all three cases, the loss of the religious substance of myth—the result of modern secularization—makes it a secular figure of enchantment or, rather, a nonreligious way to rediscover the sacred.

The sinister perversion of myths by German Fascism, their manipulation as national and racial symbols (not to mention the mediocre philosophical imaginings of an Alfred Rosenberg [*Le mythe du XXᵉ siècle,* 1930]) went a long way toward discrediting mythology after the Second World War, especially in Germany. The protests of anti-Fascist German intellectuals against this perversion carried very little weight. Still, Mann wrote in 1941 that "we have to tear myth away from intellectual Fascism and make it change function in a human direction (*ins Humane umfunktionieren*)." Bloch, in turn, believed in the possibility of saving myth from the blot inflicted by the Nazi ideologues—provided that myth is illuminated by "the utopian light of the future."[63]

At the outset, in the *Frühromantik,* the first German Romanticism, this light is omnipresent; it illuminates from within the idea of the "new myth," invented at the dawn of the nineteenth century by Schlegel and Schelling. If we return to this original source, the contrast with the mythological affectations promoted by the Third Reich is striking.

For the Frühromantik, the new myth is not "national-Germanic" but human-universal. In a course given in Wurzburg (1804), Schelling explained:

> Mythology is not the manifestation of an individual or even of a species, but that of a species gripped and animated by an artistic instinct. The possibility of a mythology refers us thus to an even higher requirement: humanity must again become one, in general and in particular. In the meantime, only a partial mythology will be possible, one that, like Dante, Cervantes, Shakespeare, and Goethe, draws its material from history: a universal mythology, endowed with a general symbolics, will continue to be lacking.

Schlegel too, in his "Rede über die Mythologie" (1800), dreams of a mythology without frontiers, which would seek its inspiration not only in European literature and in antiquity but also in the "treasures of the East" and in India, thus leading to a universality "that would probably make the meridional ray that makes Spanish poetry so attractive to us right now seem very pale and very Western."[64]

Schlegel's "Rede über die Mythologie" is probably among the most visionary of the so-called theoretical texts of German Romanticism. Inseparably associating poetry and mythology, it makes a utopian ferment of nostalgia for the past:

> Our poetry lacks a center such as mythology was for the poetry of the ancients. The chief weakness of modern poetry, in comparison to ancient poetry, can be summarized in these words: we have no mythology. However, I will add that we are close to acquiring one; or, more precisely, it is time to work together seriously to bring one to the light of day. Why should what has been not be renewed? In a different way, to be sure; but why not in a higher, more beautiful form?

In other words, the Romantic Schlegel does not want to restore the archaic myths; his ambition, unprecedented in the history of culture, is to create freely a new poetic, nonreligious, modern mythology. This is the opposite of the historicist and archaeological undertaking of the late Romantics (Johann Joseph von Görres, Friedrich Creuzer, Johanas Arnold Kanne, Johann Bachofen), who were fascinated by the past. Throughout Schlegel's entire text, we find no reference to any ancient mythic figure: rejecting archaistic regression, he turns resolutely toward the future.[65]

The new mythology is not only not a pale imitation of the ancient forms; it is also radically distinct from them by its very nature, by its spiritual texture, so to speak: whereas the ancient mythology was linked in an immediate way with what was closest and most alive in the perceptible world, the new mythology has to be constituted on the basis of "the most intimate depths of the spirit" (*tiefsten Tiefe des Geistes*). Arising from this internal source, the new mythology is thus produced by the spirit from the spirit itself; whence its elective affinity to idealist philosophy (here Schlegel is thinking in particular of Johann Fichte), which also creates "from nothing" (*aus Nichts entstanden*). This "mythopoetic" interiority arising from the depths cannot accept the limits imposed by rational reason: it is the realm of "what always escapes consciousness," of the "fine disorder of the imagination" and of the "originary chaos of human nature." This does not mean that the new myth is unattuned to the external world: it is at the same time "a hieroglyphic expression of the nature around us transfigured by imagination and love."[66]

In a well-known fragment published in 1798 in the journal *Athenäum,* Schlegel wrote: "The French Revolution, Fichte's theory of science, and Goethe's *Meister* are the greatest trends of the era." Two years later, in "Rede über die Mythologie," the term "revolution" reappears three times: he refers to a "great revolution," to "the spirit of that revolution," and to the "eternal revolution." This is not merely a reference to the French Revolution but an evocation of a radical change in life and culture, one that is translated into every realm of the spirit and that explains the "secret cohesion and ultimate unity" of the epoch (*das Zeitalter*).[67]

In the conclusion of this astonishing text, which is replete with startling intuitions, Schlegel turns his gaze toward the future: our epoch, that of a universal rejuvenation of the species, will be that of the rediscovery, by human beings, of their divinatory power (*divinatorischen Kraft*) — a power that will allow us "an incomparable broadening of the spirit." We shall thus be able to know and recognize "the poles of humanity as a whole," from the action of the first human beings to the "character of the golden age which is yet to come": "This is what I mean by the new mythology." By situating the Golden Age in the future, not in the past, Schlegel transfigures the myth into utopian energy and invests mythopoetry with a magical power.[68]

This utopian quality is absent from the mythological works of late Romanticism. Still, even the work of a conservative spirit such as Bachofen could lend itself to quite varied interpretations: a celebration of matriarchy among socialists and libertarians (from Engels and Jean-Jacques-Elisée Reclus to Erich Fromm and Walter Benjamin), an irrational cult of the archaic in Ludwig Klages, and finally a sacralization of the patriarchal Roman state by the Nazi ideologue Alfred Bäumler.

The Quantification of the World

As Max Weber sees it, capitalism was born with the spread of merchants' account books, that is, with the rational calculation of possessions and duties (*l'avoir* and *le devoir*), of receipts and expenses. The ethos of modern industrial capitalism is Rechenhaftigkeit, the spirit of rational calculation.

Many Romantics felt intuitively that all the negative characteristics of modern society—the religion of the god Money (Carlyle called it mammonism); the decline of all qualitative, social, and religious values; the death of the imagination and the novelistic spirit; the tedious uniformization of life; the purely utilitarian relations of human beings among themselves and with nature—stem from the same source of corruption: market quantification. The poisoning of social life by money and the poisoning of the air by industrial smoke are understood by several Romantics as parallel phenomena, stemming from the same perverse root.

Charles Dickens offers an illustrative example of the Romantic charge against capitalist modernity. Dickens was one of Marx's favorite authors, although he was in no way given to socialist thinking. His *Hard Times,* a novel published in 1854, contains an exceptionally well-articulated expression of the Romantic critique of industrial society. This book does not offer as explicit a homage to precapitalist (generally medieval) forms as do the works of most English Romantics (Burke, Samuel Taylor Coleridge, Cobbett, Walter Scott, Carlyle—to whom *Hard Times* is dedicated—and William Morris), but reference to the moral values of the past is an essential component of its atmosphere. In what is only superficially paradoxical, these values have found refuge in a circus, a somewhat archaic but authentically human community in which people still have "tender hearts" and make "natural gestures," a community situated outside of, and in pronounced opposition to, "normal" bourgeois society.

In *Hard Times,* the cold, quantifying spirit of the industrial age is magnificently personified by a utilitarian ideologue and member of Parliament, Mr. Thomas Gradgrind (the name suggests someone who "grinds up to suit"). This is a man "with a rule and a pair of scales, and the multiplication table always in his pocket"; he is always "ready to weigh and measure any parcel of human nature, and tell you exactly what it comes to." For Gradgrind everything in the universe is "a mere question of figures, a case of simple arithmetic," and he organizes the education of children strictly according to the salutary principle that "what you couldn't state in figures, or show to be purchaseable in the cheapest market and saleable in the dearest, was not, and never should be." Gradgrind's philosophy—the harsh, bitter doctrine of political economy, strict utilitarianism, and classic laissez-faire ideology—was based on the principle that "everything was to be paid for. Nobody was ever on any account to give anybody anything, or render anybody help without purchase. Gratitude was to be abolished, and the virtues springing from it were not to be. Every inch of the existence of mankind, from birth to death, was to be a bargain across a counter."[69]

In contrast with this powerful and evocative portrait—almost a Weberian ideal type—of the capitalist ethos, whose miserable triumph will be achieved when "romance is utterly driven out" of human souls, Dickens offers his faith in the vitality of human "sensibilities, affections, weaknesses," which constitute a force "defying all the calculations ever made by man, and no more known to his arithmetic than his Creator is." He believes—and the whole story of *Hard Times* is a passionate plea in favor of this belief—that in the hearts of individuals there are "subtle essences of humanity which will elude the utmost cunning of algebra until the last trumpet ever to be sounded shall blow even algebra to wreck." Refusing to bow to the machine-for-grinding-everything-up-to-suit, he clings to values that cannot be reduced to figures.[70]

But *Hard Times* does not deal merely with the way souls are ground up; the novel also illustrates how modernity has eliminated qualities such as beauty, imagination, and the colorful aspects of the material life of individuals, by reducing everything to a sullen, wearying, and uniform routine. Dickens describes "Coketown," a modern industrial city, as "a town of machinery and tall chimneys, out of which interminable serpents of smoke trailed themselves forever and ever, and never got uncoiled." Its streets were all alike, "inhabited by people equally like one another, who all went in and out at the same hours, with the same sound upon the same pavements, to do the same work, and to whom every day was the same as yesterday and tomorrow, and every year the counterpart of the last and the next."[71]

For industrial civilization, nature's qualities do not exist: it takes into account only the quantities of raw materials that it can extract from nature. Coketown, consequently, was an "ugly citadel, where Nature was as strongly bricked out as killing airs and gases were bricked in"; its tall chimneys "puffing out their poisonous volumes" hid the sky; the sun was "eternally in eclipse through a medium of smoked glass." Those who were eager for "a breath of fresh air," who wanted to see a green landscape, trees, birds, a bit of blue sky, had to travel several kilometers by railway and walk in the fields. But even there they were not at peace: deserted wells, abandoned after all the iron or coal had been wrested from the earth, were hidden in the grass, like so many deadly traps.[72]

Dickens was a moderate in favor of social reforms; the Romantic critique of quantification can also take conservative and reactionary forms. For instance, Adam Müller and other figures of political Romanticism defended traditional feudal property as representing a qualitative form of life, in contrast to monetarism and the market alienation of property. Anti-Semites identified Jews with money, usury, and finance and saw them as factors of corruption and subversion in the Old Regime. Edmund Burke's pamphlet on the French Revolution offers a classic example of a counterrevolutionary use of the Romantic argument about modern quantification: denouncing the humiliation inflicted on the French queen by the revolutionaries in 1790, he exclaims: "The age of chivalry is gone. That of sophisters, œconomists, and calculators, has succeeded; and the glory of Europe is extinguished for ever."[73]

The Mechanization of the World

In 1809, Franz von Baader published *Über den Begriff dynamischer Bewegung im Gegensatze zur mechanischen* (On the concept of dynamic motion as opposed to mechanical) a work that was to have considerable reverberations among the Romantics. In the name of the natural, the organic, the living, and the dynamic, the Romantics often manifested a deep hostility to everything mechanical, artificial, or constructed. Nostalgic for the lost harmony between humans and nature, enshrining nature as the object of a mystical cult, they observed with melancholy and despair the progress of mechanization and industrialization, the mechanized conquest of the environment. They saw the capitalist factory as a hellish place and the workers as damned souls, not because they were exploited but because, as Dickens put it in a gripping image in *Hard Times,* they were obliged to follow mechanical movements, the uniform rhythm of the steam engine's piston, which "worked monotonously up and down like the head of an elephant in a state of melancholy madness."[74]

The Romantics were also haunted by the terrifying prospect that human beings themselves could be mechanized, from the time of Hoffmann's "Sandman," in which Olympia's movements "seem to stem from some kind of clockwork" and whose music is "unpleasantly perfect," to the future Eve of Auguste de Villiers de l'Isle-Adam. In a commentary on Hoffmann, Walter Benjamin observed that his tales are based on an identification of the automatic with the satanic, the life of modern man being "the product of a foul artificial mechanism governed by Satan from within."[75]

Thomas Carlyle's "Signs of the Times" (1829) does an admirable job of summing up the Romantics' anxiety and discomfort before the mechanization of the world: "Were we required to characterise this age of ours by any single epithet, we should be tempted to call it, not an Heroical, Devotional, Philosophical, or Moral Age, but, above all others, the Mechanical Age. It is the Age of Machinery, in every outward and inward sense of that word." Not only are all the traditional activities of the human species disappearing, replaced by machines, but "men are grown mechanical in head and in heart, as well as in hand." Social and political life, learning, religion, all these are themselves subjected to this logic of mechanization: "Our true Deity is Mechanism." Yet humanity's greatest conquests were not mechanical but dynamic, impelled by an infinite aspiration. This is true of the rise of Christianity, the Crusades, and even the French Revolution: "Here too was an Idea; a Dynamic, not a Mechanic force. It was a struggle, though a blind and at last an insane one, for the infinite, divine nature of Right, of Freedom, of Country."[76]

One of the most important aspects of this problematics is the Romantic critique of modern politics as a mechanical system — that is, artificial, "inorganic," "geometrical," lifeless, and soulless. This critique can even go so

far as to challenge the state as such: for example, in an anonymous document (probably written by the young Schelling), from 1796 – 97 discovered by Franz Rosenzweig and published under the title *Das älteste
Sustem des deutschen Idealismus* (The oldest system of German idealism), we
find this appeal: "We must go beyond the State! For every State necessarily
treats free human beings like a mechanical system of gears [*mechanisches
Räderwerk*]." Without going that far, many Romantics considered the modern state, based on individualism, property, contracts, and a rational bureaucratic administration, to be as mechanical, cold, and impersonal a system as a factory. According to Novalis, "in no State has the administration
so perfectly resembled a factory as in Prussia since the death of Friedrich
Wilhelm I." In the same spirit, Müller denounced those who reduced the
state to "a manufacturing plant, or an insurance company," while Schlegel
complained of a "certain mathematical conception of the State and of politics [that] was not the responsibility of the republican or liberal party alone,
but that was found in many legitimate governments."[77]

We find echoes of this Romantic rejection of the machine state and modern politics up to the twentieth century, for example in a text by Martin
Buber published in 1919. Buber presents the state as a fully wound up
mechanical doll (*wohaufgezogene Staatspuppe*) that wants to take the place of
the organic life of the community.[78] Another example occurs in Péguy's
famous opposition of the mystical to the political — that is, of what stems
from heroism or sainthood to what stems from modern political degradation, and in particular from the modern (parliamentary) forms of the state.

Most Romantics converge in criticizing the modern (bourgeois) perception of the political bond as a mathematical contract between proprietary
individuals and in denouncing the modern state as an artificial scaffolding
of wheelworks and balances, or as a blind machine that takes on a life of its
own and crushes the human beings who created it. However, the alterna-
tives proposed are not only diverse but also often contradictory, going from
the traditionalist return to an organic state (generally monarchic) of the
past to the anarchist rejection of any form of state in the name of the free
social community.

Rationalist Abstraction

According to Marx, the capitalist economy is based on a system of abstract
categories: abstract work, abstract exchange value, money. For Max Weber,

rationalization is at the heart of modern bourgeois civilization, which organizes all economic, social, and political life according to the requirements of rationality-with-respect-to-goals (Zweckrationalität, or instrumental rationality) and bureaucratic rationality. Finally, Mannheim shows the connection among rationalization, disenchantment, and quantification in the modern capitalist world: according to him, "this 'rationalising' and 'quantifying' thinking is embedded in a psychic attitude and form of experience with regard to things and the world which may itself be described as 'abstract.' . . . [This] rationalism . . . has its parallel in the new economic system" oriented toward exchange value.[79]

Some of the Romantic critiques of rationalist abstraction are launched from within rationalism itself: this is the case with Hegelian and neo-Hegelian dialectics, whose connection with Romanticism has been noted by many writers. This approach aims to replace the analytic rationality (*Verstand*) of the Enlightenment by a higher and more concrete level of reason (*Vernunft*). This is also the case, a century later, with Theodor Adorno and Horkheimer's *Dialectic of Enlightenment,* which is positioned as an instance of "self-criticism on the part of Reason" and an attempt to counter instrumental rationality — in the service of domination over nature and over human beings — with substantive human rationality.

The Romantics' ideological struggle against abstraction often takes the form of a return to the concrete: in German political Romanticism, the concrete, historical, traditional laws of every country or region are opposed to abstract natural laws; the concrete "freedoms" of each social state are opposed to "Freedom" in the abstract; national or local traditions are opposed to universalist doctrines, and the concrete, particular, specific aspects of reality are opposed to general rules or principles.

One of the most important forms of this "concrete thinking" is historicism: confronting a reason that wants to be seen as atemporal and abstract/human, the Romantics rediscover and rehabilitate history. The historical school of law (Karl von Savigny, Gustav Hugo), the conservative German historiography (Leopold von Ranke, Johann Gustav Droysen), the surge of historical novels (the works of Walter Scott, Victor Hugo's *Notre-Dame de Paris,* Alexandre Dumas's many novels), the relativist historicism in the social sciences in the late nineteenth century (Dilthey, Simmel) — these are all manifestations of the Romantic historicization of culture as a whole.

The Romantic opposition to rational abstraction can also be expressed as a rehabilitation of nonrational and/or nonrationalizable behaviors. This applies in particular to *the* classic theme of Romantic literature: love as a pure emotion, a spontaneous attraction that cannot be reduced to any calculation and that is in contradiction with all rationalist strategies of marriage — marriage for money, marriage "for good reasons." There is also a revalorization of intuitions, premonitions, instincts, feelings — all these terms are intimately linked to the conventional use of the term "Romanticism" itself. This approach may lead to a more favorable evaluation of madness, as the individual's ultimate break with socially instituted reason. The theme of mad love in surrealist literature and poetry is the most radical expression of this tendency.

The critique of rationality may also take rather obscurantist and disturbing forms: irrationalism; hatred of reason as "dangerous," "corrosive" toward tradition; religious fanaticism; intolerance; the irrational cult of a charismatic "leader," nation, or race; and so on. These elements are present in certain currents of Romanticism, from its beginnings up to the present day, but to reduce Romantic culture to irrationalism would be a serious error, short-circuiting the difference between the irrational and the nonrational (that is, between the programmatic negation of rationality and the delimitation of psychic spheres that are not reducible to reason), and overlooking the Romantic currents that spring directly from the rationalist tradition of the Enlightenment.

The Dissolution of Social Bonds

In a striking passage from *The Condition of the Working Class in England in 1844*, Engels points out an essential contradiction of modern life:

> The hundreds of thousands of people of all classes and ranks crowding past each other [in London], are they not all human beings with the same qualities and powers, and with the same interest in being happy? . . . And still they crowd by one another as though they had nothing in common, nothing to do with one another. . . . The brutal indifference, the unfeeling isolation of each in his private interest, becomes the more repellent and offensive, the more these individuals are crowded together, within a limited space.[80]

But the German Romantic Clemens Brentano had already reacted against that phenomenon in observations he made about Paris in 1827: "All those I saw were walking in the same street, side by side, and yet each seemed to be going his own lonely way; no one greeted anyone else, everyone pursued his own personal interest. All this coming and going struck me as the very image of egoism. Everyone has only his own interest in mind, like the number of the house toward which he is hurrying."[81]

Indeed, the Romantics are painfully aware of the alienation of human relationships, the destruction of the old organic and communitarian forms of social life, the isolation of individuals in their egoistic selves, which taken together constitute an important dimension of capitalist civilization, centered on cities. Saint-Preux in Rousseau's *Julie* is only the first in a long line of Romantic heroes who feel lonely, misunderstood, unable to communicate in a meaningful way with their fellows, and this is the case at the very center of modern social life, in the "urban desert."

In literary representations of this theme, isolation, "solitude in society,"[82] is experienced in the early stages of Romanticism, above all by privileged souls—poets, artists, thinkers; but starting with Flaubert (his *Sentimental Education* in particular), a large number of works show and analyze the failure of communication as being the universal—and tragic—condition of all human beings in modern society. We see reflections of this preoccupation not only at the thematic level but also in literary forms, such as internal monologues or non-omniscient narration—that is, narration in which the narrator is enclosed within his or her own consciousness and manages only partially, or not at all, to penetrate the subjectivity of others: Marcel in Marcel Proust's *Remembrance of Things Past* is an exemplary case.

Modern literature offers various simultaneous attempts to rediscover the lost community and bring it into the imaginary universe: the circle of pure souls gathered around Daniel d'Arthez in Balzac's *Lost Illusions,* the bands of adventurers, soldiers, and revolutionaries in André Malraux's novels and Antoine de Saint-Exupéry's stories, to mention just a few examples.

This dual concern—an acute awareness of the radical deterioration of the quality of human relations in modernity and a nostalgic search for authentic community—is by no means limited to literature. It is also present in pictorial art. In *Promenade,* a drawing by the German abstract expressionist August Macke, we see a certain number of human forms, each one on a different level and facing in a different direction, all with sad, shuttered, neutral faces. This drawing would make an excellent illustration for the remarks by Engels and Brentano cited above. We may think, too, of paintings by the American Edward Hopper, in which everything — the choice of subject, the quality of light and shadow, the arrangement of the surfaces — reinforces a stifling feeling of individual isolation. To be sure, in painting we also find images — idealized and nostalgic images — of unified groups, of solidarity and harmony, as in scenes of peasant life or exotic locales.

This thematics plays a major role, at the same time, in the realm of ideas. A primordial element of existentialism is the anguish of individuals confined within their own existences, facing their own particular death. This leads religious existentialists to envision the quest for God in the first place as a search for authentic communication: Martin Buber's I-Thou relation. Thus, in Christianity, according to Nicolas Berdiaev, "from the ontological standpoint solitude implies a longing for God as the subject, as the Thou."[83]

But we must also keep in mind that, entirely apart from both the secular and the religious existentialist tendencies, this problematic found its sociological-theoretical expression on the one hand in Tönnies's classic work, *Gemeinschaft und Gesellschaft,* which establishes a contrast between earlier communities — held firmly together by organic bonds — and modern society with its mechanical and contractual character, and on the other hand in Cooley's work on "primary relations."

THE GENESIS OF THE PHENOMENON

In addressing the question of the origins of Romanticism, we must first distinguish clearly between words and things, between the lexical history of the terms "Romantic," "Romanticism," and so on and the history of the cultural phenomenon that we are analyzing here, while recognizing that the two histories are nevertheless connected. The phenomenon had existed for more than half a century before anyone began to use nouns such as "romanticism," "*romantisme*" or "*romanticisme*" (French), and "*Romantik*" (German) to characterize contemporaneous cultural movements. The adjectives, on the contrary ("romantic," "*romantique*," "*romantisch*") appeared well before the actual advent of the phenomenon, although they did not yet have the meaning of intellectual and artistic current that they would later acquire.

Friedrich Schlegel seems to have been the first — in the early nineteenth century — to associate the adjective "romantic" with a philosophical-literary movement, that of the first German Romanticism.[84] Subsequently, and through a slow and complicated process, the nouns took hold as names of cultural trends that belonged at once to the contemporary period and to the recent past. In England, the school of the Lake Poets — Coleridge, Words-worth, Robert Southey, who began to be known in the early years of the eighteenth century — acquired the name Romanticism only retrospectively, several decades later.[85] As for France, the use of the noun increased during the 1820s, and the term came to designate the young literary movement associated with Vigny, Alphonse de Lamartine, and Hugo.

The adjective can be found as early as the seventeenth century, however, particularly in England and Germany. It was originally used to describe whatever was perceived as characteristic of novels, *romans,* from the Middle Ages and beyond: exalted sentiments, extravagance, the marvelous, chiv-alry, and so forth. The two focal points are emotion and freedom of the imagination. These were negative values in the seventeenth century, but they became more and more positive during the century that followed, when the adjective began to be applied frequently to scenes of nature, in a related but different sense: "Romantic . . . is the landscape before which one feels the sentiment of nature, or the epic grandeur of the past, or a mixture of both: ruins in a wilderness. But romantic, as well, is the sensibility capable of responding to this spectacle. . . ."[86] If to the associations already invoked we add Gothic on the one hand and utopian on the other (as in the following citation, referring to biblical prophecies: "a romantick state, that never has nor ever will be" [1690]),[87] we can measure the extent to which the term's linguistic prehistory anticipates the cultural phenomenon.

But when did this phenomenon actually begin? There is considerable confusion on this point. Depending on which national tradition one is investigating, the date is earlier or later: for example, English Romanticism can be said to start with Coleridge and Wordsworth at the beginning of the nineteenth century, while the French version does not begin until the 1820s. Recently, the predominant tendency has been to take at face value the labels applied either by contemporaries or by the later tradition — in short, to conflate words and things.

As a result, the origins of Romanticism are rarely situated before the French Revolution. Everything from the earlier periods that resembles more or less closely what had come to be called Romanticism has been christened "pre-Romantic."[88] Different terms were sometimes invented to characterize the pre-Romantic periods and movements: the German Sturm und Drang has been called the "Age of Genius," and according to an article by the American critic Northrop Frye, the second half of the eighteenth century in England was the "Age of Sensibility."[89]

Still, there have been some discordant voices. At the heart of the Romantic movement of the first half of the nineteenth century, in his *Histoire des idées littéraires en France* (1842), Alfred Michiels recognized that all Romanticism was already present in the work of Louis-Sébastien Mercier, whose literary career began in the 1860s.[90] In 1899, H. A. Beers published *History of English Romanticism in the Eighteenth Century,* and in 1912 Daniel Mornet's *Le Romantisme en France au XVIIIe siècle* appeared. The tendency to extend the notion of Romanticism properly speaking back to the heart of the eighteenth century has increased markedly in recent years.[91]

In the context of our own way of conceptualizing the Romantic phenomenon, it seems clear in fact that the movement's genesis has to be located in the course of what has been customarily called "the century of Enlightenment," and more specifically around the middle of that century. We are in overall agreement on this point with the perspective of Jacques Bousquet, who produced an anthology of eighteenth-century Romanticism. For this scholar and theoretician of Romanticism, especially though not exclusively the French version, Romanticism represents a vast cultural movement closely connected with "the whole of modern civilization." He rightly notes that "no culture has an absolute beginning or end. But it is still not impossible to see in what period, if not at what moment, one cultural tendency predominates over the others." For Bousquet, then, whereas in the seventeenth century and the first half of the eighteenth, "anticipatory signs" could be noted, although they "remained in the minority," in the second half of the eighteenth century a "reversal" comes about; and "the adventure that began around 1760 is not yet over today. . . . we still belong to the great Romantic era."[92]

The anticipatory signs of Romanticism in the seventeenth century have been spotted by others besides Bousquet, in particular Barbéris, who points out a line of affiliation leading to Romanticism among moralists like François de Salignac de la Mothe Fénelon, Louis de Rouvroy, duc de Saint-Simon, and Jean de La Bruyère. Barbéris comments on La Bruyère's *Characters,* his major work, as follows:

Whereas the bourgeoisie has already taken possession of broad zones of social life and rules it with an iron hand, in the eyes of a feeling person starved for justice, what is the weight of its claims to offer a better explanation of the physical universe? . . . The demands of what could already be called *sentiment* entail the condemnation of all harshness, all inhumanity. Here we have the seeds both of the return to religion that will be affirmed by Rousseau and the condemnation of "progress" that has not brought about the reign of greater love, but only new forms of force and extortion. In *Characters,* sentiment is already rising up against certain claims to a "modernism" that is more technical than human.[93]

But we can go even further back: in the writings of Martin Luther and the German reformers we find a virulent denunciation of their age, in which large-scale commerce and finance are rapidly expanding. They condemn usury, avarice, and the spirit of profit, and they glorify the traditional peasant society, expressing nostalgia for a lost Golden Age—a thematics that relies on a theological current that was already widespread in the Middle Ages.[94]

We can also mention the tradition—lay or pagan—of the "pastoral" in the Renaissance and the seventeenth century, a tradition that is itself modeled on the pastorals of ancient Rome, especially those of Horace and Virgil. The latter contrast the city—a place of commerce governed by ambition and greed, productive of insecurity—with the country, which always retains traces of an ancient era of perfect happiness. The most celebrated expression of this view is doubtless Horace's *"Beatus ille, qui procul negotiis . . .":* "Happy the man who, far away from business cares, / Like the pristine race of mortals, / Works his ancestral lands with his steers, / From all money-lending free."[95]

Thus there is a prehistory of Romanticism that has its roots in the ancient development of business, money, cities, and industry and that is manifested later, especially in the Renaissance, in reaction to the evolution and the abrupt forward surges of progress toward modernity. Like its antithesis, capitalism, Romanticism evolved over a prolonged historical period. But these two antagonists truly come into being as fully developed structures—as Gesamtkomplexe—only in the eighteenth century.

Although we have just evoked a number of themes that can be said to be parts of Romanticism, we cannot yet speak of an integral worldview; these are only separate elements of the whole that is later known as Romanticism, but so far they have always been expressed within the framework of other, older forms of thought and sensibility. For Romanticism properly speaking, that is, as an overall cultural response to a generalized socioeconomic system, is a specifically modern phenomenon. It corresponds to a qualitative leap in the historical development of societies, the advent of an unprecedented new order that contrasts in a decisive way with everything that has gone before.

The well-known Austro-Hungarian economist Karl Polanyi, in *The Great Transformation* (1944), rightly stresses the absolutely unprecedented character of this mutation. For him, what is happening is the "metamorphosis of the caterpillar" in which, for the first time in human history, the economic realm, in the form of the self-regulating market, becomes autonomous and dominant with respect to the entire set of social institutions; at the same time, at the level of social psychology, one of the multiple motives (custom, law, magic, religion, and so on) that determined action in earlier societies acquires primacy: the profit motive. In a triple process of unification, extension, and emancipation of the market economy, we reach a total reversal of the principles governing all past societies: the new principle consists in subordinating "the substance of society itself to the laws of the market."[96]

What was once a means becomes an end in itself; what was an end becomes a simple means. Rousseau betrays his awareness of this dizzying reversal fraught with consequences when, in 1764, in *Lettres écrites de la montagne,* he addresses the following remarks to the bourgeois citizenry of Geneva concerning their political life:

> The ancient peoples are no longer a model for the moderns; they are too foreign in every respect. You, especially, Genevans, stay in your place. . . . You are neither Romans nor Spartans; you are not even Athenians. Leave those great names alone; they do not become you. You are merchants, artisans, bourgeois, always occupied with your private interests, your work, commerce, profits; you are *people for whom freedom itself is only a means toward untrammeled acquisition and secure possession.*[97]

The acquisition of property becomes a value in itself; accordingly, as the British intellectual historian Alfred Cobban has noted, in the eighteenth century "the absolute rights of private property had come to possess in and for themselves and apart from fulfillment of function a sacrosanct character such as they had never had before."[98] It is in this context that one has to understand the radical critique of private property developed by Rousseau in his two *Discourses*.

Historians and economists generally agree in seeing two key moments, two points of rupture in the slow, centuries-long transition between feudalism and capitalism: first, the Renaissance, at different times in different countries, a period during which the medieval social bonds were loosened and the process of primitive accumulation got under way; next, and more definitively, the nineteenth-century Industrial Revolution that led to the hegemony of the system of capitalist production based on the laws of the marketplace. It was thus during this second and last moment — when the tendencies that had been at work for a long time became a system, when the bases of modern industry were created, and when the grip of the market over social life as a whole took on concrete form — that Romanticism arose.

Now in this generalization of the marketplace, culture, art, and literature were by no means spared; in the second half of the eighteenth century, intellectuals, artists, and writers became, to a vastly greater extent than before, free agents in the various marketplaces for their cultural products. The system of patronage increasingly gave way to the sale of books and paintings. The producers of culture thus found themselves confronted with a contradiction between the use value and the exchange value of their own products; the new socioeconomic system affected them in their innermost reaches.

The socioeconomic transformation is accompanied by an ideological evolution, which begins in the Renaissance but is taken to its logical extreme only in the second half of the eighteenth century: systematic skepticism, rationalism, the scientific and technological spirit, materialism, numerical individualism (Simmel). In the spirit of the Enlightenment, the model of the natural and mathematical sciences is often applied to the understanding of human beings and the resolution of their problems. This spirit takes a particularly empiricist and utilitarian form in England, with John Locke, David Hume, and especially Jeremy Bentham.

It is thus against this phenomenon as a whole — the various effects of the unprecedented advent of a market economy and in particular its penetration of culture life but also certain ideological facets of the spirit of the

Enlightenment and quite specifically of those aspects that are most closely bound up with the new reification of life, which reduced human aspirations to egoistic calculations — that late eighteenth-century Romanticism rises up to protest. And if it is true, as Eric Hobsbawm has suggested, that the Romantic critique of this period is not always directed against a bourgeoisie that has not yet gained political power (the Romantic themes could even be used for the "glorification of the middle class"),[99] it is just as true that, to cite Marilyn Butler, an eminent historian of British literature, "the most obvious feature common to all the arts of Western nations after 1750 was the refusal to validate the contemporary social world."[100]

Up to now we have spoken of the origins of Romanticism in general terms, without focusing on the particular countries in which this genesis took place. We must now raise the following question: Can the source of Romanticism be localized in one country rather than another, as has sometimes been claimed? To begin with, one element seems clear, namely, that the "kernel" or heart of the phenomenon can be situated in three countries: France, England, and Germany.[101] For it is in these relatively developed countries that Romanticism arose earliest, in the second half of the eighteenth century, most intensely and in the most pronounced manner. Furthermore, elsewhere and later on, these countries exercised a massive influence over the development and expansion of the various Romanticisms.

But is there one country that supplied the first thrust, chronologically preceding and decisively influencing the birth of Romanticism in the other two? Does one country have the right to be called the creator of this vast intellectual and artistic movement? Both Germany and England have been proposed as candidates for this distinction, the first often because of a particular vocation associated with its national character and destiny, the second because of its socioeconomic head start. However, if we look closely at the cultural history of these two countries and France in the eighteenth century, such assertions appear debatable, and we agree with Mannheim that Romanticism appeared at roughly the same time in all three European nations.[102]

In his *Anthologie du XVIIᵉ siècle romantique,* Jacques Bousquet convincingly refutes the idea that France was considerably behind the others. He not only recalls that some first-rate French texts (e.g., Rousseau's *Julie*) appeared before their counterparts in the other countries (e.g., *Werther*), but he also shows even more compellingly that in eighteenth-century

France a strong Romantic flavor characterized a great number of secondary works and authors that are now forgotten except by a handful of specialists. Thus in France, as in Germany and in England, there was a dense Romantic cultural fabric; it was not just a matter of a few outstanding works. As for the question of the presumed Anglo-German influences, Bousquet demonstrates that the influence of German authors was not very important and that the English influence was much less significant than has been claimed. The texts translated were often the least "Romantic" of the period, or were adulterated in translation.[103]

We shall thus retain the idea that Romanticism emerged on more or less equal terms, independently and simultaneously, in the three countries in question, the ones that were relatively most advanced in the process of the modernization and development of capitalism. But this formulation may raise a second question: Why is Germany included in the triad? How can we explain, in the framework of our theory, how this destitute country, lagging economically several decades at least behind England and France, could have participated on equal terms with these other countries in the genesis of Romanticism?

We can offer several suggestions in answer to that question. In the first place, and in a general way, it is important to recall that the development of capitalism was initially a European phenomenon, then a worldwide one; its effects were felt everywhere in the zones it touched, and the earliest and most violent reactions did not always come from the center. The Russian and Chinese revolutions can suffice as examples.

But so far as the genesis of Romanticism in Germany is concerned, there is a more important explanation. For, as Lukács emphasized,[104] the famous *"deutsche Misere,"* German destitution, lends itself to abusive simplifications. Germany underwent large-scale industrialization in the eighteenth century and was even in the lead in some areas (iron, coal, and so on).[105] Capitalism took firm hold in Germany during this period, especially from midcentury on, but in a more state-controlled form than in England or France. As Henri Brunschwig asserts in his fine book *Société et romantisme en Prusse au XVIIIᵉ siècle:* "Whereas the growing freedom of trade favors the development of large-scale private capitalism in England and France, Prussia becomes the country of state capitalism. . . ."[106] It was Frederick the Great who, starting in 1740, undertook to rationalize and modernize the Prussian economy by means of a state-controlled bureaucracy; the state became the principal trader, banker, and industrialist. This is why the critique of political modernity was to take on special importance in German Romanticism.

At the same time, Frederick encouraged the emergence of an Aufklärung, partially imported from France.[107] This Aufklärung was actively cultivated by the educational establishment and the official church and reached its apogee in Berlin at the end of the eighteenth century. It constituted the basis for a thriving bourgeois culture, which was on the way to becoming predominant — and this suggests a second explanation for Germany's meriting special attention — in this period when the nobility was still the leading social force in the country. Brunschwig speaks of a "quasi-monopoly of the culture that the bourgeoisie took over in Prussia . . .": Members of the bourgeoisie "do most of the writing. They impose their formulas on those who claim to think. . . . the noble who wants to think can only do so in a bourgeois way, and the public opinion of the Prussian monarchy is that of the bourgeois order. . . ."[108] The bourgeois mentality is rooted on the one hand in a certain religious moralism and on the other hand in an ethic of education, rationality, and method in all activities of life, work, and individual success.[109]

We are asserting, then, that Germany possessed both an essentially capitalist economic system and a bourgeois Enlightenment culture, against which the earliest manifestations of Romanticism arose. This is certainly not to deny the existence of a deutsche misere. On the contrary, German poverty played a considerable role in the development of German Romanticism, and it may help to account for the specific character of that movement, namely, the relative weakness of its leftist or progressive wing, its orientation largely toward conservatism and reaction.[110] In fact, according to Karl Mannheim in *Conservatism,* the economic lag and the lack of a sufficiently large and powerful bourgeoisie prevented a synthesis of Romanticism with Enlightenment and instead produced an alliance with the aristocratic-feudal resistance to absolutist bureaucracy.[111]

As for the countries on the periphery, both in terms of socioeconomic development and in terms of the kernel of Romanticism, their Romantic movements clearly arose later, generally starting in the 1820s. In the countries of Eastern Europe (Russia, Poland, Hungary, the Balkans, and so on), in Italy, and in Spain, the early impulse is primarily nationalist (opposition to foreign occupiers or support for national unification), and in the absence of a significant bourgeois element it is often directed against a decadent local aristocracy.[112] But given the international character of capitalist development and evolution toward modernity, we can understand how these countries too, though they may be only slightly — or not yet at all — imbued with the new tendencies, are just as subject as the kernel countries to the Romantic challenge.

Let us now look briefly at the origins of Romanticism as they took shape — in an autonomous way, despite reciprocal influences — in each of the three principal countries.

England

Beginning in 1760, a cultural change became manifest in England.[113] The symptoms of this transformation are broadly apparent in literature and the arts and to a somewhat lesser extent in philosophy and political and social thought, which were by and large dominated by the utilitarian tendency. In the arts especially, then, a certain number of Romantic elements took hold and spread widely, the most important being nostalgia for the past.[114]

Nostalgia for the Middle Ages and the English Renaissance predominated (in fact the two were often viewed as part of a single past era), but there was also nostalgia for "barbarian" societies (Nordic, Gaelic, Scottish, and so on), as well as for primitive Greco-Roman antiquity or traditional peasant society. At the same time, a cult of sentiment and subjectivity was emerging, with an emphasis on their lugubrious and melancholic dimensions, along with a celebration of nature and a critique of the market spirit and industrialization.

Nostalgia for the past is manifested in particular in the Ossianic poems (1762) of James Macpherson; in the Gothic novel, beginning with Horace Walpole's *Castle of Otranto* (1764); and also in the fashion for imitating various ancient styles in architecture and the decorative arts. Regarding sentiment and nature, let us mention the Graveyard School of Thomas Gray, Edward Young, and William Collins.

And let us cite one example among many others, Oliver Goldsmith's "The Deserted Village" (1770), a poem that brings all these themes together and denounces the commercialization of England from a Tory perspective:

Ill fares the land, to hastening ills a prey,
Where wealth accumulates and men decay . . .
But a bold peasantry, their country's pride,
When once destroyed, can never be supplied.

A time there was, ere England's griefs began,
When every rood of ground maintained its man;
For him light labour spread her wholesome store,
Just gave what life required, but gave no more . . .

But times are altered; trade's unfeeling train
Usurp the land and dispossess the swain. . . .[115]

France

The movement of ideas in France was very heavily dominated by the *Ency-clopedia* and the Enlightenment in the second half of the eighteenth century. Early French Romanticism was expressed mainly in the arts and literature but was also found in religion, especially starting around 1770 with the burgeoning of illuminist and theosophic sects, which were often apocalyptic, millennial. Auguste Viatte studied these sects as "hidden sources of Romanticism."[116]

In his *Anthologie du XVIIIe siècle romantique,* Jacques Bousquet lists a large number of characteristic Romantic themes that appear frequently in the literary works of the period, among major authors as well as minor ones (e.g., Baculard d'Arnaud, Tiphaigne de la Roche, Laoisel de Tréogate): sensibility, melancholia, dreams, mal du siècle (Weltschmerz), the urban desert, idyllic nature and savage nature, the return to religion, and so forth. Concerning nostalgia for the past, Bousquet declares that during this period the medieval period did not yet play the role it would take on after the Revolution; people longed rather for the Nordic barbarian times and for classical antiquity. As for the latter, Bousquet notes that "neoclassicism is not a final appearance of classical wisdom and order; it is one of the aspects of Romantic nostalgia; antiquity is no longer a source of models, as it was in the sixteenth century, but has become a theme of reverie."[117]

Rousseau is the key author in the genesis of French Romanticism, for he was able to articulate the entire Romantic worldview in the mid-eighteenth century. For Bousquet, "not all of Rousseau is Romantic, but almost all of

Romanticism is already in Rousseau," and Octavio Paz remarks that "if modern literature begins as criticism of modernity, the figure in whom this paradox becomes incarnate is Rousseau."[118] In Rousseau we can see a Romantic configuration that begins to emerge with *Discourses* (1750, 1755) and *Julie, or the New Heloise* (1761), but that continues in *Confessions* and *Rêveries du promeneur solitaire* from his later years.

Whereas Denis Diderot, without being fully Romantic himself, has a Romantic dimension, especially in his valorization of the imagination, disciples of Rousseau such as Jacques-Henri Bernardin de Saint-Pierre and Restif de la Bretonne are wholly Romantic, the first in his tragic idyll, *Paul et Virginie,* and the second in his communist, patriarchal, and peasant utopias.[119] Chateaubriand can be located in this Romanticism that precedes the French Revolution, because he wrote his *Tableaux de la Nature* between 1784 and 1790.

Germany

In contrast to the French and English forms, German Romanticism in its beginnings was embodied just as much in thought as in the arts, in particular with the pietist theologian Hamann (1730–1788) and his disciple the philosopher Herder, in whose work we find a celebration of backward states of development (*die Rückständige*), of the organic, and of intuition. These same tendencies are evidenced in the Sturm und Drang movement of the 1770s, which includes the young Schiller and Johann Wolfgang von Goethe (*Werther,* 1764). In fact, as Henri Brunschwig asserts, "*Sturm und Drang* is not a new school. It takes its place in a continuous series from pietism to Romanticism, illustrated by Hamann, Möser, Herder, Jacobi, and Jung-Stilling."[120]

Religion — Lutheran pietism and certain more or less occult or "illuminated" sects — played a particularly important role in the birth of German Romanticism. Eighteenth-century mystical Swabian pietism, especially that of Johann Albrecht Bengel and his disciple Friedrich Christoph Oetinger (themselves inspired by Meister Eckehart and Jakob Böhme), was to have a direct influence on Romanticism's *Naturphilosophie,* from Schelling to Baader. Religious feeling is manifested as well in other phenomena that mark the Romantic cultural upheaval of the second half of the century: the appearance of the Rosicrucians and the transformation of the Masonic lodges. During this period, the latter, which had been conceived in the purest spirit of the Enlightenment, adopted the "Scottish rite," which had a quasi-religious character, replacing discussion and rational free examination with mystery, ritual, and hierarchy. The Rosicrucian order was created in the same spirit; it also claimed to give its initiates alchemical and healing powers.[121]

To conclude this chapter, we still need to make a few remarks about the relation between Romanticism and the Enlightenment. For these two spiritual tendencies have too often been opposed to one another in an absolute way, sometimes with the claim that the century of Enlightenment, the eighteenth, had been rejected and replaced by a Romantic century, the nineteenth; or, in cases where the existence of Romantic or "pre-Romantic" tendencies in the eighteenth century are acknowledged, they are seen as basically alien and antagonistic to the dominant current of the Enlightenment.

But this is not at all an accurate picture. In the first place, it is fair to say that Romanticism and the Enlightenment have coexisted in all periods of modernity, from the eighteenth through the twentieth century. Second, their relation has always been variable and complex. As we have already noted, while the opposition between Romanticism and classicism is completely unnecessary in the framework of our conceptualization, the opposition between Romanticism and the Enlightenment is more pertinent for us, given the undeniable connections between the spirit of Enlightenment and the bourgeoisie. But in no case should we construe these connections in a simplistic and mechanical way, as if the Enlightenment were the ideological reflection of the capitalist system or its dominant class; for if the spirit of the Enlightenment is closely related to the "spirit of capitalism" (Weber), like any cultural production it maintains relative autonomy and has been used toward ends that go beyond capitalist goals or that even tend to subvert them. In short, there is more than one Enlightenment.

In the same sense, there is more than one Romanticism. We shall need to circumscribe and organize its diversity in certain typical configurations. The relations among the various Romanticisms and the spirit (or spirits) of the Enlightenment are not constant. One can hardly conclude, then, that Romanticism represents, in general and necessarily, a total rejection of the Enlightenment as a whole. To take an example from the century of Romanticism that interests us here, Hamann and his disciple Herder have radically different outlooks on the Enlightenment: the former rejects it violently and categorically—after having been briefly tempted by it—while the latter always maintains the highest respect for reason and comes close, in some respects, to the Enlightenment movement in France (especially as represented by Diderot).[122] Like Herder, many later Romantic authors such as Shelley, Heinrich Heine, or Victor Hugo are far from being adversaries of the Enlightenment.

In fact, we find all sorts of blends, articulations, juxtapositions, hesitations, and passages between the two perspectives, which are certainly divergent but not totally heterogeneous. In the celebrated cases of Schiller and Goethe, we observe the passage from a predominant Romanticism to a predominant Enlightenment spirit, without there being a complete break between two mentalities in their pure state.

Romanticism often appears, in addition, as a radicalization, a transforming continuation of the social critique of the Enlightenment. Mannheim observes this in a general way, whereas Ernst Fischer notes more specifically that the Sturm und Drang movement both prolongs and surpasses Gotthold Lessing.[123] In particular, the social critique developed by the Enlightenment against the aristocracy, privileges, and the arbitrary use of power can be extended to a critique of the bourgeoisie and the reign of money. Goethe's *Werther* represents a critique of bourgeois as well as aristocratic milieux and mentalities.

A form of radicalization of the Enlightenment exists in the writings of perhaps the greatest Romantic author—by virtue of the value and the influence of his work—of this period of Romanticism's origins, namely, Rousseau. And he illustrates at the same time the juxtaposition of perspectives, for some of his texts are rooted primarily in the Enlightenment.

Let us acknowledge, then, the diversity of the relations between Romanticism and Enlightenment. In the next chapter, we see that, while it is possible to bring them together throughout the typology we propose, certain forms of Romanticism manifest greater or lesser affinity with its enemy brother.

2

Romanticism: Political and Social Diversity

In the vast scaffolding of the Romantic worldview as we have just outlined it in general terms, can we identify typical forms that will allow us to organize the field in a useful way? And beyond such a structuring, are we in a position to establish the foundations for a sociology of Romanticism? To answer these questions, we must also ask whether we can identify the social forces that produced the Romantic weltanschauung. These are the two problems to which we now turn: the creation of a typology of Romanticism on the one hand and the sociology of Romanticism on the other.

OUTLINE OF A TYPOLOGY

In the effort to develop a typology of Romanticism, it is clear that one can divide up the terrain, for example, according to national tradition, historical period, or cultural field. However, if we define Romanticism as a reaction against industrial capitalism and bourgeois society, it seems more consistent to constitute types according to the attitude or position adopted with respect to that society, according to the specific way the problem of modernity is envisaged and perhaps resolved. We are dealing, then, with various politics of Romanticism, but not in the narrow sense of the term; our typology will be more like a grid that brings together the economic, social, and political realms.

We shall in fact be presenting "ideal types" in Max Weber's sense; by this we mean theoretical constructions that on the one hand do not purport to be the only possible or valid ones and that on the other hand often turn out to be articulated or combined in the work of a single author. In citing examples, we shall say that a given thinker or writer belongs to a particular type when this type constitutes the dominant element in his or her writings.

Before discussing each type in turn, let us list — proceeding roughly from right to left on the political spectrum — what we see as the major types of Romanticism if we analyze the phenomenon in terms of the position adopted toward modern society: the particular modalities of the critique and the solutions — or lack thereof — offered to the dilemma facing the Romantic. We have identified the following types of Romanticism:

1. restitutionist
2. conservative
3. fascistic
4. resigned
5. reformist
6. revolutionary and/or utopian

Within revolutionary-utopian Romanticism, one can distinguish several distinct tendencies:

1. Jacobin-democratic
2. populist
3. utopian-humanist socialist
4. libertarian
5. Marxist

Let us emphasize from the outset that this attempt at a typology — proposed here simply as a working hypothesis — has to be handled with care, for often a given cultural expression does not correspond entirely to any of these ideal types (this is characteristic of such Weberian constructions); we also have to take into account the transmutations, reversals, and renunciations that are so characteristic of Romanticism, as they are manifested through the displacement of a given author from one position to another within our typological gamut. Let us recall, to cite some examples, that Friedrich Schlegel and Johann Joseph von Görres went from Jacobin republicanism to the most conservative monarchism, William Morris from nostalgia for the Middle Ages to a Marxist-leaning socialism, Georges Sorel from revolutionary unionism to the right-wing Action française (and vice versa), György Lukács from a tragic and disenchanted Romanticism to Bolshevism.

For some authors these mutations may lead to a complete break with the Romantic spirit and to a reconciliation with the status quo of modernity, but they are exceptional cases. In most of the itineraries in question, we see a displacement within a single intellectual field. And it is precisely the homogeneity of the Romantic sociocultural matrix that makes it possible to understand these seemingly astonishing metamorphoses. The fundamentally ambiguous, contradictory, and hermaphrodite character of this worldview makes the most diverse solutions — and the shift from one to another — possible, without a need for the author to break with the foundations of his previous problematic.

This unity-in-diversity is also embodied in certain cultural movements such as symbolism and expressionism, which traverse the various types without being captured by any; the same holds true for certain back-to-nature social movements, like the *Jugendbewegung* (youth movement) in Germany at the beginning of the twentieth century, or the contemporary ecological movement.

We shall thus try to examine more closely each of the categories we have proposed, chiefly by studying an author whose work comes very close to the ideal-typical characteristics of the figure in question.

Restitutionist Romanticism

In the constellation of Romanticisms, "restitutionism" occupies a privileged place; thus it constitutes a logical point of departure in the discussion of types. This articulation of the worldview may indeed be deemed the most important of all, from both the qualitative and the quantitative viewpoints. In the first place, we note that the greatest number of significant Romantic writers and thinkers fall in this category. In addition, it is obvious that the restitutionist perspective is in a way the closest to the essence of the overall phenomenon, given that nostalgia for a precapitalist state lies at the heart of this worldview. Now the restitutionist type is defined precisely as aspiring to the restitution — that is, the restoration or the re-creation — of this precapitalist past. Neither resigned through realism to a degraded present nor oriented toward a transcendence of both past and present, restitutionism seeks the return of the past, the restoration of the object of nostalgia.

Restitutionist Romanticism is not identical to the reactionary version; the latter refers directly to counterrevolutionary reaction, and this would cover only part of our category. The term "restitutionist," borrowed from the work of the sociologist of religion Jean Seguy, strikes us moreover as decidedly preferable to terms such as "retrograde" or "backward-looking," which are excessively pejorative.

The past that is the object of the restitutionists' nostalgia is sometimes a traditional agrarian society (among the Russian Slavophiles or among the Agrarian southern writers in the United States between the world wars), but restitutionism is most often associated with the Middle Ages. This idealizing focus on the medieval past, especially in its feudal form, can probably be explained by the relative temporal proximity of the Middle Ages (compared for example to ancient or prehistoric societies) and by the radical difference between that era and the aspects of the present that restitutionists reject: the medieval past is close enough for its restoration to be imagined, but at the same time its spirit and structures are completely opposed to those that characterize modern life.

Another general characteristic of this tendency is that its most notable representatives are mainly literary figures. While the restitutionist perspective is also expressed in philosophy (Friedrich Schelling) and in political theory (Adam Müller), for example, the fact remains that it presents particular affinities with artists. The predominance of artists seems to be explained chiefly by the growing self-evidence of the nonrealist and even nonrealizable character of the desire to bring back a period of the past that is definitively over. The dream of returning to the Middle Ages or to an agrarian society nevertheless holds considerable suggestive power over the imagination and lends itself to visionary projections. It thus attracts, first and foremost, sensibilities oriented toward its symbolic and aesthetic dimensions.

If we list the major writers who share the restitutionist vision, we note that many of them come from Germany. Restitutionism is highly developed in the intellectual milieu — including both thinkers and artists — of the *Frühromantik,* the early Romantic period in Germany. This movement was initially characterized, however, by enthusiastic support of the French Revolution and for the values and hopes that it embodied, which demonstrates that restitutionism does not always have its roots in a fundamentally reactionary or rightist viewpoint. Still, disillusioned by the direction that the Revolution had taken in its later years, and especially dismayed by the Napoleonic period, the German Romantics turned toward the ideal of resurrecting a medieval period whose dominant values were the hierarchical ideal of the *Stände,* interpersonal feudal bonds, communion of the entire social body in religious faith, and love of the monarch. Developed by Franz von Baader, Görres, and Müller at the level of political and economic thought in opposition to the liberalism of Adam Smith, and by Ritter, Friedrich Schleiermacher, and the Schlegel brothers (August Wilhelm and Friedrich) at the level of philosophical and theological reflection, this vision of an idealized Middle Ages that contrasted in every respect with the new bourgeois order was expressed in the literary realm first by Ludwig Tieck, Wilhelm Wackenroder, and Novalis.

Novalis provided its classic formulation in his essay *Die Christenheit oder Europa* (1800), in which he contrasts not only the sterile rationalism of the Aufklärung to the lost marvelous aspects of religion but also "commercial life" (*Geschäftsleben*) with its "selfish preoccupations" (*eigennützige Sorgen*) and "men greedy for possessions" (*habsuchtiger Mensch*) to medieval culture united in the spiritual communion of the church.[1] Subsequently, we find the restitutionist outlook in E. T. A. Hoffmann and Joseph von Freiherr Eichendorff, and it appears again in the neo-Romantic tendencies of the late nineteenth and early twentieth centuries.[2]

In England, a phenomenon similar to the one that marked the Frühromantik emerged in the group known as the Lake Poets: after initial enthusiasm for the French Revolution, Robert Southey, William Wordsworth, and Samuel Taylor Coleridge lost their illusions and turned — Coleridge and Southey in particular — toward a form of medieval restitutionism. Walter Scott later expressed the same viewpoint in his novels at the level of the imagination, while Thomas Carlyle gave it discursive expression in his essays; the viewpoint is found later still among the English Pre-Raphaelites. As for France, the ideological reversal that occurred within Romanticism is precisely the opposite: the first perspective, more or less imbued with restitutionism, of François-René de Chateaubriand, Alfred de Vigny and Alphonse de Lamartine, Félicité Robert de Lamennais and Victor Hugo, gave way under the pressure of events to positions that were politically more liberal or democratic.

If at the end of the nineteenth century and in the twentieth, restitutionism has a tendency to yield to some extent to resigned, revolutionary, or fascistic Romanticism, it nevertheless remains in the front ranks. To give some idea of its persistence right up to the Second World War, we can mention its influence on Oswald Spengler and the *Kulturpessimisten* of the German right, on William Butler Yeats, T. S. Eliot, and G. K. Chesterton in England. It survives today with Alexander Solzhenitsyn.

As the exemplary case of restitutionism, let us take a French writer from the period between the two world wars: Georges Bernanos. His case is interesting first of all because it seems to bring the perspective of a significant sector of French youth at the beginning of the twentieth century to literary expression. In his youth, before the First World War, Bernanos was a militant in an extreme right-wing student organization whose very name, the King's Camelots, indicates its restitutionist character. Between the wars, along with other members of the Camelots, Bernanos joined the Action française; but while a significant part of this organization — and of the French right as a whole — was gradually leaning toward fascism, Bernanos remained faithful to his first ideal: the medieval Christian monarchy. Thus despite an anti-Semitism that disfigures some of his early writings, his vision is totally different from that of the twentieth-century Romantics who let themselves be drawn into the Fascist ideology, and he remains a particularly pure instance of restitutionism.

In the original title — *Les grands cimetières sous la lune* — of the book called *A Diary of My Times* in English translation, Bernanos offers a metaphoric image for his conception of modern society: everything is stricken with spiritual death in a world illuminated solely by the value of money. In the same work he denounces in modern humanity "the extreme loneliness of a society that recognizes between its members no longer any links but those of money."[3] *The Diary of a Country Priest* projects the same conception as a social microcosm; the rural parish. According to one of the characters, "the titulary gods of the modern world — we *know* 'em; they dine out, they're called bankers." The representatives of the true spiritual values in the novel oppose this uniformly degraded world, to the ideal of the old medieval Christianity; if it had survived up to the present, "we would have torn from the very heart of Adam . . . that sense of his own loneliness."[4]

The great spiritual challenge of the parish priest, who is a sort of modern saint, is to try to awaken his flock to true values and thus to create a propitious terrain for re-creating the Christianity of times past. This calling is strikingly similar to that of the German restitutionists, defined by Schlegel as early as 1805: "It is the declared goal of the new philosophy to restore the old German constitution, that is, the system of honor, liberty, and loyalty, by working to form the state of mind on which a true free monarchy rests: a state of mind which . . . alone has a character of saintliness."[5] The restitutionist project could not be better defined in its continuity from the earliest German Romanticism to that of France between the wars. The project stands in opposition not only to the reign of trade and money but also to modern politics: the bureaucratic state for the Romantics, parliamentarianism for Bernanos.

However, in Bernanos's novel, this project is destined to fail. The modern malady runs too deep, and the priest's struggle to save the soul of his parish is completely hopeless. The relative optimism of the German Romantics is replaced in Bernanos by a radical pessimism. Still, Bernanos does not become resigned for all that. In the universe of his novels, the only acceptable attitude is commitment to a struggle to restore the lost paradise, a struggle that is absurd, a lost cause from the start. This is the desperate visage that restitutionism can assume in late capitalism.

Conservative Romanticism

Conservative Romanticism aims not to reestablish a lost past but to maintain the traditional state of society (and of government) to the extent that it has managed to persist from late eighteenth-century Europe into the second half of the nineteenth century; it seeks to restore the status quo that had obtained before the French Revolution. It is thus a question of defending societies that are already well along on the road toward capitalist development, but these societies are valued precisely for what they preserve of the ancient, premodern forms.

In addition, there is a non-Romantic conservatism that justifies the capitalist order and seeks to defend it against all criticism, whether the critiques are made in the name of the past or the future. One can speak of conservative Romanticism only to the extent that a certain critique of capitalist-industrial modernity, based on the organic values of the past, is immanent to its discourse. This will also be true, of course, for the other types that we shall consider shortly.

Conservative Romanticism is manifested in particular in the work of political thinkers situated in the early periods of Romanticism (the late eighteenth century and the first half of the nineteenth). Their basic aim was to legitimize the established order as the natural result of historic evolution:

we find evidence of this in the historic school of law (Gustav Hugo, Friedrich Karl von Savigny), in Friedrich Julius Stahl's positive philosophy of the state, in Benjamin Disraeli's Tory ideology. Among the great philosophers of Romanticism, it is probably Schelling who comes closest to this position; in political economics Thomas Malthus can be linked with it to some extent.

The borderline between conservative Romanticism and restitutionist Romanticism is blurry; certain authors such as the "ultras" Joseph de Maistre and Louis de Bonald seem to be located somewhere in a transitional zone. One of the characteristics that nevertheless allows us to distinguish between the two types is the acceptance or nonacceptance of elements in the capitalist order. The total rejection of modern industry and bourgeois society is an essential feature of the restitutionist outlook; full acceptance of these phenomena characterizes non-Romantic thinking, no matter how large a place is granted to tradition, religion, or authoritarianism; this is true, for example, of Auguste Comte's positivism. Conservative Romanticism takes an intermediate position, accepting the situation that prevailed in Europe during the periods in question, in which emerging and flourishing capitalism shared the terrain with significant feudal elements.

Edmund Burke's thought offers a concrete example that will help us spell out the features of this tendency. His work is unquestionably embedded in Romanticism: passionately hostile to the philosophy of the Enlightenment ("this literary cabal"), in his famous pamphlet against the revolution of 1789 (*Reflections on the Revolution in France,* 1790) he contrasts the chivalric traditions and the old feudal spirit of vassality to those of the era of "sophisters, œconomists, and calculators" established by the revolutionaries. He sets the ancient, wise social prejudices, the fruits of a "Gothic and monkish education" against the barbarian philosophy produced by "cold hearts"; the venerable institution of land ownership, the legacy of our ancestors against the sordid speculation of agitators and Jews.[6] Hence the extraordinary impact of his book in Germany, where he contributed to shaping the conceptions of political Romanticism.

Nevertheless, unlike the restitutionist Romantics, Burke is not an unambiguously antibourgeois thinker: his doctrine includes a liberal dimension that is typical of the Whig party to which he belongs. His previous political interventions, favorable to reconciliation with the rebellious American colonies and to the principles of Parliament against the royal absolutism of

George III, had earned him a reputation for liberalism, to such an extent that Thomas Paine could believe that Burke was prepared to join the camp of English supporters of the French Revolution.

In reality, Burke's political and social ideology was the expression of a compromise between the bourgeoisie and the landed property owners that governed the course of the English state after the Glorious Revolution of 1688, to which Burke moreover fervently adhered. In a very revealing passage of *Reflections on the Revolution,* Burke regrets that in France, unlike England, the mutual convertibility of land into money and money into land has always been difficult, since this tradition, along with the great mass of real property in the hands of the crown and the church, "had kept the landed and monied interests more separated in France, less miscible, and the owners of the two distinct species of property not so well disposed to each other as they are in this country."[7]

Despite his admiration for the hereditary aristocracy and the great rural landowners, Burke has no desire to see them keep a monopoly on power. This has to be the privilege of all property owners, or of what he calls a "natural aristocracy," which includes not only the nobility but also judges, professors, and "rich traders, who . . . possess the virtues of diligence, order, constancy, and regularity."[8]

Nostalgia for a chivalrous Middle Ages is not absent from Burke's work, but the past does not play the same role that it plays for the Romantic restitutionists. Burke uses the past much more to justify England's present than to criticize it: he legitimizes the laws, customs, institutions, and social hierarchies of England in 1790 as both natural and providential products of organic growth, as an ancestral legacy transmitted through the centuries by each generation, as part of what Burke calls "the whole chain and continuity of the commonwealth."[9]

Burke's influence is by no means limited to the German Romantics. The adoption of his views by antirevolutionary bourgeois liberalism, from his day to ours, attests to the ambiguity that is peculiar to this conservative Romantic. It is revealing that a North American political scientist, William McGovern, for whom the German Romantics, along with Jean-Jacques Rousseau and Carlyle, are the precursors of the totalitarian doctrines of the twentieth century, insists, on the contrary, that "the political philosophy of Burke was truly liberal" and that "Burke was anti-despotic, and to this extent a believer in democracy."[10]

Fascistic Romanticism

In approaching the fascistic type of Romanticism, we should begin by emphasizing that for us this is just one type among others, and it is a long way from being the most important or most essential aspect of the overall phenomenon. In this respect we are setting ourselves apart from those scholars—both fascist and antifascist and among the latter, both liberal and Marxist—who have interpreted the entire history of Romanticism as a prelude to fascism, and Romanticism as inseparably linked to the fascist ideology. As the discussion of the other elements in the typology ought to show clearly enough, this is not at all the case: the Romantic worldview is manifest in many diverse perspectives that are totally foreign to fascism.

Moreover, the fascist and immediately prefascist ideologies—Spengler's Kulturpessimismus, the "conservative revolution" (Carl Schmitt, Ernst Jünger)—cannot be identified in any simple way with the Romantic perspective. This is easy to observe in the case of Italian Fascism, in whose ideology, despite a nostalgic reference to a certain Roman antiquity, a different thematics has priority, that of the "futurists": praise of urban, industrial, and technological society, the cult of modern warfare, and an appeal to go still further in the direction of modernity.

But the disparity between Romanticism and fascism also pertains in the German case, where the Nazi ideology may seem more purely past-oriented: in favor of traditional peasant life as opposed to the frenzy of large cities, in favor of the old gemeinschaften as opposed to today's gesellschaft. It is true that Nazism unquestionably drew this theme, along with others (e.g., the specificity of the Germanic nation and the mythology of its origins, the *völkisch* ideology, the radical critique of Enlightenment thought and of liberal-democratic ideals), from the cultural arsenal of Romanticism, and it is also true that some German Romantic authors were anti-Semites. Nevertheless a fundamental difference remains between the ideology of the Nazis and some of their direct precursors on the one hand and the Romantic worldview on the other, namely, the modern, industrial, and technological dimension of the Nazi phenomenon, a dimension that is expressed both in its culture and in its practices. We need to recall in particular the crucial role played by industry, especially military and paramilitary industry (steel production), and the "death factories" we know as concentration camps.

Analyzing the ideological precursors of Nazism, Louis Dupeux rightly observed: "The conservative revolution manifests undeniable modernity, but this modernity is partial, and it is directed against modernism and progressivism in particular . . . or, in a word, the *modern reaction*. . . . This tendency . . . responds to the 'challenge of modernity'; it favors large-scale industry, technology, and a certain rational organization of society." Gilbert Merlio develops the same reasoning in a discussion of Spengler: "One must fight against progress with its own weapons, empty it of its meaning, that is, of all the elements of individual or collective liberation that it implies, even while accepting the means of power it makes available to us; hence Spengler's affirmation of technology, industrial dynamism, and the total mobilization of the nation by a State of functionaries and soldiers."[11]

We encounter this attitude again in the National Socialist ideology itself. In *Mein Kampf,* Hitler presents Aryan culture as a synthesis of the Greek mind and Germanic technology. And in 1930, Peter Schwerber, a Nazi ideologue, published a book titled *Nationalsozialismus und Technik* (National Socialism and technology), which put forward the idea that, far from being antitechnological, Nazism sought to free technology from the domination of money and "Jewish materialism."[12]

The North American sociologist Jeffrey Herf has recently studied this aspect of German Fascism, showing the continuity between the reactionary modernism of the conservative revolutionaries and that of the National Socialists, through a detailed analysis of the writings of Spengler, Ernst Jünger, Werner Sombart, and the principal Nazi ideologues. According to Herf,

> the paradoxical combination of irrationality and technics was fundamental to Hitler's ideology and practices and to National Socialism. This tradition began in Germany's technical universities in the late nineteenth century, was nurtured by the national engineering associations, given new life by Weimar's conservative revolutionaries, and became a constituent component of Nazi ideology from the early 1920s up to 1945. This synthesis of political reaction with an affirmative stance toward technological progress emerged well before 1933 and contributed to the ongoing ideological dynamism of the regime after 1933.[13]

Nazi ideology — and fascist ideology more generally — and the Romantic spirit do not coincide. That said, it is undeniable that Nazism exercised a fascination over a not inconsiderable number of authentically Romantic intellectuals during the period between the two world wars. Apart from the (fairly numerous) cases of mediocre or worthless neo-Romantic authors (the expressionist Hanns Johst, for example), a certain number of writers of quality allied themselves with fascism; we can cite in particular Pierre Drieu la Rochelle, Ezra Pound, and Knut Hamsun.

What are the defining features of Romanticism in its fascistic form? First, the rejection of capitalism is blended with a violent condemnation of parliamentary democracy as well as of Communism. Furthermore, its anticapitalism is often tinged with anti-Semitism: capitalists, the wealthy, and those who represent the spirit of cities and modern life are depicted as Jews. Next, the Romantic critique of rationality is taken to its outer limits; it becomes a glorification of the irrational in the pure state, a glorification of raw instinct in its most aggressive forms. Thus the Romantic cult of love turns into its opposite, spawning praise of force and cruelty. Finally, in its fascistic version the individualist pole of Romanticism is severely attenuated, if not entirely suppressed: in the fascist movement and the fascist state the unhappy romantic self disappears. Nostalgia for the past focuses most characteristically on the instinctive and violent barbarian prehistory of the human race; on Greco-Roman antiquity in its warmongering, elitist, slaveholding dimensions; on the Middle Ages (in Nazi painting Hitler sometimes appears as a medieval knight); on the rural *Volksgemeinschaft*; and on the mythic time of origins.

To illustrate this type, we shall take the case of Gottfried Benn, for it brings out the nature of fascist Romantics in a particularly striking way. Benn, one of the most prominent representatives of German expressionism, publicly supported the Hitler regime as soon as it came to power; unlike many others, however, he very quickly changed his tune. Benn actively supported Nazism for only two years (from 1933 to 1935), but there is a basic overall continuity in his work, and we find the same themes — except for any explicit reference to the Fascist cause — before his adherence. In his earlier work he spills forth his hatred of the modern world in its bourgeois, capitalist, urban, scientific, and also democratic and socialist aspects, and he dreams of a primitive past of instinctual life, above all in *Primal Vision* (1929). Then during his brief period of adherence to Nazism, Benn wrote some ten prose texts that all express fascist ideology in a very concerted way. But in two of these texts the Romantic aspect of his vision is exceptionally clear.

The first, and the less important of the two, is a laudatory review of a book by another Romantic, Julius Evola, called *Erhebung wider die moderne Welt* (Revolt against the modern world). Benn presents — and espouses —

the chief project of this book, which is to define and glorify what Evola calls the *Traditionswelt:* the world of primitive societies from the period between the Homeric era and that of Greek tragedy, in the Orient and in the Nordic countries as well as in Greece. After this period, there is decadence (*Verfall*), the advent of the degenerate modern world. According to Evola (and Benn agrees with him), fascism and Nazism make it possible for the first time to reestablish a connection between peoples and the lost Traditionswelt. Let us add, however, that for Benn — and this holds true for fascistic Romanticism in general — it is not a question of a simple return to the Traditionswelt. In another text written during his fascist period, Benn declares that in his eyes "it is only now that the history of mankind, its danger, its tragedy, begins,"[14] thereby suggesting that humanity will shortly reach a higher stage. In reality, the fascist perspective is oriented toward the new as well as toward the old, as we can see from numerous terms such as "new order," "new Europe."

The past for which Benn is nostalgic is amply fleshed out in a long article titled "Dorische Welt." The Doric world — that is, the world encompassing the Greek states up to the fifth century B.C.E. — is the Traditionswelt Benn favors. In depicting this world, he portrays war, sport as preparation for war, slavery and antifeminism, racism and xenophobia, elitism, and the unscrupulous powerful state as basic and necessary features. In fact, the image he offers looks remarkably like National Socialist society. But Benn stresses another characteristic of the Doric world: there is no private property in the modern sense, since land is inalienable; and there is not really such a thing as money, only not-very-useful iron coins. As a result, "desire is not drawn to gold, but to sacred things, to magical weapons."[15] Benn's ideal past is thus specifically noncapitalist. It is interesting to note here that, in the text in which Benn expresses his disappointment with Nazism for the first time ("Art and the Third Reich," written in 1941), he accuses the Nazis of wanting to get rich, thus of not representing a true alternative to bourgeois society. This reveals the essential consistency of Benn's Romanticism. Unfortunately, like many others, he believed he had found in fascism the realization of his dreams.

Resigned Romanticism

Resigned Romanticism arises most notably starting in the second half of the nineteenth century, when capitalist industrialization appears more and more to be an irreversible process and when the hope for a restoration of precapitalist social relations — which had still been conceivable at the beginning of the century — was tending to fade away. Romantics of this type are thus led to conclude, though with deep regret, that modernity is a fact to which one has to resign oneself. The grudging acceptance of capitalism brings resigned Romanticism close to the conservative type, but its social critique of industrial civilization is more intense. Depending on the authors (and here is an example of the possible superimposition of two different perspectives), this type of Romanticism can give rise to a tragic worldview (positing an insurmountable contradiction between values and reality) or to a reformist undertaking that seeks to remedy certain of the most flagrant evils of bourgeois society by means of the regulatory role of institutions translating precapitalist values.

Many writers whose work belongs to what Lukács called "critical realism" can be viewed as sharing in this form of Romanticism, for example Charles Dickens, Gustave Flaubert, and Thomas Mann; Honoré de Balzac is perhaps at the crossroads between restitutionist and resigned Romanticism. But it is in turn-of-the-century Germany that we find the most characteristic expression of this current, above all in the milieus of the university hierarchy, among the first great German sociologists; their main ideological center was the *Verein für Sozialpolitik,* with which Ferdinand Tönnies and Max Weber allied themselves, and their social philosophy was known as *Kathedersozialismus* ("lectern sociology").

Other German academics from that period may also be viewed as close to resigned Romanticism. Max Weber probably expressed an attitude shared by many in this group when he wrote in 1904, in the journal *Archiv für Sozialwissenschaft und Sozialpolitik,* that it was necessary to accept capitalism "not because we find it better than the old forms of social structure, but because it is virtually inevitable."[16] Some of these authors were more traditionalist (Adolph Wagner), others more modernist (Lujo Brentano, Max Weber); some were even close to unions and the social-democratic movement (Tönnies). In spite of its reformist tendency, this current conveys a tragic dimension to the extent that its social and cultural values appear condemned to decline and disappear in the present reality.[17]

The most typical representative of the contradictions of resigned Romanticism is probably Ferdinand Tönnies, who is considered the founder of German sociology. In his famous work *Community and Society (Gemein-*

schaft und Gesellschaft, 1887), he contrasts two forms of sociability: on the one hand there is "community" (families, villages, traditional small towns), a universe governed by concord, custom, religion, mutual assistance, and *Kultur,* and on the other hand there is "society" (big cities, national states, factories), driven as a whole by calculation, profit, the struggle of all against all, *Zivilisation* as technological and industrial progress. Tönnies's book is intended as an objective comparison, "free of value judgments," between these two structures, but the author's nostalgia for the "organic" rural gemeinschaft is transparent: "Gemeinschaft . . . is the lasting and genuine form of living together. In contrast to Gemeinschaft, Gesellschaft is transitory and superficial. Accordingly, Gemeinschaft should be understood as a living organism, Gesellschaft as a mechanical aggregate and artifact." Whereas the family economy is "based on liking or preference, viz., the joy and delight of creating and conserving," urban life and society in general represent the decay and destruction of the people.[18]

The opposition between these two forms — or between Kultur and Zivilisation — became one of the principal themes of neo-Romanticism in Germany at the turn of the century. But what characterizes Tönnies as a resigned Romantic thinker is the tragic conviction that the return to gemeinschaft is an illusion, that social decadence is inevitable, like the decline of a living organism that can no longer return to its first youth.[19] Although Tönnies looked with sympathy on labor unions and consumer cooperatives as neocommunitarian organisms correcting certain excesses of modern society, he saw the possibility of a restoration of the authentic gemeinschaft of the past as out of the question.

Reformist Romanticism

This type cannot be identified with the reformist tendency of resigned Romanticism, which envisaged reforms simply as palliative measures for an inexorable situation; in contrast reformist Romanticism properly speaking was convinced that the old values could come back. However, the measures reformist Romantics advocated to reach that goal were limited to reforms: legal reforms, an evolution of the consciousness of the ruling classes. In this type of Romanticism, we thus often find a striking contrast between the radicalism of the critique and the timidity of the solutions imagined.

In this regard, we can observe that while the reformers — like the Jacobin-democrats mentioned earlier — regularly invoked the French Revolution and its values, they were referring primarily to its moderate elements, to the Girondins rather than to the Jacobins, and their revolutionary inspiration had a tendency to be expressed in a sentimental, vague, or mythic register.

The most prominent instances of reformist Romanticism are concentrated in the first half of the nineteenth century in France: Lamartine, Charles-Augustin Sainte-Beuve, Julee Michelet, Lamennais, Hugo — and the latter could just as well be called "liberal," as certain Romantics of this persuasion identified themselves at the time.[20] We prefer the term "reformist," however, as indicating more clearly the essential thrust of this current. The term "liberal" is notoriously ambiguous, and at the beginning of the nineteenth century it had at least two distinct meanings: on the one hand it designated a political current connected with a party whose ideology and practice translated the interests of the rising bourgeoisie against the aristocratic and ecclesiastic reaction, and on the other hand it designated a much broader movement of ideas that would be called "progressive" today in the broadest sense of orientation toward change and the future. The Romantic reformers identified themselves especially with this second meaning of liberalism, but in some of them, at certain points, we find leanings toward liberal ideology understood in the first sense. Generally speaking, it is fair to say that, like the conservatives, the reformers did not display the wholesale, coherent radicalism that characterized the other types.

The work of Lamennais, an essayist and writer of religious and political tracts who had a strong influence on intellectual trends in France in the decades conventionally designated as Romantic (1830–1850), illustrates particularly well the gap between the perceptive and acerbic diagnoses that the reformist Romantics often produced about their own era and the relative weakness of the remedies they proposed. This sincere and fervent Catholic, a royalist at the outset, became a republican and an advocate of "the people" in the early 1830s.

In articles, pamphlets, and books, and above all in *Words of a Believer* (1834), Lamennais denounced the evils of the society of his own day in extremely violent terms. He condemned the oppression practiced in earlier times by kings and nobles in collusion with the established church (Rome), but he criticized the new domination of the bourgeoisie still more harshly. For "the aristocracy based on birthright was replaced by an aristocracy based on the right of money," which led to a moral decline "in the name of

industrial and commercial prosperity, material interests placed in the es-
timation of the government above all others, transformed into a sort of
religion." For Lamennais, the new aristocracy and the new oppression are
worse than the old ones, and the new capitalist oppressors are worse than
tyrants; as for the former, "Hell alone can furnish a name."[21]

Lamennais's lost paradises are the Garden of Eden, when the earth was
beautiful and before the earliest form of oppression (royalty) was instituted, then early Christianity, when the tree of life "flowered again." And
in the apocalyptic Eden of *Words of a Believer,* Lamennais hints at the immi-
nent return of the kingdom of God on earth, the City of God: "And this
time shall be as the time when all men were brethren"![22]

When Lamennais gets around to representing — in other, less lyrical essays, but also in *Words of a Believer* — how the world ought to change, his
tone becomes more modest, however, and the nature of the transformation
is surrounded by restrictions. He specifies that, since the bourgeoisie is
"closer to the people than to the oligarchy that arose from its breast, and
that holds it in a bondage no less harsh than ancient servitude, its interests
are the same . . . as those of the people"; in general, class differences are
rooted in misunderstanding.[23]

At the same time, Lamennais asserts that "equality of fortunes" is against
nature (he found it necessary to add a chapter to *Words of a Believer* to refute
the accusation that he was against property), that there will always be poor
people (but fewer and fewer), that the true solution to the problem of
poverty lies in giving the people access to property.[24] Thus what Lamennais
is appealing for, in the last analysis, looks much more like an adjustment of
existing arrangements than a genuine fresh start; it resembles reform more
than utopia.

Revolutionary and/or Utopian Romanticism

The revolutionary and/or utopian type of Romanticism — which encompasses a whole range of subtendencies that we shall discuss in turn — goes
beyond the types already mentioned to invest the nostalgia for a precapitalist past in the hope for a radically new future. Rejecting both the illusion of
a pure and simple return to the organic communities of the past and the
resigned acceptance of the bourgeois present or its amelioration by means
of reforms, revolutionary or utopian Romanticism aspires — in a way that

may be to a greater or lesser extent radical, to a greater or less extent contradictory — to the abolition of capitalism or to an egalitarian utopia in which certain features or values of earlier societies would reappear.

Jacobin-Democratic Romanticism

The very existence of this type is in itself eloquent testimony against any assertion of an absolute opposition between Romanticism and the spirit of the Enlightenment. The two movements are by no means necessarily in contradiction and conflict; in fact, an important sector of the former is the spiritual heir of the latter, with Rousseau, situated at the crossroads between the two, often serving as the connecting link. This type of Romanticism is characterized by a radical critique both of the oppression of past forces — the monarchy, the aristocracy, the church — and of the new bourgeois oppressions. This double critique is carried out (except, of course, in the case of writers — especially Rousseau — who came earlier) in the name of the French Revolution and the values represented by its principal and most radical tendency: Jacobinism.

This current is sometimes paralleled by a Bonapartist tendency, to the extent that Napoleon is seen as an effective and heroic extension of Jacobinism; admiration for Bonaparte often stops, however, with the 18 Brumaire events. Unlike the reformers, the Jacobin democrats call not for slow transformations, for compromises and moderate solutions, but rather for revolutionary breaks and profound upheavals. Most often, they take their precapitalist references from the Greek city-state and the Roman republic.

We put the Jacobin-democratic current in first place among the revolutionary-utopian Romanticisms quite simply because it comes first chronologically. This current, which is distinctly different from a purely rationalist radicalism (William Godwin's, for instance), is manifested in all the major countries in which Romanticism first took hold — and naturally first of all in the home country of the Revolution. After Rousseau, we can include the Jacobins themselves in the French lineage, for their passionate reference to an idealized antiquity attests to a quintessentially Romantic nostalgia, and many of them were shaped much more by Rousseau's school than by the Enlightenment. However, we must note that Jacobinism in its most radical version — in the case of Philippe Buonarroti and François-Noel Babeuf (Gracchus) — comes close to communism and thus tends to depart from the type. In the postrevolutionary years, among those who were at once Jacobins and Bonapartists, we should mention Stendhal, of course, but also Alfred de Musset, the Musset of the introduction to *Confession of a Child of the Century.*

In Germany, where the members of the earliest Romantic movements were Jacobin democrats for a brief period before becoming restitutionists, some important writers never gave up the first perspective, Friedrich Hölderlin and Heinrich Heine in particular. The latter, an anti-Romantic who ended up acknowledging that he was a Romantic at heart after all, saw the Revolution as the agent of humanity's redemption: "Freedom is a new religion, the religion of our age. . . . The French . . . are the chosen people . . . , Paris is the new Jerusalem, and the Rhine is the Jordan which divides the consecrated land of freedom from the land of the Philistines."[25] At the end of his life, after several shifts to the left and to the right of this position, Heine reaffirmed as the principle of unity of his thought "an unchanging devotion to the cause of humanity, to the democratic ideas of the Revolution."[26]

The case of Heine is particularly interesting where his nostalgia for the past is concerned: in the "confessions of the author" at the end of *Concerning Germany,* he reveals that, whereas he was once a Hellenophile (like most of the Jacobin democrats), he has recently turned back toward his Jewish antecedents. Heine concludes that it is neither ancient Greece, with its slavery, nor Rome with its legalistic chicanery, that prefigures the French Revolution, but rather Mosaic law and the values of ancient Judaism.

As for England, we can begin by citing William Blake, whose poem "The French Revolution" (1790–91) reveals a Jacobin perspective, then George Gordon, Lord Byron and Percy Bysshe Shelley for their radicalism. The Lake Poets were initially enthusiastic about the Revolution, shifting only later to a reactionary viewpoint. But Coleridge, in particular, was never truly a Jacobin — his position was paradoxically at once more moderate politically and more radical socially. We analyze this position in detail, along with the multiplicity of possible relations between Romanticism and the Revolution, in chapter 4.

Jacobin-democratic Romanticism was rather narrowly limited in time: beginning with Rousseau, it was concentrated chiefly in the revolutionary period and its immediate aftermath. Heine may well have been its last representative. Its short life can be explained by its very nature, which was that of a radical indictment of modernity presented in the name of revolutionary values. With the Revolution's transformation into a myth of the foundation of the victorious bourgeoisie, a radical critique of the present (and of the past) could not remain radical and continue to refer to the Revolution alone. With the birth of the socialist and workers' movements, an authentically radical critique oriented toward the future had to be transformed if it was to avoid contradicting itself.[27]

Along with Shelley, Heine, who — especially during the period of his association with Karl Marx — was fascinated and tempted by Communism without ever joining the Party, represents the extreme limit of Jacobin-democratic Romanticism beyond which it turns into other revolutionary-utopian types. With Heine and Shelley, the worldview is on the point of changing, a situation that differentiates its later representatives from the earlier ones. Lukács points out the difference between Hölderlin and Shelley, rightly declaring that "a later Hölderlin who did not follow Shelley's course would not have been a Hölderlin, but rather a narrow classicist liberal."[28]

The difference is so obvious that some have gone as far as to represent Shelley as a socialist. In particular, Marx's daughter and son-in-law — Eleanor Marx Aveling and Edward Aveling — tried to demonstrate this in a brochure titled *Shelley's Socialism*.[29] They assert that there is a fundamental difference between Byron's radicalism, which is essentially bourgeois radicalism, and that of Shelley, who is already speaking in the name of the proletariat. But although the difference between Byron and Shelley is indeed quite real, in our view it is a matter of a variation within the same type of Romanticism, and it is an interpretive distortion to present Shelley as a socialist.

For, although in several poems — in particular "The Mask of Anarchy" (1819) — Shelley casts himself as the advocate of the cause of rebelling workers and violently denounces working-class conditions as slavery, he never goes so far as to challenge private property, and his ideological reference always remains Jacobin-democratic radicalism.

Indeed, his political viewpoint does not change between his earliest poem, "Queen Mab" (1812), and "Ode to Liberty" (1820) or "Hellas" (1821), written the year before his death. It is probably in the latter works that his historical, social, and political vision is expressed most fully (at least so far as his poetry is concerned). Unlike Rousseau, for example, Shelley is not given to nostalgia for primitive man; for, according to Shelley, if freedom was inscribed in the nature of the world itself by God at the creation, it succeeded in asserting itself for the first time, after long epochs of barbarity, only in ancient Greece: "Let there be light! said Liberty, / And . . . Athens arose!"[30]

After a brief continuation of its reign in Rome, freedom suffered a long eclipse, owing first to the tyrannies of throne and altar, then to the oppressions born of the thirst for money. In the modern era of revolutions, freedom is preparing to return to earth, but this time at a higher level, and permanently. For Shelley, "The coming age is shadowed on the Past / As on a glass," and "The world's great age begins anew, / The golden years return." But in ancient Greece only "Prophetic echoes flung dim melody," and the world to come will be "A brighter Hellas," "Another Athens." It will constitute a return, but a return to the mythical and utopian age of Saturn: "Saturn and Love their long repose shall burst . . . / Not gold, not blood, their altar dowers, / But votive tears and symbol flowers."[31]

The future—for Shelley as for others with a future-oriented perspective—will thus be not the mere re-creation of a real past but instead the full enjoyment of all the qualities that were only in bud in the previous era, a total realization that has never existed before, a utopia of love and beauty.[32]

Populist Romanticism

This form of Romanticism is opposed both to industrial capitalism and to monarchy and servitude, and it aspires to save, reestablish, or develop, as an alternative to contemporary society, the peasantry and the artisanal forms of production and communitarian life of premodern "peoples."

While J.-C. S. de Sismondi's work introduces populism as an economic doctrine, the tendency is most fully elaborated as a social philosophy and a political movement in Russia, for reasons that have to do with the social structure of the country and with the situation of its intellectuals during the second half of the nineteenth century. Economists more or less influenced by Sismondi (for example, Efroussi, Vorontsov, and Nicolaion) and "nihilist" revolutionary philosophers such as Herzen are the chief representatives of a populist Romanticism that sees the traditional Russian rural community (*obschtchina*) as the basis for a specifically Russian path to socialism; this form of Romanticism rejects both the czarist autocracy and the capitalist civilization of the West. Its political expression will be the *Narodnaya Volya* movement (The will of the people), which seeks to "go to the people" to win the peasantry over to the new revolutionary ideas. Of all the great Russian writers, Leo Tolstoy doubtless shows the greatest affinity for the populist cult of the peasantry.

Sismondi was hardly a revolutionary, but his rigorous and radical critique of capitalism won Marx's admiration. Unlike that of the classical economists, Sismondi's analysis of economic reality had a moral basis: "I shall always fight the system of industrialization, which has cheapened human life."[33] Sismondi rejected the quest for wealth as a goal in itself (he called it "chrematism") and the reduction of men to the condition of machines.

Sismondi's critique of capitalism is Romantic in that it constantly refers to a precapitalist Golden Age—chiefly situated in the medieval Italian republics—and dreams of a patriarchal society of small artisans and peasant landowners, brought together in structures of the corporatist or communitarian type. In a passage that is characteristic of his major work, *Nouveaux principes de l'économie politique* (1819), Sismondi writes: "In countries where the farmer owns his land, and where the harvest belongs exclusively to the men who have done all the work, countries in which we shall call the form of exploitation patriarchal, we see at every turn signs of the love the cultivator feels for the house he lives in, for the land he tends."[34] The author insists nevertheless that he is not an "enemy of social progress," and he stresses that he seeks not to restore what has been but rather to create "something better than what is," on the basis of specific social transformations (the sharing of large properties and businesses, and so forth).

The continuity between these economic ideas and those of the Russian populists is undeniable, even if the latter ended up giving a much more revolutionary cast to the program. In an 1897 pamphlet called "A Characterization of Economic Romanticism (Sismondi and Our Native Sismondists)," Lenin settled his accounts with the populists and forcefully condemned Sismondi's work as reactionary. But, as we shall see, Rosa Luxemburg defended Sismondi against Lenin (in *The Accumulation of Capital*, 1911), by affirming that the French writer raises questions that are essential for the development of a Marxist political economy.

Utopian-Humanist Socialist Romanticism

The specifically Romantic authors linked with this type construct a model for a socialist alternative to bourgeois-industrial civilization, a collectivist utopia, while they refer to certain social paradigms and ethical and/or religious values of the precapitalist type. They present their critique not in the name of a class (the proletariat) but in the name of humanity as a whole, and especially the part of humanity that is suffering; it is addressed to all persons of good will. The authors usually known as "utopian socialists" do not always share the Romantic sensibility: Robert Owen and Claude Henri de Rouvroy, Comte de Saint-Simon, in particular are first and foremost men of the Enlightenment, in favor of progress and industry. However, with the socialist Romantic type we can associate authors and tendencies such as Charles Fourier and Pierre Leroux (and, up to a point, his literary disciple George Sand), the German Karl Grün with his "true socialism," the expressionist Ernst Toller, and the Marxist humanist Erich Fromm.

A clarifying example of this undertaking is found in the work of Moses Hess, the German Jewish socialist who had a formative influence on Marx and Engels, especially through his early writings (1837–1845). His first work, *Die heilige Geschichte der Menschheit* (The sacred history of humanity, 1837), is probably the one in which the Romantic presence is strongest: Hess develops a messianic and political interpretation of history that locates in antiquity an era of social harmony based on the community of goods. Private property has destroyed this original equilibrium, allowing the rise of industry and trade, with their cortege of inequalities, selfishness, and social injustices. The messianic task of the future will consist in eliminating inheritance and private appropriation of property, "so that the primordial equality among men may be reestablished," thus opening the way to the advent of the New Jerusalem, a new Eden, that is, the kingdom of God on earth.[35] Strongly inspired by Fourier, whose concept of social harmony is the underlying theme of the book, Hess sketches a radical critique of the new monied aristocracy and of industry, which is increasing the wealth of a few at the expense of the many.[36]

Unlike his first book, which aroused very little interest, the book Hess published in 1841, *Die europäische Triarchie* (The European triarchy), had a considerable impact on the critical intelligentsia, especially among its neo-Hegelian sector, in Germany. In this later book Hess proposes the constitution of Europe as a unified organism, starting with a spiritual alliance between France, Germany, and England, which would lead to the establishment of the kingdom of God on earth. In a typically Romantic shortcut between past and future, he writes: "What the sacred Jewish State was in Antiquity, what the Holy Roman Empire was in the Middle Ages, Romano-German Europe will be in the future: the pupil of the eyes of God, the central point from which the world's destiny will be directed."[37]

The socialist ideas implicit in these works are expressed little by little in a series of essays and articles published by Hess from 1842 through 1845, in *Rheinische Zeitung, Deutsch-Französischen Jahrbücher, Neuen Anekdoten,* and *Rheinische Jahrbücher.* These works contrast the communist principle of humanity with the principle of selfishness, the spirit with Mammon, the socialist community of the future with the selfish and inorganic individual of bourgeois society. Hess's essay on the essence of money is probably the most important of these texts; written in 1843 and published in 1845, it had considerable influence on the young Marx.

This text offers a passionate critique of the domination exercised by divinized money over men; it attacks the system of putting human liberty up for sale that characterizes modernity. For Hess, the modern world of bargaining (*moderne Schacherwelt*), of which money is the essence, is worse than ancient slavery because it is "not natural, and inhuman, that one should sell oneself voluntarily." The task of communism is to abolish money and its evil power and to establish an organic community that is authentically human.[38]

Libertarian Romanticism

Libertarian, anarchist, or anarcho-syndicalist Romanticism, which takes its inspiration from collective precapitalist traditions of peasants, artisans, and workers qualified to lead a struggle that targets the modern state as much as it does capitalism per se, seeks to establish a decentralized federation of local communities; it reached its apogee in the late nineteenth and early twentieth centuries. We also find in anarchism an Enlightenment tendency that is rather remote from Romanticism. But most of the classical libertarian thinkers, such as Proudhon, Mikhail Bakunin, Pyotr Kropotkin, or Jean-Jacques-Elisée Reclus, share the Romantic outlook to a great extent.[39]

At the same time, it seems that in Spain, where anarchism's hold as a social movement was most powerful, the movement was Romantic in the sense that it sought to prevent the establishment of capitalism. Thus as Franz Borkenau remarks in his excellent eye-witness account of the Spanish civil war,

The Spanish popular movement is directed not towards overcoming capitalism . . . after its complete unfolding, but against its very existence at any stage of its possible progress in Spain. . . . The materialist conception of history, based on the belief in progress, meant nothing to [the Spanish worker]. . . . In a word, the Spanish labour movement is based on a mentality directed against the introduction, not against the indefinite continuance, of capitalism. And this, in my opinion, is the explanation of the preponderance of anarchism in Spain.[40]

One of the most typical representatives of libertarian Romanticism was Gustav Landauer. A writer, literary critic, social philosopher, and leader of the Munich Commune in 1919 (he was assassinated by the counterrevolution after the defeat of the Bavarian Republic of Consuls), in his youth Landauer was influenced by Richard Wagner and Friedrich Nietzsche before becoming an anarchist. However, from the beginning he distinguished himself from his masters not only by his revolutionary orientation but also by his attraction to religious spirituality; in 1903 he published a translation of the mystical writings of Meister Eckehart. Indeed, Landauer shared with classical German Romanticism a deep nostalgia for medieval Christianity: "Christianity, with its Gothic towers and battlements . . . with its corporations and fraternities, was a people in the strongest and highest sense of the term: an intimate fusion of the economic and cultural communities with a spiritual bond [*Geistesbund*]."[41]

In contrast, modern England (as of the nineteenth century), "with its desolate factory system, with the depopulation of the countryside, the homogenization of the masses and of misery, with economies geared to the world market instead of to real needs," is for Landauer a grim dustbin. He bitterly reproaches Marx, a "son of the steam engine," for admiring the technological successes of capitalism. The task of socialism does not consist in helping people find culture, the mind, freedom, or community.[42] Radically hostile to the state and to bourgeois society, Landauer exhorted the socialists to retreat from that corrupt and decadent social universe to establish autonomous rural communities united by a free federation. Rather than general strikes or insurrection, the path leading to libertarian socialism requires abandonment of the capitalist economy and construction of the socialist Gemeinschaft, here and now, in the countrysides.[43]

It would be wrong, however, to present Landauer as a partisan of a pure and simple reestablishment of the sociocultural forms of the past. He recognizes the value of certain acquisitions of civilization — the Aufklärung, the fading of superstition, the burgeoning of science — and he wants to create, on the basis of a marriage between modern Zivilisation and premodern Kultur, an authentically new society, without state or social classes.

Marxist Romanticism

In the excursus we offer in chapter 3, we focus on the relationship between Romanticism and Marxism, and we pursue several key examples at some length. Here, therefore, we propose to offer only a brief preliminary presentation. First, we may say that there is a significant, if not truly dominant, Romantic dimension in the work of Marx and Engels themselves — a dimension that has not often been noted and that was later shed by official Marxism (strongly marked by evolutionism, positivism, and Fordism), the Marxism of both the Second and the Third Internationals. In the writings of such thinkers as Karl Kautsky, Georgii Valentinovich Plekhanov, or Nicolai Ivanovich Bukharin, not to mention Joseph Stalin, one would look in vain for traces of a Romantic legacy.

But the Romantic dimension that is present in the work of Marxism's founders becomes more central for certain authors who claim to be Marxists but who are marginal or eccentric in relation to the orthodoxy. The first important attempt to produce a neo-Romantic interpretation of Marxism was made by William Morris, at the end of the nineteenth century; we must specify, though, that Morris actually occupied a position on the border between Marxism and anarchism. An essayist, poet, artist, and director of the Socialist League, Morris was first of all a disciple of Carlyle and John Ruskin, and his poems sang of the lost charms of the Middle Ages. Close to Edward Coley Burne-Jones, to Dante Gabriel Rossetti and the Pre-Raphaelite Brotherhood (defined by Burne-Jones as a "crusade and holy war against the epoch"), he actually belonged, in a first phase, to restitutionism.

But with his conversion to socialism and his discovery of Marx in 1883–84, Morris did not abandon his earlier vision of the world: "The dominant passion of my life," he wrote in 1894, "has been and still is the hatred of modern civilization."[44] In his utopian novel of 1890, *News from Nowhere,* he describes an ideal future society, the product of a proletarian revolution and civil war, resembling the fourteenth century in many respects but actually constituting a new type of society, simultaneously anarchist and communist. For a long time Morris was completely rejected by the Marxist camp because of his unorthodox perspective; recently, however, two British Marxists who share his Romantic tendencies, E. P. Thompson and Raymond Williams, have shed light on the critical importance of his thought for Marxism.

Outside of this British lineage, it is particularly in the German cultural sphere of influence — and independent of the British developments — that we find Marxist authors and currents powerfully tinged with Romanticism: György Lukács, Ernst Bloch and the Frankfurt School (especially Walter Benjamin and Herbert Marcuse). In France, however, we can at least cite Henri Lefebvre.[45]

What distinguishes this approach from that of the other socialist or revolutionary currents of Romantic sensibility is the central preoccupation with certain essential problems of Marxism: the class struggle, the role of the proletariat as a universal emancipating class, the possibility of using modern productive forces in a socialist economy, and so on — even if the conclusions reached in these areas are not necessarily identical to those of Marx and Engels.

HYPOTHESES FOR A SOCIOLOGY OF ROMANTICISM

Now that we have developed the broad outline of a possible typology of the politics of Romanticism, at the end of which we see clearly how Romanticism unfolds from one end of the political gamut to the other, passing through virtually all the intermediate positions, we still have to propose some necessarily schematic and provisional sociological hypotheses. What are the social bases for Romanticism? Is it possible to connect this worldview with one or more social groups? While Marxist texts on Romanticism do not offer many highly developed hypotheses on this point, we nevertheless find in them a certain number of schematic and circumstantial sociological explanations of their object. Yet these explanations most often appear inadequate.

Some see Romanticism as merely a form of bourgeois consciousness: according to Arnold Hauser, the fact that the Romantics' audience is made up of members of this class shows that "romanticism was essentially a middle-class movement."[46] The reduction of Romanticism to a bourgeois ideology — a practice present even among critics otherwise endowed with genuine talent — is often the common site of a certain dogmatic deformation that violently represses the affinities between Marxism and Romanticism. And this occurs at the price of ignoring the essential characteristics of Romanticism: for, although a certain number of its writers and a portion of its audience belong to the bourgeoisie, Romanticism constitutes a profound challenge to that class and to the society it dominates. To be sure, in several elements of our typology — for example, the "conservative" and "reformist" types — there can be reconnections with the bourgeois spirit and the status quo of a bourgeois present. In our own view, however, these are actually extreme cases in which Romanticism runs the risk of denying itself.

Marxist analyses sometimes associate Romanticism with other social classes, in particular the aristocracy and the petite bourgeoisie. In a passage cited earlier (chapter 1), Jacques Droz claims that whereas most German Romantics may belong to the latter group, they express the ideology of the former.[47] For the East German critic Gerda Heinrich, on the contrary, this same German Romanticism articulates the "class interests of certain levels of the petite bourgeoisie," and Ernst Fischer finds that, more generally, "the Romantic attitude could not be other than confused, for the petty bourgeoisie was the very embodiment of social contradiction."[48] In our view, these interpretations remain one-sided; they are not incorrect, but they need to be incorporated into a more complete explanation.

The work of Pierre Barbéris has the advantage of offering a multilateral approach. At the origin of French Romanticism Barbéris sees a historical conjunction between the aspirations and interests of various social levels marginalized by capital: in particular, the aristocrats who have been dispossessed by the bourgeoisie, and the young bourgeois generations that have not been "provided for, that run into the obstacle of money, that do not find work."[49] It strikes us as insufficient, however, to look only at aristocrats and the petite bourgeoisie (or young members of the bourgeoisie who have not yet "arrived"), at least if one is proposing to account for the overall phenomenon as we have defined it.

Furthermore, while Barbéris rightly sees that the Romantic movement is nourished by the various victims of the triumphant bourgeoisie and its social framework, most often he conceives of the revolt of petit bourgeois youth or of the bourgeoisie in general above all as a reaction to a situation that frustrates their ambitions while denying them adequate outlets. Now, while this motive undoubtedly played a role, it cannot account all by itself for the violence and depth of this challenge to an entire socioeconomic order. Much more essential is the experience of alienation and reification, and sociological analysis should pose the problem in terms of a differential sensitivity to this experience.

From this standpoint, it seems to us that most of the usual analyses of the social frameworks of Romanticism reach an impasse when they come to one essential category: the intelligentsia, a group made up of individuals of diverse social origins, whose unity and (relative) autonomy result from a common position in the process of cultural production. One of the exceptions is Mannheim, who shows, in his 1927 essay on conservative thought in Germany, that the bearers of the Romantic movement were *freischwe-bende Intellektuellen* (unattached intellectuals).[50] Generally speaking, it is clear that the producers of the Romantic worldview represent certain traditional segments of the intelligentsia whose way of life and culture are hostile to bourgeois industrial civilization: independent writers, religious thinkers or theologians (many Romantics are pastors' sons), poets and artists, university mandarins, and others. What is the social basis for this hostility?

The traditional intelligentsia (let us recall the cenacle in Balzac's *Lost Illusions*) lives in a mental universe governed by qualitative values — ethical, aesthetic, religious, cultural, or political; all their activity of "spiritual production" is inspired, oriented, and shaped by these values, which constitute, as it were, their raison d'être as intellectuals. Given that capitalism is a system whose workings are entirely determined by quantitative values, there is a fundamental contradiction between the traditional intelligentsia and the modern social environment, a contradiction that generates conflict and rebellion.

The old-style intelligentsia does not escape, of course, as industrial capitalism develops, from the necessity of selling its spiritual products. And some members of this social category end up frankly accepting the hegemony of exchange value, by making internal adjustments — sometimes even enthusiastically — to its requirements. Others, faithful to their precapitalist cultural universe, refuse to accept what is called in Balzac's cenacle "the propensity to traffic in one's soul, one's mind, one's thought" and become the productive foyer of Romanticism.[51]

If the creators and transmitters of the various figures of Romanticism thus emerge from this classical intelligentsia (as distinguished from an intelligentsia of a more modern type: scientists, technicians, engineers, economists, administrators, "mass-media" experts), its audience, its social base in the fullest sense, is much larger. It is made up potentially of all classes, segments of classes, or social categories for whom the advent and development of modern industrial capitalism provoke a decline or a crisis in their economic, social, or political status, and/or threaten their way of life and the cultural values to which they are attached.

This can include, for instance, the various levels of the aristocracy, landowners, the old rural and urban petite bourgeoisie, the clergy, and a whole range of traditional intellectuals, including students. We should add that women, independently of their class origin and as writers, readers of novels, militants in feminist movements (in other words, simultaneously creators, consumers, and transmitters), maintain a privileged relation with Romanticism from the outset. This link can probably be explained by the fact that women were historically excluded from the creation of the principal values of modernity (by scientists, businessmen, industrialists, politicians) and that their social role was defined as centered on qualitative values: family, feelings, love, culture.[52] In the case of the various social groups as well as in the case of women, we are dealing only with an objective possibility—a "behavioral probability," as Max Weber would say—whose actual realization depends on a series of concrete historical, social, and individual conditions.

Beyond this overall sociology of Romanticism, is it possible to define the specific social bases of each of the types we have analyzed? In a general way, we can posit that the utopian-revolutionary forms find their audience primarily among the nondominant layers of society, but any attempt at a more precise determination strikes us as problematic—all the more so in that, as we have noted, the same individuals often pass from one position to another within the gamut of the politics of Romanticism.

The foregoing sociological remarks have a limitation, nevertheless: they tend to reduce Romanticism's audience, its social public, to certain "pockets of resistance" that are archaic, traditional, or on the margins of modern society. If that were correct, this worldview would be a phenomenon on the decline, condemned to disappear by the development of modernity itself. But this is not at all the case: not only is a significant part of contemporary cultural production profoundly influenced by Romanticism, but we are also witnessing the rise of new social movements that are strongly tinged with Romanticism.

It is as if capitalist-industrial civilization had reached a stage in its development in which its destructive effects on the social fabric and on the natural environment have taken on such proportions that certain Romantic themes — and certain forms of nostalgia — exercise a diffuse social influence going well beyond the classes or categories with which they were once primarily associated.

3

Excursus: Marxism and Romanticism

KARL MARX

With the exception of authors such as William Morris or the youthful Ernst Bloch (since both of these writers are more Marxist-leaning than Marxist in the traditional sense of the word), what characterizes the posture of Marxism toward the Romantic worldview is a certain ambivalence: even the thinkers most drawn to Romantic themes maintain a critical distance that is inspired by the progressive legacy of the Enlightenment.

To illustrate this ambivalence, this attraction/repulsion with respect to Romanticism, we shall examine the approach of Karl Marx himself and that of two preeminent Marxist thinkers of the twentieth century, Rosa Luxemburg and György Lukács. As we see it, similar attitudes characterize the other Marxist authors and tendencies with a Romantic sensibility whom we mentioned in our typological section (the Frankfurt School, the English school of social historiography, and so on).

On the surface, Marx had nothing in common with Romanticism. To be sure, during his youth he was not impervious to the seductive hues of Romantic culture. According to Auguste Cornu, his biographer, the baron of Westphalen — the philosopher's future father-in-law — "filled Marx with enthusiasm for the Romantic school, and while his father read Voltaire and Racine with him, the baron read him Homer and Shakespeare, and these remained his favorite authors all his life." Under such conditions, it is not surprising that, during his years of study at the University of Bonn, he chose to attend courses on Homer offered by an old Romantic, Friedrich Schlegel. Marx's early writings—poems, dramas, plays (of mediocre literary quality, it should be noted in passing)—bear the visible mark of Romantic literature (they manifest particular affinities with E. T. A. Hoffmann's writings), and they bear witness to a typically Romantic revolt. In addition (somewhat surprisingly), Marx's first attempt to produce a critique of Georg Wilhelm Friedrich Hegel was strongly influenced by Friedrich Schelling's *Naturphilosophie*.[1]

After his conversion to Hegelian dialectics, materialism, and the philosophy of praxis (1840–1845), Marx left his initial youthful Romanticism behind: his new philosophy of history seems to have had no room for nostalgia. In the *Manifesto of the Communist Party* (1848), Marx and Engels reject as reactionary any dream of returning to craftsmanship or other precapitalist modes of production. Marx celebrates the historically progressive role of industrial capitalism, which not only developed productive forces on a vast and unprecedented scale but also unified the world economy—an essential preliminary condition for future socialist humanity. He also praised capitalism for having torn away the veils that had concealed exploitation in precapitalist societies, but this type of praise has ironic overtones: by introducing more brutal, more open, and more cynical forms of exploitation, the capitalist mode of production favors the development of consciousness and class struggle on the part of the oppressed. Marx's anticapitalism seeks to produce not an abstract negation of modern (bourgeois) industrial civilization but rather its *Aufhebung*: it is to be abolished, while its greatest conquests are maintained; it is to be surpassed by a superior mode of production.

Still, Marx was not unaware of the other side of this civilizing coin; in a typically dialectical approach, he saw capitalism as a system that transforms every instance of economic progress into a public calamity.[2] It is through the analysis of the social disasters provoked by capitalist civilization—as well as through his interest in precapitalist communities—that he rejoined the Romantic tradition, at least to a certain extent.

Both Marx and Friedrich Engels greatly respected certain Romantic critics of industrial capitalism, and they recognized their own intellectual indebtedness to these precursors. Their work was significantly influenced not only by economists such as J.-C. S. de Sismondi and the Russian populist Nikolai Danielson, with whom they corresponded over a twenty-year period, but also by writers such as Charles Dickens and Honoré de Balzac, by social philosophers such as Thomas Carlyle, and by historians of ancient communities such as Georg Ludwig von Maurer, Barthold Georg Niebuhr, and Lewis Morgan—not to mention Romantic socialists such as Charles Fourier, Pierre Leroux, and Moses Hess. In reality, Romanticism is one of Marx's and Engels's neglected sources, a source perhaps as important for their work as German neo-Hegelianism or French materialism.

Among the Romantic critics of capitalist society, Thomas Carlyle was probably one of those who had the greatest impact on Marx's and Engels's intellectual formation. In 1844, Engels published an enthusiastic review of *Past and Present* (1843); he cites approvingly Carlyle's tirades against "mammonism," the religion of the god Mammon that reigned in England. Even as he criticizes the author's conservative choices, he recognizes a decisive connection between these choices and the social interest of the work: "Thomas Carlyle . . . was originally a Tory. . . . This much is certain: a Whig would never have been able to write a book that was half so humane as *Past and Present*." His philosophy is inspired by "vestiges of Tory romanticism," but Carlyle is nonetheless the only Englishman from the "respectable" class who had "kept his eyes open at least toward the facts" and had "correctly apprehended the immediate present."[3] As for Marx, he read Carlyle's little book on Chartism in 1845 and copied many excerpts into his notebook. In one of these passages there is a marvelous Romantic image for industrial capitalism: "If men had lost belief in a God, their only resource against a blind No-God, of Necessity and Mechanism, that held them like a hideous World-Steamengine, like a hideous Phalaris' Bull, imprisoned in its own iron belly, would be, with or without hope, —*revolt*."[4]

Engels returned to Carlyle in an 1850 article; although he categorically rejects the latter's most recent writings, he sketches an analysis of Carlyle's work from the 1840s that is quite illuminating:

To Thomas Carlyle belongs the credit of having taken the literary field against the bourgeoisie at a time when its views, tastes and ideas held the whole of official English literature totally in thrall, and in a manner which is at times even *revolutionary*. For example, in his history of the French Revolution, in his apology for Cromwell, in the pamphlet on Chartism and in *Past and Present*. But in all these writings, the critique of the present is *closely bound up with* a strangely unhistorical apotheosis of the Middle Ages, which is a frequent characteristic of other English *revolutionaries* too, for instance Cobbett and a section of the Chartists.[5]

This remark contains two propositions that strike us as fundamental in the Marxist approach to Romanticism: first, the Romantic critique of the capitalist present is "closely bound up with" nostalgia for the past, and second, in certain cases this critique may take on an authentically revolutionary dimension.

An equally important influence on Marx and Engels was exercised by someone who may be considered one of the most biting Romantic critics of bourgeois civilization: Balzac, from whose work Engels acknowledged having learned "more than from all the professed historians, economists, and statisticians of the period."[6] This phrase reiterates almost word for word, moreover, the judgment Marx had pronounced several decades earlier on English writers such as Dickens, Charlotte Brontë, and Mrs. Gaskell, "the present splendid brotherhood of fiction-writers in England, whose graphic and eloquent pages have issued to the world more political and social truths than have been uttered by all the professional politicians, publicists and moralists put together."[7]

It is clear that their reading of Carlyle and Balzac is highly selective: both Engels and Marx categorically reject the backward-looking illusions of the two writers. But they appropriate unhesitatingly the latters' critique of bourgeois-industrial modernity, even though that critique is deeply invested with precapitalist ethical and sociocultural values.

This appropriation is evident in as seemingly "modernist" (that is, favorable to capitalist progress) a text as the *Manifesto of the Communist Party*. Although they categorized the Romantic currents as "reactionary," Marx and Engels recognized very explicitly the value of the social critique these currents contributed. Even "feudal socialism," a sui generis blend of the "echo of the past" with the "menace of the future," despite its "total incapacity to comprehend the march of modern history," has the undeniable merit "at times, by its bitter, witty and incisive criticism, [of] striking the bourgeoisie to the very heart's core." As for "petit-bourgeois socialism" of Sismondi and his followers, despite its limitations, Marx and Engels admitted that this school

dissected with great acuteness the contradictions inherent in the conditions of modern production. It laid bare the hypocritical apologies of

economists. It proved, incontrovertibly, the disastrous effects of machinery and division of labour; the concentration of capital and land in
a few hands; over-production and crises; it pointed out the inevitable
ruin of the petty bourgeois and peasant, the misery of the proletariat,
the anarchy in production, the crying inequalities in the distribution of
wealth. . . .[8]

Here is a rather impressive acknowledgment of an intellectual debt! In
reality, Marx and Engels integrate the entire analysis of the social calamities
of capitalism by this petit bourgeois Romantic current into their vision of
bourgeois society, although they unambiguously reject the positive solutions it offers. However, they are unsparing in their admiration for the
eminently revolutionary role of the conquering bourgeoisie and its economic achievements, which are superior to the pyramids of Egypt and the
Roman aqueducts — achievements that pave the way, in their eyes, for the
material conditions of the proletarian revolution.

Thus Paul Breines's remark on the *Manifesto* appears particularly pertinent:

In the "Manifesto" and Marx's previous writings, the capitalist industrial revolution and the entire world of objectified relations it creates
are grasped as simultaneously liberating and oppressive. . . . the Enlightenment and its Utilitarian progeny had stressed the former side of
the picture; the Romantic current, the latter. Marx stood alone in
transforming both into a single critical vision.[9]

However, we cannot follow Breines when he asserts that in the writings of
Marx and Engels in the second half of the nineteenth century, the utilitarian
root alone flourishes, while the Romantic aspect withers. This is far from
obvious, to the extent that, from the 1860s on, Marx and Engels manifested
increasing interest in and sympathy for certain precapitalist social formations — a characteristic theme of the Romantic vision of history. Their fascination with primitive rural communities — from the Greek *gens* (the clan
structure of prehistoric antiquity) to the old Germanic *Mark* (rural community) and the Russian *obschtchina* (traditional rural commune) — stems
from their conviction that these ancient forms incorporated social qualities
that modern civilizations have lost, qualities that prefigured certain aspects
of a future communist society.

Their discovery of the works of Maurer, the historian of ancient Germanic communities, and later of Lewis Morgan, was what led Marx and Engels to give new value to the past. Thanks to these authors, they could refer to an exemplary precapitalist formation — the primitive community — which was distinct from the feudal system exalted by the traditional Romantics. Marx expresses clearly this political choice of an alternative past in a letter to Engels dated 25 March 1868, in which he is discussing Maurer's book:

> The first reaction to the French Revolution and the Enlightenment bound up with it was naturally to regard everything as medieval, romantic, and even people like Grimm are not free from this. The second reaction to it is to look beyond the Middle Ages into the primitive age of every people — and this corresponds to the socialist tendency, though these learned men have no idea that they are connected with it. And they are then surprised to find what is newest in what is oldest, and even EGALITARIAN TO A DEGREE which would have made Proudhon shudder.[10]

Engels, too, was struck by Maurer's research, which inspired among other things a brief essay on the old Germanic mark, an essay in which Engels proposes "reviving the mark" as a socialist program for rural areas.[11] He even goes beyond Maurer, who seems to him still too marked by the evolutionism of the Aufklärung: in a letter to Marx dated 15 December 1882 he complains about the persistence in Maurer of the "enlightened presupposition that, since the dark Middle Ages, things *must* have changed steadily for the better; this prevents him from perceiving, not only the antagonistic nature of true progress, but likewise individual setbacks."[12] This passage strikes us as a remarkably accurate synthesis of the basic position held by both Engels and Marx on this problematic: first, rejection of a naive and linear if not apologetic progressism, which views bourgeois society as universally superior to earlier social forms; second, insistence on the contradictory nature of the progress undeniably brought about by capitalism; third, a critical judgment of industrial-capitalist civilization as representing, in certain respects, a step backward, from the human point of view, in relation to communities of the past.

This last proposition is moreover one of the principal themes of *The Origin of the Family:* starting from Morgan's studies on the gens, Engels emphasizes the regression that civilization constitutes, to a certain extent, with respect to the primitive community:

> And a wonderful constitution it is, this gentile constitution, in all its childlike simplicity! No soldiers, no gendarmes or police, no nobles, kings, regents, prefects, or judges, no prisons, or lawsuits — and everything takes its orderly course. . . . All are equal and free — the women included. . . . And when we compare their position with that of the overwhelming majority of civilized men today, an enormous gulf separates the present-day proletarian and small peasant from the free member of the old gentile society.

The criteria that allow Engels to speak of stepping backward are above all social (freedom, equality), but they are also ethical: the dissolution of the gens by private property was inevitable, but it amounted nevertheless to "degradation, a fall from the simple moral greatness of the old gentile society."[13]

In the late nineteenth-century struggle against Russian populism (especially with the writings of Georgii Valentinovich Plekhanov), a radically anti-Romantic Marxism began to emerge: a modernizing, evolutionist strain that viewed capitalist-industrial progress with unconditional admiration. It is true that this tendency was based on some texts by Marx and Engels, but nothing more clearly reveals the difference between this deromanticized Marxism and the thinking of Marx himself than Marx's own work on the Russian rural commune. Without sharing all of the *Narodniki*'s presuppositions, Marx believed as they did in the future socialist role of the traditional Russian commune. In his view, as he stated explicitly in a letter of 8 March 1881 to Vera Zasulich, "this commune is the fulcrum of social regeneration in Russia, but in order that it may function as such, it would first be necessary to eliminate the deleterious influences which are assailing it from all sides, and then ensure for it the normal conditions of spontaneous development."[14] Marx insisted, of course, on the need for Russian rural communes to appropriate the technological conquests of European industrial civilization for their own use, but his analysis nevertheless converged to a large extent with the Narodniki wager on the possibility of sparing Russia all the horrors of capitalist civilization. The future laid bare the illusory character of that hope, but Marx's undertaking contained a highly fertile rational kernel.

A draft of the letter to Vera Zasulich also contains remarks on precapitalist rural communities in India, comments that point up the evolution of Marx's views from the 1850s on. In 1853, Marx was depicting the role of English colonization in India as both monstrously destructive and, in spite of everything, progressive (owing to the introduction of railways, for example); progress took the form of "that hideous, pagan idol, who would not drink the nectar but from the skulls of the slain."[15] In the 1881 letter, however, he wrote: "As for the East Indies, for example, everyone except Sir Henry Maine and others of his ilk realises that the suppression of communal landownership out there was nothing but an act of English vandalism, *pushing the native peoples not forwards but backwards.*"[16] This judgment is not in contradiction with the one he formulated in 1853, but here he stressed the regressive aspect of capitalist modernization in human terms.

Besides nostalgia for a lost communitarian paradise, the other major dimension of Marxist thinking that is undeniably Romantic in inspiration is the critique of certain fundamental aspects of industrialist-capitalist modernity. Contrary to what is commonly supposed, this critique is not limited to the question of the private ownership of means of production: it is much broader, deeper, and more radical. The entire existing mode of industrial production and the whole of modern bourgeois society are called into question—with arguments and attitudes often similar to those of the Romantics.

One of the earliest authors to observe the parallelism or affinity between the Marxist and Romantic modes of opposition to the rationalized culture of the bourgeoisie was Karl Mannheim, in "Das konservative Denken" (1927). He shows that a number of oppositions—concrete versus abstract, dynamic or dialectic versus static, totality versus fragmentation, a totalizing grasp of history versus an individualist approach—are features shared by both the right and the left in their critiques of *bürgerlich-naturrechtliche Denken* (bourgeois thinking about natural law). However, most of the examples of the Marxist position that he puts forward are drawn from Lukács's *History and Class Consciousness,* a book that is already a combination of Marxism with German sociology as inspired by Romanticism. In addition, Mannheim is more interested in the methodological similarities between the revolutionary-Marxist and the conservative-Romantic styles of thinking than in the possible convergence of their concrete critiques of bourgeois-industrial *society.*[17]

Following Mannheim, a number of sociologists or historians of literature referred to the connection between Romanticism and Marxism. Alvin Gouldner insisted on the presence of "important *components* of Romanticism" in Marx's thought; Ernst Fischer asserted that Marx had incorporated into his socialist vision "the romantic revolt against a world which turned everything into a commodity and degraded man to the status of an object." Unquestionably, the Marxist concept of alienation is strongly tinged with Romanticism; as Istvan Meszaros has shown, one of the major sources of Marx's thought is the Rousseauist critique of the alienation of the self as "selling one's freedom." Both Fischer and Gouldner — along with M. H. Abrams — see the dream of integral humanity, beyond fragmentation, division, and alienation, as the chief link between Marx and the Romantic legacy. More recently, Jürgen Habermas has characterized the thinking of the young Marx as "Romantic socialism," to the extent that "the idea of a free association of producers has always been loaded with nostalgic images of the types of community — the family, the neighborhood and the guild — to be found in the world of peasants and craftsmen that, with the violent onset of a competitive society, was just beginning to break down, and whose disappearance was experienced as a loss." According to Habermas, the very idea of a society in which individuals cease to be alienated in relation to the product of their work, other human beings, and themselves, is rooted in Romanticism.[18]

These authors do not concern themselves in any more direct way with the specific parallels between the Romantic and Marxist critiques of modern capitalist civilization.[19] As we see it, however, these parallels are particularly striking in relation to the crucial question of quantification.

The critique of the quantification of life in (bourgeois) industrial society occupies a central place in Marx's early writings, especially in *Economic and Philosophic Manuscripts of 1844*. According to this text, the power of money is such, in capitalism, that it permits capitalism to destroy and dissolve all human and natural qualities by subjecting them to its own purely quantitative measure. "The quantity of money becomes more and more its sole important property. Just as it reduces everything to its own form of abstraction, so it reduces itself in the course of its own movement to something quantitative." The exchange among concrete human qualities — love for love, confidence for confidence — is replaced by the abstract exchange of money for merchandise. The worker is reduced to the condition of merchandise, human merchandise (*Menschenware*), becoming a damned creature, physically and spiritually dehumanized (*entmenschtes*). "Man reverts once more to living in a cave, but the cave is now polluted by the mephitic and pestilential breath of civilization." Just as a trader who sells precious stones sees only their market value and not the beauty or the particular nature of the stones, individuals in capitalist society lose their material and spiritual sensitivity and replace it by the exclusive sense of possession. In a word: *being,* the free expression of the richness of life through social and cultural activities, is increasingly sacrificed to *having,* the accumulation of money, merchandise, and capital.[20]

These themes of Marx's early writings are less explicit in *Capital,* but they are present nonetheless, especially in the well-known passage in which Marx compares the ethos of modern capitalist civilization, exclusively focused on production of more and more goods and in the accumulation of capital (that is, on "quantity and exchange value"), with the spirit of classical antiquity, which holds "exclusively by quality and use value."[21]

The principal issue addressed in *Capital* is the exploitation of labor, the extraction of added value by the capitalist owners of the means of production. But it also contains a radical critique of the very nature of modern industrial labor. In its charge against the dehumanizing character of capitalist-industrial labor, *Capital* is still more explicit than *Economic and Philosophic Manuscripts of 1844,* and there is very probably a connection between the critique it formulates and those of the Romantics.

Marx clearly does not dream, as John Ruskin did, of reestablishing the medieval craft system, but he nevertheless perceives industrial labor as a socially and culturally degraded form in relation to the human qualities of precapitalist labor: "The knowledge, the judgement, and the will . . . [that] are practiced by the independent peasant or handcraftsman" are lost by the piece-work laborers of modern industry. Analyzing this degradation, Marx draws attention first to the division of labor, which "converts the labourer into a crippled monstrosity, by forcing his detail dexterity at the expense of a world of productive capabilities and instincts"; in this context he cites the conservative (Tory) Romantic David Urquhart: "To subdivide a man is to execute him, if he deserves the sentence, to assassinate him if he does not. . . . The subdivision of labour is the assassination of a people." As for machines, in themselves elements of progress, in the contemporary mode of production they become a curse for the worker; they strip work of all interest and confiscates "every atom of freedom, both in bodily and intellectual activity." With the capitalist machine, work "becomes a sort of torture" because — here Marx cites Engels's book, *The Condition of the Working Class in England in 1844* — the worker is reduced to "the miserable routine of endless drudgery and toil in which the same mechanical process is gone through over and over again, is like the labor of Sisyphus. The burden of labour, like the rock, keeps ever falling back on the worn-out labourer." In the modern industrial system, the whole organization of the process of work crushes the worker's vitality, freedom, and independence. To this already dark picture, Marx adds the description of the material conditions under which work is carried out: insufficient space, light, and air; deafening noise; a dust-filled atmosphere; the risk of being mutilated or killed by a machine; and countless illnesses stemming from "the dangerous and unwholesome accompaniments of the productive process."[22] In short, the natural and cultural qualities of workers as human beings are sacrificed by capital to the purely quantitative aim of producing more goods and obtaining more profits.

The Marxist conception of socialism is intimately connected with this radical critique of modern bourgeois civilization. It implies a qualitative change, a new social culture, a new way of life, a different type of civilization that would reestablish the role of the "human and natural qualities" of life and the role of use value in the process of production. It requires the emancipation of labor, not only by the "expropriation of the expropriators" and the control of the production process by the associated producers but also by a complete transformation of the nature of work itself.

How to achieve this aim? This is a problematic that Marx addresses above all in *Grundrisse* (1857–58): in the socialist community, in his view, technological progress and mechanization will drastically reduce the time needed for "necessary labour" — the labor required to satisfy the fundamental needs of the community. Most of the hours in a day will thus be left free for what Marx, after Fourier, calls attractive labor: that is, truly free labor, work that is the self-realization of the individual. Such work, such production (which can be material as well as spiritual) is not simply play — and here Marx separates himself from Fourier — but can require maximum effort and maximum seriousness: Marx mentions musical composition as an example.[23]

It would be quite mistaken to deduce from the foregoing remarks that Marx was a Romantic: he owes more to the philosophy of the Enlightenment and to classical political economics than to the Romantic critiques of industrial civilization. But the latter helped him perceive the limits and the contradictions of the former. In a very revealing passage of the *Economic and Political Manuscripts of 1844,* he refers to the contradiction between the old landowners and the new capitalists, expressed in a polemic between Romantic authors (e.g., Justus Möser) and political economists (David Ricardo, John Stuart Mill): "This contradiction is extremely bitter, and each side tells the truth about the other."[24] Similarly, a recurrent theme of his late economic writings is that Sismondi is capable of seeing Ricardo's limitations, and vice versa.

Marx's ideas were neither Romantic nor modernizing, but constituted an attempt at a dialectical Aufhebung between the two, in a new critical and revolutionary worldview. Neither apologetic for bourgeois civilization nor blind to its achievements, Marx sought a higher form of social organization, one that would incorporate the technological advances of modern society along with some of the human qualities of precapitalist communities — and above all one that would open up a boundless field for the development and enrichment of human life.

ROSA LUXEMBURG

Like Marx, Rosa Luxemburg would seem to be at the opposite pole from Romanticism. In her writings on the question of Polish statehood, she rejects — as a utopian dream sustained by the precapitalist social strata, such as the archaic petite bourgeoisie and the aristocracy — the restoration of an independent Polish nation. Her demonstration is based on an analysis of the irreversible consequences of the capitalist industrialization of Poland, which modernized its economy by integrating it into the Russian market — thus making any hope of reviving the independent national past anachronistic.

Nevertheless, we find an undeniable Romantic component in her economic writings, manifested at several levels. Like Marx — but unlike most twentieth-century Marxists — Luxemburg shows great interest in Sismondi's economic Romanticism, stressing its "supremely lucid" character, Sismondi's "profound grasp of the real contradictions in the movements of capital," and "his profound insight into historical connections." It is highly characteristic of Rosa Luxemburg's attitude that she considers the Romantic Swiss economist as carrying the day in some respects with regard to Ricardo himself: "Sismondi shows himself superior to Ricardo in yet a third point: he represents the broad horizon of the dialectic approach as against Ricardo's blunt narrow-mindedness with its incapacity to conceive of any forms of society other than those of bourgeois economics." Rosa Luxemburg's entire *Accumulation of Capital* is in fact based on a rehabilitation and a critical surpassing of economic Romanticism, and in particular Sismondi's, through reference to Marx himself. In this context, she defends Sismondi as opposed to Lenin, whose scornful critique of economic Romanticism she finds constricted and unjust.[25]

The other Romantic aspect of Luxemburg's economic writings is her passionate interest in precapitalist communities. The central theme of her *Einführung in die Nationaloekonomie* (an unfinished manuscript published by Paul Levi in 1925) is the analysis of social formations — which she calls "primitive communist societies" — and their opposition to capitalist market society.[26] A wholly original approach to the evolution of social formations, which runs counter to linear "progressive" views, is outlined in this text.

What lies behind Luxemburg's interest in so-called primitive communes? On the one hand, it is obvious that she seeks to use the very existence of such ancient communist societies as a tool to shake up and even destroy "the old notion of the eternal nature of private property and its existence from the beginning of the world." It is because bourgeois economists cannot even conceive of communal property and cannot comprehend anything that does not resemble capitalist civilization that they stubbornly refuse to recognize the historical phenomenon of communities. On the other hand, Luxemburg sees primitive communism as a precious historical reference point for criticizing capitalism; for unveiling its irrational, reified, anarchic character; and for bringing to light the radical opposition between use value and exchange value.[27] Luxemburg's aim, then, is to find and save everything in the primitive past that may prefigure modern socialism, at least up to a point; her undertaking is characteristic of the (revolutionary) Romantic vision.

Like Marx and Engels, Luxemburg looked closely at Maurer's writings on the ancient Germanic commune (Mark); like Marx and Engels, she marveled at the democratic and egalitarian functioning of this formation and at its social transparency:

> One cannot imagine anything simpler and more harmonious than the economic system of the ancient German communes. The whole mech-

anism of social life is there in plain view. A rigorous plan and a robust organization frame the activity of each member and integrate him as an element of the whole. The immediate needs of daily life and their equal satisfaction for all, such is the point of departure and the destination of this organization. All work together for all and decide together about everything.

Luxemburg highlights the features of this communitarian formation that oppose it to capitalism and make it in certain respects humanly superior to modern bourgeois civilization: "Two thousand years ago and more, then, among the Germanic peoples there reigned a state of affairs fundamentally different from the current situation: no State with written and constraining laws, no division between rich and poor, between masters and workers."28

Relying on the work of the Russian historian Maxime Kovalevsky, in whom Marx had been quite interested earlier, Luxemburg stresses the universality of the agrarian commune as a general form of human society at a certain stage of its development, a stage one finds among American Indians, the Incas, and the Aztecs, as well as among the Kabyls, African tribes, and the Hindus. The Peruvian example seems most significant, and here too she cannot refrain from suggesting a comparison between the Inca *Marca* and "civilized" society: "Modern art, being exclusively nourished by the work of others and making of leisure the attribute of power, was foreign to this social organization in which common property and the general obligation to work constituted deeply rooted popular customs." She thus manifests her admiration for "the incredible resistance of the Indian people and of the agrarian communist institutions of which, despite the conditions, vestiges have been preserved right into the nineteenth century."29 Some twenty years later, the eminent Peruvian Marxist thinker José Carlos Mariategui, who also displayed Romantic tendencies, advanced a thesis that presented striking convergences with Luxemburg's ideas, though very probably he was unacquainted with her remarks on Peru: to win over the peasant masses, modern socialism has to look to the indigenous traditions that go back to Incan communism.

The most important author in this area for Luxemburg — as for Engels — was the American anthropologist Lewis Morgan. Starting from his classic work *Ancient Society* (1877), Luxemburg went further than Marx and Engels: she developed an entire grandiose vision of history, a heterodox conception of the age-old evolution of humanity, in which contemporary civilization "with its private property, its class domination, its masculine domination, its constraining state and marriage" appears as a mere parenthesis, a transition between primitive communist society and the communist society of the future. The revolutionary-Romantic idea of the link between past and future lies at the heart of this visionary perspective:

> The noble tradition of the remote past thus held out a hand to the revolutionary aspirations of the future, the circle of knowledge closed harmoniously, and, in this perspective, the current world of class domination and exploitation, which claimed to be the *nec plus ultra* of civilization, the supreme goal of universal history, was no longer anything but a minuscule and transitory stage on the great forward march of humanity.[30]

From this standpoint, the European colonization of Third World peoples struck Luxemburg as a fundamentally inhuman and socially destructive enterprise. The English occupation of India was a revealing case in point: it ravaged and shattered the traditional communist agrarian structures, with tragic consequences for the peasantry. Rosa Luxemburg shared Marx's conviction that imperialism brings economic progress to colonized nations, even if it does so "by the ignoble methods of a class society."[31] Still, while Marx, without concealing his indignation at such methods, emphasized the economically progressive role of the railways introduced by England into India, Luxemburg placed greater stress on the socially harmful consequences of capitalist progress:

> The old ties were broken, the peaceful isolation of communism apart from the world was shattered and replaced by quarrels, discord, inequality, and exploitation. This produced huge farm holdings on the one hand, millions of farmers without means on the other. Private property made its entrance into India, and with it typhus, hunger, and scurvy, which became permanent guests on the plains of the Ganges.[32]

This difference from Marx probably corresponds to a distinct historical stage that allowed a new way of looking at colonized countries, but it is also the expression of Luxemburg's particular sensitivity to the social and human qualities of primitive communities.

This argument is developed not only in the *Einführung die Nationaloekonomie* but also in *The Accumulation of Capital,* where Luxemburg again criticizes the historical role of English colonialism and expresses outrage at the criminal scorn that the European conquerors displayed toward the old system of irrigation. Capital, in its blind unbridled greed, "is incapable of seeing far enough to recognise the value of the economic monuments of an older civilisation"; colonial politics provoked the decline of this traditional system and as a result, starting in 1867, famine began to claim millions of victims in India. As for French colonization in Algeria, she saw it as characterized by a systematic and deliberate attempt at destruction and dislocation of communal property, leading to the economic ruin of the indigenous population.[33]

Above and beyond any specific examples, Luxemburg denounced the entire colonial system — whether Spanish, Portuguese, Dutch, English, or German, in Africa or in Asia. She adopted the viewpoint of the victims of capitalist modernization: "For primitive peoples, in the colonial countries where primitive communism once reigned, capitalism constitutes an unspeakable misfortune full of the most frightful suffering." According to her, the struggle of the indigenous populations against the imperial metropolis admirably manifests the tenacious resistance of the old communist traditions against the quest for profits and against capitalist Europeanization. Reading between the lines, one can discern here the idea of an alliance between the anticolonial struggle of these peoples and the anticapitalist struggle of the modern proletariat as a revolutionary convergence between the old and the new communism.[34]

Does this mean, as Gilbert Badia believes, that she presents the ancient structures of colonized societies in an excessively rigid "black-and-white contrast with capitalism"? (Badia, the author of a remarkable biography of Rosa Luxemburg, is one of the rare scholars who has examined this aspect of her work critically.) According to Badia, Luxemburg contrasts the old communities, "endowed with every virtue and conceived as virtually immobile," with the "destructive function of a capitalism that no longer has any progressive aspects whatsoever. We are far removed from the conquering bourgeoisie evoked by Marx in the *Manifesto.* "[35] Badia's objections strike us as unjustified, for a number of reasons. In the first place, Luxemburg did not conceive of the old communities as immobile or frozen; on the contrary, she shows their contradictions and transformations. She stresses that "through its own internal evolution, primitive communist society leads to inequality and despotism."[36] Second, she does not deny the economically progressive role of capitalism, but she does denounce the ignoble and socially regressive aspects of capitalist colonization. Third, while she highlights the most positive aspects of primitive communism, in contrast with bourgeois civilization, she does not fail to point out its flaws and limitations: locally restricted outlooks, a low level of labor productivity and of development toward civilization, helplessness in the face of nature, brutal violence, a permanent state of war between communities, and so on.[37] Fourth, in fact, Luxemburg's approach is very different from the one Marx adopted in his 1848 hymn to the bourgeoisie; in contrast, it is very close to the spirit of chapter 31 of *Capital* ("Genesis of the Industrial Capitalist"), where Marx describes the "barbarities" and "atrocities" of European colonization.

Furthermore, on the topic of the Russian rural commune, Luxemburg's view is much more critical than Marx's. Taking Engels's analysis of the late-nineteenth-century decline of the obschtchina as her starting point, Luxemburg highlights the historical limits of traditional communities in general and the need to surpass them.[38] Then, looking toward the future, she parts company from economic Romanticism in general and from the Russian populists in particular, insisting on "the fundamental difference between the worldwide socialist economy of the future and the primitive communist groups of prehistory."[39]

Be that as it may, Luxemburg's writings on this theme are much more than an erudite glance at economic history: they suggest another way of conceiving of the past and the present, of social historicity, progress, and modernity, an approach whose affinity with certain aspects of revolutionary Romanticism is significant. By confronting capitalist industrial civilization with humanity's communitarian past, Rosa Luxemburg breaks with linear evolutionism, positivist progressivism, and all the banally modernizing interpretations of Marxism that prevailed in her day.

GYÖRGY LUKÁCS

Unlike Luxemburg, Marx, and Engels, the young György Lukács looked neither to primitive communism nor to a determined economic formation for precapitalist models, but rather to certain cultural configurations: the Homeric universe of ancient Greece; Russian literary or religious spirituality; Christian, Hindu, or Jewish mysticism. Here and there one can also find a mention of medieval Catholicism, particularly in relation to the art of painters such as Giotto or Giovanni Cimabue, but these are not central references. In another respect, Lukács was much closer than Luxemburg to classical German Romanticism and to the various late-nineteenth-century currents in literature, philosophy, and sociology inspired by Romanticism. The Romantic critique of capitalism was probably the decisive factor in the intellectual and political radicalization that was to lead him toward socialism—initially in the form of Sorelian anarcho-syndicalism, then Bolshevism.[40]

When Lukács joined the Hungarian Communist Party in December, 1918, this Romantic dimension did not disappear; for quite some time, it was blended with the Marxist worldview in a profoundly original and subtle ideological fusion expressed most fully in the essay "Alte Kultur und neue Kultur," written during the Hungarian Workers' Councils revolution (1919). The text is built around the contrast between the culture of past societies and the "nonculture" of capitalism. Lukács's analysis does not distinguish among differing modes of precapitalist production: he refers to "periods that preceded capitalism" as if they constituted a whole presenting certain common features in contrast to the capitalist revolution. On the one hand, an artistic spirit dominated all productive activity; on the other hand, *Kultur* resulted from a slow, organic growth arising from the soil of social beings, and this organic quality gave it a harmonious and grandiose character. The examples of organic culture Lukács mentions are Greece and the Renaissance, but his argument could have been applied equally well to medieval culture. With the advent of capitalism, "everything has ceased to be evaluated for itself, for its intrinsic value (e.g., artistic or aesthetic) and has values only as goods that can be bought and sold in the marketplace." The revolution in production brought about by capital requires the manufacture of so-called novelties, with rapid modifications in form or quality unrelated to the product's aesthetic value or usefulness: this is the tyrannical domination of fashion. (Similar insights can be found in some of Walter Benjamin's texts on fashion and the false novelty of merchandise.) However, fashion and culture designate realities that are mutually exclusive by their very nature. With generalized mercantilization, culture in the genuine sense of the word begins to decline: capitalism is destructive of culture. It is true that in precapitalist eras culture was the exclusive province of the dominant classes, but in capitalism itself these classes are subjected to the movement of goods and are incapable of authentic cultural creation. With the socialist revolution, the possibility arises of a culture open to all, a new culture that Lukács envisages as a true cultural restoration: owing to the abolition of capitalism and the mercantile character of products, organic development becomes possible once again; social activities lose their mercantile function and their proper human finality is restored.[41] Such expressions offer a striking illustration of the author's revolutionary-Romantic approach. For Lukács, socialist society reestablishes the cultural continuity broken by capitalism: the new culture brought into being by the revolution is linked to the old culture of precapitalist societies.

The same problematic appears, in a different form, in a lecture Lukács gave in 1919 on the changed function of historical materialism. Starting from the Hegelian distinction between the objective spirit (social relations, law, the state) and the absolute spirit (philosophy, art, religion), he notes that precapitalist societies are characterized by the determining role of the absolute spirit: for example, religion in the era of early Christianity. In the capitalist era, in contrast, all the active social forces exist only as manifestations of the objective spirit (which is itself determined by the economic base): religion becomes a social institution—the church—comparable to the state, the army, or the university. Socialism will inaugurate a period in which once again the absolute spirit—that is, philosophy, culture, and science—will reign over economic and social life.[42]

In *History and Class Consciousness* (1923), Lukács seems to distance himself from Romanticism: in his view, after Rousseau the concept of organic growth (the same one he himself had invoked in 1919) "was converted from a protest against reification into an increasingly reactionary slogan" in the course of "the historical development leading from German Romanticism via the historical school of law, Carlyle, Ruskin, etc." But at the same time he recognizes that Carlyle and authors like him had understood and described, well before Marx, "how capitalism violates and destroys everything human." A hint of Romantic nostalgia is sometimes perceptible, especially when Lukács is comparing capitalist subjection of all forms of life with mechanization and rational calculation, with the "organic process within a community" such as a traditional village. In reality, the book's central project, the critical analysis of reification (*Verdinglichung*) in all its forms (economic, legal-bureaucratic, cultural), is largely inspired by the Romantic variant of German sociology: Ferdinand Tönnies, Georg Simmel, Max Weber. Lukács is quite clearly reformulating sociological themes within a Marxist critique of market reification. But in other sections of the book he proceeds in the opposite direction: taking certain passages from *Capital* as his point of departure, he develops an overall critique of the mechanization of work and the quantification of time, a critique whose affinities with Romanticism are undeniable. Such a procedure is possible, however, only to the extent that Marx's work itself includes a Romantic aspect, as we have seen: Breines is not mistaken when he writes that the young Lukács tried to restore to Marxism "its lost Romantic dimension."[43]

Lukács's literary writings from 1922 to 1923 also include references to Romanticism, especially in connection with the author who represented for the young pre-Marxist Lukács of *Theory of the Novel* (1916) the most radical spiritual rejection of modern bourgeois civilization: Fyodor Dostoevsky. In "Strawrogins Beichte" (Stavrogin's confession), an article published in 1922 in *Rote Fahne* (the German Communist Party newspaper), Lukács salutes Dostoevsky's capacity to evoke a utopian world, "a world from which everything in capitalist society that is mechanical, inhuman, soulless, and reified is banished." And in another text published in the same newspaper, in 1923, we seem to hear a direct echo of the final chapter of *Theory of the Novel:* Dostoevsky is the precursor of the man of the future, "already socially and economically liberated," living his inner life to the fullest.[44]

It is only toward the end of the 1920s that Lukács's thinking veers toward hostility to Romanticism, and even then there are contradictions and sudden reversals. Lukács's position may conceivably have been linked to his forced reconciliation with Stalinism, for which industrialization was the alpha and omega of the "construction of socialism in a single country" (this was during Stalin's first five-year plan, 1929–1934) and which certainly has no room for Romantic nostalgia. But the relationship between Stalinian dogma and Lukács's attitude toward Romanticism is more complex than this: as we shall see, Lukács changed his position ten years later. One might also try to establish a link between his cultural analyses and the rise of Nazism, which he — along with many others — perceived as the logical result of the reactionary Romantic tradition of German culture. But in this case, too, the parallelism is far from obvious, and it cannot explain the author's astonishingly divergent interpretations of Dostoevsky in 1931, 1943, and 1957.

It would seem that for some forty years Lukács was being pulled in two different directions. The dominant tendency was the classical aufklärung, the liberal-democratic and rationalist ideology of progress (which he tried to reconcile with the harsh realities of the Soviet state); the competing tendency was the "anticapitalist Romantic demon" from which he never succeeded in freeing himself and which sometimes resurfaced in an unexpected way. While we cannot examine all the stages of this tortured, tortuous, and rather opaque itinerary here, we can point out a few of the most illuminating examples.

In 1928 Lukács published a very laudatory review of a book by Carl Schmitt on political Romanticism. He accepted without reservation the book's thesis—which in our view is very superficial—concerning the occasionalism and absence of political content of Romantic thought. Following in Schmitt's footsteps, he stressed the Romantics' incoherence, their antiscientific subjectivism, and their exaggerated aestheticism.[45]

The term "Romantic anticapitalist" appeared for the first time in a 1931 article on Dostoevsky, in which Lukács condemned the Russian writer—who had been the chief inspiration behind his own revolutionary Romanticism up to 1918—as reactionary. According to this text published in Moscow, Dostoevsky's influence resulted from his ability to transform the problems of Romantic opposition to capitalism into internal, spiritual problems, thus helping a significant segment of the petit bourgeois intelligentsia to deepen its worldview in the direction of a pseudorevolutionarism with a religious coloration (*religiöselnde Salonrevoluzzerei*)—a concept that could presumably be applied to his own early writings or to those of his friend Bloch. In *Theory of the Novel* (1916), Lukács closely linked Leo Tolstoy and Dostoevsky—although he stressed the superiority of the latter—as prophets of a new world; in 1931 he celebrated Tolstoy as the representative of the "classical tradition of the rising revolutionary bourgeoisie"—a strange definition for a writer who scorned urban luxury and admired the life style of the impoverished peasantry—while contrasting him with Dostoevsky, whose writings represented "the subterranean Romantic currents of the petite bourgeoisie." At his worst, Dostoevsky is nothing but "the writer of the Black Hundreds and of czarist imperialism"; at his best, he is the artistic representative of the "petit bourgeois Romantic anticapitalist intellectual opposition," a social level that oscillates between left and right, but for which "a broad avenue opens up toward the right, toward reaction, today toward Fascism, and on the contrary a narrow and difficult path toward the left, toward revolution." The conclusion of this fascinating document of dogmatic frenzy is that with the inevitable decline of the petite bourgeoisie, "Dostoevsky's fame will vanish ingloriously."[46]

With that article a type of analysis appeared that was to be found in most of Lukács's later references to Romantic anticapitalism: on the one hand, a recognition of the contradictory character of the phenomenon; on the other hand, a sometimes exaggerated tendency to consider the reactionary and even fascist predisposition as the dominant pole. It was no accident that the article aroused the indignation of his revolutionary Romantic friend Bloch and contributed to a cooling of their relations.[47] In an essay published some months after the article on Dostoevsky, Lukács refers once again to the existence of a direct link between German Fascism and the "theoretical arsenal of Romantic anticapitalism." But at least he established a distinction between "the subjective honesty that is still present in Sismondi and the early Carlyle" and the manipulations of Fascist propaganda.[48]

Lukács could not fail to be aware that his own evolution toward Marxism and revolution had its roots in Romantic anticapitalism. Far from nuancing his analysis, this awareness led him to an act of public self-criticism, in a 1933 manuscript on the cultural origins of Fascism: according to this text, *History and Class Consciousness* (1923) is a dangerous work containing "the gravest concessions to the bourgeois-idealist worldview." Stressing the continuity between the development of German thought and Fascism, he added: "As a disciple of Simmel and Dilthey, as a friend of Max Weber and Emil Lask, as an enthusiastic reader of Stefan George and Rilke, I myself have undergone the whole evolution described here. . . . I have had to see many a friend from my youth, sincere and convinced Romantic anticapitalists all, carried away in the tempest of Fascism."[49] Thus he refuses to examine the crucial connection between the Romantic vision and his own adherence — along with that of many other German intellectuals, in particular those of Jewish origin, such as Bloch, Ernst Toller, Gustav Landauer, Walter Benjamin, and others — to the cause of socialist revolution.

This manuscript from 1933 — something like a first version of *The Destruction of Reason* — sketches a more general and more systematic analysis of the renaissance of Romantic culture from the late nineteenth century on. While the text calls the whole set of cultural critiques of capitalism "reactionary-Romantic" (or even precursors of Fascism), it makes an interesting distinction between two periods of "neo-Romanticism": the first, the period before 1914, was inspired in particular by early Romanticism, where we still find a certain ambiguity that leaves room for leftist interpretations: Friedrich Nietzsche, Tönnies, Simmel, Weber, the philosophy of life, Ricarda Huch; and the second, the postwar period, invokes late Romanticism and is openly reactionary, if not fascistic: Martin Heidegger, Ernst Jünger, Oswald Spengler, Hans Freyer, Alfred Bäumler, Alfred Rosenberg. The change is manifested by a growing inclination toward irrationalism and myth.

Lukács is particularly interested in "the Nietzsche case." In 1934, he wrote an article titled "Nietzsche als Vorläufer der faschistischen Aesthetik" (Nietzsche as precursor of the fascist aesthetic), presenting the author of *Thus Spoke Zarathustra* as continuing the tradition of Romantic critiques of capitalism. Like them, "he constantly contrasts the present lack of culture (*Kulturlosigkeit*) with the high culture of precapitalist periods or early capitalism. Like all Romantic critics of human degradation through capitalism, he combats fetishized modern civilization, opposing to it the culture of economically and socially more primitive stages." Lukács does not seem to recognize that this type of cultural critique — which indeed plays a retrograde role for Nietzsche — may take on a revolutionary character in a different context. Nevertheless, he credits Nietzsche with sincerity, with good intentions that were degraded by the Nazis' manipulation of his ideas: "Fascism has to liquidate everything progressive in the bourgeois legacy; in Nietzsche's case, it has to falsify or deny the moments in which a subjectively sincere Romantic critique of capitalist culture is manifested."[50]

Lukács's approach to expressionism has a similar basis. In a well-known essay titled "Expressionism: Its Significance and Decline" (1934), Lukács relates expressionism to Romantic anticapitalism and compares it to the approach Georg Simmel adopted in his *Philosophy of Money*. Unaware of the revolutionary dimension of expressionism, he perceives it only as "one of the many tendencies in bourgeois ideology that grow later into fascism."[51] Three years later, the Nazis organized their sinister exhibit of "degenerate art," featuring work by most of the known expressionist painters. In a note added to his essay in 1953, Lukács remained impassive: "That the National Socialists later condemned expressionism as a 'decadent' art in no way affects the historical correctness of the above analysis."[52]

This position led Lukács to a polemical confrontation with his old friend and alter ego Bloch. In 1935, Lukács wrote a critical review of Bloch's *Heritage of Our Times,* based on the argument that, since Bloch defended the Romantic anticapitalist ideology in a critical fashion, his conception of Marxism could only be "fundamentally false." Curiously, but quite insightfully, Lukács compared Bloch to the "social-democrat Herbert Marcuse," who sought to contrast the authentic *Lebensphilosophie* (that of Wilhelm Dilthey and Nietzsche) with the false one represented by the Fascists.[53] In a 1938 article that was part of his polemic with Bloch, as well as in other writings, Lukács distinguishes between the sincere "subjective intentions" of certain expressionist artists and the "objective" reactionary content of their work. He includes his own early writings among the examples he mentions to illustrate this contradiction: whatever its aim may have been, "*Theory of the Novel* was a completely reactionary work," full of idealist mystique. Retrospectively, he even considers *History and Class Consciousness* a reactionary book because of its idealism.[54]

Starting with the article on Dostoevsky in 1931, Lukács thus appears to have embarked on an interpretive paradigm that focuses almost exclusively on Romanticism's prefascist and reactionary dimension (which undeniably exists). Yet a few years later, in several essays written in Moscow between 1939 and 1941, a point of view emerges that is astonishingly favorable to certain Romantics, for example Balzac and Carlyle. By entering into polemics with some Soviet literary critics (Valerii Iakovlevich Kirpotin, Knipovitch) who contrast progressive bourgeois thinking with Balzac's reactionary conceptions, Lukács rejects what he calls a liberal-bourgeois ideological tradition: "the mythology of a struggle between 'Reason' and 'Reaction,' or, in another variant, the myth of the struggle of the luminous angel of bourgeois progress . . . with the black demon of feudalism." For him, Balzac's pitiless critiques of capitalism, or Carlyle's, are profoundly clairvoyant, especially in relation to the role of capitalism as destroyer of culture. Now this critical aspect cannot be mechanically separated from Balzac's or Carlyle's overall worldview—and especially not from their conservative ideology or their idealization of the Middle Ages.[55]

Lukács's 1943 article on Dostoevsky is still more impressive. The critic not only rehabilitates the great Russian writer; he also sketches a luminous and penetrating analysis of Romantic anticapitalism—although this term does not appear in his essay. All of Dostoevsky's work, Lukács writes, manifests "a revolt against the moral and spiritual deformation of human beings resulting from the development of capitalism." To this degradation he opposes a certain nostalgia, the dream of a Golden Age — symbolically represented by archaic Greece, as Claude Lorrain imagined it in his painting *Acis and Galatea* — characterized by harmony among all people:

> This dream is the authentic core of what is most precious in Dostoevsky's utopia, a world in which . . . culture and civilization will not be an obstacle to the development of the human soul. The spontaneous, wild, and blind revolt of Dostoevsky's characters comes about in the name of that Golden Age. Their rebellion is Dostoevsky's poetic and historically progressive greatness: here truly arises a light that brightens the paths of humanity's future.[56]

"The Golden Age of the past that lights the way to the future": it would be hard to imagine a more propitious, more precise, and more striking formula to sum up the revolutionary-Romantic Weltanschauung with which Lukács here manifests undeniable sympathy and affinity.

In February 1946, in a preface to a collection of articles on Russian realist writers, Lukács again salutes Dostoevsky as a progressive figure. This time he inverts the explanatory model he had used in 1931: even as he criticizes mystical and reactionary aspects of Tolstoy's and Dostoevsky's subjective intentions, he declares that what really counts is their objective, historical signification:

> The important moment is the human and artistic bond of the writer with a great progressive popular movement. . . . Tolstoy's roots are in the peasantry, Dostoevsky's in the suffering urban *plèbe,* and Gorki's in the proletariat and in the poorest elements of the peasantry. But all three are rooted through their innermost souls in this movement that was both seeking its way and struggling for the liberation of the people."[57]

During the first years after the Second World War, the previous anti-Romantic attitude became dominant once again. It is easy to observe the development of this tendency by comparing the various interpretations Lukács proposed to explain the enigmatic and provocative figure of Leon Naphta, the revolutionary-conservative-obscurantist-Communist-Jesuit Jew in Thomas Mann's *The Magic Mountain.* In 1942, Lukács denounced Naphta's ideology as "reactionary demagogy," but he also recognized that Mann used this individual to bring out the "seductive, spiritual, and biting character of Romantic anticapitalism," along with "the accuracy of some aspects of his critique of contemporary social life."[58] Just a few years later, Lukács calls the young Naphta "the spokesman of the reactionary, Fascist, anti-democratic *Weltanschauung.*" His analysis very closely resembles a sophisticated version of the mythical combat between the bourgeois angel of Enlightenment and the dark feudal demon about whom he wrote so ironically in 1941. The central theme of *The Magic Mountain* is defined as "the symbolical duel between the representatives of light and darkness, the Italian humanist democrat Settembrini and the Jesuit-educated Jew, Naphta, spokesman of a Catholicising, pre-Fascist ideology";[59] Lukács thus reduces (somewhat simplistically) the character's ambivalent and "seductive" Romantic anticapitalist ideology to its reactionary and obscurantist component.

This narrow conception runs through all Lukács's postwar writings. It reaches its apogee with *The Destruction of Reason* (1953), which presents the entire history of German thought, from Friedrich Schelling to Tönnies and from Dilthey to Simmel, as a vast confrontation between reaction and reason, and all the Romantic currents "from the historical school of law to Carlyle" as leading ineluctably to a "general irrationalization of history" — thus, in the last analysis, to Fascist ideology.

The Destruction of Reason is generally viewed today as a Stalinist tract. This judgment is incorrect, to the extent that the work's leitmotiv is not — as it is for Andrei Aleksandrovich Zhdanov and his disciples — a confrontation between proletarian science (or philosophy) and bourgeois science, but only between reason and nonreason. Its principal limitation, in our view, is that it fails to take into account what the Frankfurt School calls the "dialectic of Enlightenment," that is, the transformation of reason into an instrument at the service of merchandise and myth. Paradoxically, the concept of Romantic anticapitalism appears very seldom in this book. The Romantics and their disciples are simply labeled "reactionaries" and "irrationalists." One of the rare authors to be explicitly designated as a Romantic anticapitalist is Tönnies, who is presented in a relatively favorable light:

> If we compare Toennies with the older Romantic anti-capitalists, we
> will notice the particular and subsequently important nuance that he
> was not voicing a desire to revert to social conditions now sur-

mounted, and certainly not to feudalism. . . . his position provided the basis for a cultural critique which strongly emphasized the problematic, negative features of capitalist culture, but which also underlined that capitalism was ineluctable and a product of fate.

However, the opposition between gemeinschaft and gesellschaft, which constitutes the scaffolding of Tönnies's work, only distorts in a subjective-irrationalist, Romantic anticapitalist way, according to Lukács, the realities of capitalist development already noted by Marx.[60]

At each stage in Lukács's spiritual evolution, his relation to Dostoevsky is symptomatic of his general attitude toward Romantic anticapitalism. In the postwar period, the prevailing tendency is anathema; we find another echo of this in *The Meaning of Contemporary Realism* (1957), one of Lukács's most questionable works. Lukács recognizes the critical power of the Russian writer: "His hero's sufferings derive from the inhumanity of early capitalism, and particularly from its destructive influence on personal relationships." But the essential point is that the "protest against the inhumanity of capitalism is transformed into a sophistical, anticapitalist romanticism, into a critique of socialism and democracy." According to Lukács, the evolution begun by Dostoevsky was systematized by Nietzsche and led in the final analysis to Fascism: This "rejection of progress and democracy . . . helped to prepare the way for Hitler's demagogy."[61]

It is only much later, in the last five years of his life, that Lukács returned to a more nuanced, more open approach to Romanticism, almost always in relation to youthful memories. For example, in his preface to the 1967 edition of *History and Class Consciousness,* he acknowledges that, "for all its romantic anti-capitalistic overtones, the ethical idealism [he] took from Hegel made a number of real contributions" to his thinking, and that, although they first had to be "modified fundamentally," these elements had been incorporated into his neo-Marxist outlook. Similarly, in a 1966 interview with Wolfgang Abendroth, he confessed: "I do not at all regret today that I took my first lessons in social science from Simmel and Max Weber and not from Kautsky. I don't know whether one cannot even say today that this was a fortunate circumstance for my own development."[62]

Once again, Lukács's attitude toward Dostoevsky is characteristic of his overall approach. In his 1969 preface to a 1933 Hungarian collection of essays titled "Mein Weg zu Marx" (My path to Marx), he refers to his own

"Romantic anticapitalist rebellion, directed against the very foundations of the established system," and he stresses his ties to a "revolutionary interpretation of Dostoevsky." He is even more explicit in the 1969 preface to another collection, *Littérature hongroise, culture hongroise:* "That is how I have integrated into my own universe the great Russian authors, first and foremost Dostoevsky and Tolstoy, as determining revolutionary factors. . . . It was at that point in my evolution that anarcho-syndicalism influenced me considerably. I was never able to adapt to the social-democratic ideology of the period, and especially not to Kautsky."[63]

From these diverse autobiographical observations it seems unmistakably clear that the young Lukács was nourished by various forms of Romantic thinking, from German sociology to Russian literature, and was led to oppose the social-democratic version of the dominant liberal-rationalist and evolutionist ideology and to subscribe to radical and revolutionary movements that challenged the bourgeois order: first anarcho-syndicalism, then Communism.

However, between 1928 and 1939, then from 1946 to the 1960s, through a curious ideological blindness, Lukács seemed to see in these multiple manifestations of what he called Romantic anticapitalism only their reactionary, irrational, proto-Fascist aspects. How can we account for these surprising changes of perspective? Do they correspond to some internal evolution in Lukács's philosophy, to precise historical circumstances (the rise of Fascism, the world war), or to shifts in the Komintern line? We have found no satisfactory explanation for these strange palinodes; in any event, this angle of approach presents the Hungarian philosopher in a new light, which does not correspond to the traditional outline of his political and intellectual evolution (pre-Marxist, Marxist, Stalinist, post-Stalinist).

This tortuous and contradictory itinerary, to which we do not yet have all the keys, reveals Lukács's thinking — comparable to that of Hans Castorp, the hero of his favorite novel, *The Magic Mountain* — as continually oscillating between poles represented by a "progressive Settembrini" and by a "revolutionary Naphta." Lukács never managed to surmount the antinomies of his own thought through a dialectical synthesis that would transcend the contradiction between Romanticism and rationalism.

It is clear, then, that some twentieth-century Marxists, like Marx himself, were not indifferent to the nostalgic charm of the Romantic worldview. Yet while this may have helped considerably to enlarge and deepen their critique of bourgeois civilization, it still raises some difficulties.

Although the "Romantic" Marxists did not share the restitutionist illusions that were so frequent in other forms of Romanticism, they had no concrete answers to the questions implied by their social utopia: How can a community be articulated with the wealth of individual aspirations that arise with modernity? Are we not irreversibly committed to complex societies that are incompatible with the "primitive" transparency that fascinated Marx? If the return to a premodern past is impossible in an urban civilization, in what sense might one restore the organic culture of precapitalist societies? If we acknowledge the insurpassable reality of certain of civilization's technological and scientific conquests, how can archaic social forms serve as our inspiration and model?

These questions apply to the entire Romantic current that is utopian and/or revolutionary in orientation, but they are particularly pertinent for Marx and his disciples to the extent that these thinkers situate themselves explicitly on the ground of the acquisitions of modern civilization. Such questions in themselves do not necessarily invalidate the Marxist historical perspective, but they cannot be answered simply by reference to the dialectic between thesis (the commune), antithesis (private property), and synthesis (the new commune).

4

*Visages of Romanticism in
the Nineteenth Century*

From the Romantic perspective, the French Revolution constituted a very ambiguous historical development. On the one hand, the Revolution was a manifestation of great idealism, and it offered the perspective of a millennium of human brotherhood, often conceived as a return to an ancient state of beatitude (Arcadia, Greco-Roman antiquity, and so on). On the other hand, it was also the way in which the bourgeois class consolidated its growing economic hegemony, both politically and juridically.[1] While it shared some dreams with Romanticism, the Revolution simultaneously contributed to the triumph of the very modernity the Romantics abhorred.

This ambivalence may help explain why Romantic attitudes toward the French Revolution ran the gamut from categorical rejection to acceptance of the most radical positions and actions. With some German Romantics, as well as William Wordsworth, Samuel Taylor Coleridge, and others, initial enthusiasm rapidly turned into resolute opposition. There were also considerable divergences among Romantic partisans of the French Revolution. The democratic Jacobin Romanticism we discussed in chapter 2 (of which Percy Bysshe Shelley, Stendhal, and Heinrich Heine are noteworthy examples) identified with the Revolution in general and with its most radical political wing in particular.

In another type of Romantic involvement, of which Coleridge can serve as our example, we find a paradoxical perspective: politically moderate, attracted by the Gironde more than by the Montagne, and very harsh in its condemnation of the excesses of the Revolution, this strain of Romanticism was nevertheless more radical than the Jacobin variety on social issues. It aspired to a utopian communism that sought to abolish private property (or at least to divide it up in a rigorously egalitarian manner), whereas the Jacobins sanctified it in their legislation and accepted its inequalities at least in part.

This second modality of revolutionary Romanticism is inherently contradictory. Its proponents were partisans of the Revolution but also among its severest critics, and they formulated their critiques from a viewpoint that was politically on the right but socially on the left. We find several literary expressions of this tendency in France, in the work of the Rousseauists Restif de la Bretonne and Jacques-Henri Bernardin de Saint-Pierre.[2] Here we explore a noteworthy English example, Samuel Taylor Coleridge, the great poet of the Lake School, and we examine the relation between his vision of the French Revolution and what might be called his "utopian moment."

Let us begin by looking briefly at the principal stages in Coleridge's political-philosophical evolution. One is struck at the outset by the fact that, despite his later wholesale adherence to conservatism, he never disavowed his own youth.[3] Speaking later about his early enthusiasm for the Revolution (in *The Friend*, 1809–10), Coleridge says: "My feelings . . . and imagination did not remain unkindled in this general conflagration; and I confess I should be more inclined to be ashamed than proud of myself."[4] Later still, in *Biographia Literaria* (1817), he says about his youth: "Oh never can I remember those days with either shame or regret. For I was most sincere, most disinterested. My opinions were, indeed, in many and most important points erroneous; but my heart was single."[5]

The word "disinterested" provides the key to understanding the continuity between the two phases in Coleridge's political stance. For throughout his life, self-interest—the very principle of the modern world—remained the chief enemy. In other words, continuity for Coleridge was rooted in his own Romantic vision of the world. While his political ideas and attitudes changed radically, Coleridge never ceased to be Romantic.

In the passage from *The Friend* cited above, Coleridge makes it clear that, while he participated in the general movement stimulated by the Revolution, his "little world" moved in its own "orbit" there—a personal orbit characterized by utopianism. Coleridge declares in *Biographia Literaria* that his principles at the time "were almost equidistant from all the three prominent parties, the Pittites, the Foxites, and the Democrats."[6] In short, Coleridge deemed that he had been as far removed from the liberal and radical reformers as from the conservatives.[7] The reformer John Thelwall was also of this opinion, for he noted in the margins of his copy of *Biographia:* "that Mr C. was indeed far from Democracy, because he was far beyond it, I well remember—for he was a down right zealous leveller. . . ."[8]

In fact, Coleridge's utopian enthusiasm had little more in common with reformism than with conservatism, for the poet was not prepared to settle for amelioration of the present state of affairs; he aimed at nothing less than the achievement of the Ideal. In a 1794 letter to his brother, Coleridge protests that he is certainly not a democrat. To make the distinction clear, he characterizes his own attitude as follows: he is aware that "the present is *not* the *highest* state of Society" and he believes he can "see the point of *possible* perfection at which the World may perhaps be destined to arrive," even while acknowledging that he does not know exactly how it will be achieved.[9] It would be hard to produce a better definition of the utopian spirit, in our view.

For a relatively brief period, between 1794 and 1796, Coleridge was an active advocate for this approach. In his writings and lectures, in his journalistic pursuits, and in his project for a utopian colony, he sought to invent paths toward the Ideal. His vision was deeply tinged with religiosity—a sort of apocalyptic Unitarianism that awaits the establishment of God's kingdom on earth and works to hasten its coming. In this same period, he engaged in a sustained and passionate reflection on the French Revolution: he was an ardent supporter, but he had major reservations. The Revolution was integrally linked, although in a problematic way, with his utopianism.

Coleridge's meeting with Robert Southey in June 1794 was the catalyst for the poet's public advocacy of the utopian cause. The new friends immediately formed a plan: they would leave for America with family and friends to create a pantisocracy, an ideal community in which all would be equal and would share equally in government. A short time after their meeting, the two men jointly wrote "The Fall of Robespierre," a dramatic poem about the Revolution. Significantly, this new phase in Coleridge's life began toward the end of the Terror, just before Thermidor. It arose out of a twofold awareness: the Revolution was destined to fulfill a historical mission, but its achievements were seriously compromised.

Coleridge's subsequent reflection on the Revolution posed the problem of means and ends. Whereas the goals of the Revolution were noble and pure, utopian, they were undermined by the means employed. France offered the painful and paradoxical perspective of "a nation wading to their Rights through Blood, and marking the track of Freedom through Destruction."[10] The means ought on the contrary to be in harmony with the ends: the inner transformation of individuals. Only general illumination can produce an authentic and lasting revolution that will bring about paradise on earth.

That is why Coleridge tried, between 1794 and 1796, to advance the cause of utopia in his own orbit—first, by planning the creation of an enclave consisting of elite individuals who had been transformed from within, and later, after the initial project was abandoned, by advocating "general illumination" through the newspaper he founded, *The Watchman*. In "Religious Musings," a long poem that he continued to revise throughout the period in question, the poet nevertheless represents the French Revolution as an integral part of the divine Providence that was preparing the millennium; despite the evil stirred up by the Revolution, ultimate Good would arise from it in the long run. When "the storm begins," the Virtues, "with fearful joy / Tremble far-off," while the "Giant Frenzy" wreaks havoc. But the poet recalls the Virtues, reassuring them that "the kingdoms of the world are your's."[11] He thus remained convinced, though with increasing doubts, that the French Revolution would ultimately be the vehicle for utopia, and he saw his own activities both as part of the historical movement inaugurated by that event and as its rectification, a necessary reorientation of the revolutionary impulse.

The utopian phase of Coleridge's life came to an end at the culmination of a twofold evolutionary process. On the one hand, all his personal efforts had ended in failure; on the other hand, the revolutionary regime itself had changed. The end of the Terror had raised the hope that the Revolution would take a more positive turn;[12] but in 1795–96 the installation of the Directoire and the offensive moves by Napoleon's army made the perspective according to which the Revolution was the agent of the millennium harder and harder to maintain.[13] Thus throughout 1797 Coleridge's attitudes were changing rapidly, and the transformation was complete by 1798.

In "Religious Musings" (begun in late 1794), the "tempest" that destroyed the Revolution had been an instrument of the divine project for humanity; in 1798, it was nothing but a meaningless natural disaster. In March of that year, Coleridge declared in a letter: "Of the French Revolution I can give my thoughts the most adequately in the words of Scripture — 'A great & strong wind rent the mountains & brake in pieces the rocks *before* the Lord; but the Lord was not in the wind; and after the wind an earthquake; but the Lord was not in the earthquake: and after the earthquake a Fire — & the Lord was not in the fire.'"[14] In his famous poem of retraction ("France: An Ode," 1798), the poet went further still: France and the Revolution become the enemy of the ideal — Freedom — in whose name they are perfidiously disguised. The poet asks Liberty to pardon him for having been led astray by appearances and wishes he had never had "one thought that ever blessed your cruel foes!"[15] The recent French invasion of Switzerland had pushed Coleridge to that extreme conclusion.

The change of attitude went further still. Not only was the Revolution no longer a vehicle for achieving utopia and not only did it become the enemy; the utopian ideal itself was also henceforth an undesirable and impossible goal for the disillusioned young man. Abandoning a future-oriented utopianism based on nostalgia for a lost paradise, Coleridge adopted a point of view uniquely oriented toward the past: in contemporary land ownership and aristocracy, anchored in the feudalism of yesteryear, he found the remnants of an already fully realized ideal that could supply an antidote from within to the ills of bourgeois modernity. As for utopia, it did not completely disappear, but it was internalized and aestheticized; it continued to lead a subterranean existence in the form of poetic imagination.

But let us look at the utopian period more closely. At the most general level, we can say that the "nowhere" of utopia constituted a revolt against what Coleridge in one of his lectures called the "Tyranny of the Present."[16] This expression cuts two ways: it means both that the present is characterized by the exercise of tyranny and that being imprisoned in the present is a form of tyranny. Furthermore, the tyrannical present is perceived not as an inherently political system (the monarchy, inherited from the past) but as a socioeconomic situation. In several texts Coleridge suggests clearly that this modern system of exploitation — based on avarice — is worse than the feudal exploitation that preceded it. In another lecture, he claims that there is nothing in the superiority of Lord to Gentleman, so mortifying in the barrier, so fatal to happiness in the consequences, as the more real distinction of master and servant, of rich man and of poor. Wherein am I made worse by my ennobled neighbor? . . . But those institutions of Society which should condemn me to the necessity of twelve hours daily toil, would make my *soul* a slave, and sink the *rational* being in the mere animal.[17]

The principle that engenders this modern form of slavery is selfishness, which isolates each human being from the others and from society as a whole. In "Religious Musings," the decline of modern man is depicted in the following terms: "A sordid solitary thing, / Mid countless brethren with a lonely heart / Through courts and cities the smooth savage roams / Feeling himself, his own low self the whole."[18]

Both in his personal relations and in his observations of the larger stage of history, Coleridge judges people and events according to the degree to which they have been corrupted by egotism and the mercantile spirit, which is in his eyes the primordial evil of the epoch. This is what is at stake in particular in his quarrel with Southey. For, although he had been impressed in the beginning by the latter's purity and disinterestedness, Coleridge soon notices that the dominant social values have not left his friend unscathed. The poet reproaches Southey for saying "I — I — I will do so and so — instead of saying as you were wont to do — It is all *our Duty* to do so — for such & such Reasons — ." For Coleridge, the modifications proposed by Southey to the pantisocracy project undermine it entirely by reducing it to "some 5 men *going partners* together"; and in the final letter, which makes the break definitive, Coleridge accuses Southey of being a "Selfish, money-loving Man."[19]

The French Revolution, in contrast, embodies a noble and universalist mentality (in fact Coleridge initially saw Southey as an austere republican, completely committed to the Revolution, only to discover later on that his friend did not live up to this image). It is precisely the universalism of the French Revolution that makes it a truly decisive historical event in Coleridge's eyes, unlike the American Revolution. In *The Watchman* of 18 April 1796, the poet observes acidly that

When America emancipated herself . . . , we beheld an instructive speculation on the probable *Loss and Gain* of unprotected and untributary Independence; and considered the Congress as a respectable body of Tradesmen . . . who well understood their own worldly concerns, and adventurously improved them. France presented a more interesting spectacle. Her great men with a profound philosophy investigated the interests common to all intellectual beings, and legislated for the WORLD. The lovers of Mankind were every where fired and exalted by their example. . . .[20]

Coleridge is similarly critical of Thomas Paine, the radical ideologue of the American Revolution, because he advocated an economic system based on business and private industry.[21]

Robespierre, on the contrary, brings the purity of the universalist perspective to its culmination. In the first act of "The Fall of Robespierre" (written by Coleridge; the remaining acts were Southey's), the man who was nicknamed "the Incorruptible" justifies the Terror by arguing that the only alternative would have been to appeal to avarice to combat the Revolution from the inside:

> Say, what shall counteract the selfish plottings
> Of wretches, cold of heart, nor awed by fears
> Of him, whose power directs th' eternal justice?
> Terror? or secret-sapping gold? The first
> Heavy, but transient as the ills that cause it;
> And to the virtuous patriot rendered light
> By the necessities that gave it birth:
> The other fouls the fount of the republic,
> Making it flow polluted to all ages:
> Inoculates the state with a slow venom,
> That once imbibed, must be continued ever.[22]

Robespierre and the French Revolution are thus opposed, in the young Coleridge's mind, to the zeitgeist of the nascent capitalist world. But Coleridge nevertheless discovers—in England—a certain type of bourgeois supporter of the Revolution whose motives are selfish: "They anticipate with exultation the abolition of privileged orders. . . . Whatever is above them they are most willing to drag down; but alas! they use not the pulley! Whatever tends to improve and elevate the ranks of our poorer brethren, they regard with suspicious jealousy."[23] It is probably because Coleridge observed the players in the French Revolution only from a distance (unlike Wordsworth, Coleridge never visited revolutionary France) that he tends to identify the French revolutionaries solely with purity and universalism, whereas he notices other traits in his fellow citizens—whom he knows firsthand.

In the same way, Coleridge does not seem to see the contradiction between his own social ideal and that of the Jacobins. For him, since the essence of evil in the present is the system of relations of property, the essence of the utopian dream is communism. Thus Coleridge wrote to Southey on the subject of the pantisocracy: "I have positively done nothing but dream of the System of no Property every step of the Way since I left you."[24] In 1802, long after his utopian phase had ended, when Coleridge tried to define the Jacobin credo, he specified that this credo includes the notion that each citizen "has an equal right to that quantity of property, which is necessary for the sustenance of his life and health," but that "all property beyond this [is] not . . . itself a right."[25] At this later date, he is thus aware that Jacobinism does not postulate the abolition or even the equal sharing of property. But for the Coleridge of 1794–1796, this characteristic of Jacobinism was not a problem.

For the young poet, only the abolition of private property could create the conditions that would allow his key value—human community, that is, unity and fraternity among human beings—to be realized concretely. But this was the ultimate goal of the French Revolution as well as that of his utopian project. In the poems Coleridge wrote on the theme of pantisocracy, the experimental colony that was supposed to be created along the banks of the Susquehanna was above all undivided; but in "Religious Musings" a visionary Coleridge also predicted that the Revolution would culminate in a "vast family of Love."[26]

The young Coleridge was nevertheless aware of some specific points of potential incompatibility that threatened this apparent identity of goals at the most general level. First of all, he continued to be troubled by the abstract character of the revolutionary ideology, since, for him, fraternity had to be rooted in concrete human ties and affections. As he wrote to Southey, "the ardour of private Attachments makes Philanthropy a necessary *habit* of the Soul. I love *my Friend*—such as *he* is, all mankind are or *might be!* The deduction is evident—. Philanthropy (and indeed every other Virtue) is a thing of *Concretion*—Some home-born Feeling is the *center* of the Ball that, rolling on thro' Life collects and assimilates every congenial Affection."[27]

Along with friendship, family was the other essential concrete bond on which the generalization of human brotherhood had to be based. "Domestic Happiness," Coleridge declared, "is the greatest of things sublunary."[28] In the future pantisocratic community, friendships (especially that of Coleridge and Southey) and family groups were to serve as points of departure for the development of "philanthropy."

But the Revolution turned out to be hostile to domestic happiness and friendship. A significant detail: in *The Fall of Robespierre,* which is simply a series of discussions among the principal political leaders, all men, Coleridge introduced one woman, Madame Tallien (she is called Adelaide in the play), who complains as follows:

> O this new freedom! at how dear a price
> We've bought the seeming good! The peaceful virtues
> And every blandishment of private life,
> The father's cares, the mother's fond endearment,
> All sacrificed to liberty's wild riot.

Then she begins a song in which she aspires to "domestic peace" in a country retreat, far from "the rebel's noisy hate."[29] Adelaide is associated with emotion and art (by virtue of her song), and she advocates living in the bosom of nature as the only way to be happy. While Coleridge does not overtly oppose this set of values to those of the Revolution as a general rule, he thematizes it only in relation to his own utopian project.

Thus pantisocracy was to be an agricultural society in which part of the day would be devoted to working in the fields, part to tranquil communion with nature. It was to be a place not only "where Virtue calm with careless step may stray" but also where "dancing to the moonlight roundelay, / The wizard Passions weave an holy spell."[30] And in the second version of his "Monody on the Death of Chatterton" (1794), Coleridge imagines that, had Chatterton lived, the poet-victim of society would have chosen pantisocracy over suicide.[31] The Romantic values of nature, feeling, imagination, and magic are thus integral components of Coleridge's personal utopian projections.

The poet's nostalgia for a precapitalist past is also linked to his utopian vision. Pantisocracy was supposed to entail a return to primitive rural communism, though at a higher level; Coleridge wrote in *The Friend* that it "was to have combined the innocence of the patriarchal age with the knowledge and genuine refinements of European culture."[32] Utopia, for Coleridge, recalls the Golden Age to which the "fable of the maddening rain" refers, a fable recounted in a June 1796 lecture that reflects the author's profound disillusionment at that particular moment. After the fall of the Golden Age, with the advent—symbolized by a rainstorm—of private property and trade, "the word *our* was no longer understood." The only man who remembered (since he had protected himself against the rain) and regretted the lost paradise was deemed mad; he was stoned, "till the affrighted Prophet was weary of being wise, and observing a quantity of the Rain yet remaining in a neighboring Ditch he leapt into it and returned so mad and so wicked that the whole Multitude voluntarily elected him for their Priest and Governor."[33]

Later in the same lecture, Coleridge asserts that Jesus forbade "all property" and taught "that accumulation was incompatible with . . . Salvation." His first disciples, along with the "immediate Converts," understood and applied this message: "In Acts II.44.45. we read 'And all that believed were together, & had all things in common—and sold their possessions & goods and parted them to all men, as every man had need.' But this part of the Christian Doctrine, which is indeed almost the whole of it, soon was corrupted."[34] Thus for Coleridge the lost paradise also existed in the early Christian communities.

The same nostalgia can also be found in connection with the Revolution, as in the passage from "Religious Musings" in which the poet has a vision of "the odorous groves of Earth reparadis'd."[35] On the whole, however, all the characteristic Romantic themes are much more discreet in Coleridge's discourse on the Revolution than in texts in which he evokes a personal utopian realm. This suggests that, in spite of all that has transpired, the relation between the Revolution and Coleridge's utopian aspirations continued to be problematic, probably in an unconscious or semiconscious way.

Coleridge maintained his faith in the Revolution against all odds until the evolving situation had reached a point where he could take no more. In a poem published in *The Watchman* in March 1796, he reaffirmed the historical optimism of *Religious Musings* but in terms that indicate that he had undergone severe testing. In the article in which the poem appears, Coleridge acknowledged: "In my calmer moments I have the firmest Faith that all things work together for Good. But alas! it seems a long and dark process."[36]

The turning point came shortly thereafter. Deeply troubled by reading the correspondence between representatives of the British government and the Directoire, published in English newspapers in mid-April, Coleridge drafted a "Remonstrance to the French Legislators" that appeared in *The Watchman* a few weeks later. This correspondence in fact revealed to Coleridge that the French had rejected the peace overtures made by the English and that they had refused to give up their principal territorial conquests. He inferred from this that the French were no longer motivated by the interests of humanity as a whole, but rather by "ambition," that is, by the narrow self-interest and self-glorification of a single nation.[37]

This loss of illusions with regard to France is analogous to what Coleridge had already experienced the previous year on a personal level in his relation with his friend Southey. If France had given up its universalist vocation to become "egotistical," in a way, it could no longer be the agent of utopia. The "long and dark process" no longer promised to lead to the dawn of the millennium. Although it did not explicitly go that far, the article in *The Watchman* already contained the seeds of the message of "France: An Ode," to be written two years later.

The "Remonstrance" appeared just a few weeks before *The Watchman* ceased publication. With the journal's demise, Coleridge underwent a period of doubt and moved on gradually to a whole set of new positions. After 1798, the question of the French Revolution was resolved: it became an abomination. And in his quest for an agency that could fill the void left behind, Coleridge turned toward the same social force that the Revolution had conquered: the aristocracy. But for an intense and fecund, if brief, period, Coleridge's enthusiasm for the French Revolution and his Romantic utopianism had fused in an explosive thrust.

ROMANTICISM AND THE INDUSTRIAL REVOLUTION: THE SOCIAL CRITIQUE OF JOHN RUSKIN

An art critic, a professor of drawing and art history, an essayist and lecturer who dealt with the most diverse subjects, and one of the great sages of the Victorian era, John Ruskin is a key figure in British Romanticism. At a peculiarly significant moment in the development of modernity, he was an exemplary witness and a mediator not only among several generations but also between cultural criticism and economic criticism, between aesthetics and social protest. His literary career extends from the mid-nineteenth century to the 1880s, at almost equal distance from the inception of Romanticism to our own day, and it corresponds *grosso modo* to the period in which the capitalist system triumphed in the country where it developed earliest and most powerfully from the start.

This period, coming after the Chartist upheavals and before the late-nineteenth-century socialist movements, constitutes a moment of (relative) stabilization, in the course of which the capitalist industrial system reigned more or less unchallenged and could seem incontestable, but during which its harmful effects on the overall human environment were nevertheless being felt in an increasingly general way: having been concentrated in cities at first, industrial capitalism was now radically transforming the countryside, re-creating the English language in its own image.

In this context in which the tendencies of modernity were maturing, Ruskin's thought became a crossroads of influences in the English tradition of Romantic critiques of modern civilization. On the one hand, Ruskin assimilated the earlier Romantic tradition; on the other hand, his work and his life played a crucial role for contemporary artists, writers, and Romantic movements, with which he was in direct relations; his influence eventually extended into the twentieth century.

Ruskin drew certain elements of his feeling for nature from the early nineteenth-century Romantics, especially Wordsworth; this is the poet Ruskin cites most often in his great work of art criticism, *Modern Painters*.[38] His social philosophy took its inspiration from the same source (we know, for example, that in his youth he had read Southey's *Colloquies on the Progress and Prospects of Society*).[39] But of this whole generation of Romantics, Ruskin's deepest admiration was probably reserved for Walter Scott and his historical novels; Scott's great merit, in Ruskin's eyes, was that through his art he brought privileged moments of the past to life — in the strong sense of making their powerful vitality virtually tangible.

Among the works that came out somewhat later, Ruskin also greatly admired Charles Dickens's novels for their satiric tableau of society in his day, and in particular *Hard Times*, which Ruskin found "in several respects the greatest he has written."[40] But the essential influence on Ruskin comes from Thomas Carlyle, the only one of his predecessors with whom he identified completely and whom he venerated unreservedly. For Ruskin judged harshly — especially in later years — what he saw in Dickens finally as something like a soft spot for modern life. In a letter written at the time of Dickens's death, he even claimed that "Dickens was a pure modernist — a leader of the steam-whistle party *par excellence*. . . . His hero is essentially the ironmaster; in spite of *Hard Times,* he has advanced by his influence every principle that makes them harder — the love of excitement, in all classes, and the fury of business competition, and the distrust both of nobility and clergy."[41]

This judgment, formulated in 1870, may appear excessive, but it highlights with precision the extreme intransigence of Ruskin's outlook. Similarly, ten years later, Ruskin judged that even his beloved Scott had been partly corrupted by "modern conditions of commercial excitement, then first, but rapidly, developing themselves. There are parts even in his best novels coloured to meet tastes which he despised."[42] Only Carlyle escaped the indictment, for only Carlyle manifested an opposition to modernity that was as violent, as pure, and as absolute as Ruskin's own.

Carlyle's *Past and Present* (1843) — the quintessence of the Romantic vision that contrasts a present degraded by machinism and mammonism (the worship of the god Money) to a monastic community of the medieval past — was read by Ruskin when it was first published (this was at roughly the same time as Southey's *Colloquies,* but it had a vastly greater impact on Ruskin). Almost thirty years later, Ruskin advised his listeners and readers to read the third book of *Past and Present,* the one that spells out Carlyle's critique of modern life, and learn it "by heart."[43] More generally, he declared at other points that Carlyle was "the greatest of our English thinkers" and that in some of his key books (including *Past and Present*) one finds "all that has been said."[44] It is thus impossible to overestimate Carlyle's importance for Ruskin.

Ruskin's own influence was enormous. It began with the contemporary artistic and literary movement of the Pre-Raphaelites, a movement characterized on the one hand by a focus on nature and on the other hand by a return to the styles, themes, atmospheres, and religious sentiments of the Middle Ages and the early Renaissance. Ruskin's writings were instrumental in the development of the program of the "P.R.B." (the Pre-Raphaelite Brotherhood), as the founders — William Holman Hunt, John Everett Millais, and Dante Gabriel Rossetti — called their movement; later, Ruskin's active support helped the group gain strength. But the relation between Ruskin and the Pre-Raphaelites was not one-sided: the latter in turn undoubtedly had considerable influence on Ruskin.[45] At the other end of the spectrum, it was partly through his influence on William Morris that Ruskin continued to count in the twentieth century, as we shall see toward the end of this chapter.

In studying Ruskin, we must begin by noting the profound unity of his work (which extends for nearly half a century), despite some appearances to the contrary. Ruskin himself is at the origin of the idea, a rather widely held one until recently, that there was a radical break between the work of the art critic of the 1840s and 1850s and the prophetic work of the social critic of the 1860s, 1870s, and 1880s. In a lecture given in 1877, Ruskin described the year 1860, with the publication of the essays from *Unto This Last* (reprinted in book form in 1862), as the great turning point in his life.[46] Charles Eliot Norton, the American academic and a personal friend of Ruskin's, situates the turning point three years later, when Ruskin published his first book to focus on the social and economic aspects of the artistic phenomenon, *The Political Economy of Art* (1857).[47]

Other abrupt and profound changes seem to be manifested in the realm of Ruskin's religious beliefs: by his own account, he underwent a sort of unconversion in 1858, followed some fifteen years later by a second experience in which he regained his faith. Here, too, then, there seem to be two distinct Ruskins: the devout and fervent Ruskin of the beginning and end of his career, and the atheist he claimed to be in a conversation with William Holman Hunt in the 1860s.[48] Moreover, above and beyond these breaks, a certain general lack of coherence in Ruskin has often been noted: we are confronted, we are told, with a thinker who was unsystematic, vacillating, and contradictory in many of his specific judgments, and, at least according to one commentator, "one can find almost any view in his work."[49]

Now, if one can hardly deny that Ruskin evolved in several areas or that there were variations and contradictions in his positions, the fact remains that in a more fundamental sense the man and the work were remarkably homogeneous. First of all, as far as his religious perspective is concerned, despite a quite genuine crisis of belief in the late 1850s, Ruskin continued to formulate his thought within the framework of his earlier religiosity, constantly citing and referring to biblical texts, speaking as if his faith were intact, to such an extent that if we did not know he had lost his faith, a reading of many of his texts from the atheist period would convince us of the contrary. (We should add that no one has clearly demonstrated that Ruskin ever entirely lost his faith.)

Thus during his entire literary career Ruskin expressed himself in a consistent Judeo-Christian idiom. But both the periods during which he believed in God and the period in which he no longer believed (or in which he at least underwent a spiritual crisis) manifest the same religion at a deeper level, and not only as the language in which he expressed his ideas. This — one might call it the religion of humanity-in-nature — was Ruskin's true religion, transcending belief and nonbelief in church dogma. This is where the sacred is really situated for Ruskin, a sacred dimension that was respected in the past, is soiled in the present, but is potentially recoverable in the future.

As for the move from art criticism to social criticism, it is less a question of the complete substitution of one problematics for another than of a shift in emphasis or perspective within a single problematics. The basic problem that Ruskin raised consistently involved the realization of true human value (humanity-in-nature), and the conditions of possibility of that realization. And this true human value was simultaneously and indissolubly aesthetic and moral-and-social. For the conviction of human unity also subtends Ruskin's thinking: human faculties, activities, and the conditions of human life are part of a whole and are intimately and necessarily interrelated.[50]

From the outset, Ruskin was aware, then, that aesthetics and morality are integral parts of the social whole, and he expressed his rejection of the state of contemporary society very early in the name of his aesthetic-moral values. We find a rebellion of this sort in letters he wrote for the *Times* in 1852, which he never sent to the newspaper because his father was shocked by their radical content.[51] Another manifestation can be found the following year, in the central chapter of the second volume of *Stones of Venice* (its "keystone," as it were), "The Nature of Gothic." But this critique of contemporary society actually goes back much further, to the period when Ruskin was a student at Oxford. In 1841, in fact, he composed a fantastic tale — "The King of the Golden River" — that already contained the mature Ruskin's entire social criticism and worldview. Northrop Frye was not mistaken when he claimed that *Unto This Last* and Ruskin's other socioeconomic writings constituted "essentially a commentary" on that work of imagination.[52]

Given the unity of Ruskin's work (which is not marred by the author's personal oscillations and inconsistencies, since these never bear on the essential elements), we consider it more appropriate to deal with his social thought thematically (that is, as a set of structured themes), taking up any work that contributes a relevant element to each theme, rather than reviewing the major works in chronological order. In the same spirit, while we may privilege the second part of Ruskin's career, in which he focuses more directly and exhaustively on the social question, we shall not neglect the considerable — indeed, crucial — contribution of the first period to the question that fundamentally traverses all his work.

It is fortunate that we are under no obligation to situate Ruskin within our typology of the politics of Romanticism (chap. 2) and to identify him with a particular vein of sociopolitical thought. We would be hard put to do so, for from this standpoint he is difficult if not impossible to classify; indeed, he illustrates perfectly the characteristic feature of Romanticism demonstrated in the typology taken as a whole, namely, that Romanticism is a political hermaphrodite, manifesting itself at the two extremes and all across the gamut of ideas in this realm. We find the same ambivalence and multiplicity in Ruskin himself.

This may explain the great gulfs between the evaluations offered by Ruskin's various exegetes and commentators. Ruskin has been seen by turns as a protofascist, a partisan of the providential state, a reformer, and so on, and he has been situated for the most part on either the right or the left. While a recent analysis, without denying Ruskin's other facets, finds him most authentically Tory, the playwright George Bernard Shaw claimed on the contrary that Ruskin's Toryism masked his true visage, that of a Communist, and that his real heirs were Lenin and the Bolsheviks![53]

Ruskin himself willingly contributed to the confusion, taking obvious pleasure in muddying the waters in his political self-portraits. Coming from a conservative Tory family, he sought for a long time to stress that his views were in line with his father's. In *Unto This Last* (1860) Ruskin was still trying to establish his distance from socialism (he had been accused of joining its ranks); however, he later identified both with a form of socialism or communism and with a particular strain of Toryism.

In *Fors Clavigera*, a series of open letters to the workers of England, Ruskin presents himself (in a letter dated July 1871) as a "Communist," "reddest also of the red," whereas only two months later he could repeat insistently that he was not and that he never had been anything but a Tory. But in each case he took pains to stress that he was "of the old school": he rejected the modern communism of the French communards and aligned himself with the old communist school, that of Horace (!) and Thomas More's *Utopia;* in the same way, he claimed not to resemble the contemporary Tories but rather to follow the model of Walter Scott and Homer.[54] Because he supported a version of socialism or communism that did not include the abolition or equal distribution of private property and a Toryism that did not seek to protect the privileges of the property-owning classes and did not identify with any current monarchy, Ruskin's conceptions do not correspond to the conventional meanings of the terms.

Moreover, he felt more at ease when he was countering common attitudes. In an 1851 letter to his father, he reported his wife's opinion that he was "a great conservative in France, because there everybody is radical, and a great radical in Austria, because there everybody is conservative," and he added: "I suppose that one reason why I am so fond of fish . . . is that they always swim with their heads against the stream. I find it for me the healthiest position."[55] Ruskin thus categorically refused to play the game of parliamentary politics. According to his biographer, W. G. Collingwood, he is supposed to have said: "I care no more either for Mr. D'Israeli or Mr. Gladstone than for two old bagpipes with the drones going by steam."[56] He never voted, did not seek the extension of suffrage to workers since it would bring them nothing, and thought that all reforms of the system were useless.

The best way to define Ruskin's politics is to say that he was a radical in the etymological sense of the term, that is, someone who attempts to get to the root of a problem and tries to solve it. His attitude during a discussion with a government minister about poverty is characteristic: seeing the minister dismiss one of his propositions as unpractical, Ruskin said nothing, "feeling that it was vain to assure any man actively concerned in modern parliamentary business, that no measures were 'practical' except those which touched the source of the evil opposed."[57] Let us look beyond political labels, then, to see precisely what constituted the root in Ruskin's eyes.

A particular view of human history pervades and grounds all Ruskin's work: that of a fall or decline starting from an initial stage of plenitude. Drawing on both the Greek myth summarized in Plato's *Critias* and the biblical story of the Fall (he is conscious of their structural identity, since both relate "the same first perfection and final degeneracy of man"),[58] Ruskin reads in the actual history of mankind the embodiment of that tragic fate.

The fall took place in stages, the beginning of the end being the waning of the Middle Ages: the evil that was eating away at the old world was the seed of what was to come, for "it was the *selling* of absolution that ended the Mediæval faith."[59] The Renaissance saw the harmful development of individual luxury and vanity (see the passages on the Renaissance in the third volume of *Modern Painters*), but it is only in the modern world that the end is really achieved: in *Unto This Last*, Ruskin denounces the era of "political economy founded on self-interest," the political accomplishment of the fall of the angels.[60]

The modern era, radically fallen, nevertheless offers the possibility of redemption, and it is this possibility that provides the scaffolding for the tale "The King of the Golden River" (1841). As a result of the sins of selfishness and avarice, three brothers find themselves expelled from a valley that resembles the Garden of Eden but is reduced, through the fault of two of the three, to a desert. The purity of the third brother nevertheless ends up bringing the place back into flower: "And thus the Treasure Valley became a garden again, and the inheritance, which had been lost by cruelty, was regained by love."[61]

The earthly paradise is represented in particular by a place in which humanity lives in harmony with nature, and nature probably offers a primordial visage of what has been lost. In his autobiography, *Praeterita* (1885–1889), Ruskin evokes his first glimpse of the Alps as "a blessed entry into life," and he declares that the array of mountaintops that arose before his eyes was like "the seen walls of lost Eden."[62] But Ruskin's nostalgia is also focused on certain historical periods: his admiration falls more or less equally on the Greece of history (especially its earliest years: the Homeric epoch and Sparta at its apogee) and myth (the Athens of King Theseus and the fabled island of Atlantis) and on the Gothic Middle Ages (including what would now be called the early Renaissance).[63]

Ruskin also occasionally evokes successful communities from less remote periods, late survivals of a similar state of mind, most notably clans of brigands in the Scottish highlands and farm families from the Scottish borderlands (his inspiration clearly comes from the novels of Walter Scott). He also refers to the spirit of childhood in us that retains traces of plenitude (a Wordsworthian echo): in a striking phrase, Ruskin invites the listeners to one of his lectures to let themselves "slide back into the cradle, if going on is into the grave."[64]

The historical moments on which his nostalgia is focused share several key features. First of all, a communion of humanity with nature, perceived as a universe animated by supernatural or divine presences. In the third volume of *Modern Painters* (1856), for example, we find an extended discussion of the Homeric concept of nature inhabited by the gods; elsewhere, we read that in the era of the "Gothic school of Pisa" the sky was "sacred," a place where "every cloud that passed was literally the chariot of an angel."[65] The world of these lost societies is first and foremost an enchanted world.

Next, the enchantment of the world stimulates the imaginative faculties, and these are in turn the source of great art, for, in Ruskin's eyes, only a noble conception of the universe can produce a noble art. Among the features that Ruskin attributes to the pinnacle that Gothic art (based on unalienated craftsmanship) represents for him, we find sympathy with nature and the burgeoning of the imagination first and foremost.[66] In addition to the aesthetic-religious type of well-being that humans experience in the bosom of nature, the past of nostalgia also offers the image of a community united by bonds of solidarity and love; thus Ruskin admires the "perfect affection" of the members of the Scottish clans.[67]

Far from being egalitarian and peaceful, however, these communities are bound together by the absolute authority of their leaders and by war. Fraternal bonds among the clan's members are accompanied by obedience to the leader even to the death. And Ruskin sees no contradiction between the warlike spirit and the other ideals: as proof, he cites Sparta, where men sacrificed to the Muses and to the god of Love before setting out to do battle.[68] Authoritarian commandment and war are thus not envisaged as evils that partially darken an otherwise idyllic tableau; on the contrary, they generate value: submission to a just authority was a fundamental principle for Ruskin, and he had a highly idealized notion of the nature of ancient and medieval warfare.

While Ruskin may sometimes seem to take these privileged moments from the past as embodiments of perfection, he nevertheless finds weaknesses and even major defects in them: a certain perversion of religious beliefs in the Middle Ages as well as in ancient Greece, but also the harshness of the oppression of the poor by the upper classes. Such considerations lead him to state on several occasions that he does not want to limit himself to restoring the past.[69]

In a particularly striking way, Ruskin's writings repeatedly compare those past moments — which, while they were not without flaws, nevertheless allowed human beings an essential fulfillment, for the most part — with modern society, which leaves them almost entirely unfulfilled. In dramatizing the contrast, Ruskin follows the example of his great master, the author of *Past and Present*. But to do this he employs several discursive techniques that owe nothing to Carlyle. One literary device in particular recurs frequently: it involves the account of a walk the author has just taken in the countryside or in what was once countryside but has now become a suburb or even part of the city. The narrator imagines, or remembers, the happiness and rustic beauty that once reigned there (sometimes the degradation has been rapid and of recent date), and he describes the aspect of the place as he sees it at present: the sky darkened by smoke from factory chimneys, springs and rivers dreadfully polluted, fields stripped of their plantings and covered with buildings and industrial or commercial detritus.[70]

Another device, more generalized and more fundamental, consists in offering the listener or reader an existential choice between two modes of life: that of the past (which might need to be improved, corrected) and that of the present. After sketching these life styles or social and cultural environments (sometimes, but not always, through the staging of a walk), Ruskin turns to his readers to ask them to reflect and act accordingly. The title of one of his works, *The Two Paths,* is emblematic of an approach that is omnipresent in his writings.[71]

Ruskin is convinced that the choice is clear-cut: it amounts to deciding between life and death. He reverses the usual terms, applying to modernity the label that the Enlightenment and the era of progress had used to express their scorn for the Middle Ages: "the Dark Ages."[72] The obscurity of modernity is that of death and death's master, Satan. Hell is not in some other world; it is here among us. But Ruskin cannot be certain that his interlocutor, shaped by modernity, will be convinced in spite of everything by the self-evidence of this choice. As George Bernard Shaw pointed out, what shows Ruskin that modern human beings are not only in hell but in the "uttermost depths of damnation" is that they do not know that they are there and delight in the wretchedness of their lives.[73]

The critical analysis to which Ruskin subjects this modern condition (his point of view on what was conventionally called the "state of England question," a question that Ruskin applied to Europe and America as well) is extremely rich: very insightful and multifaceted, presented with passion and with extraordinarily powerful stylistic effects, it represents perhaps the most important and most lasting contribution of his work, although until recently it has not received much attention from traditional literary history.

Ruskin usually does not display a systematic spirit, and in most of his works we find a variety of themes mixed together in no particular order. But if we look at the entire array of statements on modernity, we can identify three major axes: a critique of the effects of modern science, a critique of the domination of modern life by money, and a critique of industrialism. The degradations characteristic of modernity are sometimes closely associated with one of these aspects in particular, but most often several elements are in play at the same time.

Ruskin's attitude toward science is much more ambivalent than the attitude he manifests toward the other two aspects of modern life. For him it is unquestionably a tragedy that advances in scientific knowledge are progressively destroying religious faith, the sense of the sacred, the sense that nature is animated by a supernatural presence. He sees this loss of the supernatural as inevitable, and all (Romantic) efforts to reanimate the world as futile. Modern art often commits the famous "pathetic fallacy," the attribution of sentiments to objects in the natural world — a concept developed by Ruskin in the third volume of *Modern Painters* (1856). This device is only an ineffective palliative against the modern vision of the world as a set of dead things, "governed by physical laws, and so forth." And art is thereby weakened, as Ruskin tries to demonstrate by comparing verses from Homer and John Keats.[74]

Moreover, Ruskin sometimes claims that the scientific approach to nature does not interest him at all. Astronomers, he asserts, can tell us everything about the sun, moon, and stars; nevertheless, "I do not care, for my part, two copper spangles how they move. . . ."[75] Ruskin also complains about the "dreadful Hammers" of the geologists who cut gashes into the Christian faith.[76] But this same geology actually fascinated him, as did botany, and he devoted several books to elements of both these sciences. It seems clear that Ruskin does not condemn science as such, nor does he challenge its discoveries, but that he does deeply regret the decline of religious sentiments, the disenchantment of the world, and the anxiety and lack of inner peace that inevitably accompany these changes. This attitude may account for the absence of a truly penetrating critique of the scientific spirit in Ruskin's work. The same does not apply to the other two aspects of modernity, and we may say that for Ruskin mammonism and industrialism truly represent the two heads of the monster.

Mammonism — that is, the fetishizing of money and exchange value, which Ruskin more traditionally calls "avarice" at times — has become the true religion of the English. He identifies their principal goddess as "Britannia of the Market," whereas in ancient Greece Athena Agoraia was only a subordinate power.[77] The English have reached the point of thinking and acting as if "commodities [were] made to be sold, and not to be consumed."[78] Consumption is the phase in the economic process in which the product's use value and quality assert themselves, and for Ruskin one of the worst consequences of mammonism is indifference to the qualities of things and to the qualitative values to which mammonism gives rise.

Recounting an allegorical dream, Ruskin offers an emblem of this deplorable situation. Among the children invited to a spring party in a lovely and luxurious house (the world), a certain number decided to take away the copper nails decorating the armchairs, claiming that "nothing was of any real consequence, that afternoon, except to get plenty of brass-headed nails; and that the books, and the cakes, and the microscopes [that had been made available to them], were of no use at all in themselves, but only, if they could be exchanged for nail-heads."[79]

A second series of consequences that follow from the mammon mentality is the narrow selfishness of *homo oeconomicus,* the relations of hostility and greed instituted by competition among those people thus motivated, hence a total lack of human community and cooperation. Ruskin often denounces aspects of modernity in particularly bitter tones, as when he recalls the Greek etymology of the word "idiot" — "entirely occupied with his own concerns" — and even more so when he speaks of capitalists as a "yelping, carnivorous crowd, mad for money and lust, tearing each other to pieces."[80]

Mammonism also results in the creation of unjust wealth. For Ruskin there is such a thing as just individual wealth: it is wealth based on what individuals produce by their own work. But the desire to accumulate money leads people to profit from the work of others, which is equivalent to stealing. In the modern era, the rich steal from the others — an act that is both crueler and more cowardly than the thievery practiced in earlier times by barons or highway robbers, for thieves of that sort usually stole from the rich.[81]

Ruskin notes that "whenever material gain follows exchange, for every *plus* there is a precisely equal *minus*":[82] trade for profit, like speculation and usury, are thus stealing. The way some people steal from others produces a monopoly, held by a minority, on all the good things in life. But, more important, wealth unjustly gained exercises a corrupting power throughout the social fabric. Wealth in monetary terms is equivalent to power over people, and this power, badly exercised, makes its harmful effects felt in many ways, in a concatenation of causes that usually go unnoticed. To designate this sort of wealth, Ruskin, who often invents highly suggestive neologisms, transforms the word "wealth" — signifying riches but etymologically related to the idea of well-being, *weal* — into "illth."[83]

"Political economy" is the ideology of mammonism, with its various disastrous ramifications, and Ruskin attacks it energetically (especially in *Unto This Last,* where he singles out his contemporary John Stuart Mill): according to Ruskin, modern political economy considers the human being "merely as a covetous machine" and "founds an ossifiant theory of progress on this negation of a soul."[84] For him it is a pseudoscience based on bad postulates, and in his eyes Mill partially redeems himself precisely to the extent that he contradicts his own principles from time to time, allowing glimpses of the moral considerations "with which Mr Mill says political economy has nothing to do."[85]

Ruskin has been much criticized for his lack of knowledge of the theories that he claims to be challenging, and he readily recognizes his relative ignorance in this respect (indeed, he virtually boasts of it). But this does not in any way invalidate the challenge he poses to political economy, for his argument is not drawn from within the conceptual universe (a quantitative, morally neutral universe) of political economy; he displaces the debate onto a radically other terrain, that of the choice of values, qualitative life choices.

Ruskin's critique of industrialism encompasses two major themes above all: the transformation and degradation, in the era of mechanization and large-scale industry, of work on the one hand, of the environment on the other. The first theme is masterfully developed in a famous section in the second volume of *Stones of Venice* (1853), "The Nature of Gothic," in which

Ruskin contrasts craftsmanship, which involves workers' natural creativity (since they mobilize a multiplicity of human faculties), with modern industrial labor.

According to Ruskin, the origin of the revolutionary wave that has just rolled over the European nations has to be situated in spiritual rather than physical poverty: "It is not that men are ill fed, but that they have no pleasure in the work by which they make their bread." More than that, they are aware that their work reduces them to being "less than men." As he often does, Ruskin redefines the terms of the customary discourse, suggesting that it is wrong to speak of the "division of labor": "It is not, truly speaking, the labour that is divided; but the men: — Divided into mere segments of men — broken into small fragments and crumbs of life. . . . we manufacture everything [in industrial cities] except men."[86]

Industrial workers are thus shrunken and stripped of their full humanity, but those who have other occupations, or who do not work, are also diminished. Tradesmen and capitalists, by their very functions, distort their own human nature. The worst cases, however, from Ruskin's perspective, are people of leisure (aristocrats or other do-nothings) and the unemployed, who are entirely cut off from the vital source of humanness constituted by work.

Now if modern occupations or activities tend to alienate human beings from what they can be, from what they are in their essence, the global environment reinforces that tendency, first and foremost in large cities, which Ruskin saw as deserts of ugliness, filth, and disease. Over the course of his career, his conviction of the corrupting power of cities grew stronger. In a well-known passage from the fifth volume of *Modern Painters,* "The Two Boyhoods" (1860), Ruskin compared the physical spaces in which Giorgione (Venice, late fifteenth century) and William Turner (London, early nineteenth century) spent their childhoods. Turner grew up in a decidedly less propitious atmosphere, in the slums on the banks of the Thames, surrounded by soot, smoke, garbage, noise, and brutality; and yet he succeeded in becoming, in Ruskin's view, one of the greatest painters of all time.

Turner is obviously an exception, and Ruskin notes that he knew "nature" later on in Yorkshire, but the fact remains that for the author of *Modern Painting* the city does not seem to be a place that corrupts inexorably and absolutely. Twenty years later, in "Fiction, Fair and Foul," Ruskin offers the following diagnosis: the illness of the city is incurable — a city life is so cut off from natural rhythms, so monotonous, that facile or dishonest excitement is required—and the modern literature that takes the city as its object suffers from the same malady.

But what upsets and annoys Ruskin even more than the city itself is the tentacular extension of industry and its multiple effects, direct and indirect, on the suburbs (transforming into city what was country before), the countryside (railroads, mines, and so on), and even the heart of wild nature. He is profoundly shocked to see the Alps invaded by vacationers who treat those mountains—sacred sites to his eyes—as sporting grounds, and pollute them with their leavings. He rails at his contemporaries: "You have despised Nature. . . . The French revolutionists made stables of the cathedrals of France; you have made race-courses of the cathedrals of the earth. Your *one* conception of pleasure is to drive in railroad carriages round their aisles and eat off their altars."[87]

Ruskin sometimes goes beyond mere description of the devastation that he sees around him: he imagines what England will become if current development continues. The north, he says, is already an immense coal mine, and if no one stops the process, soon the south will be only a construction site of bricks and the mountainous regions will be vast quarries. This vision of an industrialized future can become a nightmare or a hallucination, as when Ruskin sees the emergence of a world lit entirely by gas lights because the light of the sun is hidden by factory smoke, or a world made of metal because the earth has become "the vast furnace of a ghastly engine."[88] His great fear, then, is that nature will be totally destroyed by the (inhuman) actions of modern humanity.

Under the conditions defined chiefly by the reign of money and industrialism, but also by the scientific outlook on the world, modernity becomes a true desert, imperiling human life and nature. And the harmful influence of the principles that govern modernity pervades all aspects of existence. Ruskin lays particular stress on their effects in three areas he sees as crucial: war, religion, and culture.

While his conception of the wars of earlier times can appear astonishing in its naïveté (people often fought for "just causes," and in any event the combatants were moved by great collective enthusiasms and the outcome of the ordeal demonstrated which of the two camps was the "best"), Ruskin is lucid and free from illusions where modern wars are concerned. Their source must be sought, he claims, in the greed of thieves—that of the

European nations, and more particularly of their capitalists, who finance wars out of a desire to appropriate their neighbors' goods and lands for themselves. The rich who start wars do not do the fighting themselves; they send poor men to die in their stead. War in the modern era is crueler than ever before, because it is becoming "chemical and mechanical," deploying scientific and technological means, the fruits of "progress." Victory is reserved for the side that possesses the greatest quantity of these industrial means of destruction.[89]

As for religion, as we have already suggested, it no longer exists in the fullest sense, according to Ruskin. What remains is an immense hypocrisy, for the social and economic life of a country like England constitutes "systematic disobedience to the first principles of its professed religion."[90] Religion is completely eliminated from everyday life; it is restricted to churches and Sunday services, where it functions mostly as a soporific destined to tranquilize the working masses (here, as on other points, Ruskin's critique converges with Marx's).[91]

But Ruskin is perhaps most perspicacious and most subtle when he analyzes the degradation to which cultural life has been subjected. For the incursions of society or civilization into the realm that ought to be opposed to them, culture (art and thought), cause him great pain, and he examines the many forms these incursions take. First, he denounces the transformation of artistic and intellectual productions into merchandise; this is one of the principal themes of *The Political Economy of Art* (1857), a work to which he gave an ironic title in a later edition: *A Joy for Ever (and Its Price in the Market)*.[92] At the same time, he sees the public becoming less and less capable of understanding these products and appreciating their real value, since modernity has led to a degradation of sensibility, the intellect, and the aesthetic sense. One of the lectures included in *Sesame and Lilies* (1865) focuses especially on reading, and Ruskin claims that "the insanity of avarice" is depriving the contemporary British public of its ability to read in the real sense of the term.[93]

From the internal standpoint, modern works of art and thought are themselves often vitiated or diminished. For one thing, they can become ugly by becoming mere reflections of the ambient physical and moral ugliness; for another, if they take a stance against the modern ethos, cultural works are more and more cut off from life as a whole, and they often serve chiefly as a safety valve that allows their audience to slake its thirst for beauty, sensations, and emotions that are lost everywhere else but are found here in a weakened form. Ruskin sometimes seems to be suggesting that Romantic and neo-Romantic culture is doomed to failure, incapable of reproducing the intensity of ancient art (Keats or Wordsworth rather than Homer), at once betrayed and marginalized by civilization (the Gothic Renaissance in architecture). As he grew older, he increasingly saw modern civilization as a total system—we would call it "totalitarian" today—that invades and colonizes every nook and cranny of human and natural existence, making any resistance futile.

From the late 1870s on, Ruskin was so thoroughly despairing that he lapsed into periods of madness; he collapsed completely a decade later. (He wrote nothing between 1880 and his death in 1900.) But he did not yield without waging an epic battle against the dragon. For in the face of triumphant modernity, Ruskin began by positing an ideal, projecting a vision of a possible future society, and undertaking to bring it about.

The goal was a complete transformation of England, Europe, and indeed all humanity—a transformation of individuals and societies that would allow a renewal of human sensibility, in relation to work, nature, and one's fellowman. In *Unto This Last,* Ruskin returns ironically to the utilitarian formula while adding a significant element: the goal for the greatest number of human beings must not be simply that they be happy but that they be noble and happy.[94]

The form appropriate to a society of noble and happy individuals is often described in rather vague terms (Ruskin sets forth his most concrete and detailed proposals in *Time and Tide* [1867]), but we can identify some general principles, characterized chiefly by their paradoxical nature. In Ruskin's utopia, inequalities of fortune will not disappear, nor will poverty itself; however, these inequalities will be "just," because they will grow out of fair exchanges and salaries. Private property will be maintained, but it will be strictly limited and will constitute only a modest proportion of the overall wealth. Furthermore, this utopia will be modeled on medieval society but will not be identical to it: in principle, it will offer everyone the time, abundance, and possibilities needed for the development of human faculties, assets that were much less broadly distributed in the days of chivalry.[95]

The utopian social structure is to be organic, woven of close bonds of responsibility and duty, affection and trust; but it also resembles medieval society in that it is to be rigidly hierarchical. Ruskin's most common analogies are with the family (headed by a beneficent paterfamilias) and the army (in the old style); in *Time and Tide* he compares the ideal society to the crew of a ship struggling against the elements on the high seas, all members working to the best of their abilities, sharing the rations, helping the weak and the sick, and obeying the captain.[96] Ruskin's utopia is to be a directed society par excellence: marriage, for example, would no longer be determined by supply and demand, but would be the object of an authorization granted after a certain age in recognition of a life worthy of this privilege.[97] Against the harmful and unjust disorder or anarchy constituted by modern capitalism, Ruskin wants to establish (or reestablish) a fruitful order rooted in justice.

He never settled for pairing his denunciation of the status quo with a mere dream of what ought to be, however; he sought to act to hasten the coming of God's kingdom. In the beginning, he set out to play a role chiefly through his writings; each of his lectures is a passionate appeal to his listeners, confronting them with the choice between two paths, proposing rules of behavior, showing them the consequences they ought to draw, on the basis of what they purport to believe. In a first phase (roughly from the late 1850s to the late 1860s), he addressed all classes, attempting to trigger consciousness-raising at the level of the individual. Initially optimistic about his chances of success (see the preface to *The Political Economy of Art,* 1857), he was soon disillusioned; in 1868 he described himself as "a mind which has surrendered its best hopes, and been foiled in its favourite aims."[98]

Later, Ruskin turned increasingly to the working class as the element of contemporary society that was most apt to understand him: *Fors Clavigera* is chiefly addressed to the workers of Great Britain (although the terms of the subtitle — "workmen" and "labourers" — allow for a broader interpretation). At the same time, he undertook a number of extraliterary projects conceived less as utopian experiments properly speaking than as pedagogical demonstrations: they were designed to demonstrate a collective will to live his ideas and to show that these ideas were not chimerical.

Initially the focus was on attempts to surmount the breach between intellectual work and manual labor: on several occasions in the early 1870s, Ruskin engaged in strenuous physical labor to improve public spaces (city street cleaning, road repair). Then he set up a much more ambitious long-term project, creating the Guild of St. George, a society modeled after medieval guilds, as its name suggests. The associates put part of their income into a common fund, acquired both factories and agricultural lands, and put into practice the principles of cooperative craftmanship that Ruskin advocated. Conceived and inaugurated in 1871, the association actually began to take shape around 1875. Ruskin devoted himself to it with intensity during the latter half of the 1870s, but the Guild did not succeed in satisfying his hopes and he gradually withdrew from it in the early 1880s.[99]

Deeply disappointed in his efforts to combat the modern sickness and prey to periodic attacks of mental illness, Ruskin gave two final lectures in 1884 that brought his anguished vision to its apogee. This series, titled "The Storm-Cloud of the Nineteenth Century," expressed his conviction that "month by month the darkness gains upon the day," and it offered a hallucinatory description of a sinister cloud mixed with poisonous fumes (nature and humanity, both wholly vitiated, participate in this phenomenon) that seems to threaten the world with destruction and to announce the Last Judgment.[100] This was the final, most terrible, and most desperate expression of Ruskin's condemnation of the world in which he lived.

It is not hard to find weaknesses in Ruskin's thought. In the first place, his strategies for reconquering the lost world unquestionably entail a good dose of naïveté: ignorant of the structural imperatives that govern modernity, Ruskin seems to put all his hopes in individual awareness and action. More important still, in certain of his viewpoints, he fails to transcend his own position as a great lord or his sexual identity as a male in Victorian culture: the solutions he advocates are in general authoritarian and paternalistic in the extreme, and he often addresses women and "the people" as if he were speaking to children. In many places, his critique of modern society is blended with an antisexual puritanism that we can only call pathological. Finally, the violence of his social critique sometimes leads him to reject all modern artistic developments altogether as mere reflections of a corrupt society.

Despite these problematic aspects, which must not be overlooked or underestimated, it seems to us that Ruskin nonetheless made a major contribution to Romantic thought — and the impact of his writings and thinking attests to this. He had a decisive influence, as we noted earlier, on William Morris, for whom "The Nature of Gothic," read while he was a student at Oxford, was a revelation. For him as for others, Morris said later, this chapter of *Stones of Venice* "seemed to point out a new road on which the world should travel."[101] In "How I Became a Socialist" (1894), Morris declares: "It was through [Ruskin] that I learned to give form to my discontent. . . . Apart from the desire to produce beautiful things, the leading passion of my life has been and is hatred of modern civilization."[102] Like Carlyle's influence on Ruskin, Ruskin's influence on Morris seems paramount.

In part through Morris, but also more directly, Ruskin's influence continued into the twentieth century. Despite the scornful recommendation addressed to the English by the futurist Emilio Marinetti at the beginning of the century ("When will you disembarrass yourself of the lymphatic ideology of that deplorable Ruskin. . . . With his morbid nostalgia for Homeric cheeses and legendary wool-gatherers . . ."),[103] Ruskin played a role in the intellectual, artistic, and political development of important individuals and movements in England and elsewhere. Frank Lloyd Wright drew the inspiration for his conception of organic architecture from Ruskin's *Seven Lamps of Architecture*. Gandhi admired *Unto This Last* enough to translate it into an Indian dialect. And Clement Atlee, the historic leader of the British Labour Party, converted to socialism after reading Ruskin and Morris.[104]

Ruskin's influence on the formation of the British labor movement seems in fact fairly widespread. The results of a questionnaire distributed to the first group of Labour candidates elected to the House of Commons suggest that *Unto This Last* is the book that counted the most in their evolution. If we are to believe George Bernard Shaw, the Ruskinian line had an impact even on the most radical left: "I have met in my lifetime some extremely revolutionary characters; and quite a large number of them, when I have asked, 'Who put you on to this revolutionary line? Was it Karl Marx?' have answered, 'No, it was Ruskin.'"[105] The irony is patent, but it is an irony characteristic of Romanticism that this disciple of the archreactionary Carlyle, who proudly called himself a Tory to the end of his days, should have been a spiritual father to William Morris and to a significant sector of the left in the twentieth century.

5

Visages of Romanticism in the Twentieth Century

In our introduction, we sought to show that, in temporal terms, Romanticism includes not only the mid-eighteenth century but also our own day. In chapters 1, 2, and 3, to illustrate our perspective on Romanticism, we frequently drew our examples from the twentieth century. It is time now to justify this second extension of the concept and to look more closely at the shapes of twentieth-century Romanticism.

The continuity we are asserting is not self-evident. The persistence of a Romantic culture up to the present day has by and large been ignored, denied, and perhaps even repressed. Literary history, having for a long time limited the Romantic phenomenon to movements that had adopted—or had been assigned—the Romantic label, has sometimes ended up recognizing the continuation of Romanticism in the second half of the twentieth century, but without giving it much closer scrutiny. At the beginning of the twentieth century, modernism—a tendency understood to be radically antagonistic to Romanticism—was thought to have supplanted the older movement. As for the other realms of cultural and political life, the principal reference to a possible twentieth-century Romanticism was the one whose validity we have just challenged, the one that linked historical Romanticism with fascism and Nazism.

Some historians have nevertheless accurately noted that a significant number of twentieth-century authors and trends share a common matrix with nineteenth-century Romanticism. With a few exceptions, this recognition has come about only recently, in the 1980s in particular. The realm of

Anglo-American literary studies can serve to illustrate the evolution of the historical perspective. In 1949, Graham Hough gave the title *The Last Romantics* to a work dealing with John Ruskin, the Pre-Raphaelites, William Morris, and other late nineteenth-century writers, and he concluded with William Butler Yeats, the only author in the group whose work, although begun in the nineteenth century, continued up to the eve of the Second World War. A few years later, in *The Romantic Survival* (1957), John Bayley studied what he deemed a renaissance of Romanticism in the twentieth century; its most illustrious representatives, besides Yeats, were W. H. Auden and Dylan Thomas—two poets whose careers were just beginning when Yeats's was drawing to a close.[1]

Starting in the late 1970s, a growing number of literary critics began to associate some contemporary British poetry and certain major twentieth-century authors, such as Hart Crane or William Carlos Williams, with Romanticism.[2] In the last decade of the twentieth century, a considerable number of works published in the area of German studies attributed a Romantic coloration to the cultural and social movements we are about to discuss.[3]

It is also sometimes suggested that Romanticism has been (and remains) present in a much more global manner, even in our contemporary culture. For example, in the commentary that accompanies their anthology of the German Romanticism of the *Athanäum* (1798–1800), Philippe Lacoue-Labarthe and Jean-Luc Nancy spell out the interest their subject may have for us: "What interests us in romanticism is that we still belong to the era it opened up. The present period continues to deny precisely this belonging, which defines us (despite the inevitable divergence introduced by repetition). A veritable romantic *unconscious* is discernable today, in most of the central motifs of our 'modernity.'"[4] A similar perspective underlies the approach of the influential North American critic Jerome McGann in *The Romantic Ideology* (1983). While contemporary culture nurtures the illusion that it has nothing in common with nineteenth-century Romanticism, it is perceived by these critics as participating fully in the Romantic movement.

Lacoue-Labarthe and Nancy do not pursue this insight very far, however (their book has other aims), and in McGann's case the argument suffers, in our view, from an obvious lack of sympathy with what McGann calls the Romantic "ideology." But we fully share the idea that certain trends in contemporary art and culture perpetuate the Romantic legacy: not just by "repeating" it, as Lacoue-Labarthe and Nancy suggest, but also by transforming and developing it further.

Our hypothesis might be formulated as follows. If our key assumptions — that Romanticism is a critique of capitalist-industrial civilization, that this civilization (which we have called "modernity") still exists, although in modified form, and that certain social groups conveying the Romantic worldview are also still among us — are accepted, then it is reasonable to suppose that Romanticism continues to play a key role.

Now there is no doubt that capitalism has evolved tremendously since the end of the nineteenth century. Phenomena such as monopolization, state intervention, the growth of the tertiary sector, the development of consumerism, and so on are clearly changes of considerable import. But the fact remains that the undergirding, the basic principle — what Karl Polanyi sees as the unprecedented rupture brought about by the institution of capitalism — remains entirely intact: the domination of society by the economy in the form of omnipotent exchange value.

At the same time, it is obvious that the social strata and categories that are vehicles for the Romantic worldview (see chap. 2) have not been eradicated. While the aristocracy has grown smaller and smaller, the petite bourgeoisie continues to reproduce itself as the functional sector of contemporary economies; and although traditional intellectuals, especially those who are the producers of Romantic culture, face competition from the increasing number and power of the technocratic intellectuals, they nevertheless continue to play their role to the hilt (and their own numbers are probably growing as the student population increases). One can also point to the ascendancy that the various religions — and consequently theologians, religious thinkers, clergy, members of religious orders, and others — continue to exercise over contemporary culture.

In particular, alongside this persistence of groups that have traditionally been especially attuned to the Romantic worldview, we note that in late capitalism, a kind of globalization of the phenomenon is being produced: a diffusion of the system and its effects — the latter becoming more radical in the process — to virtually all the worldwide human community and to the entire natural environment of the planet. This globalization may tend to broaden the potential audience for a Romantic critique well beyond the groups drawn to it earlier.

A very suggestive study of American science fiction by a specialist, Gérard

Klein, seems to reinforce this hypothesis.[5] In an analysis inspired by Lucien Goldmann's work, Klein traces a tripartite evolution in the science fiction novel, whose producers and consumers tend to be recruited, he claims, chiefly from the sector of the middle class constituted by scientists and technicians: in short, they are the new intellectuals, a group that in theory should not be very susceptible to the appeal of the Romantic worldview. In a first phase, before the Second World War, American science fiction indeed lay at the opposite end of the spectrum from Romanticism, projecting positivist techno-scientific utopias to show that all contemporary problems have scientific and technological solutions. But after the Second World War and during the 1950s, doubt and skepticism took over, and in a third phase, from the 1960s on, science fiction has given us dark visions of wholesale disintegration, ecological disaster, and ultimate destruction of the world.

Thus we start with the observation — and this is what we attempt to demonstrate and to illustrate in this chapter and the next — that significant aspects and elements of twentieth-century culture can be found that derive from the Romantic worldview, not only in the most traditional domains but also in the most innovative ones.

Now if there is continuity between the earlier Romanticism and certain forms of twentieth-century culture, there are also specific differences that should be mentioned. In the first place, twentieth-century authors and movements do not call themselves — and are generally not called — "Romantic." What is more, they often see themselves — and are seen — as anti-Romantic. Octavio Paz holds this view, noting with regard to Ezra Pound and T. S. Eliot that their "denial of Romanticism was also Romantic."[6] Eliot especially, in the wake of Thomas E. Hulme, rejected the Romantic spirit of the nineteenth century in the name of a new classicism, even though as a partisan of the authority and discipline embodied in Christianity and the traditional monarchy he fully shared the Romantic worldview. The confusion arises because, for Eliot, the term "Romantic" referred first and foremost to an aesthetic notion linked with a literary sensibility and the corresponding practices of the previous century. But as we have already emphasized, it is perfectly possible to reject specific artistic techniques and subjective attitudes associated with the term "Romantic" and with the so-called Romantic movements of the nineteenth century while remaining indebted at a deeper level to the same weltanschauung that critiques the capitalist present in the name of the past.

Another difference between nineteenth- and twentieth-century Romanticism is that the twentieth-century version is undeniably less hegemonic. There is probably a certain truth in Morse Peckham's title, *Romanticism: The Culture of the Nineteenth Century*. While Romanticism was already present in the eighteenth century, it shared the arena of culture more or less equally with the Enlightenment (the two movements were not necessarily in contradiction, but Romanticism nevertheless constituted a divergent perspective with considerable impact). In the nineteenth century, on the contrary, although not everything was in tune with Romanticism (far from it: movements such as utilitarianism, liberalism, and positivism were quite distinct), cultural spheres such as art, literature, and philosophy were thoroughly imbued with nostalgia for a lost paradise. In the twentieth century, as in the eighteenth, Romanticism found itself once again up against serious competition.

In *Shifting Gears: Technology, Literature, Culture in Modernist America*, Cecelia Tichi has shown to what extent the world of industry, machines, and technological constructs, with its ideology of efficiency and speed, permeated the general culture — daily life, the popular novel, but also high art and literature — in the late nineteenth and early twentieth centuries in the United States.[7] She identifies the effects of the new technologies and their ideologies in some major writers: John Dos Passos, Ernest Hemingway, Williams. Her book reveals a fascination with modern life and its novelty that is not limited to the United States. But Tichi herself recognizes that the authors she studies are ambivalent (partly nostalgic, partly enthusiastic about modernity), and that in many other writers nostalgia is the dominant mode.

One final difference between the twentieth century and the nineteenth stems from the presence in the twentieth century of a new type of society. Whereas earlier societies were either precapitalist or (more or less) capitalist, the twentieth century witnessed the emergence (and eventually, in some instances, the dissolution) of what might be called bureaucratic noncapitalist societies. "Socialist" in name only, these latter nevertheless represented a structure different from capitalism, based on state control of the means of production and the exercise of dictatorship over needs (Agnes Heller), centralized bureaucratic planning, and so forth. (Totalitarianism, as Hannah Arendt showed, is not specific to this type of society: it can also be found in the capitalist world.) Heller, a Hungarian philosopher, was a follower of Georg Lukács and a Marxist-democratic critic of the authoritarian socialist regime in Hungary, which she defined as a dictatorship over needs. Exiled in Australia and later the United States, she distanced herself from Marxism and the Lukácsian heritage.

The intimate connection between modernity and capitalism, which is one of the premises of our analysis of Romantic culture, remains valid in any event for the history of Romanticism from the Industrial Revolution to the Russian Revolution. But is it still valid for the twentieth century? Seemingly not, to the extent that, starting in the 1920s (and especially after Stalin's first Five-Year Plan, 1929–1934), a noncapitalist form of modernity appears, one that is also a target for a critique of the Romantic type. Nevertheless, for the great majority of twentieth-century Romantics (writers, artists, and philosophers), the chief — if not the only — object of their anxiety and rejection remains bourgeois industrial society.

It is true that both in the West and in the East there are a certain number of Romantic critics whose hostility is also directed toward noncapitalist modernity. However, the aspects of this modernity they denounce are mainly the ones it shares with capitalist civilization: hyperindustrialization and technologizing, utilitarian rationality, productivism, the alienation of work, the instrumentalization of human beings (for Stalin, humans were "the most precious form of capital"), the domination and exploitation of nature, and so on. For some of these critics, the Soviet Union and societies constructed on the same model are only variants of the capitalist-industrial system, a form of state capitalism. As early as the 1920s, we find this sort of analysis among libertarian socialists and, later, among Trotskyite dissidents (C. L. R. James, Raya Dunayevskaya, Tony Cliff). All these critics share the conviction that the so-called socialist societies have broken with the modern capitalist-industrialist paradigm in only a limited and partial way.

A different approach is developed in certain conservative milieus, among both religious fundamentalists and pre-Fascists (and Fascists, especially before 1933): in this view, capitalism and "communism" are simply two sides of the same coin, two forms of the same decadent and perverse modern civilization.

In still another context, we see the emergence of the idea that the two forms of modernity, despite their apparent differences at present, are headed toward a similar future, which will be the exacerbated expression of all the negative features of industrial civilization. Here we can identify the inspiration for several great twentieth-century literary dystopias: Aldous Huxley's *Brave New World* (1932), a society whose god is the founder of the modern automobile industry ("Our Ford"), and George Orwell's *1984* (1948).

Finally, we can point to the Romantic critics who emerged from within noncapitalist societies. Even if their works display characteristic features that distinguish them from their Western homologues (especially the centrality of the problem of the totalitarian bureaucratic state), for the most part they present an identical worldview. This is true of the ecological movements of Eastern Europe, for example, and, at the other end of the political spectrum, of the restitutionist movements with their nostalgia for the "old" (czarist and/or Christian) Russia, whose most illustrious literary representative is Alexander Solzhenitsyn. In these two cases as in others (such as the religious neofundamentalists), the similarities with respect to their Western counterparts are more striking than the differences. What distinguishes these Romantic critics from the other internal adversaries of societies built on the Soviet model (liberals, modernists, and other Occidentalists) is their suspicion of — if not scorn for — the economic structures and lifestyle of the industrialized capitalist countries.

These diverse considerations have led us to the tentative conclusion that the existence of noncapitalist forms of industrial modernity for half a century (though we may now be witnessing the gradual disappearance of the model) no doubt introduces an additional dimension into our analytic framework, but it does not call this framework into question. The basic point to be stressed is that in no case have these societies achieved a genuine break with capitalist civilization; on the contrary, they have retained most of its essential features, reproducing them in modified forms. Under these conditions, it is not surprising that these societies too have given rise to Romantic protests from within.

In short, despite the differences we have just identified between nineteenth- and twentieth-century Romanticism, we are obliged to recognize that during the entire period in question we find the same structure of thought and the same themes that we examined in chapter 1: the disenchantment of the world and the critique of quantification, mechanization, rationalist abstraction, the modern state, modern politics, and the dissolution of social bonds. Discussions of twentieth-century art and thought have often included the various iconoclastic and innovative trends that flourished in the early twentieth century (and even late in the nineteenth), using terms that stress their modernness: "modernism" in art and literature, "modern thought," sometimes known as "modernity." More recently, and on the basis of this conceptualization, critics have spoken of "postmodernism" and "the postmodern" to account for some of the cultural trends of recent decades. The question that necessarily arises for us, since we define Romanticism as a critique of modernity in the name of the past, is how to understand the relationship between these designations and twentieth-century Romanticism.

The answer to this question seems fairly clear: since our concept is of a different order from those proposed by modernism and postmodernism, it traverses them, yet without either identifying with them or opposing them. For these designations have to do with what is modern — that is, new — in culture (art, thought), whereas for us Romanticism constitutes a rejection of the modern social realm. It is obviously possible to be enthusiastic about the most audacious forms of artistic experimentation or thought processes even while categorically rejecting modern capitalist society, just as it is possible to be at once a cultural conservative and a supporter of modern bourgeois society. Indeed, every combination is possible: Romantic and non-Romantic modernism, Romantic and non-Romantic postmodernism, and so on. To take just one set of examples, from this standpoint Italian futurism is a case of artistic modernism with a non-Romantic tonality, while surrealism is an instance of Romantic modernism.

Among the new forms taken by the Romantic critique of civilization in the twentieth century, certain avant-garde cultural movements occupy a central position. The transition between nineteenth-century Romanticism and these movements is achieved by way of symbolism; and expressionism, which comes immediately afterward, can already be read as an initial expression of the modernist Romanticism of the new century.

The art historian Philippe Jullian has aptly defined symbolism as "a walled garden in which all those who were horrified by Zola's world, those who were afraid of machines and scornful of money, took refuge at the end of the materialistic nineteenth century." Artists such as Odilon Redon, Fernand Khnopff, and Alfred Kubin; writers such as Joris K. Huysmans and Oscar Wilde; and poets such as Stéphane Mallarmé and Francis Viélé-Griffin share a certain esoteric, mystical, inspired, decadent cultural universe, in radical opposition to the bourgeois aesthetic and the positivist realism of the official ideology. Irony, melancholia, and pessimism are the dominant tonalities of a state of mind that results from the permanent rejection of the dull, prosaic reality of the modern world.[8]

The symbolist nebula contained Catholic traditionalists (such as "Sâr" Péladan or Auguste de Villiers de l'Isle-Adam) as well as anarchists such as Bernard Lazare and his friends from the journal *Entretiens politiques et littéraires*. What brought them together despite their differences was the Romantic hostility to bourgeois society and its disenchanted culture — as is evidenced by the astonishing homage to Villiers de l'Isle-Adam that Lazare published in his journal in November 1882, in which he celebrates the "contempt for the modern world" and the "hatred of contemporary social manifestations" exhibited by the author of *L'Eve future*.

Expressionism inherited some features of the symbolist movement, but its roots go much deeper, back to the German *Frühromantik* of the early nineteenth century. It is widely acknowledged that expressionism is neither a structured movement nor a literary or artistic school. The affinities among authors such as Gottfried Benn, Ernst Toller, and Franz Marc can be attributed not to a shared doctrine or aesthetic but rather to a certain *Stimmung,* that is, an atmosphere, a climate — a mix of utopia, anguish, despair, and revolt. There is also a common style, consisting in a negation of reality — especially among painters, who used harsh colors and lighting — and a concern for expressing the inner life and its torments.[9]

Kurt Pinthus's introduction to the well-known collection of poems *Menschenheitsdämmerung: Dawn of Humanity: A Document of Expressionism,* first published in 1919, is fairly representative of this atmosphere. Criticizing the alienation of modern life, Pinthus observes that humankind has become "totally dependent on its own creations, on its science, on technology, statistics, commerce and industry, on a rigidified communal order, on bourgeois and conventional practices. This recognition signifies at the same time the start of the struggle against the times [*die Zeit*] and against their reality." The poets brought together in this collection (Else Lasker-Schüler, Gottfried Benn, Walter Hanseclever, Georg Heym, Jakob von Hoddis, Johannes Becher, Franz Werfel, Albert Ehrenstein, Yvan Goll, René Schickele, Ludwig Rubiner, and many others) had foresight: "From the bursting blossom of civilization the stinking breath of decay wafted toward them and their presentimental eyes already saw as ruins an unsubstantially bloated culture and an order of humanity built up on the mechanical and conventional."[10]

Nostalgia for a communitarian past is less pronounced than in nineteenth-century Romanticism, but, as Jean-Michel Palmier observes, "the poetic scripture of Novalis is also found among the expressionists, where it is more somber, more despairing, given the supplement of soul they require, the pathos, the anticapitalist Romanticism, the hatred of technology and of cities, the blend of fear and love they feel for Berlin."[11]

The movement was fairly heterogeneous politically: while most artists involved were on the left (in particular through their opposition to war), only a few, such as Ernst Toller, the Bavarian People's Commissar in 1919, participated in the revolutionary movement, or, like Johannes Becher, in the Communist Party. Even rarer were those who, like Gottfried Benn, joined the Nazis. The most astonishing case is that of the mystical pacifist poet Hanns Johst, who became president of the Nazi Chamber of Literature and an SS *Obersturmführer*. At the other extreme, the author and playwright Arnolt Bronnen first supported Nazism, then shifted to the opposition, and eventually became a Communist.

In his well-known article "Expressionism: Its Significance and Decline" (1934), György Lukács is thus not mistaken when he stresses the intellectual confusion and political ambiguity of expressionism, with its "anti-middle-class ideology" whose "emotional roots undoubtedly lie in a romantic anti-capitalism" that attacks only the ideological symptoms of capitalism and not its economic foundations. However, as we have seen, he seriously distorts reality when he claims that expressionism was at bottom just one of the countless tendencies leading to Fascism.[12]

We do not claim of course to be offering even a minimally comprehensive treatment of the vast subject represented by the Romantic component of twentieth-century culture; to do it justice would take an entire book.[13] In this chapter and the next, we focus on three key expressions of twentieth-century Romanticism: religious, utopian, and feminist critiques of modernity, illustrated respectively by Charles Péguy, Ernst Bloch, and Christa Wolf. In chapter 6, we evoke what we take to be among the most significant Romantic cultural configurations specific to the twentieth century, starting with surrealism and leading up to the present and into the future.

ROMANTICISM AND RELIGION: THE MYSTICAL SOCIALISM OF CHARLES PÉGUY

The "return of the religious" as a form of resistance to modernity and the recourse to religious traditions as an inexhaustible arsenal of symbols, values, and arguments against bourgeois society are not phenomena specific to early Romanticism: we also find them in the twentieth century, despite the growing secularization of social life.

Charles Péguy (1873–1914) is an eminent representative of the second great wave of religious renaissance, which appeared at the beginning of the twentieth century. A socialist converted to Christianity, he sought to fuse two belief systems that are traditionally opposed and considered mutually exclusive. Péguy's work is often disconcerting or irritating, blending strange digressions, petty polemics (and sometimes calumny: see his delirious attacks on Jean Jaurès's supposed "pan-Germanism"), and patriotic jeremiads. But it also contains profound intuitions, visionary insights, and startling illuminations, written in a somber, majestic style.

Péguy interests us as a thinker in several respects. On the one hand, he attacks not isolated aspects of bourgeois civilization but rather the modern *world* as a whole, and he does so with passion, rage, bitterness, a desperate and tragic violence unequaled in the twentieth-century movement of ideas; on the other hand, he embodies in an exacerbated form all the ambiguities, contradictions, and ambivalences of a certain Romanticism.

Indeed, it is difficult to imagine a more contradictory figure. At once conservative and revolutionary, authoritarian and libertarian, nationalist and internationalist, Catholic and anticlerical, "on the right" and "on the left," Péguy seems totally resistant to categorization. Sometimes he criticizes military service as passive obedience and servitude, sometimes he defends it as authentic freedom; similarly, he can denounce the barbarity of the French colonial wars and then celebrate those same wars as carrying out the glorious and heroic task of defending the culture. Under these conditions, it is not surprising that both the fundamentalist right and the Christian left (Emmanuel Mounier, the journal *Esprit*) claim him as their own, as do both Vichy and the Resistance (Edmond Michelet, *Témoignage chrétien*). If Marshall Pétain's National Revolution could not fully co-opt him, it was chiefly because Péguy remained stubbornly loyal to his Dreyfusard convictions and his solidarity with the Jewish people: the ideologues of Pétainist anti-Semitism were unable to assimilate an author who presented the Jewish anarchist Bernard Lazare as a prophet of the era (in *Notre jeunesse,* 1910).

Péguy's views unquestionably evolved (some would say they regressed): the man who saw Jaurès (in 1900, in *Le triomphe de la République*) as a "simple and great worker in thought and action" was not the same man who denounced the socialist leader (in 1913, in *L'argent*), calling him "the man who represents German imperial policies in France." However, there are sometimes contradictions within a single text, or within the same time period: beyond the incidental shifts and ideological reversals (which Péguy did not acknowledge; he claimed to be consistently defending the same ideas), there is nevertheless an underlying continuity and consistency in his thought. If we set aside nationalism (or more precisely anti-German chauvinism, in its most rudimentary form), which is probably the element that led him to veer toward the reactionary camp (without ever belonging to it fully), his thought seems to pivot around three essential axes: the Christian religion, the critique of modernity, and socialist mysticism. And it is Romanticism that holds these axes together and gives Péguy's thought its contradictory unity.

It may seem paradoxical to speak of Romanticism in connection with Charles Péguy, since the writer endlessly denounced that movement and vaunted the moral and artistic superiority of classicism. But his declarations are hard to take at face value, given that Péguy fervently identified with the legacy of Victor Hugo and Jules Michelet and also with the Romantic poets: in a text from 1911 he mentions in one breath, as it were, Aeschylus, Pindar, Sophocles, Virgil, Pierre de Ronsard, Pierre Corneille, Blaise Pascal, Jean Racine, Lamartine, Hugo, Alfred-Victor de Vigny, Michelet, and Alfred de Musset.[14] In addition, as Simone Fraisse demonstrates convincingly (in a collection titled *Péguy, un romantique malgré lui*), Péguy's writing offers something like a mirror image of all the characteristics of Romanticism he himself criticizes: an exalted sensibility, disorder, excess; he attacks Romanticism as a Romantic, with passion, exaggeration, dramatization. His "Hymn to Night" is wholly comparable in spirit to Novalis's poem by the same name, and it is clear that Péguy unwittingly participates in the "Romantic soul." Moreover, in a critical note written in 1910, Henri Ghéon observed that Péguy was the only living representative of "the ultra-Romantic type of writer who gives himself over to his demon."[15]

The various literary dimensions of Péguy's work refer, in the final analysis, to a deeper core: Romanticism as a worldview, which inspired not only his style and his writing but also his semiheretical religiosity, his fierce critique of modernity, and his mystical socialism.

In a first period running from 1897 — the year of publication of his first *Jeanne d'Arc,* dedicated to "all those who will ever have died their human death for the establishment of the universal socialist republic"—to his religious conversion in 1907, Péguy was a socialist infused with ethical idealism and a declared adversary of Catholicism. An active Dreyfusard, he sometimes defined himself as an anarchist, and he manifested his fraternal solidarity with the Jewish people, to whom "we owe a good deal in the extension of socialism, anarchism, and just rebellions." He denounced with passion the "infamous machinations of the Jesuits" during the Dreyfus affair, and he assailed "Tartuffes like Barrès," "the Tartufied Church," and the sectarian teaching dispensed by religious orders; however, by also denouncing "prevarication and the profanation of the sacraments, the sacrilege of communion for bread coupons," he seems implicitly to accept certain religious values betrayed by the clergy.[16]

Péguy's rejection of Catholicism was nevertheless more profound than a simple critique of the (unworthy) attitude of the church during the Dreyfus affair. What he was wholly unable to accept—on principle, out of political and moral conviction—was the dogma of eternal damnation. He explained his position beautifully in 1900:

> I shall thus attack the Christian faith. What is most foreign to us about it, and I shall even say what is most odious, what is barbaric, what we shall never accept, the reason the best Christians have fled, or silently turned away . . . is this: the strange combination of life and death that we call damnation. . . . No man who has been given his share of humanity, or who has claimed it, will ever accept that. No citizen will accept it, out of simple solidarity. As we are one with the wretched of the earth . . . we are one with the eternally damned. We do not accept that there are human beings treated inhumanly. . . . We shall never consent to the prolonged exile of some miserable wretch. All the more strongly do we refuse to accept categorical eternal exile. Individual, particular, national, international, political and social events are not the only things that set the socialist revolution in opposition to the reactionary posture of the Church. But these events are the expression, and I would almost say that this opposition is a symbol, of a fundamental and invincible incompatibility.[17]

Rarely has such a stern moral condemnation been formulated by a socialist against Catholicism.

Despite this categorical spiritual opposition to the dogmas of the

Church, Péguy never ceases comparing socialism to Christianity, by presenting it as a lay equivalent of Christian mysticism, and by charging it with an ethical exigency analogous to religious faith. It is as if, in Péguy's spiritual economy, the socialist faith occupied the very same place as the religion he has rejected. The same 1900 text that proclaims the "invincible incompatibility" between Christian dogma and socialism draws parallels between the power of socialist communion and "the strength of Christian communion, and in particular Catholic communion," between socialist solidarity and Christian charity (in Pascal's sense of the term); better still, he wonders whether solidarity does not have for socialists, "making the appropriate adjustments in the respective attributions, the same function that God himself has for Christians." Conversely, in a text from 1902 ("De Jean Coste"), he compares damnation with the hell that can exist in society: "When we speak with the common people of hell . . . we mean precisely that poverty is in economics what hell is in theology."[18]

Péguy returns to these parallels in "Avertissement au Cahier Mangasarian" (1904), one of his most astonishing texts. After manifesting his deepest contempt for the anticlerical policies of the minister Emile Combes (that is, for the "anti-Catholic bourgeois politicians" and the "Voltairian bourgeoisie" of the radical party), he concludes that this shabbily political anticlericalism can do nothing against Christian mysticism and morality: only a socialist morality, only a libertarian socialism can stand up to religion. In other words: "Politics does not displace religion; politics does not displace mysticism; morality displaces religion; social philosophy, economics displace mysticism. To the eternal idea, the infinite, Christian, and in particular Catholic idea, of eternal salvation, a single idea can be opposed . . . a single idea can measure up: the socialist, economic idea of temporal salvation."[19] We can already see the seeds of the idea that is at the center of Péguy's writings in 1908–1912: only a mystical socialism can measure up to Christian mysticism. However, after 1908 the talk is no more of displacement but rather of convergence between the two.

Péguy also offers another analogy between revolution and Catholicism: they are not only worths of the same order, but also, and much more profoundly, "worths of the same species, of the same nature," in that they both refer to a tradition. In a typically Romantic — and paradoxical — fashion, he accounts for what distinguishes revolution from a traditional institution (such as the Catholic Church):

A revolution is an appeal from a less perfect tradition to a more perfect tradition, an appeal from a less profound tradition to a more profound tradition, a surpassing in depth; a search for deeper sources; in the literal sense, a resource. . . . At bottom a revolution is a full-fledged revolution only if it is a fuller tradition, a fuller conservation, an earlier tradition, deeper, truer, older, and thus more eternal.[20]

By this revolutionary traditionalism, with its strong ethical connotation ("The revolution will be moral or it will not be," as the *Cahiers de la Quinzaine* proclaims), Péguy occupies a place in socialist thought in France that has some affinity with the "morality of producers" cherished by Pierre-Joseph Proudhon and Georges-Eugène Sorel.

At the other extreme from this libertarian socialist faith nourished by tradition, from the "revolutionary forces of Dreyfusism, socialism, and anarchism" with which Péguy identifies, he places political corruption, parliamentary and administrative machinations, the ritual cult of the state, and state domination. Whence his overt hostility to the policies of radical governments owing to which "everything that has been lost by the Church has been gained by the State. . . ; neither justice nor liberty has gained a whit."[21]

But administrative and parliamentary policy is only one aspect of a more general deterioration known to us as the "modern world." From 1905 on and to an increasing extent, the struggle against the modern world became the critical issue at stake in Péguy's writing and in his activity as director of the *Cahiers de la Quinzaine*. This commitment preceded and probably prepared the way for his religious conversion; it was accompanied by a classically Romantic idealization of the past, the medieval past in particular. In a 1905 text that was not published until much later, "Par ce demi-clair matin," Péguy asserted that, since the beginning of the corruption characteristic of the modern era, the fate of humanity had been under greater threat than ever before. In contrast, medieval society represented "a perfect community, I would say a perfect communism"! The partisans of modern progress denounce the Middle Ages as an era of immobility and stagnation, yet "there was a hundred times more movement, appearances notwithstanding, a hundred times more . . . real life, under the feudal cloak of inertia . . . a hundred times more organic movement . . . more interior life in medieval French feudal society than in our modern societies."[22]

That year (1905) also marked the beginning of Péguy's shift toward nationalism, in reaction to Wilhelm II's threatening discourse in Tangiers; Péguy discovered the new chosen people in the French populace. His ex-alted anti-Germanism stops short of revanchism, however, as he is opposed to any war of invasion: "If, impossibly, a reactionary Caesarian military government were as openly preparing, were executing a military invasion of the Rhenan provinces to crush the national, political, and social freedoms of the Germans . . . we would be the first to give not only the precept but the example not only of desertion but of insurrection and revolt."[23]

In 1906, in the first "Situation," Péguy denounced the "incurably bour-geois" character of the modern world, and its "informed boycotting" of everything that challenged its dominance — the reason why "intellectual activities in the modern world are less numerous than ever before, in any world, less important, certainly less free, less fresh, less new, less promi-nent." The modern decline does not even spare the Catholic Church, whose position in the debate with Ernest Renan and in similar confrontations is "much more modern than Christian, sometimes entirely modern and not at all Christian, and therein lies the secret of its present weakness."[24] Whereas the terms "bourgeois" and "modern" are directly linked, "Christian" and "modern" already appear as two antithetical and mutually exclusive poles.

Between 1907 and 1912 Péguy's socialism was increasingly colored by Christian religiosity. His conversion to Catholicism — around 1907, made explicit during a confession to his friend Joseph Lotte in September 1908 — was irreversible, but he refused to break with his past and to submit to the authority of the Catholic Church. Out of respect for his wife, who remained an atheist, he did not have his children baptized and did not regularize his marriage, which meant that he could not receive the sacraments and did not participate in religious services. In addition, he persisted in rebelling against the dogma of eternal damnation. This theme recurred obsessively in his major poetic works on religious topics, *The Mystery of the Charity of Joan of Arc* (1910) and *The Portico of the Mystery of the Second Virtue* (1911). As Romain Rolland observed, Péguy was torn between his ardent need for God and "the terrifying impossibility of accepting an unjust and inhuman God, a God who condemns to damnation."[25]

Having become a fervent Catholic, Péguy nevertheless remained a merci-less critic of the church and the clergy. As he saw it (in *Notre jeunesse,* 1910), modernism's greatest coup was to modernize even the church and Christianity, transforming them into a "religion of the rich." Thanks to its wretched and miserable efficiency, the modern world has succeeded in modernizing everything: "That modernism of the heart, the modernism of charity itself, has caused the failure and collapse in the Church, in Christianity, in Christendom itself." Between the French Christianity of the fifteenth century, "in an age when there were saints," and the world of modern Catholics, "modern in so many, in almost all, senses," there is a huge gulf. This modern corruption is expressed in various realms, including clerical politics, the manipulation of religion by clerics and reactionaries in total contradiction with authentic Christian mysticism.[26] In a ferocious witticism, Ernest Lavisse (the director of the Ecole normale supérieure) described Péguy in 1911 as an anarchist who had put holy water in his gas tank. The terms of the comparison can just as well be reversed: Péguy was an anarchist who added gas to others' holy water. Each image points to a rather heterodox mix of profane and sacred liquids, which explains why Péguy remained profoundly alienated from the Christianity of his day.[27]

Péguy's indictment of the modern world—a critique that only intensified after 1907—was inspired by both socialist and Christian arguments: "One too quickly forgets that the modern world, from another angle, is the bourgeois world, the capitalist world. It is even an amusing spectacle to see how our anti-Christian socialists, especially the anti-Catholics, unconcerned with contradiction, praise the modern world as modern and condemn that same world as bourgeois and capitalist." Capitalism and modernity are for Péguy simply two sides of the same coin, inseparable, solidary, and homogeneous. Why? First of all because, contrary to the "ancient worlds"—a generic term that for Péguy conflates all forms of social life from antiquity to France under the Old Regime—in which spiritual powers still existed (and in which even the temporal powers were more or less imbued with a spiritual dimension), the modern bourgeois world knows only one power: money. This is why the world is a "vast dead corpse," which spoils everything it touches: cities, men, love, women, children, nations, families.[28] If one had to sum up in a word what the modern world lacks, the word would be "mysticism." For Péguy the term means something quite different from a form of contemplative religiosity: it implies active belief; militant faith; devotion and sacrifice to a cause; an ideal; absolute values, whether religious or secular. However, the modern world belongs to those who believe in nothing ("not even in atheism"), who do not devote themselves or sacrifice themselves to anything — *"More precisely:* the world of those without a *mystique.* And who boast of it." The de-Republicanization of France and its de-Christianization are two necessarily linked forms of the modern tendency that constitutes "one and the same movement, a profound demystification." From this viewpoint, the modern world is opposed not only to the Old Regime in France but also to "all old cultures . . . to everything which is culture, everything which is the city."[29] What positivist thought would categorize as "demystification" is taken up pejoratively by Péguy through the neologism "demystication," a term more likely to evoke "domestication." Péguy's famous opposition of mysticism to politics refers to an analogous and equivalent contradiction between the postmodern (or antimodern) and the modern.

Péguy's antimodern polemic was enriched and theorized in the great unpublished philosophic dialogues from 1909 to 1912, *Clio et Véronique.* Here the author not only denounces the modern world as "the inexpiable reign of money," "without any reservation, without any limitation or flaw," as a world whose very substance is the implacable omnipotence of money, but he also sheds light on the other aspects that create "the affinity, the deep kinship . . . between the modern world and bourgeois capitalism." This intimate link is manifested with particular clarity in the theory of progress, "the reigning theory if ever there were one," which is "at the heart of the modern world and its philosophy and politics and pedagogy." This essentially inorganic theory is a doctrine of capitalization, of accumulation — in short, a savings-bank theory. It presupposes a certain conception of temporality: homogeneous time, spatial time, geometric time, mathematical time. Now this fictional time is "quite precisely that of savings banks and major lending institutions . . . ; it is the time of the progress of interests earned by capital; it is the time of trade agreements and effects, and the anxiety of due dates; it is a truly homogeneous time, since it translates or transposes into a (mathematical) language the countless varieties of anxieties and fortunes." At the opposite pole from this homogeneous time of progress, "modeled on space," reduced to an "absolute, infinite" line, there is the organic time of past cultures, whether pagan or Christian. Here we have an entirely different temporality, consisting of an authentic duration "that we really have to call Bergsonian": it is the time of memory, of "organic remembering," of the inner gaze that comes back to the surface, the time of the work of the chroniclers and memorialists — a time that is not homogeneous but that has "full and empty spaces."[30]

Péguy's critics and commentators often complain that his criticism of the modern world is unjust, excessive, too pessimistic, or too exaggerated. Those who see it, on the contrary, as an extraordinary manifestation of lucidity are much harder to find. Among the latter, we discover revolutionaries such as Walter Benjamin, who wrote in a letter to his friend Gerschem Scholem on 15 September 1919: "I have again read some things by Péguy. In this instance, I feel that I am being addressed by an unbelievably kindred spirit. Might I be permitted to say that *nothing* written has ever impressed me so much because of how close it is to me, because of my feeling of oneness with it. . . . Immense melancholy that has been mastered." There is no evidence that Benjamin ever read *Clio* (published in 1931), but the parallel with his own critique of the ideology of progress and of the concept of homogeneous and linear time is striking, especially in Benjamin's 1940 theses on the concept of history.[31] To explain Péguy's antimodern — and anticapitalist — rage, his pessimism and bitterness, some critics refer to the circumstances of his life, and in the first place to his precarious financial situation, to the difficulties he had keeping *Cahiers de la Quinzaine* afloat, and so forth.[32] This type of explanation strikes us as somewhat cursory and ultimately rather superficial. Romain Rolland's sociological hypothesis is more interesting: Péguy's "incurable melancholia" resulted from the "fatal struggle of his class" (that of craftsmen), which was eliminated by "the rise and forward thrust of big enterprise, department stores, industrial and commercial capitalism, the world of Money." Certain passages in *L'argent* celebrate the craftsman's "devotion to the work well done" (craftsmen being similar in this regard to cathedral builders), the honor of one's trade, the ancient laborer's love for his work, and especially the virtues of the petite bourgeoisie, which has become today "the unhappiest of all social classes, the only one today that really works, the only one that has subsequently retained the working-class virtues intact"; these passages seem to confirm Rolland's analysis.[33]

The ideology of revolutionary syndicalism, with which Péguy sympathized in certain respects, was not without an analogous artisanal sensibility. Nevertheless, it seems to us that the thrust of Péguy's critique of modernity goes well beyond the anguish of a declining artisanal class (the class into which Péguy was born: his mother worked as a chair upholsterer). His critique gives a singularly radical expression to the feelings and intuitions of various social strata — intellectual as well as popular — that had been jolted by the process of accelerated industrial modernization experienced in France starting in the late nineteenth century (it is no accident that Péguy often identifies the 1880s as the beginning of the modern era). Above all, from a theoretical standpoint this critique represents one of the first attempts (along with Sorel's) within the socialist camp to call into question the ideology of progress and its epistemological presuppositions.

Until 1911, Christianity and antimodernism were closely linked with socialism in Péguy's major texts. Even though he established considerable distance between himself and the socialist worker movement (in both its political and its syndicalist dimensions), and even though his polemics against Aimé-Marie-Edouard Hervé, Jean Jaurès, and the Confédération Générale du Travail took on an increasingly reactionary (and nationalist) slant, he did not go so far as to renounce his youth. Henri Guillemin, who was not inclined to be indulgent toward Péguy, observed nevertheless that the writer

> did not push his renunciation all the way, [being] incapable of doing so, unable to debase himself to that extent. He had been viewed, for a while, on the right, as a zealous auxiliary; hence the nice things said about him at first in the national newspapers. This did not last, after it became apparent that in *Notre jeunesse* he had staked out the limits that he would not consent to cross. . . . Péguy kept his neck too stiff, unsuited to certain movements.[34]

His itinerary was not dissimilar to Sorel's, except for two details: he never indulged in anti-Semitism (this was even the reason for his break with the author of *Réflexions sur la violence*) and he never agreed to join forces with the Action française.

Invoking his Dreyfusist and socialist past in *Notre jeunesse,* Péguy interprets it in the light of his religious and antimodern convictions:

> It is undeniable that in all our socialism there was infinitely more Christianity in the whole of the Madeleine together with Saint-Pierre-de-Chaillot and Saint-Philippe-du-Roule and Saint-Honoré-d'Eylau. It was essentially a religion of temporal poverty. It is therefore the religion that will never be acclaimed in any way in modern times. . . . Our socialism was never a parliamentary socialism, nor the socialism of a rich parish. Our Christianity will never be a parliamentary Christianity, nor the Christianity of a rich parish.[35]

The struggle in favor of Captain Dreyfus becomes, in this retrospective light, a confrontation between Christian mysticism and the political forces of the church, and a movement of socialist mysticism taken over by parliamentary socialist politics.

The concept of mysticism is now invested with a directly religious content: "Our socialism was a religion of temporal salvation, nothing less. And even today it is nothing less than that. We sought nothing less than the temporal salvation of humanity through the improvement of the worker's world. . . ." It was not a uniquely Christian matter: Bernard Lazare, the Jewish anarchist, embodies more than anyone else the Dreyfusist socialist mystique: for Péguy, he is "one of Israel's greatest prophets; in Lazare, despite his declared and sincere atheism, "there resonated, with incredible power and gentleness, the eternal Word; with an eternal power; with an eternal gentleness; whose like I have never found anywhere else." In Lazare, spiritual power, contempt for temporal power, and libertarian hatred for the state were intimately blended: he was a man, or rather a prophet, "for whom the whole apparatus of powers, reasons of state, temporal powers, political, intellectual, and even mental powers did not weigh an ounce in the face of a revolt, a movement of conscience itself."[36] Simultaneously a restitutionist and utopian anticapitalist, Péguy defined his socialism as a doctrine of restoration—an ambiguous formula that lends itself to numerous misunderstandings; "Our socialism was essentially, and moreover officially, a restoration, a general and even universal restoration." More specifically, its objective was "restoring health to work, . . . giving work back its dignity" by a cleansing, an organic, molecular restructuring, of the world of work and thus of "the whole industrial economic world."[37]

In "Un nouveau théologien, M. Fernand Laudet" (1911), Péguy took up the cause one last time, in an effort to save socialism—"our socialism"— from political degradation and the contamination of modernity. Once again he refuses to recant: "We shall never renounce an atom of our past." With respect to this past, there has been no "turning back" or "distortion" or "revulsion" but only "deepening": because, even during the Dreyfus affair, "our socialism was a mystical socialism and a deep socialism, profoundly related to Christianity, a trunk growing from the old root, already (or still) a religion of poverty."[38] This assertion is both false and true. It is false to the extent that, starting about 1905, Péguy's thought underwent an undeniable conservative (and nationalist) inflection; it is true to the extent that a mystical element was already present, in secular form, in his youthful socialism. The continuity between the two periods is assured by Péguy's Romantic rejection of capitalist modernity.

This rejection continued to intensify during the last two years of Péguy's life. While the two 1913 essays on money deal essentially with themes he had already sketched out in his earlier writing, in his last major text, "Note conjointe sur M. Descartes" (1914), an ethical and philosophical, radical and acerbic critique of modern capitalist, quantification becomes more explicit than before. Money, master of the modern world, has instituted a universal venality, by destroying all qualitative values, by transforming everything that was once "supple, untrammeled, alive, free of charge, graceful, fecund" into an "object of calculation . . . convertible into money, comparable, marketable, venal." Everything becomes homogeneous with money, exchangeable, and at once "the whole world falls into commerce." Elements that could not originally be sold, counted, measured, or calculated became "countable, measurable, calculable: convertible into money." In short: "All the debasement of the modern world . . . comes from the fact that the modern world had no respect for values that the ancient world and the Christian world considered nonnegotiable. It is this universal negotiation that produced the universal debasement." Money, which was supposed to be a simple instrument of measurement and evaluation, has destroyed the entire scale of values: The instrument has become "the matter and object" of the world. It is, for Péguy, a rather new cataclysm, an event as monstrous as if the clock began to *be* time, and numbers with their arithmetic began to be the counted world.[39]

However, a new inflection appears in the texts Péguy wrote in the last few years of his life. Much more than before, the maleficent character of the modern world is defined in religious terms: it is the world of the Antichrist, of which the savings passbook is the quintessence — "just as the Scriptures are a complete expression of Christian thought." And, much more than before, the alternative becomes the past, the old France, the loyalty and heroism of Christian chivalry, the just Christian wars of Saint Louis. The word "socialism" tends to disappear from his vocabulary, and the insults directed at Jaurès ("agent of the German party") become frankly hateful.[40] If Péguy rejects any complicity with Charles Maurras and the Action française, it is because he views them as reactionary modernists: "They are essentially modern men and generally modernists. . . . They are reactionary, but they are infinitely less conservative than we are." That said, certain elements of his past — should we say vestiges? — are still present in his discourse. In "L'argent suite," he invokes socialism one last time as "an economic system of the healthy and just organization of work in society," and he proclaims his fidelity to the social revolution: "I am an old revolutionary . . . I am for the Paris Commune . . . I am for Proudhon's policy and for Blanqui's policy against the dreadful little Thiers."[41]

In its most nationalist and reactionary aspect, Péguy's legacy was to be manipulated by the Vichy ideologues; in its most profound and radical aspect, its mystical socialism, it went on to inspire Emmanuel Mounier and, through him, the Latin American Christian left and liberation theology.

ROMANTICISM AND UTOPIA:
ERNST BLOCH'S DAYDREAM

The work of Ernst Bloch illustrates in a remarkable way a paradox that is at the heart of all revolutionary Romanticism: how can thought that sees itself as entirely oriented toward the utopian future draw the heart of its inspiration from the past? The dialectic that unfolds in Bloch's writings represents an original solution to this contradiction. Unlike most other Romantics, Bloch does not refer primarily to premodern forms of life and social conditions; the references for his utopian project are mainly daydreams, the anticipatory aspirations and unfulfilled promises conveyed by past cultures.

A comparison between the young Ernst Bloch and Charles Péguy reveals some surprising affinities. They share not only a mystical and libertarian socialism, a visceral rejection of bourgeois modernity and a strange fascination with Catholicism but also the same blindness during the First World War, which makes them see Clemenceau's France as the incarnation of the principles of the Revolution of 1789 in the face of Wilhelm II's Prussia.

In one of the rare texts in which Bloch mentions Péguy (an article on socialism published in 1919), the latter is presented, along with Léon Bloy (spelled "Blois"), Leo Tolstoy, Thomas Münzer, Wilhelm Weitling, Immanuel Kant, and Franz von Baader—a philosophical and literary mix typical of the "Bloch laboratory"—as the representative of a powerful tradition of fraternity, radical socialism, and "warm-hearted anarchist Catholicism" (*herzlich anarchischen Katholizität*);[42] this last concept also belongs exclusively to the rather heterodox political-religious universe of the young Bloch.

Péguy is not often mentioned in the later writings of the German Jewish philosopher, but obvious traces of his influence pop up here and there. For example, in the section titled "Faith without Lies," which appears at the end of *Heritage of Our Times* (1935), certain phrases repeat the French writer's criticisms of the Catholic Church almost word for word:

> Its spirit, formerly cunning, also bold, colourful and broad, but today "harmonious" and without its bite, has become one of the savings bank, not of transubstantiation. . . . The papal Church does not even stick to this, at least relative contrast to the Now, but rather it is practically total modernism, it affirms and defends capitalism . . . far from abstractly rejecting practical mechanism . . . , the Church chooses an unwise compromise, a harmony based on incompatibility, namely, practical modernism with Gothic ornamentation.[43]

If the reference to Péguy is understandable on the part of the young libertarian mystic in 1919, it is much more surprising in the Soviet Communist sympathizer in 1935. But the example attests to one of the distinguishing features of Bloch's intellectual itinerary: the persistence of antimodern Romantic sources and themes throughout his political and philosophical career.

Ernst Bloch was born in Ludwigshafen in 1895. In numerous autobiographical texts and interviews, he stresses the contrast between that industrial city, the seat of the great chemical company I. G. Farben (which was to distinguish itself during the Second World War by making intensive use of slave labor at Auschwitz), and the old neighboring city of Mannheim, situated on the other side of the Rhine. While the first revealed the ugliness and feeling of uprootedness (*Heimatlosigkeit* — literally, "homelessness") of the modern city, the second — a ducal residence with a magnificent castle and the largest theater in Germany — embodied not only reactionary nostalgia for the good old days but also the powerful archetype of "home" (*Heimat*). According to Bloch, this sharp contrast resonated throughout all his philosophic activity, for what he had found in the old ducal city was not only tradition but also the future in a past that spoke to him and assigned him a mission.[44]

In 1911, in one of his earliest texts, the young Bloch describes the Germany of his day in terms that no doubt echo his feeling about the modern city of Ludwigshafen: that region has lost its soul, "its angular, pious, dreamy old soul," and it has become a barracks courtyard and it swims in dirty chemical waters that poison everything. Thought must rediscover Germany's "forgotten essence," which is unacquainted with either chemical runoff or Prussian helmets, and the most radical left has to be won over for a new memory, the memory of poets and thinkers of an earlier time.[45]

In the old castle of the city of Mannheim there was a library where the young student first read philosophy—in particular the four volumes of Friedrich Schelling's *Philosophie der Mythologie und Offenbarung:* a source that was to prove decisive for the evolution of the future "Marxist Schelling" (the expression is Jürgen Habermas's).

A student of Georg Simmel in Berlin, which is where he met Lukács, Bloch left with his Hungarian friend in 1912 for Heidelberg, where they participated in Sunday gatherings at Max Weber's home. The sociologist Paul Honigsheim, another member of "Max Weber's Heidelberg circle," describes Bloch (quite accurately) in his memoirs as an "apocalyptic Jew with Catholic leanings."[46] One has only to read Bloch's correspondence with Lukács from this period to discover both apocalyptic themes and a penchant for Catholicism. Around 1911–12, Bloch was very close to Friedrich Wilhelm Foerster, an (anti-Prussian) Catholic pacifist and (medievally inclined) restitutionist Romantic, whose writings Bloch often recommended to Lukács, as in a letter dated 28 August 1911: "Works like Foerster's show me with a certainty that is already determinable from a purely historical viewpoint that we . . . are at the end of the modern age, and on the eve of its sudden transformation into a renewed medieval period and a renewed Catholicism—this time enriched by Protestantism." And he adds, with a grain of salt, that he will need social democracy if he is to become the Pope Innocent III and the Thomas Aquinas of this new medieval world.[47]

Notions of an apocalypse and the Middle Ages are also at the heart of Bloch's first great work, *Geist der Utopie* (*The Spirit of Utopia*), written between 1915 and 1917, published in a first version in 1918 and in a second, considerably revised, in 1923. The book's hermeneutic, esoteric, and above all expressionist writing has often been criticized. Nevertheless, its style is inseparable from its content: as Theodor Adorno observes, Bloch's philosophy is the philosophy of expressionism, in that it is both an attempt to break through the encrusted surface of life and a protest against the reification (*Verdinglichung*) of the world.[48] It also shares with expressionism the explosive articulation between a radical *Zivilisationskritik,* a "modernist" artistic sensibility and a pacifist and social-revolutionary tendency.

The first aspect is particularly striking at the very beginning of the book, where Bloch launches into a conventional, fiercely ironic attack on the pretensions of modern technology. Responsible for the "destruction of the imagination" (*Phantasiemord*), machines are a capitalist invention whose purpose is not at all to make human work easier but is solely to foster mass production in view of greater profits. Mechanical production is lifeless (*leblos*) and subhuman (*untermenschlich*), and the "great works" it is capable of constructing—the modern equivalent of the Gothic cathedrals—are bathrooms! The spirit of modern sanitary installations, as an a priori of industrial merchandise, is surreptitiously present in even the most sophisticated architectural productions of our times. Carried away by his antimodern passion, Bloch goes so far as to foresee that one fine day the mechanical loom will join the cannon in "the same peculiar museum." Citing Ruskin, he observes that machines have killed joy in the overall work of craftsmanship, leaving no traces, and have destroyed "the old perfection, the deliberateness and piety of the old masters"; he hopes nonetheless that soon, once the aberrant capitalist deviation (*die kapitalistische Abirrung*) has been left behind—the expression is a marvelous condensation of the young Bloch's philosophy of history!—the peasantry and craftsmanship will be reestablished: the world to come will see the rise of a new type of human being, "a pious and chivalrous peasant."[49]

This extreme restitutionist attitude and antitechnological maximalism were attenuated in the 1923 version of the same text, which is more sober and more deeply marked by the Marxist problematic. Even while repeating the most important of his criticisms, Bloch now acknowledges that turning back is impossible: "The old craftsmen will not return." Thus Bloch aspires to a new, humanistic technology and to a limited, controlled, and functional use of machines.[50]

The counterpart of this visceral rejection of capitalist modernity, defined as a universe of "transcendental uprooting"—the German expression "transcendantale heimatlosigkeit" again appeals to the concept of heimat— is passionate praise for medieval Christian culture and Gothic art above all. The 1918 and 1923 editions of *Geist der Utopie* both celebrate the Gothic form with mystic fervor as the supreme expression of the "spirit of the resurrection": unlike Egyptian or Greek ornamentation, "only the Gothic has this fire at the center, over which the deepest organic and the deeper spiritual essences bring themselves to fruition." In the Gothic world, stones flourish and bear fruit while the domes of cathedrals are thrust upward toward God like stone ships. The Egyptian art of the pyramid, a crystal of inorganic death, is located at the opposite pole from this living organicity. According to Bloch, an intimate bond connects modern buildings of glass, cement, and stone to the Egyptian pyramids, and only the inconsistency of the modern world prevents it from slipping entirely toward the Egyptian model. Similar comparisons come back often in the Zivilisationskritik of the era — including, in a different form, those found in the famous conclusion to Max Weber's *The Protestant Ethic and the Spirit of Capitalism,* haunted by the specter of a new bureaucratic empire of the Egyptian type.[51]

In the 1923 edition, Bloch distinguishes his position from that of restorationist Romanticism more explicitly: even though he identifies with medieval Christian humanism, he criticizes the "Romanticism of the latest reaction" for replacing the true German popular tradition — that of the peasant war — with the cult of feudal fortified castles.[52]

Despite Bloch's many references to medieval Christianity, the young critic's religiosity cannot be reduced to a Romantic variant of Catholicism: it is rather a matter of an original and very personal form of heretical Judeo-Christianity with a Gnostic tinge. Even as he reproaches the Jews for failing to recognize Jesus as the Messiah, he declares, faithful to Jewish tradition, that the last Messiah has not yet come. And he not only distinguishes, following Gnostic doctrine, between the god of creation, lord of the world, and the god to come, lord of salvation, but he also salutes — taking his inspiration from the Ophite heresy — the biblical serpent, Lucifer, and original sin as legitimate forms of rebellion that prepare the way for the last god, still a long way off.[53]

These rather esoteric mystic reveries do not keep Bloch from concluding his book — after an excessively long digression about the philosophy of music — with a political-religious socialist and revolutionary apocalypse: the famous chapter titled "Karl Marx, Death, and the Apocalypse." Here he is of course presenting a reinterpretation of Marx, which singles out the aspects of Marx's thought that are compatible with the Romantic worldview, for example, "the synthetic-dialectic restoration, accepted by Marx, of the state of liberty, equality, fraternity, as it reigned among the old communist *gens.*" He also offers a libertarian reading, which stresses the antistate dimension of Marxist socialism: the cooperative socialist association of the future has nothing to do with a monopolist state economy — "Marx and Engels were in this sense liberals, and even 'conservatives,' that is, hostile to all contracts, nonjuridical, sufficiently irrational so that [their position] cannot be confused with state socialism" of the Lassalle type. Bloch even accepts — ungracefully — the primacy of the economy, a Marxist tenet: the revolutionary has to be able to think in purely economic terms, "like the businessman, against the businessman," like the "detective who has to force himself to resemble the criminal" if he is to fight him effectively (a rather curious comparison that Bloch uses frequently). But socialism has meaning only as a liberation of individuals from their economic worries, so they can finally open themselves to the real problems of the soul, to the inner, silent, and irrational aspects of human life, which imply "the rebuilding of the Church as educational and metaphysically centralizing an institution of salvation"![54]

The originality of *Geist der Utopie,* especially in the first version, lies in the way Bloch puts the arguments and themes of the reactionary and melancholic *Kulturpessimismus* to work in the service of an optimistic revolutionary perspective and in the way he uses the sober and resigned Weberian analysis of modernity as instrumental rationality to launch a project that is simultaneously Romantic and socialist. Bloch is persuaded that the war constitutes a historic turning point whose outcome will be the end of the modern era (*die Neuzeit*) with its capitalist economic system and its instrumentality (*Zweckhaftigkeit*): the day when the expropriators will be expropriated, presaged by the Russian Revolution. He finished writing the book in May 1917: thus he is referring to the anticzarist revolution of February 1917 (and not to the October revolution). Nevertheless, with a political intuition that is surprising in someone whose mind is more attuned to the various doctrines of the transmigration of souls than to the programs of the assorted factions of the worker movement, Bloch perceives in the "council of workers and soldiers" the main force of the future, a force "hostile to all private economy." The 1917 revolution is, in his view, a movement that breaks not only with retrograde feudalism but also with liberal superficiality, Anglo-Saxon banality, and the skeptical petite bourgeois spirit of German social democracy, and for the bourgeoisie of Western Europe it represents a much greater danger than the German army's entire arsenal: the rise in Russia of the ideas of another Germany — the socialist ideas of Karl Marx.[55]

What is this "utopian spirit," then, from which the work takes its title? This is a hard question to answer. The concept of utopia had an almost exclusively pejorative connotation at the time: one of the first socialist thinkers of the twentieth century to restore some positive dignity to the term was the libertarian Romantic philosopher Gustav Landauer, in his book *Die Revolution* (1907). Although Bloch never says so, he very probably borrowed the term from Landauer, in the sense of social ideal legitimately opposed to the existing state of affairs. He gives it a broader and deeper metaphysical scope: it is a matter of invoking what does not yet exist, of building in the unknown (literally *ins Blaue,* "in the blue"), of seeking "the true, the veritable, where the simple world of facts disappears — *incipit vita nova.*" Bloch uses the adjective "utopian" to characterize a form of reality superior to that of vulgar empirical facticity.[56]

But utopia has a dual function. It serves "to cultivate the past once again and to deliberate in a new way on the future as a whole." This is precisely the sense of the 1918 book, and it was the project Bloch pursued throughout his life in his work. As the American scholar John Ely has observed, Bloch's conception of history considers that progress is achieved through moments of return and that ultimate fulfillment requires a grasp at the origin: "From the outset, such a conception decisively shaped the philosophy of history which Bloch worked out and the manner in which he interpreted Hegel and later integrated historical materialism into the core of his work."[57]

The period of Bloch's exile in Switzerland (1917–1919) constitutes a curious parenthesis in his intellectual and political evolution. Torn between a libertarian Christian socialism and the "socialism of the Entente," he criticizes the position of the Zimmerwald internationalist socialist conference (the simultaneous rejection of both warring blocs) as stemming from "materialist economism." He has an overt preference for the Entente, which he does not hesitate to label, in a rather incredible text from 1918, "armed pacifism" and "combative Christianity." The Bolsheviks are criticized for their statism, but especially for having forgotten the mystical and communistic peasant tradition, the spirit of Tolstoy and Ivan Karamazov, in short, the "religious anarchist Russian consciousness," in favor of the industrial proletariat alone. Bloch recognizes nevertheless that "the impulse toward social revolution came into the world thanks to Russia."[58]

As Bloch says in a 1974 interview, "mythical Russia," "imaginary Russia," Russian Christianity, and the spiritual universe of Tolstoy and Dostoevsky lay at the heart of all political reflection at that time, for him as well as for Lukács. This attitude unquestionably contributed—despite a period of hesitation—to his and Lukács's commitment to Soviet Russia. Lukács had made his decision by December 1918, and Bloch made his at some point in 1920.[59]

With *Thomas Münzer als Theologe der Revolution* (Thomas Münzer as theologian of the revolution [1921]), the major political and philosophical shift begun with *The Spirit of Utopia* was completed: the articulation of revolutionary Romanticism with Marxism and Bolshevism. Bloch did not abandon his libertarian convictions, however: denouncing the satanic nature of the state, he presents Thomas Münzer as a precursor of Mikhail Bakunin and of Karl Liebknecht and Lenin. The idealization of the communitarian past and of millenarian and heretical religious forms is as intense as in the 1918 work, but a significant change has taken place in this area: the Gothic period—"the golden centuries of the Middle Ages"—is no longer represented as the true community of Christians, because the people at that time were oppressed by the ecclesiastic state, "the Caesarean legacy." The era he now privileges is the one the Aufklärung saw as a regression into barbarianism: the centuries that followed the fall of the Roman Empire, the early Middle Ages. He is pleased with the disappearance of the abstract bureaucratic form of the state and the monetary economy and with their replacement by a society based on the values of fidelity, tradition, piety, and patriarchal simplicity. Bloch seems to identify with the dream of the Anabaptist peasants who wanted things to return "to exactly the way they were before, when they were still *free* men, within free communities, when, in its first freshness, the countryside was open to everyone as a communal meadow." At the beginning of the Middle Ages there is already "a sort of agrarian communism, reasonably well suited to Christian requirements."[60]

In total opposition to the communitarian aspirations of the rebellious peasants, Calvinism represents, "as Max Weber has brilliantly shown," the developing capitalist economy which thus turns out to be "totally liberated, detached, freed from all the scruples of primitive Christianity, and also from the relatively Christian elements that remained in the economic ideology of the Middle Ages." Sacrificing the primitive Christian ethic of communistic love in favor of capitalist inequality, Calvin opened up the way for the religion of Mammon, according to Bloch.[61] The Weberian sociology of the Protestant ethic is thus deflected and placed at the service of a Christian-communist denunciation of capitalism.

Nevertheless, Bloch rejects as "inoperative" everything that "purports to suppress the modern world rather than to heal it"; he denounces the Catholic, organicist, or solidarist "Romantic reaction" as a "hypostasis of the old regime of 'states.'" His goal is not restoration but the revolutionary struggle for a "new universality," a "new Commune," a "rational, inherently millenarist socialism."[62] Here the organic, religious and heretical, popular and rural communitarian past is a source of inspiration for modern revolutionary utopias, charging the Marxist conception of history with messianic energy.

A fellow traveler of Stalin's Soviet Union during the 1920s and 1930s, Bloch nonetheless continued to be a Romantic philosopher—whence the conflict with his friend Lukács, for whom anticapitalist Romanticism could lead only to fascism. The book Bloch published in 1935, *Heritage of Our Times,* attests to this continuity and also to a certain independent-mindedness in relation to the KPD, the German Communist Party, with which he had close ties.

In this work, Bloch highlights the critical, subversive, anticapitalist, and potentially revolutionary dimension of various cultural manifestations that stem from Romanticism (in the broad sense): what he himself calls "cracks" in the Romantic soul (tales, pulp novels, occultist dreams), expressionism (a blend of archaic shadows and revolutionary light), surrealism (the book's final chapter is titled "Thinking Surrealisms"). At the same time, he subjects the reactionary and fascistic manifestations of that same culture—the works of Ludwig Klages, Carl Jung, Oswald Spengler, Martin Heidegger, and so on—to a merciless critique.

However, the principal theme of *Heritage of Our Times* is the complex and disconcerting issue of the relations between Romantic anticapitalism—Bloch borrows this term from Lukács—and Nazism. From this standpoint, the entire book—and not simply the passages on expressionism, in which Bloch enters into explicit polemics with the Hungarian philosopher—may be viewed as a response to Lukács's theses. Bloch starts with an analysis of the noncontemporaneous—that is, archaic and backward-looking—contradiction that opposes strata such as the peasantry and the petite bourgeoisie to the "death machine of capitalism." Anticapitalist Romanticism is the spontaneous form taken by this opposition, inspired by nostalgia for the past. Even as he criticizes the reactionary goal of restoration, Bloch recognizes that "the relatively more lively aspect and wholeness of earlier relations between human beings is understood."[63] Accordingly, one must be able to distinguish between this Romantic culture of noncontemporary social strata and the Fascist swindle that exploits it, by separating the "seed of the dream" that lies in the memory of ancient times from the monstrous falsifications of the Nazis.

Thus millenarism, the authentic dimension of many revolutionary utopias — since "the wish for happiness was never painted into an empty and completely new future"[64] but often implied the dream of a lost paradise (constructed from memories of the primitive commune) — could not be confused with the miserable caricature of Hitler's Third Reich.

Hence Bloch's critique of the KPD's "vulgar Marxism" (and implicitly of the Soviets), which took the progress of socialism too far from utopia toward science, abandoning the world of the imagination to the enemy. Too abstract, characterized by an overly narrow and vulgar free-thinking rationalism, partisans of a materialism insufficiently distinct from the wretched materialism of capitalist entrepreneurs, the German left in general and the KPD in particular were incapable of triumphing over Fascism in the struggle for the political and cultural conquest of the noncontemporaneous strata. Their economism allowed retrograde Romanticism to get these classes to accept "the nonsense of seeing in liberalism and Marxism only 'two sides of the same coin' (namely those of abstraction and mechanization)."[65]

What would the correct antifascist policy have been? According to Bloch, it would have been necessary to "mobilize contradictions of noncontemporaneous strata against capitalism under socialist direction" by constituting a "Triple Alliance" among the proletariat, the peasantry, and the impoverished middle strata ("under proletarian hegemony"). But to do that one would have had to be able to exploit the dialectical flaws of that Romantic anticapitalist culture, that is, to take control of its "subversive and utopian elements," by reconnecting with the millenarist tradition of socialism and replacing vulgar materialism with a pluritemporal and plurispatial dialectic. This would be a dialectic that would be capable of integrating Romanticism into the revolutionary perspective: "Romanticism has no other future than at best that of the undisposed-of past, of course. But it does have this kind of future, and it ought to be 'resolved' for it, in the precise dialectical multiple sense of this term."[66]

Bloch's analysis undoubtedly represents an innovative and original contribution to the theory of fascism; it also attests to his ability to view the policies of Stalinized German Communism from a critical distance. Unfortunately, his critique leaves intact the centerpiece of the KPD's strategy between 1929 and 1933, namely, the stubborn rejection of unified anti-Fascist action in common with other worker parties, especially with the Social Democrats (defined during this period as "Social-Fascists"). Bloch himself is careful to spell this out, in the 1934 preface to his book: "Nor has this formulation of the question the slightest thing in common either with social-democratic dilution or with Trotskyite obstructionism; since what the party did before Hitler's victory was completely correct, it was simply what it did not do that was wrong."[67] This remark harshly illuminates the limits of Bloch's political autonomy, as well as those of his alternative political strategy, for it is obvious that without the anti-Nazi unity of the worker movement itself—advocated not only by Leon Trotsky and his partisans but also, in Germany, by the SAP (Workers' Socialist Party) of Heinz Brandler, Willi Brandt, and Paul Fröhlich—it would have been impossible to win over other social strata for an alliance with the left against Hitler.

The Principle of Hope (1959), Bloch's major work, is an astonishing text in several respects. As David Gross observed in a recent commentary, no one has ever written a book like it, folding into a single philosophical soufflé the pre-Socratics and Georg Wilhelm Friedrich Hegel, Renaissance alchemy and Johannes Brahms's symphonies, the Ophite heresy and Sabbataï Tsevi's messianism, Wolfgang Amadeus Mozart's operas and Charles Fourier's utopias.[68] Opening a page at random, we come across Renaissance man, the concept of matter in Paracelsus and Jakob Böhme, Marx's *Holy Family*, Giordano Bruno's doctrine of knowledge, and Baruch Spinoza's *On the Improvement of the Understanding*.[69] Bloch's erudition is so encyclopedic that very few readers are capable of making informed judgments on every theme developed in the book (which runs to nearly fourteen hundred pages in the English translation, more than sixteen hundred in the original German). The style is often opaque, but it has a powerfully suggestive quality: as Jack Zipes has written, it is up to the reader to "sift the gems of light from the poetical and somewhat esoteric philosopher's esoteric pen."[70]

Unlike so many other thinkers of his generation—beginning with his friend György Lukács—Bloch remained faithful to the daydreams of his youth and never renounced the revolutionary Romanticism of his early writings. Thus in *The Principle of Hope* we find frequent references to *The Spirit of Utopia,* and many themes from the 1918 book return in the later text (written from 1938 to 1947 and revised in 1953 and 1959), especially the notion of utopia as anticipatory consciousness, as a figure of preappearance.

The central paradox of *The Principle of Hope* (and perhaps of Bloch's work as a whole) is that this monumental text, entirely oriented toward a future horizon, toward the front, the *Novum,* the Not-Yet, says almost nothing at all about the future. It almost never tries to imagine, anticipate, or prefigure the shape of human society to come, except in classic Marxist terms: it will be a society without classes and without oppression. Science fiction and modern futurology hold no interest for Bloch at all. Apart from the most theoretical chapters, the book is actually an immense voyage through the past, in search of images of desire, waking dreams, and landscapes of hope, dispersed among social, medical, architectural, technological, philosophical, religious, geographical, musical, and artistic utopias.

In this particular modality of the Romantic dialectic, what is at stake is the discovery of the future in the aspirations of the past—in the form of unfulfilled promises: "The rigid divisions between future and past thus themselves collapse, unbecome future becomes visible in the past, avenged and inherited, mediated and fulfilled past in the future."[71] So it is not a question of falling into a dreamy, melancholic contemplation of the past but of turning the past into a living source for revolutionary action, for a praxis oriented toward the utopian future.

Despite the Romantic revolutionary tonality of Bloch's magnum opus, Romanticism as such is not addressed in any serious way in the book. In one passage of the first volume, Bloch recognizes that

Undoubtedly, German Romanticism—this cannot be stressed often enough in view of the antiquated, abstract way it has been underestimated—also had a progressive character; precisely its instinct for what is bubbling up, becoming, growing, is relevant here, the famous "historical sense" which first created whole disciplines like legal history and German studies. . . . As the Wartburgfest of 1817 alone shows, there is definitely also a revolutionary Romantic component in German Romanticism: while even the most passionately utopianized red dawn is shot through here time and again with the above-mentioned night-thoughts of an antiquarium, with the projection of an overprized past even into the newness of the future.

According to Bloch, in English and Russian Romanticism in particular (George Gordon Byron, Percy Bysshe Shelley, and Aleksandr Pushkin), "the true feeling of homeland commensurate with man becomes explosive and future-laden, and is not sought by sinking back into the past." The examples cited—and the Wartburg festivals figure prominently—may not be the best possible choices, and the distinction among national variants is highly questionable, but the crucial point is that Bloch wants to rescue the revolutionary legacy of Romanticism from its detractors at any price. This is why, at the end of volume 3, he insists on the need to avoid confusing the aufklärung with Johann Christoph Gottsched or Christoph Friedrich Nicolai, "as if revolutionary Romanticism were identical with Quixotry."[72]

The Romantic coloration of *The Principle of Hope* is manifested first of all in an aspect that has often been missed or ignored by its commentators: its ferocious critique of Zivilization. Returning frequently to the themes he had put forth in his 1918 book, Bloch pillories the "purely despicable level" and "ruthless nastiness" of what he calls "the totally crooked business-life of today," in which "the greed for profit . . . overshadows all other human inclinations." He also attacks modern abstract, functional cities, which are no longer homes (heimat) but "housing machines," reducing human beings to the state of "standardized termites." Refusing all ornamentation and organic patterns, rejecting the Gothic legacy of the tree of life, modern constructions have returned to the Egyptian crystal of death. In the final analysis, "functionalist architecture reflects and doubles the ice-cold automatic world of the commercial society anyway, of its alienation, of its human beings subject to the division of labour, of its abstract technology." In the same spirit, he compares the "cadaverousness" of merchandise produced by machines with the qualities of earlier artisanal products—and he contrasts the modern worker's hatred and lethargy with the pleasure of the craftsman who creates his product with love. It is no accident that Bloch refers with sympathy—but also with a certain critical distance—to the "homespun socialism" of Ruskin and Morris, two "romantic anticapitalist" thinkers whose "backward utopia[s]" were "not intended in a politically reactionary way."[73]

Bloch's critique of modern (capitalist) technology is motivated above all by the Romantic requirement of a more harmonious relation with nature. Bourgeois technology maintains only a hostile, mercantile relation with nature: it "stands in nature like an army of occupation in enemy territory." Like the representatives of the Frankfurt School, the author of *The Principle of Hope* views "the capitalist concept of technology as a whole" as reflecting "more domination than friendship, more of the slave-driver" in relation to nature. Bloch does not reject technology as such, but he contrasts the technology that characterizes modern societies with the utopia of a "technology of alliance mediated with the coproductivity of nature," technology "understood as the delivery and mediation of the creations slumbering in the womb of nature" (a formula borrowed — as is often the case, without attribution — from Walter Benjamin).[74]

This preecological sensibility is directly inspired by the Romantic philosophy of nature, and by its qualitative conception of the natural world. According to Bloch, the rise of capitalism, of exchange value and market calculation, brings with it a "de-organization which completely abandons the organic" as well as a loss of the sense of quality in nature. And it is no accident that the rebellion against the new mechanical conception of nature took place above all in Germany, a country in which medieval traditions have persisted much more vigorously than in France or England: Johann Wolfgang von Goethe, Schelling, Franz von Baader, Joseph Molitor, and Hegel are among the representatives of this return to the qualitative, which has its sources in Paracelsus, Jakob Böhme, and Meister Eckehart. But Bloch also dips into the legacy of the Pythagorean symbolics of numbers, hermetic physiognomy, the cabalistic theory of signs, alchemy, and astrology to bring to light the limitations of the quantitative mechanism of the sciences of nature. He is especially fascinated by the theory of nature as a coded language — Jakob Böhme's *signatura rerum,* refashioned by Novalis, Ludwig Tieck, and Molitor. From this standpoint, Habermas is fully justified in labeling Bloch the "Marxist Schelling," to the extent that Bloch attempts to articulate, in a unique combination, the Romantic philosophy of nature with historical materialism.[75]

Bloch's other Schellingian aspect is of course the role he gives religion in his philosophy. Among all the forms of anticipatory consciousness, religion holds a privileged place because it is a utopia par excellence, the utopia of perfection, the totality of hope. In this area, too, there is a great deal of continuity between Bloch's earlier and later work, except that in *The Principle of Hope* the atheist character of his religion is much more openly stressed. He offers a kingdom of God without God, one that takes the lord of the world down from his celestial throne and replaces him with a "mystic democracy":

"Atheism is . . . so far from being the enemy of religious utopia that it constitutes its precondition: *without atheism messianism has no place.*"[76]

However, Bloch rather trenchantly distinguishes his religious atheism from any vulgar materialism, from the "bad disenchantment" conveyed by the most pedestrian version of Enlightenment (*Aufkläricht*), and by bourgeois doctrines of secularization. It is a matter not of opposing belief to the banalities of free thought but of saving — by transporting them toward immanence — religion's treasures of hope and contents of desire, treasures among which one finds the communist idea, in the most varied forms: from the primitive communism of the Bible (recollection of nomadic communities) to the monastic communism of Joachim de Flore and even the chiliastic communism of the millenarist heresies (Albigensians, Hussites, Taborites, Anabaptists). To show the presence of this tradition in modern socialism, Bloch maliciously concludes his chapter on Joachim de Flore with a little-known and rather astonishing quote from the young Friedrich Engels: "The self-confidence of humanity, the new Grail around whose throne the nations jubilantly gather. . . . This is our vocation: to become the Templars of this Grail, to gird our swords about our loins for its sake and cheerfully risk our lives in the last holy war, which will be followed by the millennium of freedom."[77]

As this reference shows, Marxism is for Bloch above all the heir to the utopian traditions of the past — not only the social utopias, from Joachim de Flore and Thomas More to Wilhelm Weitling and William Morris, as commentators have often stressed, but all the waking dreams and wishful imagery in the history of humanity. And its adversary is the "old enemy" of the human, the age-old selfishness that "has conquered as never before, in the form of capitalism," by transforming all things and all human beings into merchandise.

The new element Marxism offers is *docta spes* (informed hope), the science of reality, active knowledge directed toward a world-transforming praxis and the horizon of the future. Unlike the abstract utopias of the past (which settled for contrasting their wishful images with the existing world), Marxism starts with objective tendencies and possibilities present in reality itself; owing to this real mediation, it allows the concrete utopia to come into being.

But one must not take the metamorphosis of utopian socialism into science too far: Marxism can only play its revolutionary role in the inseparable unity of sobriety and imagination, reason and hope, the rigor of the detective and the ardor of dreams. In an expression that has become famous, the warm and cold currents of Marxism have to be fused, as both are equally indispensable—even if there is a clear hierarchy between them: the cold current exists for the warm current (*um dieses Wärmestrom willen*), for the benefit of the warm current (*für den Wärmestrom*), which needs scientific analysis in order to rid utopia of its abstractness and make it concrete.[78]

Marxism's warm current inspired in Bloch what he called his "militant optimism," that is, his active hope for the novum, for the achievement of utopia. He nevertheless distinguished quite explicitly between this militant position and "banal, automatic progress-optimism"; considering that such false optimism tends dangerously to become a new opium of the people, he thought that "even a dash of pessimism would be preferable to the banal, automatic belief in progress as such. Because at least pessimism with a realistic perspective is not so helplessly surprised by mistakes and catastrophes." He insisted accordingly on the importance of the category of danger and on "the objectively unguaranteedness" (*objective Ungarantiertheit*) of utopian hope. He returned to this question again and again in lectures and interviews in the 1960s and 1970s, to justify a "militant pessimism" that is not contemplative but disposed to action against *pessimum*. In a series of lectures on Arthur Schopenhauer in 1965, under the title "Recht und Unrecht des Pessimismus" (Legitimacy and illegitimacy of pessimism), he noted that with Auschwitz and Majdanek the horrors of the twentieth century far exceeded what Schopenhauer had been able to imagine in his bleakest pessimism (or what Dante had ascribed to the terrors of Hell in the *Divine Comedy*).[79]

Reinterpreting one of Marx's celebrated formulas ("We are still living in the prehistory of humanity"), Bloch concluded *The Principle of Hope* by affirming his conviction that "true genesis is not at the beginning but at the end." The book's last word, significantly, is "homeland" (heimat). Despite his critique of vulgar progressism, Bloch's optimism poses a problem. In a century that witnessed so many disasters, this attitude appears much less convincing than the somber lucidity of a Walter Benjamin. The concept of catastrophe does not take up much space in his philosophic system, and Auschwitz and Hiroshima are not key themes in his reflection. Nevertheless, there is a greatness of spirit in this hope against hope, which refuses to be discouraged by any fact ("facts be damned" is one of Bloch's favorite expressions). According to the homage paid him by Theodor Adorno, one of the most pessimistic thinkers of the twentieth century, Ernst Bloch is "one of the very few philosophers who does not recoil in fear from the idea of a world without domination and hierarchy."[80]

Bloch's Marxism is thus sui generis, and completely irreducible to Soviet *diamat* ("dialectical materialism"). The fact remains that from the late 1920s to the mid-1950s Bloch figured among the fellow travelers of Stalinism. In this respect, he failed to remain faithful to the rich libertarian socialist and anarcho-Marxist intuitions of his early writings.

Of all his compromises with the Stalinist variant of communism, the worst was undoubtedly the position he took during the Moscow trials. While Lukács himself, although a Party member living in the USSR at the time, maintained a prudent silence, Bloch judged it opportune to declare *urbi et orbi* his loyalty to the Soviet Union and to its revolutionary tribunals. In a 1937 article titled "Le jubilé des renégats"—which remains a black mark on his political reputation—he took it on himself to compare the left-wing intellectuals who criticized the trials to the German Romantic authors of the late eighteenth century (from Friedrich Klopstock to Friedrich von Schiller) who, shocked by the revolutionary Jacobin tribunals, denounced the French Revolution they had supported in their youth, moving into the camp of counterrevolution. Still, one sentence at the end of the article leaves the critics of the trials at least the benefit of the doubt as to their attachment to revolutionary ideals: "Contrary to what Klopstock and Schiller were still able to believe, senselessly exaggerated criticism of the homeland of the revolution will not benefit the ideal of revolution. This ideal can be furthered only by the popular front."[81]

We still need to determine—and this is the question that interests us most in the context of the present discussion—to what extent Bloch's own philosophy may have been affected in its very structure by these political compromises. It must be said that Stalin's name appears only twice in the nearly fourteen hundred pages of *The Principle of Hope* (less often than Sabbataï Tsevi, the seventeenth-century Jewish "Messiah"); there are more frequent references to the USSR (in particular the famous formula *ex Oriente lux,* which Bloch purports to transpose from the Christian realm into that of modern politics), but these are external to the substance of the argument itself. In its underlying principles, Bloch's philosophy actually manifests a profound continuity that extends from his early writings through those of the pro-Soviet period to the texts of the later, post-Stalin years.

Thus it seems to us that Oskar Negt is right when he draws the following conclusion about this debate: "Just as we cannot stamp Hegel as the philosopher of the Prussian state because he lets the development of the moral idea end in the Prussian state, we cannot reduce Bloch's thought, the philosopher in combat, to statements he made about the Moscow trials, for these statements clearly contradict his entire philosophy."[82] Still, we must add that the Prussian state occupies a much more crucial place in Hegel's political philosophy than the Soviet Union does in *Prinzip Hoffnung:* however much he may admire Soviet achievements, Bloch still conceives of utopia as a hope for the future, an unfulfilled latency-tendency, a desire-image that has not yet been realized. His philosophical system is entirely based on the category of the Not-Yet-Being and not on the rational legitimation of some actually existing state.

Furthermore, it seems to us that Bloch supported Stalin's USSR despite his revolutionary Romanticism and not because of it. In fact, a profound contradiction opposes his nostalgic sensibility and his suspicion of industrial modernity—not to mention his esoteric preoccupations and his atheist mysticism—to the ruthless bureaucratic productivism, the cult of heavy industry, and the vulgar materialism that characterize both the practice and the ideology of the Soviet regime.

Ernst Bloch's influence is closely bound up with the Romantic tonality of his philosophy of hope. In addition to his impact on contemporary philosophers such as Laura Boella, Renate Damus, Helmut Fahrenbach, Hans-Heinz Holz, Fredric Jameson, Heinz Kimmerle, Thomas Leithäuser, Arno Münster, Oskar Negt, Uwe Opolka, Jean-Michel Palmier, Gérard Raulet, Burghart Schmidt, and a number of others, Bloch fascinated many Catholic and Protestant theologians, partisans of a theology of hope that was explicitly inspired by Bloch: Jürgen Moltmann, Johannes Jetz, Hellmut Gollwitzer, Harvey Cox, and others. He also had considerable influence on the student movement of the 1960s, whose principal ideologue in Germany, Rudi Dutschke, considered himself a disciple. His influence is even felt, in a more diffuse manner, in the alternative and ecological movements of the 1980s.

Finally, Bloch was probably the twentieth-century Marxist thinker who most directly inspired the liberation theology of Latin America, especially through the work of Gustavo Gutierrez. One can view this theology as the heir both of Charles Péguy's Christian socialism (by way of Emmanuel Mounier's personalism) and of Ernst Bloch's atheist-religious Marxism.

ROMANTICISM AS A FEMINIST VISION:

THE QUEST OF CHRISTA WOLF

Few modern authors have given such powerful expression to the "elective affinity" between Romanticism and feminism as Christa Wolf.[83] When we refer to her as a Romantic writer, we take into account not only her explicit interest in the German Romantic tradition of the early nineteenth century, but also — and above all — her own Romantic worldview. In terms of our conceptualization of the latter, the importance and the specificity of the case of Christa Wolf lies in the fact that alone among the authors we have treated in detail she lived for most of her adult life not in the capitalist West but in a "noncapitalist" country — postwar East Germany. Although she was a child during the Nazi period, from adolescence at the end of the war up to the disappearance of East Germany as a separate entity, Christa Wolf lived in the environment of "actually existing socialism."

In the introductory section to this chapter,[84] we suggested that a certain number of writers and movements from within this world have manifested a Romantic worldview in the full sense. Although they can be distinguished from their Western counterparts by a preoccupation with problems specific to their societies — particularly totalitarian state control — they articulate the same basic cultural criticism of capitalist-industrial-technological modernity, in the name of qualitative and premodern values. On the other hand, in spite of certain themes they share with other internal critics of Soviet-style "socialism," their Romantic sensibilities differentiate them from the latter, leading them notably to refuse to see the capitalist West with its market economy as a panacea. We believe this to be perfectly illustrated in the case of Christa Wolf, a writer whose Romanticism belongs to the utopian-revolutionary current, reinterpreted in feminist terms.

Romanticism and feminism have not always been associated in the same intellectual configurations. Many Romantic authors, such as Pierre-Joseph Proudhon, John Ruskin, and others, actively opposed feminism and women's emancipation, harking back to a patriarchal past in order to celebrate traditional feminine roles. Nonetheless, the egalitarian and modernist approach of liberalism and even utilitarianism has attracted feminists, especially as some of its exponents, John Stuart Mill, for example, clearly supported the struggle for women's rights. However, since Romanticism's incipience, there has also existed a "philogynic" Romanticism, represented in the thought of Charles Fourier. In addition, certain female writers, such as Elizabeth Barrett Browning, George Sand, and the Brontë sisters, were simultaneously concerned with the emancipation of women and attracted by Romanticism. Christa Wolf belongs to this last tradition, although her style of thought and writing has little in common with the great female novelists of the nineteenth century.

In spite of its diversity and its undeniable evolution, Wolf's work as a whole can be characterized by this double perspective: feminism together with Romanticism in its utopian-revolutionary dimension, which in Wolf's case assumes the form of a Marxist humanism. Viewed chronologically, her literary career, begun in 1960 and producing various forms of expression — novels, short stories, autobiographical sketches, essays, interviews, and other works that resist traditional classification — exhibits certain significant changes in form and content. In regard to Wolf's feminist and Marxist-humanist vision and frame of reference, Anna Kuhn, the author of the first full-length study of Wolf's work to appear in English, has pointed to an evolution both "from Marxism to feminism" and "from the Enlightenment to Romanticism."[85]

While Kuhn's study of Wolf's developing career through detailed analyses of her works is a fine, illuminating one, Kuhn's formulations seem to suggest an either/or dichotomy in which feminism and Romanticism replace Marxism and Enlightenment. In contrast to Kuhn, we would stress an underlying continuity to Wolf's work — one to which Kuhn is, in fact, often attuned — and argue for an increasing consciousness and elaboration of Romantic and feminist problematics that were present in Wolf's writing from the start. The maturation of Wolf's feminist and Romantic awareness has not canceled her Marxist-Enlightenment perspectives; rather, these perspectives have been reinterpreted and integrated into a context in which the emphasis has shifted.

In one of the lectures connected with her novel *Cassandra* (1983), Wolf compares her recent exposure to feminism with her earlier initiation to Marxism:

With the widening of my visual angle and the readjustment to my depth of focus, my viewing lens . . . has undergone a decisive change. It is comparable to that decisive change that occurred more than thirty years ago, when I first became acquainted with Marxist theory and attitudes; a liberating and illuminating experience which altered my thinking, my view, what I felt about and demanded of myself.[86]

In no way in this passage does Wolf affirm that feminism supplants Marxism. Wolf significantly uses a camera metaphor to express her second, feminist awareness as a widening and deepening of focus rather than as a substitution of one lens for another. Moreover, in response to criticism from the same period (1983) that she was making an anti-Enlightenment retreat into Romanticism, Wolf denied that either she or the historical movements of early Romanticism and Sturm und Drang were anti-Enlightenment, calling such a claim a "very undialectical view."[87]

Yet, Wolf's early work was never that of a pure partisan of the Enlightenment (*Aufklärer*) and had always possessed a strong undercurrent of Romanticism. Her contact with historical Romantic trends — at least in the form of Sturm und Drang — dates back to her student years (the late 1940s and early 1950s). During this time, Wolf was able to read and use the Sturm und Drang writers — especially the young Goethe — who were considered politically progressive as a model; only much later did she assimilate the early-nineteenth-century German Romantics.[88]

Also during her student years at the University of Leipzig, she first came under the influence of two heterodox Marxists — Hans Mayer and Ernst Bloch — who were teaching there and who could be characterized as utopian-revolutionary Romantics. In a 1987 address to Hans Mayer, Wolf traced her relationship with him, starting with her studies under his direction and continuing through the publication of his *Outsiders* (*Aussenseiter*) in 1975, which she greatly admires.[89] In this address she claims that, like Mayer, she was drawn to the Communist movement by a "longing" (*Sehnsucht*) to belong to a "community" (gemeinschaft).[90] The impact of Bloch's philosophy on Wolf's writing has been amply documented, most notably by Jack Zipes and Andreas Huyssen. In particular, they discuss Bloch's linked concepts of "homeland" (*Heimat*) and the not-yet-attained "upright posture" (*aufrechter Gang*) of humanity, which together form a quintessentially utopian-Romantic configuration, as constituting an integral part of Christa Wolf's worldview as well.[91]

Drawing on the Romantic tradition in both its early and late stages, then, Wolf develops her own vision through a process of feminist reappropriation and reinterpretation. In what follows we explore the chronology of this intertwined elaboration of utopian-revolutionary Romanticism and feminism.

In Wolf's first published piece of creative writing—"Tuesday, September 27" (1960)—it is striking that one already finds indications of both a feminist and a Romantic sensibility. In this submission to a literary contest, proposed by the Soviet newspaper *Isvestia* on the subject "Your day of 27 September, 1960," the narrator pointedly comments that at a meeting of the Party management at the factory where she works, someone brings up the idea of inviting women to an important brigade meeting simply because that is "the trend of the times. Nobody can publicly argue against this; however, it becomes clear that the suggestion has no fiery advocates. Don't the women have enough to do with the children . . . ? says one of them."[92] At the end of the piece, the narrator speaks of the difficulty of writing a longer text (clearly what will later become *Divided Heaven*), because she is unable to animate the banality of the factory life that is her subject. This oppressive banality of her everyday reality stands in stark contrast with her lucid dream just before she falls asleep, evoked in the closing paragraph:

> A street appears leading to that landscape I know so well without ever having seen it: the hill with the old tree, the softly inclined slope up to a stream, meadowland, and the forest at the horizon. That one can't really experience the seconds before falling asleep—otherwise one wouldn't fall asleep—I will forever regret.[93]

This yearning for a communion with nature—this utopian vision of integration with the natural world—will echo throughout Wolf's later work.

Her first book, *Moskauer Novelle* (*Moscow Novellas* [1961]), in fact celebrates the happy union of its heroine with that world and with a unified human community as well. Vera, an East German pediatrician, visits Soviet Russia with a delegation of her compatriots and has a relationship with Pawel, a Russian she had known earlier as a girl. She falls in love with the Russian countryside as well as with Pawel. The natural surroundings thus become identified with the people, seen as a lyrical whole: "This is life, thought Vera longingly [*sehnsüchtig*]. This sun and this land and these people."[94] When the delegation visits a *kolkhoz* they are welcomed and feted;

Vera feels entirely a part of what seems a joyous community, just as she is more durably linked to the other members of her delegation by strong bonds of friendship. Unlike "Tuesday, September 27," *Moskauer Novelle* does not problematize the reality of actually existing socialism; in many ways, Wolf's first novel glorifies it as the ground for the realization of Romantic aspiration.

Yet the picture given us in the novel is not quite so simple. In a central passage the characters discuss the qualities they imagine the socialist human being of the future will exhibit. Pawel asserts, in Blochian language, that humankind finally "will walk upright [*aufrecht*] over the earth"; he adds that the most important characteristic of the new human being will be "brotherliness" (*Brüderlichkeit*).[95] Human relations will not be competitive and mistrustful. This picture of a future of open and affectionate communication implicitly suggests a contrast with the present; in *Moskauer Novelle* liberation remains utopian, or in Blochian terms, the not-yet-attained.[96] The love affair between Vera and Pawel exhibits the main traits of this utopia but only as a fugitive premonition (*Vorschein*); it marks a caesura in their normal lives, about which we know little and to which they voluntarily return at the end.

With *Divided Heaven* (*Der geteilte Himmel* [1963]), separated from *Moskauer Novelle* by the erection of the Wall, the tone becomes more openly critical; now the center of attention becomes normal life in actually existing socialism. The appreciation of a life close to nature in the previous novel turns here to an unhappy consciousness of the alienation of city life and of the incursions of polluting industry even into the countryside. The heroine Rita, coming from a small village with "just the right amount of woods, meadows, fields and open sky," which she loves, is assailed by loneliness when she moves to the town, and by the ugliness of industrial sights and smells both in and out of town (*DH*, p. 11).

Divided Heaven is ultimately ambiguous in its depiction of East German society in relation both to Romantic longing and to its feminist project. On the one hand, an opposition is set up between the workers and the bourgeois professorial milieu. The workers show devotion and idealistic selflessness in the herculean effort to build a new society — Meternagel is compared to "a hero in some old legend, set out upon a seemingly hopeless task" — whereas the professors are petty, egotistical, and opportunistic (*DH*, p. 75). The workers are in principle egalitarian with regard to the sexes — Rita is impressed by the equal division of housework by the Schwarzenbach couple — while the wives of the professors are dominated objects. The professors are identified with the capitalist West, to which Rita refuses to immigrate because it represents greed, a total lack of community, ideal, or hope, as well as alienation from nature. Significantly, she sees the dreary, run-down little garden in West Berlin, in which she says goodbye to Manfred, as a symbol of the West (*DH,* p. 195).

On the other hand, there is an unmistakable undercurrent of doubt as to whether East Germany constitutes a true alternative to its western counterpart. In addition to the pollution that threatens the environment, the productivist, technocratic mentality taken from the West predominates: after all, it is solely to increase industrial production that the workers sacrifice themselves. Manfred's point of view — that what people really want is "a house that runs like a well oiled machine" — is hegemonic; he only immigrates to the West because there they do the same thing, only better (*DH,* p. 106). Even Schwarzenbach admits at the end of the novel that "sometimes we think we're changing something when all we're doing is giving it a different name" (*DH,* p. 203). The conclusion also questions male-female relations among workers, when Rita visits Meternagel's wife and discovers the cost to her of his monomaniacal devotion to stepping up productivity (*DH,* pp. 216–17).[97] Although *Divided Heaven* thus does take a step further than its predecessor in critically analyzing actually existing socialism, it remains at least partially within the framework of the socialist-realist bildungsroman, with a matured Rita returning to play her part in socialist construction at the end.

Wolf's Romantic and feminist critique makes another crucial leap in her next novel, *The Quest for Christa T.* (*Nachdenken über Christa T.* [1968]), in which for the first time the heroine is an "outsider" (as they will be in following novels), a misfit who is unable to integrate herself into her society yet who is shown to be the incarnation of values that could help that society to become what it should be.[98] Christa T. manifests many characteristically Romantic traits, some of which had already appeared in earlier heroines, including, but not limited to, a love of nature, an attraction to simple peasants, and an empathy with children that comes from being in touch with the child in oneself. Some traits — in particular, the urge for self-expression and self-exploration and an openness of the self to experience — are carried much further in Christa T. than in earlier heroines. But with her emerge several new areas: fantasy, art, and the transforming power of the imagination. The new interest in the free play of the imagination had in fact already been signaled in "A June Afternoon" ("*Juninachmittag*" [1965]), notably when the narrator's family engages in a word game, similar to those of the surrealists, in which they recombine the elements of fixed, stereotyped expressions to produce marvelous, suggestive absurdities. When applied to political terminology and clichés, the game turns briefly into political satire.[99]

In Christa T., the imagination involves a double movement: a nostalgic yearning on the one hand and the opening up of possibilities on the other. She chooses to study Theodor Storm because his work is a lyrical "landscape of longing" (*QCT,* p. 97); near the end of her life she herself writes sketches of the traditional peasant communities around her new home (*QCT,* p. 171). Yet she refuses to accept limitations and gives herself up to limitless dreaming of what could and should be — an activity that Bloch calls future oriented: dreaming "forward" (*nach Vorwärts*) (*QCT,* p. 114). The imagination has a moral dimension for her as well. Such an orientation imbues her life and her Romantic sensibility — overtly nonpolitical, although Christa T. is committed to socialism and eschews the capitalist West — with political import. She is a living reproach to East German society, since she incarnates the impulse toward human liberation that it claims to be building, while she is incapable of living in that society as it really is.

A number of critics have pointed out that Christa T.'s consciousness also has a feminist dimension. In particular, Myra Love remarkably demonstrates how, although Wolf does not use the term "patriarchal" until ten years after the publication of *The Quest for Christa T.,* both the character Christa T. and the narrator break down a whole set of either/or, mutually exclusive oppositions that have marked patriarchal culture, through the process by which the narrator re-creates Christa T. and changes herself in so doing. Love also notes the utopian potential of Christa T.'s feminine consciousness: "By appropriating the sort of subjectivity which Christa T. embodies, the narrator is also appropriating, by a process of solidarity, the utopian potential of a historically female subjectivity."[100] Love's article elucidates striking similarities between Christa Wolf's novel and the work of several Western feminists, in particular Adrienne Rich and Mary Daly. Inta Ezergailis does the same in a book studying Ingeborg Bachmann, Doris

Lessing, and others.[101] In addition, Ezergailis's book makes clear the elective affinity between feminism and Romanticism; for although it does not use the term, it reveals the archetypal Romantic configuration in the authors studied: a sense of loss and the yearning to re-create a paradise.

It is difficult to know the extent to which Christa Wolf reacted to the Romantic dimension of the European events of 1968; in any case, in that year she wrote her essay "The Reader and the Writer," which contains one of the most beautiful formulations of the Romantic-utopian ethos: "We have preserved a memory of past ages [*Vor-Zeiten*] which afforded people a simple and serene way of living. This memory shapes our image of what we want for our future [*Sehnsuchtbild von der Zukunft*]."[102] One could hardly imagine a more striking summary of the Romantic dialectical bond between the past and the future, nostalgia and utopia.

The Soviet invasion of Czechoslovakia and the rather intolerant internal climate in the GDR—Wolf's *The Quest for Christa T.* had been condemned by the Party leadership at the sixth conference of writers in the GDR (May 1969)—created the historical context for a new stage in her intellectual and literary evolution, characterized by a sharp critical stand and a growing interest in the German Romantic tradition. Other GDR writers shared similar concerns. In fact, Wolf's ideas were part of a larger constellation, which included works of other well-known GDR writers like Heiner Müller, Volker Braun, and Christoph Hein. During the 1970s and 1980s, each in his or her own way developed a criticism of reification and alienation that was clearly inspired by the Romantic protest against modern *Zivilisation* (and to a certain extent by the Frankfurt School's critique of instrumental reason). They all seemed to consider that the limitations or failures of East German socialism were the result of an insufficiently radical break with Western civilization. And their apocalyptic vision of history gave back to utopia its full force. Confronted by a Western civilization doomed by the curse of its instrumental destruction, the jump into the "otherwise" becomes a question of survival for the human species.[103]

Christa Wolf's own version of this pattern is subtly colored by Romantic irony and feminist subversion. One of the first writings of this new stage, the short story "The New Life and Opinions of a Tomcat" ("Neue Lebensansichten eines Katers") written in 1970, inspired by E. T. A. Hoffmann's ironic masterpiece "The Life and Opinions of Kater Murr" ("Lebensansichten des Katers Murr"), quoted in the epigraph of Wolf's story—provides a biting satire of techno-bureaucratic, scientific ideology.[104] Max, the tomcat who tells the story, enthusiastically shares the views of his master, Prof. R. W. Barzel, and those of his associates, Dr. Lutz Fettback (a transparent reference to cybernetic feedback), a dietician and physiotherapist, and Dr. Guido Hinz, a cybernetic sociologist. Their aim is grandiose: nothing less than TOHUHA (Total Human Happiness)! Unfortunately, the present human species has not achieved the maturity to understand its needs and has to be forced to become happy. This will happen, thanks to the obligatory introduction of a strictly scientific and error-proof system called SYMAHE (System of Maximum Health of Body and Soul).

How is SYMAHE to be implemented? According to the three illustrious scholars, all that is needed is the elimination of some superfluous and useless aspects of human life, the soul (*Seele*) for instance, a reactionary illusion that serves only to assure a profitable existence for such unproductive economic branches as literature (*Belletristik*) (*NLT*, p. 124). The same applies to other anachronistic and prescientific ideas or values such as "creative thinking," "audacity," "altruism," "pity," and "pride." The result of this process of purification will be the normalized or "standard human being" (*Normalmensch*), a purely reflexive being that answers in a precisely predictable way to stimuli (*NLT*, p. 149).

In other words, the aim is an exhaustive programmation of that span of time signified by the antiquated word "life." Until now humanity has had an irrational and mystical attitude toward this time span, leading to disorder, squandered time, and wasted strength. Now, thanks to SYMAHE, we have a logically unavoidable system of rational life conduct, applying the most modern technique of calculation (*NLT*, pp. 136–37).

Women do not seem to share the faith of the three male scientists — and of their feline follower, the tomcat Max — on the virtues of SYMAHE. In general, as Prof. Barzel sadly acknowledges, they seem to resist stubbornly the most advanced experimental methods of science. Isa, the young daughter of the professor, sharply formulates feminine feelings by calling her father an "anti-progress philistine" (*Fortschrittsspiesser*) (*NLT*, p. 142).

By ridiculing this kind of scientific project, Christa Wolf not only pokes fun at the positivist ideology of the ruling elites both East and West but also draws attention to the dangers of technological dehumanization and authoritarian standardization resulting from a certain form of instrumental rationality. Like E. T. A. Hoffmann's Murr, Christa Wolf's tomcat Max is an ironic device to unmask the philistine attempt to eliminate human imagination and human feelings in the name of reason.

"The New Life and Opinions of a Tomcat" is one of three stories published under the subtitle Three Improbable Tales (*Drei unwahrscheinliche Geschichten*). In a conversation with Hans Kaufmann, Christa Wolf offers some important insights into her intentions:

> I wrote the three stories between 1969 and 1972, and they are representative of that phase of my work. . . . I hope that their "improbability," their dreamlike, utopian, and grotesque character will produce an alienation-effect towards certain processes, circumstances, and modes of thought which have become so very familiar that we no longer notice them, are no longer disturbed by them. And yet we should be disturbed by them — and I say this in the confident belief that we can change what disturbs us.[105]

The third "improbable" tale is also a critique of scientism, but this time gender is the key issue. "Self-Experiment" ("Selbstversuch"), her first work with an explicitly feminist and antipatriarchal ethos, supposedly takes place in the near future (the year is 1992!), when scientific progress will permit the transformation of women into men, thanks to a new drug: "Peterine Masculinum 199."[106] The story assumes the form of a letter, written to the professor leading the project by one of the female scientists participating in the research team, who agreed to experiment with the drug on herself. The letter is both a description of her feelings and reactions during the experience and a more general reflection on gender relations. As a man, she (or rather, he) has a love affair with the professor's daughter; but after a few weeks, a feeling of the "barbaric senselessness" of the experiment leads him/her to interrupt it and return to the female condition.

She now understands much better that the professor and his male assistants share a "superstitious worship of measurable results"; they are caught fast in their "net of numbers, diagrams, and calculations" (SE, p. 113). Believing in scientific neutrality, they try to remain always dispassionate, unattached, and impersonal; according to the narrator, the secret of their invulnerability is indifference (SE, p. 128). In their eyes, problem-burdened women, who hesitate between happiness in love and the urge to work, are like a "falsely programmed computerized mouse" "zigzagging" from one side to the other (SE, p. 120). And they don't understand "what fiendish spirit possessed me to break off the successful experiment prematurely" (SE, p. 113).

Back in her female form, the narrator opposes "the words of my inner language" to the unreal neutrality of "scientific" speech (SE, p. 113). She refuses the attitude of noninvolvement and impassivity of the male scientists and criticizes their way of life.

> Unknowingly, and without wishing it, I did indeed act as a spy in the adversary's home territory and so discovered the thing that must remain your secret if your convenient privileges are to remain inviolate: that the activity you immerse yourselves in cannot bring you happiness, and that we have a right to resist when you try to drag us into them. (SE, p. 128)

At the same time she rejects the dangerous division of labor which "gives women the rights to sorrow, hysteria, and the vast majority of neuroses while granting them the pleasure of dealing with outpourings of the soul (which no one has yet found under a microscope)" and with the fine arts, while men devote themselves to the realities: business, science, and world politics (SE, p. 128).

This improbable tale shares a key element with "The New Life and Opinions of a Tomcat": the Romantic protest against the tyrannical domination of the quantifying, calculating, cold, and impersonal form of modern scientific and technical rationality. As Christa Wolf stressed in a remark about "Self-Experiment," the story questions "certain types of positivist thought that barricade themselves behind so-called natural scientific method and ignore the human aspects."[107] However, its tone is radically distinct from the previous tale. It is not ironical or satirical but betrays unease and even bitterness. And the essential point is not the absurdity of the plans for scientific management of the soul but the intimate link between this positivist ideology and patriarchal hierarchy.

"Self-Experiment" also contributes to the continuing feminist debate on the choice of equality or difference as the main vector of women's liberation. The heroine of the experiment does not deny the need for equality, but she criticizes the assimilationist tendency of emancipated women, that is, their imitation of masculine patterns of behavior. In the above-mentioned conversations with Hans Kaufmann, Christa Wolf offers some highly personal comments on this issue:

The kind of questions I attempted to provoke through my story might be: should the aim of women's emancipation be for them to "become like men?" . . . As the material conditions allowing the sexes an equal start improve—and this must necessarily be the first step towards emancipation—so we face more acutely the problem of giving the sexes opportunity to be different from each other, to acknowledge that they have different needs, and that men and women, not just men, are the models for human beings. This does not even occur to most men, and really very few women attempt to get to the root of why it is that their consciences are permanently troubled (because they can't do what is expected of them). If they got to the bottom of it, they'd find it was their own identification with an idealized masculinity that is in itself obsolete.[108]

In their introduction to the first English translation of "Self-Experiment," Helen Fehervary and Sara Lennox highlight the tale's feminist dimension and Wolf's reinterpretation of Marxism through women's experiences:

From women's lives, Wolf derives an entirely new potential of experience and knowledge. . . . What has been attributed to Wolf in all her works as her "critical," "human," or "utopian" Marxism is her female perception of history; and the utopian "traces" and "hopes" which Bloch talks about in his theoretical works take on an indelibly material character in the reality of women mediated by Wolf. And this, indeed, is the very radicalism of Wolf's work, not as an alternative to Marxism but as a qualitatively new and autonomous dimension that is a prerequisite for its renewal.[109]

One must add, however, that the values that inspire her Marxist-feminist utopia and her rejection of positivist-patriarchal ways of life are deeply rooted in the Romantic tradition of *Zivilisationskritik*. This connection, already suggested in her earlier writings, will become central in her next works: *No Place on Earth* (*Kein Ort: Nirgends* [1997]) and the corresponding essays on Karoline von Günderrode and Bettina von Arnim.[110]

No Place on Earth is one of the most interesting expressions in the literature of the second half of the twentieth century of the subterranean continuity between the *Frühromantik* circa 1800 and the Romanticism of our times—a continuity that does not exclude, of course, very significant differences. Despite the numerous quotations from Heinrich von Kleist and his friends that appear in the dialogues, the novel is an entirely modernist one in style, content, and meaning.

Why did an East German writer of the 1970s feel the urge to write a novel about an imaginary meeting between Kleist and Karoline von Günderrode? Christa Wolf's choice should be placed in the specific cultural and political context of the GDR at that particular time. For many years the reception of Romanticism in the GDR was dominated by György Lukács's aesthetics of realism, which rejected the Romantic tradition in general and Kleist's works in particular, as subjectivist, irrationalist, and reactionary. As early as 1937, Anna Seghers had already challenged this view in her (published) correspondence with Lukács, but her standpoint was marginal in relation to the established doctrine. Only during the seventies did there begin to be a reassessment of Romanticism by East German writers and literary historians, which can be seen as part of a general tendency toward cultural criticism of the official ideology.[111] Christa Wolf's novels and essays are related to this movement, but by focusing on Romantic women writers virtually ignored by the German literary canon — such as Karoline von Günderrode or Bettina von Arnim — and their conflict with patriarchal norms, Wolf strikes a new note and creates her own, singular, and unique literary universe.

But there is also another, directly political background for her personal interest in the Romantics: the situation created by the expulsion of the dissident poet and singer Wolf Biermann from the GDR. In reaction to this arbitrary measure in November 1976, a group of concerned writers and intellectuals, including Stephan Hermlin, Christa Wolf, Gerhard Wolf (her husband), and Sara Kirsch, sent an open letter of protest to the official Party newspaper and the French news agency, urging the authorities to reconsider their action. In reprisal for this first public, collective protest, Christa Wolf and other well-known writers were expelled from the board of directors of the Berlin branch of the Writers' Union. The vice-minister of culture, Klaus Höpcke, referred to the signers of the petition as "enemies of socialism." A few months later Gerhard Wolf was excluded from the Party.

For Christa Wolf these events were a crucial turning point in her relation to the GDR power structure — soon afterward she suffered a heart attack, perhaps signaling her deep personal investment in this crisis as well. From that moment on, she felt herself to be an outsider — much as the Romantic writers perceived their relation to society. In a conversation with Frauke Meyer-Gosau some years later, Wolf tried to link her personal experience to some general patterns of modern civilization:

> What most interested me was to investigate when this dreadful split between individuals and society had really begun. . . . In industrial society . . . neither women nor intellectuals have any influence on the key processes determining our lives. It was the severity of this transformation into an outsider, which I felt within my own self existentially, that I wanted to examine. . . . Where and when did it begin? In the writings and lives of the Romantics you find an abundance of documentation on this; they perceived with some sensitivity that they were outsiders, that they were not needed in a society which was in the process of becoming industrial society, of intensifying the division of labor, of turning people into appendages of machines. . . . The fact that we really can detect similarities here to our own reactions . . . prompted me to take this so-called step into the past.[112]

In other words, the early Romantics — particularly the women among them — had already discovered, thanks to their remarkable sensitivity, some of the negative aspects of modern industrial society, as it was beginning to crystallize in the early nineteenth century. By revisiting their writings, one can find the roots of present problems, both in the East and the West. According to Christa Wolf in the same interview, there are some basic human needs that are not satisfied by the social and economic systems of the two German states:

> I mean the need for . . . poetry in one's life. For everything that can't simply be counted or measured, or put in statistical terms. And here literature has its role as a means of self-assertion. . . . And here we're back on the path that takes us straight to Romanticism again. . . .[113]

Christa Wolf's novels and essays of the late seventies are Romantic not only because their subject matter is the life of poets and writers of 1804 but also because they give literary expression to a deep elective affinity with the dilemmas, values, and desperate hopes of the early Romantics. At the same time, her specific interest in women writers and poets reflects her increasing concern with gender issues and patriarchal structures.[114]

Let us now attempt a closer examination of *No Place on Earth*. The structure of the novel is somewhat static: it describes an imaginary meeting in 1804 between Heinrich von Kleist and Karoline von Günderrode (who would soon commit suicide), at the house of Merten, a merchant, in Winkel on the Rhine. Among the other guests are the poet Clemens Brentano; the philosopher of law Karl von Savigny, who is married to Clemens's sister, Gunda; the physician Franz Wedekind; and the scientist Christian Nees von Esenbeck. Günderrode previously had an emotional attachment to Savigny but is now trying to liberate herself from this bond. During the afternoon, she and Kleist are drawn to each other by a common feeling of dissatisfaction with the shallow conversation of the tea room. They leave together for a short walk, during which they reveal to each other their innermost feelings, ideas, and doubts. They soon separate, and Kleist returns to Mainz. The first part of the novel is mainly composed of Kleist's and Günderrode's interior monologues, while only in the last part does an authentic dialogue take place between them.

The two poetic and tragic figures stand in stark contrast to the others. Joseph Merten, a "wholesale dealer in foodstuffs and perfume" and a patron of the arts and sciences, is the ideal bourgeois philistine (*NPE*, p. 40). He cannot understand why works of poetry should not be written with the same order and transparency as his own accounting books — "why should not the rules which have proved their worth in one discipline also be valid in another" (*NPE*, p. 77). Ness von Esenbeck is the classic "scientific philistine" who rejects the hypochondriacal lamentations of the literary gentlemen in the name of "the spirit of the age" and "scientific progress" (*NPE*, p. 79). His only wish would be to live two hundred years later, in the paradisiacal condition humanity will then enjoy, thanks to the development of science. Finally, Savigny, the founder of the archconservative Historical School of Law, represents the philistine intellectual who insists on the neat separation of the realm of thought from the realm of action and who categorically refuses to measure life by an ideal.

Against this gray and conformist background, Kleist's figure stands out as the embodiment of a higher spiritual imperative. In spite of his vacillating political loyalty between Napoleon and Prussia, Kleist believes in certain values that he is not willing to compromise. When Merten suggests that he make a living out of his literary production, he answers with "unexpected vehemence" that he refuses to "write books for money" (*NPE*, p. 63). He explains to Savigny that he cannot accept the established views on what is honorable and what is contemptible: "I bear an inner precept inscribed in my heart, compared to which all external maxims, where they sanctioned by a king himself, are of no value whatever" (*NPE*, p. 67). And in a debate with Esenbeck, he sharply criticizes the "unilateral, cyclopean" approach of the scientific disciplines, while praising the human thirst for knowledge and enlightenment: "without enlightenment [the human being] is not much more than an animal" (*NPE*, p. 80). However, like most of the Romantics, he believes that science has been perverted in modern society: "as soon as we set foot in the realm of knowledge, an evil magic appears to turn against us whatever application we make of our knowledge" (*NPE*, p. 80).

Kleist's state of mind is one of desperation. Deeply disappointed by his experiences in France and Prussia, he does not believe that he can find a place on earth that would fit him: "Unlivable life. No place on earth" (*NPE*, p. 108). It is in fact not so much a question of place as of time: it is the zeitgeist that makes life so miserable. And here is the point where he intuitively feels that Karoline von Günderrode shares his feelings. While people like Merten "praise the virtues of the new age as opposed to the old . . . I, Günderrode, I and you as well, I think, are suffering from the evils of the new age" (*NPE*, p. 85).

Christa Wolf's Günderrode possesses a rebellious mind. When she wants to break loose from her bonds of dependence on Savigny, he complains of her "republican attitudes" (which he defines as "a little hangover from the French Revolution" and her "exaggerated inclination to autonomy" (*outrierte Selbständigkeit*) (*NPE*, pp. 48, 58). But she clings with all her forces to this proud autonomy, whose terrible limit is the dagger she carries always with her, in order to be ready at any moment to put an end to her life. In one of her poems, published under the male pseudonym "Tian," she rejects as disloyal those (such as Savigny) who with "cold consciousness" (*kaltes Bewußtsein*) "judge," "calculate," and "measure" things of love (*NPE*, p. 75). Unlike those artists who seek only glory and success, she writes poetry from an inner need, a burning and nostalgic desire (sehnsucht) to express her life in a permanent form (*NPE*, p. 31).

While the other men at the tea party (Clemens Brentano, Savigny) treat her as an object, a sort of "private property," she finds in conversation with Kleist the possibility of a meaningful human (not necessarily erotic) exchange.[115] Beyond the barriers of reified gender identity and gender hierarchy, two human beings meet and disclose to each other their highest feelings and ideas. The following dialogue is characteristic of their shared Romantic and utopian striving:

> Kleist: Often I think: What if the primal, ideal state created by nature, which we were compelled to destroy, could never lead to that second ideal state we envisage, via that organization which we have created for ourselves?
>
> Günderrode: If we cease to hope, then that which we fear will surely come. (*NPE*, p. 117)[116]

It is difficult not to hear in this last phrase an echo of Bloch's philosophy of hope. Although many of the dialogues in *No Place on Earth* are more or less literal quotations from the writings and correspondence of the historical figures, Wolf has of course selected and reinterpreted this material, in the light of her own critical and feminist sensibility.

At the same time as she was writing the novel, Wolf prepared a collection of Karoline von Günderrode's writings (poems, prose, letters), which Wolf published in the same year (1979) with the title (taken from one of Günderrode's letters) "The Shadow of a Dream" (*Der Schatten eines Traumes*).[117] This text reveals the reasons for Christa Wolf's keen interest in early German Romanticism and the topicality of this cultural universe for the problems of the contemporary world.

First of all, Wolf emphasizes the strong antibourgeois character of the movement. The Romantics of 1800 were a small group of intellectuals — a vanguard "with no backup force (as happened so often in German history from the Peasants' War onward)"[118] — that fought a lost war against the narrow-minded spirit of the German bourgeoisie — an underdeveloped class that took from the bourgeois catechism only one commandment: "Get rich!" and whose only moral interest was "to harmonize the boundless instinct for profit with the Lutheran-Calvinist virtues of industry, thrift, and discipline" (*SD*, p. 133). They were a generation that rebelled against the arid rationalism of those times (not unlike the vulgar materialism of ours) — an "insipid dogmatism" (*Plattheit*) that pretended to explain everything but did not understand anything — against icy abstraction and the irresistible consolidation of destructive structures, against "ruthless utilitarian thinking" (*erbarmungsloses Zweckmäßiskeitsdenken*) (*SD*, p. 136). In one word, against all aspects of modernity that lead to fear, depression, and self-destruction (*SD*, pp. 133–36).

She quotes a philosophical poem by Karoline von Günderrode as a testimony to the reaction of this Romantic generation, "which had seen the great intellectual venture of the German Enlightenment reduced to pragmatic sophistry" (*SD*, p. 136), into the flat and colorless world-image of these times:

> The heaven has crashed, the pit has been filled in,
> And paved with reason, the road's easy on the shoes (*SD*,
> p. 136).

Equally opposed to narrow-minded feudalism and to "the dreary acquisitiveness" (*tristen Erwerbsgeist*) (*SD*, p. 139) of the new times, Günderrode longs for a lost paradise: "This age seems shallow and empty to me, a yearning sorrow tugs me with violence into the past" (*SD*, p. 147). As a Romantic woman poet, she is doomed to become an outsider; and in her complex relationship with three men (Clemens Brentano, Karl von Savigny, and Friedrich Creuzer) she achieves nothing but, in her own words, "the shadow of a dream" (*SD*, p. 144). According to Wolf, one can find in her letters and poems the desperate hope that "the relations between man and woman could be governed by something other than dominance, subordination, jealousy, property — that is, by equality, friendship, mutual help" (*SD*, p. 146). Through her writings, she struggles to be an autonomous subject, but "the work to become an autonomous self went against the spirit of the times, which aimed for utility, profitableness, and the conversion of all relationships into barterable goods. It was as if objects and people had been placed under an evil spell" (*SD*, p. 147).

Reading the correspondence between Günderrode and her friends (Lisette Nees and Bettina von Arnim), Wolf comes to the conclusion that these young women, the first feminist intellectuals, "experienced the start of the industrial age, the idolatry of reason, and the increasing division of labor as a violation of their nature" (*SD*, p. 153). The signs they left can only now be again perceived, accepted, and understood. Not accidentally, it was precisely among women that the evils of the times were so uncompromisingly judged. Their economic marginality and the impossibility of their striving for a position, a public charge, liberated them from the need to "justify subservience" (*Untertanen-Ungeist*) (*SD*, p. 154). By a strange inversion, it was from a situation of total dependency that "completely free utopian views" grew (*SD*, p. 154), poetically conveyed in Karoline von Günderrode's dream: "A time must come when every being will be in harmony with himself and others" (*SD*, p. 174). Poetry, comments Wolf, has an affinity with the essence of utopia, because it has "a painful yet joyous yen for the absolute" (*SD*, p. 175).

Günderrode was rescued from oblivion by her friend Bettina von Arnim, who published a revised version of their correspondence in 1840. In a postface to the 1980 republication of this book, *Die Günderrode,* Christa Wolf wrote an essay on this other impressive woman writer, too often defined only by her relation to male figures (Clemens Brentano's sister, the friend of Goethe, or the wife of Achim von Arnim); Bettina von Arnim's works are among the few that keep alive the radicalism of early Romanticism during the first half of the nineteenth century. Because of her sympathy for the proletariat, von Arnim was accused of communism and her books were forbidden by the Prussian authorities: "The soulless, mechanistic approach which derived from the rest of industrial machinery and was then transferred into social relations and applied to man was a horror to Bettine."[119]

Commenting on their correspondence, Wolf is fascinated by the way the two Romantic women "philosophized in unison" over "a religion of joie de vivre, of sensory pleasure and human attitudes," radically opposed to the male cult of aggression (*YNL*, p. 211); their friendship was a utopian experiment, an attempt to give life to a different sort of reason and progress, a kind of Enlightenment thought opposed to the "onesidedness of instrumental and reified thinking" and to "the soulless, mechanistic attitudes of 'spirit-killing [*geisttötenden*] philosophy'" (*YNL*, p. 212). They both dreamed of an alternative to the exploitation of nature, the inversion of means and ends, and the repression of all feminine elements in the new civilization. Von Arnim's melancholic writings and Günderrode's suicide bear witness to this lost battle (*YNL*, pp. 211–12). These two essays constitute one of Christa Wolf's most illuminating and articulate attempts to uncover the common roots, the secret solidarity, and the intimate kinship between Romantic protest and feminist utopia.

With the publication of *Cassandra* in 1983, the whole process of maturation of the combined feminist and utopian Romantic worldview of Wolf culminates. For in this work, Wolf gives these two tendencies — which were present from the start and which had become increasingly prominent in the course of her development — their most conscious, explicit, and elaborated form. She intertwines them into equally important facets of a single, seamless vision. While in *No Place on Earth* Wolf had linked herself with an earlier Romantic tradition, in *Cassandra* she articulates the essential core of the utopian Romantic impulse: reaching to the past for inspiration in imagining a future that can transcend a degraded present. *Cassandra* most clearly manifests the overall structure of the Romantic vision. Here also Wolf's feminism, which had remained to a certain extent latent in earlier productions, comes to be overtly and forcefully expressed as one of the central focuses of the work.

Cassandra is a series of five lectures delivered by Wolf at the University of Frankfurt in 1982, the first four made up of accounts and reflections involving her recent travels in Greece and readings in ancient Greek culture, while the last piece takes the form of a short novel that reinterprets the Cassandra legend. The first four pieces were originally published separately as *Voraussetzungen einer Erzählung* (Conditions of a Narrative), but Wolf has made it clear that these and the novel "together form an aesthetic whole."[120]

In the preface to "Conditions" Wolf states that in *Cassandra,* her "overall concern is the sinister effects of alienation";[121] the preliminary lectures are indeed first and foremost a landscape of alienation, a bleak portrait of the "barbarism of the modern age" (*CNFE,* p. 159). Beginning with her unease in the antiseptic atmosphere of airports and airplane, a microcosm of society in which no one cares about anyone else, the travel account records her discovery of modern Greece, defaced by pollution (fast destroying remnants of the past, including the most sacred sites, like Eleusis) and architectural ugliness ("concrete cubes," indicating that the Greek sense of beauty has given way to the "dominion of effectiveness over all other values" (*CNFE,* p. 203). In Athens she finds an "overcrowded, hurrying, homicidal, money-chasing city that pumps out smoke and exhaust fumes, trying to catch up . . . [with more 'advanced' countries]," in which all that holds together the "city-monads" is "the hunt for the drachma" (*CNFE,* pp. 159–60). In her later reflections, Wolf develops her thoughts on modern civilization more generally, notably focusing on technology, the alienation of labor, and the ideology of scientism and bureaucracy (*CNFE,* p. 251). Within this civilization, she evokes particularly the "desperate plight" of women, who find themselves in a worse situation even than that of Cassandra, victim of an early stage of modern development (*CNFE,* p. 195).

Wolf notes the existence of a few pockets of life held over from the past—several gypsy women who carry "a circle of relatedness around with them"

(*CNFE*, p. 163) or the traditional Greek village she visits — but they represent no solution for her, since in them community and meaningful value also imply the total subservience of women. For her religious belief is impossible as well — modern skies are "mute and meaningless" (*CNFE*, p. 158) — as is "adventure," or rather all but "an adventure of the spirit" (*CNFE*, p. 199); it is this sort of adventure that Wolf engages in as she attempts the imaginative journey from modern Greece back to ancient times.

That journey into the past reveals that the Homeric period — the period of the Trojan war and the Cassandra legend that will be her theme — is already "late": that is, by then the first, crucial historical mutations have already taken place, on the road that will lead to modernity. Classical Greek civilization worships "false gods" similar to ours (*CNFE*, p. 237). In one passage Wolf asks where the "turning points" were and also whether they were inevitable (*CNFE*, p. 251); although she does not try to pinpoint the historical moments of transition, in this and several later passages she seeks to define the nature of these transitions. This attempt attests to the integral connection between feminism and Romanticism in Wolf's thought; she sees the historical process involving simultaneously the advent of patriarchy and of a group of characteristics that will later evolve into modern, capitalist civilization: private property (*CNFE*, p. 282); class hierarchy (*CNFE*, p. 296); and the early pursuit of economic efficiency and of "products, more and more products" (*CNFE*, p. 251). In psychological and ideological terms, this change was accompanied by the body-soul-mind split.

Before these disastrous turns were taken, there existed agricultural matriarchies that worshipped fertility and earth goddesses, in which magic was practiced by female elders or priestesses and in which a holistic interrelatedness of all aspects of life prevailed. This period, which Wolf suggests is at the very roots of humanity since it was then that the human race developed its specificity in relation to its animal ancestors, clearly exercises a great fascination on her (as does the later Minoan matriarchy that she also discusses).[122] Yet she painstakingly distinguishes her position from that of some radical feminists (represented in the text by the Americans, Sue and Helen), who make these originary cultures into idealized promised lands. Minoan society, she is aware, included feudal hierarchy and slavery; the primitive agricultural matriarchies were prerational and did not yet know individual selfhood. The fact that Wolf cannot accept such societies as a model and warns of the dangers of pure irrationality, illustrates the degree to which her Romantic perspective fully integrates Enlightenment thought within itself.

Her point of view, then, is ultimately oriented toward the future — toward the creation of a future that, while drawing on the past, would be fundamentally new, an *Aufhebung* of the past. Throughout the *Cassandra* lectures Wolf raises the question of this future, asking whether there is an alternative to the barbarism of modernity. She is assailed by doubts and sees a future transformation of life — a new Renaissance — as merely a possibility, one that the present situation makes difficult to believe in. Her only assurance is that this new future, if it were to come into being, would be at the same time a generalized human phenomenon (she decisively rejects feminist sectarianism or particularism) and one in which women would play a central role), through the contribution of positive aspects of historically constituted feminine consciousness. The last of the preliminary lectures ends by warning that the words of women, which "could have the power to cast spells," are threatened by the danger that women simply come to think like men, so that in spite of formal equality, men would continue to rule through the perpetuation of their mentality — the mentality of destructive modernity. This, claims Wolf, is "Cassandra's message today" (*CNFE,* p. 305).

The utopian-Romantic structure-of-feeling is articulated in fictional terms in the novella *Cassandra* — the dynamic of a present that is fallen in relation to the past and beyond which the possibility (but solely a possibility) of a different future remains open. The principal difference between the lectures and the novella in this respect is that, while the lectures do not identify any utopian enclave in contemporary reality, in her story Wolf is able to project a utopian vision within her imaginary Troy. This Troy — based on the one described in the *Iliad* — already has been corrupted by the vices of modernity and, in fact, can be read as an allegory of our own world.

Wolf refers to the past of this present as a Golden Age of "remotest antiquity" before there occurred a "chain of events ruinous to our city . . . under the sovereignty of a shifting succession of kings" (*CNFE,* p. 37). Thus patriarchy is well established in Troy at the time of the war, as well as in the camp of the enemy Greeks. Wolf's retelling of the Trojan war demystifies the patriarchal "hero," revealing his hypocrisy, cowardice, and brutality. She also criticizes the well-established mercantile mentality in

Troy and in Greece: in Cassandra's childhood memories she associates the "ascetic, clean odor of my father" with "the goods we traded or transported . . . the figures of our income and the debates about their expenditure" (*CNFE*, pp. 13–14). Troy at war (and even before the war per se) shows the marks of the police state; Eumelos heads this apparatus, engaging in quasi-Orwellian language manipulation and rewriting of history, as well as having Cassandra followed and then imprisoned.

Within this totally alienated society (or almost — there are some signs that the Trojans have not become quite so corrupt as the Greeks), there exists a utopian counterculture: the women who secretly worship Cybele, an ancient fertility goddess, on the slope of Mount Ida. This worship constitutes an atheistic religion, since at least the more sophisticated members of the group recognize that Cybele really stands for "the things in us that we do not dare to recognize" (*CNFE*, p. 124). A fully egalitarian society in which slave and servant women are as prized as the daughters of royal blood, a tightly knit community based on giving and sharing, and one whose activities bring into play the whole human being, this group refreshes Cassandra's waning faith in humanity, "by being different, by extracting from their nature qualities I hardly dared dream of" (*CNFE*, p. 79). Consisting mainly of women, this community is not exclusionary since it includes old Anchises, a carver of beautiful objects in wood, which he then gives away. Possibly the figure of Anchises obliquely alludes to Ernst Bloch, since he "never tired of maintaining that it was always possible" to do what their group was doing, that is, "to slip a narrow strip of future into the grim present . . ." and he "was teaching us younger ones how to dream with both feet on the ground" (*CNFE*, pp. 134–35).

The community of women thus becomes a Blochian vorschein, a glimmer in the present of what a liberated future might be. This group wonders about the human being of the future: "But more than anything else we talked about those who would come after us. What they would be like. . . . Whether they would repair our omissions, rectify our mistakes" (*CNFE*, p. 132). Whereas the group in *Moskauer Novelle* is affirmative about the future, the community of women in *Cassandra* is interrogative, reflecting Wolf's uncertainty about a future utopia. In *Cassandra*, at least, the future remains open and utopia a hope.

In the works following *Cassandra* — *Accident* (*Störfall* [1987]), *Sommerstück* (1989) and *What Remains* (*Was Bleibt* [1990]) — Wolf's pessimism deepens and hope seems to dwindle dangerously. The concluding chapter of Anna Kuhn's *Christa Wolf's Utopian Vision* addresses the pessimism in *Accident* and raises the question of whether the very basis of Wolf's vision has not crumbled under the pressure of the most recent developments. The subtitle of Kuhn's chapter is couched in the interrogative: "The Destruction of Utopia?" An examination of the totality of Wolf's last three books published to date illustrates that, despite a pessimistic tendency, Kuhn's question must ultimately be answered in the negative.

As Kuhn rightly points out, "the tension between hope and despair, so characteristic of Wolf's work since *No Place on Earth,* is the structuring principle of *Störfall,* "[123] In the face of the event that occasions that piece — the explosion of the nuclear reactor at Chernobyl — despair weighs heavier in the balance, without, however, entirely crushing hope. Wolf now sees the modern world, which brings itself to the brink of destruction with Chernobyl, as a system in which "everything fits together . . . : the desire of most people for a comfortable life, their tendency to believe the speakers on raised platforms and the men in white coats . . . seem to correspond to the arrogance and hunger for power, the dedication to profit, unscrupulous inquisitiveness, and self-infatuation of the few."[124] This system is seen as monstrous, with humankind having become a monster in relation to the natural order. The dolphins, with "their playful existence, and their friendly behavior," are favorably compared with humans; try as hard as we may, Wolf feels, "friendly we cannot be," since "we have accepted the gifts of false gods" (*A,* p. 98).

Yet the science, technology, and material, quantitative progress that have become modern gods are not rejected per se; rather they have been elevated to the status of gods, that is, of supreme values supplanting all others. Wolf recognizes the potential for good in science when she juxtaposes Chernobyl against the (successful) brain tumor operation undergone by her brother. Also, when the narrator of *Accident* reaches out mentally to her brother on the operating table, communicating with him and helping him in an intuitive, nonscientific way, she projects other values — particularly, the very friendliness of which she despairs — as a forceful alternative to the ethos of the modern world. The text ends on a dark note, with a dream in which a voice calls out, "A faultless monster," and in which a "putrescent moon" sinks out of sight (*A,* p. 109). But the conditional tense of the final sentence — "How difficult it would be, brother, to take leave of this earth" — still leaves open the door of hope.

While the next work published, *Sommerstück,* does not close that door either, it does emphasize failure and resignation.[125] *Sommerstück* recalls the attempt by a number of friends—artists, intellectuals, and others who feel marginal in relation to their society—to achieve a fulfilling community by acquiring, restoring, and living (part-time) in a number of peasant houses in a country village. This work may allow us to understand why "Conditions" of the *Cassandra* narrative does not include any utopian enclave of the kind imaginatively represented by the worshippers of Cybele in *Cassandra. Sommerstück* refers to an experience in Wolf's life that took place for the most part before the composition of *Cassandra.*[126] Since *Sommerstück* is the account of an aborted utopia, we can surmise why "Conditions" of 1982–83 did not bring in that subject matter. For in *Cassandra* as a whole, Wolf still wished to foreground the principle of hope.

The very first page of *Sommerstück* tells the reader that the experience is now over, that "destiny" did not will its success. And as it draws to a close, Ellen, the character most closely resembling Wolf herself, reflects on the basically unsatisfactory nature of retreat to an island of rural bliss on the part of people who aspire to the transformation of the whole of society. The body of the text nonetheless evokes many moments of magic and sympathy in the relations between the friends and recalls periods of contentment in the beauty of their environment. At the same time, it records tensions and conflicts and depicts how even in such a village, the human and natural environment suffers the incursions of modernity (it also includes a vision of impending ecological disaster). The effort to create conditions of life inspired by the past is threatened throughout and finally doomed. Significantly, near the end when the group conceives the idea of writing a book together with a collective name, like the art workshops of the masters in earlier times, someone comments simply that the present is not the past, and that they no longer have that freedom.

The last published book, *What Remains,* also a revision of a work first written much earlier, recounts the activities and reflections of one day in the narrator's life.[127] One of its main focuses is the possibility of a future different from the present. The situation is bleak, the prospects dim. In one passage the narrator finds that the very language in which she formulates her desire shows that she has begun to think like those who rule the present:

> If only there were a machine that could gather up all the hope left in the
> world and shoot it like a laser beam at this horizon of stone, melting it,

breaking it open. Now you're thinking like them. Machines, radiation, violence. Now you're extending their little bit of current power into the future. Then they'd have you where they want you. (*WR*, p. 270)

The conditional of the final sentence, though, reaffirms that all is not lost, and the conclusion of the work as a whole firmly reestablishes the Blochian perspective of hope.

For at a talk the narrator gives at the end of the day, a young woman asks during the question period, "how a livable future for ourselves and our children was going to grow out of this present situation?" The question sets off an impassioned discussion of the idea of the future, in which someone softly speaks the "utopian" word "brotherhood"; the atmosphere then becomes relaxed, "as on the eve of a celebration" (*WR*, pp. 286–88). The terms in which Wolf describes this scene leave no doubt that it has itself become a glimmer of a liberated future. The conclusion of the story reveals the meaning of the title — *What Remains* is precisely the future, clearly signaling that utopia has not been entirely destroyed for Christa Wolf.

What Remains also largely focuses on the narrator's surveillance by the Stasi; this aspect of the work threw its author into a violent political controversy immediately on the book's publication. For since she waited to publish it until after the fall of the Wall and of the East German regime, Wolf was accused of compromising herself with the latter (she has been called by some a state poet [*Staatsdichterin*]). Further fueling the controversy, Wolf revealed in January 1993 that she had herself been an informal collaborator with the Stasi between 1959 and 1962. Although a full treatment of this question clearly falls outside the framework of this study of Wolf's Romantic-feminist vision, in conclusion we will offer a few remarks on the controversy, particularly insofar as it relates to our conception of her work.

With regard to Wolf's actual collaboration with the Stasi, several things should be emphasized. First, this "pact with the devil" took place over a short period, early in Wolf's career; corresponding to the composition of *Moskauer Novelle,* it was a period in which Wolf was quite naive politically and still strongly swayed by an inferiority complex in relation to the antifascist aura of the regime's leaders. It was also a limited collaboration, about which Wolf had misgivings and which apparently proved to be rather unfruitful for the Stasi.[128] But more important, her collaboration was short-lived — unlike that of many other East German artists.[129] Wolf's attitude became increasingly critical, and beginning in 1968 — with her refusal (along with Anna Seghers) to sign the Writers' Union statement of support for the Soviet repression in Czechoslovakia — she became suspect herself and was harassed by the Stasi for incomparably longer (more than twenty years) than the period of small-scale collaboration.

As for the doubts cast on Wolf's position in the later period and the suggestions that she was guilty of hypocrisy, they seem highly unfair. As was pointed out by one of her supporters among prominent intellectuals, Günter Grass, she never relinquished hope in the possibility of a transformation of East German society.[130] Indeed, for Wolf's utopian-Romantic sensibility the capitalist West — the very root of modernity — was never an attractive alternative. After all, the so-called socialist countries were at least founded on an emancipatory project, although ultimately they had completely travestied it. Christa Wolf chose the contradictory path of affirming the utopian hope of true human self-realization within the constraints of "actually existing socialism." One must admit, as she herself does, that her political criticism of the East German regime was insufficient; however, her achievement as a writer far overshadows this weakness. As David Bathrick has pointed out, while she never questioned the fundamental political structures of the GDR (the one-party system, the lack of democracy), she at least is "someone who at a moment of danger spoke the unspeakable," denouncing aspects of East German society that resembled the West and creating "a genuine cultural alternative"[131] — one, we would add, that is indissolubly feminist and Romantic.

6

The Fire Is Still Burning:
From Surrealism to the
Present Day and Beyond

The Romantic fire continued to burn throughout the twentieth century, even though the light of its flames took on unfamiliar shapes, far removed from earlier aesthetic or cultural canons. Among the Romantic configurations of the century that has just ended, we focus first on the two that strike us as most significant: the major avant-garde movement known as surrealism and the "spirit of May 1968." Next, we attempt to bring to light the Romantic dimension that is present in twentieth-century mass culture and in some social and religious movements of the period. Then, after evoking contemporary debates over the nature of modernity, we look at some recent French and English critiques of modern civilization that extend and renew the Romantic perspective. Finally, we venture some remarks on the future of Romanticism.

SURREALISM

Of all the avant-garde movements of the twentieth century, surrealism is probably the one that brought the Romantic aspiration to reenchant the world to the peak of its expression and that most radically embodied Romanticism's revolutionary dimension. Intellectual rebellion and social revolution, transformation of life (Arthur Rimbaud) and of the world (Karl Marx): these two polestars have oriented the Romantic movement since it began, pulling it toward a perpetual search for subversive cultural and political practices. At the cost of multiple schisms and defections, the core surrealist group gravitating around André Breton and Benjamin Péret never abandoned its intransigent rejection of the established social, moral, and political order — or its jealous autonomy, despite its attraction and even its commitment to the various tendencies of the revolutionary left: first Communism, then Trotskyism, and finally anarchism.

In one of its earliest documents, "La révolution d'abord et toujours" (1925), the surrealist movement proclaimed its irreducible opposition to capitalist civilization: "Wherever Western civilization reigns, all human bonds have given way, except those based on interest, 'payment in hard cash.' For more than a century, human dignity has been reduced to the level of exchange value. . . . We do not accept the laws of Economy and Exchange, we do not accept the slavery of Labor. . . ."[1] Much later, recalling the movement's first stirrings, Breton observed: "At this point, surrealism rejects everything: no political movement could harness its energies. All the institutions on which the modern world is resting and that have led to the First World War we deem aberrant and scandalous."[2] This rejection of social and institutional modernity does not prevent the surrealists from identifying with the same cultural modernity that Charles Baudelaire and Rimbaud had invoked in their day.

The privileged targets of the surrealist attack on Western civilization are abstract, blinkered rationalism; flatfooted realism; and positivism in all its forms. Starting with the first "Manifesto of Surrealism," Breton denounced the attitude that would banish everything with a chimerical aspect, "under the pretense of civilization and progress"; confronted with this sterile cultural horizon, he asserted his belief in "the omnipotence of dream."[3] The search for an alternative to Western civilization remained present throughout the history of surrealism, including the moment in the 1970s when a group of French and Czech surrealists published *La civilisation surréaliste*, with Vincent Bounoure as editor.

Breton and his friends never hid their deep attachment to the German Romantic tradition of the nineteenth century (Novalis, Achim von Arnim) as well as the English tradition (the Gothic novel) or the French (Victor Hugo, Pétrus Borel). Criticizing the pompous official celebrations of the centenary of French Romanticism in 1930, Breton comments in "Second Manifesto of Surrealism":

> We say, and insist on saying, that this Romanticism which we are today willing to [be considered, historically] as the tail, *but then only as an amazingly prehensile tail,* by its very essence [in 1930] remains unmiti-

gated in its negation of these officials and these ceremonies, and we say that to be a hundred is for it to be still in the flower of its youth, that what has been wrongly called its heroic period can no longer honestly be considered as anything but the first cry of a newborn child which is only beginning to make its desires known through us. . . .[4]

It would be hard to imagine a more categorical twentieth-century declaration of the contemporaneousness of Romanticism.

To be sure, the surrealists' reading of the Romantic legacy is highly selective. What attracted them to "Hugo's gigantic facades," to certain texts by Alfred de Musset, Aloysius Bertrand, Xavier Forneret, and Gérard de Nerval, as Breton wrote in "Marvelous versus Mystery," was the "original impetus to emancipate man *totally.*" In addition, "a good number of Romantic or post-Romantic writers . . . such as Pétrus Borel, Flaubert, Baudelaire, Daumier, and Courbet" are attracted by a "completely spontaneous hatred of the typical bourgeois" and share "a common will not to compromise in any way with the reigning class," whose domination is "a sort of leprosy against which — if one wishes to prevent the real meaning of the most precious human attainments from being distorted and from contributing only to the greater and greater debasement of the human condition — it was no longer sufficient merely to brandish the whip: rather, it will some day be necessary to apply a red-hot iron to it."[5]

The use of premodern cultural traditions and forms was also selective: the surrealists drew unhesitatingly on alchemy, occultism, the Kabala, magic, astrology, and the so-called primitive arts of Oceania, Africa, and America. In all their activities, their goal was to go beyond the limits of "art" — as a separate, institutionalized, ornamental activity — and embark on the limitless adventure of reenchanting the world. However, as revolutionaries inspired by the spirit of the Enlightenment, by Georg Wilhelm Friedrich Hegel, and especially by Marx, they were the most resolute and intransigent adversaries of the values that lie at the heart of reactionary-Romantic culture: religion and nationalism. As "Second Manifesto" declares: "Everything remains to be done, every means must be worth trying, in order to lay waste to the ideas of *family, country, religion.*"[6] At the entrance to the surrealists' lost paradise, a well-known libertarian inscription is written in flaming letters: neither God nor Master!

In the late 1930s, the premodern form of myth became a key element in the spiritual and emotional apparatuses of surrealism. Breton and his friends presumably viewed that myth as too precious a gem to be abandoned to the Fascist mythmakers. In 1942, at the worst moment of the war, Breton believed more than ever in the necessity of a counterattack in this area: "Faced with the conflict which is at present shaking the world, even the most recalcitrant mentalities are beginning to admit the vital necessity of a myth which can be set up in opposition to that of Odin and various other belligerent gods."[7] Other anti-Fascist intellectuals, Germans such as Ernst Bloch (and Thomas Mann) or Frenchmen such as Roger Caillois and — not without regrettable ambiguities — Georges Bataille, had the same concern. In *Prolegomena to a Third Surrealist Manifesto or Not* (1942), Breton identifies Bataille, Caillois, Georges Duthuit, André Masson, Pierre Mabille, Leonora Carrington, Max Ernst, René Etiemble, Péret, Nicolas Calas, Kurt Seligmann, and Georges Henein as among those who share his interest in myth.

The surrealists' attraction to myth also has to do with the fact that (along with the esoteric traditions) it constituted a secular alternative to the religious stranglehold on access to the universe of the nonrational. This is the sense in which we have to interpret a remark Breton made (intended as a provocative and iconoclastic image) in his dedication on a copy of *L'Amour fou* to his friend Armand Hoog: "Churches, beginning with the most beautiful: demolish them, leave no stone standing on stone. *And then let the new myth live!*"[8]

Breton first suggested in "Nonnational Boundaries of Surrealism," in 1937, that the task of surrealism should be "elaborating a *collective myth* appropriate to our period in the same way that, whether we like it or not, the gothic genre must be regarded as symptomatic of the great social upheaval that shook Europe at the end of the eighteenth century." Why this analogy between the new myth and the English Gothic novel? On the one hand, because the Gothic type of fantastic literature carried an explosive psychic charge: "The pleasure principle has never more obviously taken its revenge on the reality principle." On the other hand, because, as the above statement shows, the Gothic novel is inseparable from the intellectual and social process that led to the French Revolution (Breton cites the Marquis de Sade's comment that the Gothic genre was "the indispensable fruit of the revolutionary upheavals whose effects were felt all over Europe"). These two characteristics, this doubly subversive dimension, emotional and social, must be at the heart of the new myth. The 1937 text adds that, to create such an imaginary configuration, surrealism has to "bring together the scattered elements of that myth, *beginning* with those that proceed from the oldest and strongest tradition."[9]

Breton and his friends continued to explore and reinvent these "scattered elements" in the years to come, drawing on the mythos of Romanticism and the Gothic novel, Celtic myths, and indigenous myths of Mexico and North America. However, mythology in all its forms is by no means their own recourse: as Breton wrote in 1942 in an article on Max Ernst, the new myth is inspired by the prophetic power of certain visionaries of the past — such as Rimbaud, Friedrich Nietzsche, Søren Kierkegaard, Sade, and Isidore Ducasse Lautréamont — or the present, such as Ernst, whose work presents a mythological and anticipatory character, prefiguring "events destined to be realized on the plane of reality" and even "the *very order* in which these events will occur."[10]

In myth, then, what is at stake is thus the future itself: the function of myth is eminently utopian. In his "Prolegomena to a Third Surrealist Manifesto or Not," Breton asks (and asks himself) "in what measure can we choose or adopt, and *impose,* a myth fostering the society that we judge to be desirable?"[11] Everything thus seems to indicate that, for him, myth and utopia are inseparable: if they are not identical, they nevertheless remain connected by a system of communicating vessels that allow desire to pass in both directions.

The surrealists did not succeed in imposing a collective myth, but they did create one, using the Romantic method: by drawing on "the most intimate depths of the spirit" (Friedrich Schlegel) or, in Breton's own words, "the innermost emotion of a human being . . . in its haste to [express itself], being unable to externalize itself within the confines of the real world, . . . has no other outlet than to yield to the eternal lure of myths and symbols."[12] If they were unable to constitute "a universal mythology, endowed with a general symbolics" (Friedrich Schelling), or to discover, with the help of esoteric myths, "the mechanism of universal symbolism,"[13] they nevertheless managed to invent — in the alchemical sense of the term — a new myth, destined to hurtle across the sky of modern culture like a shooting star in flames.

What is this myth? To answer the question, we can usefully return to Breton's most "mythological" work, *Arcanum 17* (1944). Transposing an assortment of myths (Isis and Osiris, Melusine, woman as agent of earthly salvation, Satan, the Angel of Liberty), Breton incorporates the astrological myth of Arcanum 17 and above all "a very powerful myth [that] continues to have a hold on [him]": the myth of mad love, "love that seizes power" and in which all the world's regenerative force resides. In the conclusion of this book, which is one of the most luminous texts of surrealism, all these mythical figures flow like rivers of fire toward an image that contains them all, and that is in Breton's eyes "the supreme expression of Romantic thought" and "the most lively symbol it has bequeathed to us": the morning star — " 'born from a white feather shed by Lucifer during his fall' " (Breton is citing Hugo here) — is an allegory of rebellion. This symbol signifies that "rebellion itself, rebellion alone is the creator of light. And this light can only be known by way of three paths, poetry, liberty, and love. . . ."[14]

So what is this new myth that contains revolt, poetry, liberty, and love (in their modern forms), bringing them together (without ranking them) and unifying them (thanks to their elective affinities)? It can only be surrealism itself, in its "divinatory force" (Schlegel), in its utopian gaze turned toward "the golden age to come" (Schlegel). As a poetic myth, surrealism inherited the program announced 150 years earlier by the *Frühromantik* movement. Still, surrealism has the distinguishing property of being a myth in motion, always incomplete and always open to the creation of new figures and mythological images. As it is first and foremost an activity of the spirit, surrealism cannot be frozen into a grail to be conquered or a reified sur-reality: perpetual incompleteness is its elixir of immortality.

MAY 1968

The youthful rebellion of the 1960s was clearly not limited to France. Analogous or comparable movements unfolded throughout the world, and in particular in the United States, Germany, and Italy, in the form of pacifist mobilizations, Third World movements, counterculture initiatives (both urban and rural), antipsychiatry experiments, and so on. A Romantic dimension was present in varying degrees in most of these movements, in the critiques addressed to modern industrial societies as well as in the utopian aims that inspired them.

May 1968 in France counts as one of the moments of universal crystallization of this worldwide wave of protest. Antibourgeois Romanticism was unquestionably an essential component of the diffuse and explosive mix of social, political, and cultural radicalism that has been called "the spirit of

May" — especially in the challenge to capitalist modernization and consumer society, and in the attempt to put imagination in power.

"Pourquoi des sociologues?" — a famous tract written in March 1968 in Nanterre by Daniel Cohn-Bendit and his friends — condemned sociologists who supported modernization, that is, the "planning, rationalization, and production of consumer goods according to the economic needs of organized capitalism." The critique of technocracy is a theme running like a red thread through many documents of the student movement, for example a tract from Censier titled "Amnistie les yeux crevés": "Students, if they treat you as *privileged,* it is so they can better integrate you into the industrial bureau-technocracy of profits and progress by deceiving you with economico-scientific imperatives . . . Let us categorically reject the ideology of PROFIT and PROGRESS and the pseudoforces that go by the same name. *Progress will be what we want it to be.* . . . We no longer want to be governed by the 'laws of science' any more than by the laws of the economy or technological 'imperatives.' "[15]

The sociologist Alain Touraine, an outside observer, noted this dimension of the May movement in his own way: "The revolt against the 'one dimensionality' of the industrial society governed by the economic and political structures could not break out without involving some 'negative' aspects, that is, without opposing the immediate pressure of its desires to the constraints — accepted as natural — of growth and modernization."[16]

The Romantic gust of May '68 is not limited, however, to negativity. It is also manifested in the feeling of a rediscovered human community, in the experience of the revolution as a festival, in the ironic and poetic slogans written on walls, in the appeal to collective imagination and creativity as a political imperative, and finally in the utopian notion of a society free of all alienation and reification.

The influence of surrealism on the culture of May '68, attested by numerous graffiti, has not been sufficiently highlighted. More generally, there is a family resemblance between the May '68 culture and the surrealist requirement of total emancipation. The surrealists of Paris were right when they recognized the movement as the surging forth of their own dreams: "What is being born magnificently before our eyes, what is being born in us, is much more than a heresy or a utopia: neither an end point nor a pause; every arrival is a departure. Whatever may happen to the contrary, we know better today that man is a new idea — and that his desire is his sole reality."[17]

Beyond the impact of surrealist writings on the generation of the 1960s, we must also note that the role of the situationist International (which may be considered up to a point as a dissident branch of surrealism) did not go unnoticed. It was an active presence and the direct inspiration for many of the movement's catchwords through the writings of Guy Debord, Raoul Vaneigem, and especially an anonymous brochure written in 1966 (in fact written by Mustapha Khayati), "De la misère en milieu étudiant," whose call for a new poetry, "poetry made by all, the beginning of the revolutionary festival," did not go unheeded.[18]

Two intellectual figures—who owe a good deal to surrealism themselves—played an important role in the gestation of this protest ideology, establishing a bridge between the revolutionary-Romantic cultural critique of the 1920s and 1930s (György Lukács, Breton, the Frankfurt School) and the new generation that manifested itself around May '68: Herbert Marcuse and Henri Lefebvre—the former above all in the United States and Germany, the latter chiefly in France.

In his first text, a doctoral thesis on the artistic novel in Germany ("*Der deutsche Künstlerroman,*" 1922), Marcuse shows how nineteenth-century works featuring an artist as hero (Novalis, E. T. A. Hoffmann, and others) incorporate a Romantic protest against the growing industrialization and mechanization of economic and cultural life, processes that are responsible for the marginalization or destruction of all spiritual values. The burning aspiration of many Romantic or neo-Romantic writers to transform life radically by breaking through the narrow confines of philistine bourgeois materialism is comparable, as Marcuse sees it, to Charles Fourier's utopian socialism.

Whereas, in his work during the 1930s and 1940s, Marcuse placed special emphasis on the critical and emancipatory function of rationalism, in particular in his major work on Hegel, *Reason and Revolution* (1941), in his work from the 1950s and 1960s, such as *Eros and Civilization* (1955) and *One-Dimensional Man* (1964), he returned to the Romantic themes of his early texts. The two dimensions do not strike him as at all contradictory: as he writes in *Eros and Civilization,* Johann Gottfried Herder and Friedrich von Schiller, Hegel and Novalis developed the concept of alienation in almost identical terms, using it to express their criticism of the industrial society that was coming into being, governed by the principle of performance. And in the 1960 preface to *Reason and Revolution,* he puts forward the common ground underlying both rational dialectics and poetic language: the negation, the Great Refusal of the existing state of affairs.[19] Marcuse's work is thus a concrete demonstration of the inadequacy of the classical analyses according to which irrationalism would be the very quintessence of his critique of modernity.

Like many twentieth-century revolutionary Romantics, Marcuse was fascinated by surrealism, the most radical heir to the intuitions of early Romanticism. In *One-Dimensional Man,* he writes:

> The traditional images of artistic alienation are indeed romantic in as much as they are in aesthetic incompatibility with the developing society. This incompatibility is the token of their truth. What they recall and preserve in memory pertains to the future: images of a gratification that would dissolve the society which suppresses it. The great surrealist art and literature of the Twenties and Thirties has still recaptured them in their subversive and liberating function.[20]

But it is not a matter of surrealism alone: for Marcuse, most of the great works of art from the nineteenth century on represent an antibourgeois revolt, a passionate protest, a dissociation "from the world of commodities, from the brutality of bourgeois industry and commerce, from the distortion of human relationships, from capitalist materialism, from instrumental reason."[21] Confronted with the present state of the world and of civilization, artistic culture preserves the memory of things past—a recollection that may become the promise of a future and the source of utopia.

We find similar ideas in a 1955 talk in which Henri Lefebvre argues against the narrow vision developed by Lukács in *The Destruction of Reason:*

> Romanticism expresses the disagreement, the distortion, the internal contradiction of the individual, the contradiction between the individual and the social. It implies disharmony between ideas and practice, conscience and life, superstructures and the base. It encompasses revolt, at least virtually. For us as Frenchmen, Romanticism retains an antibourgeois allure. . . . Whether it is historical truth or error, the subversive antibourgeois character of Romanticism acts as a screen between classicism and ourselves. For my part, I do not share Lukács's radical suspicion of Romanticism. I shall not be able to sacrifice it wholesale.[22]

In reality, this bond with the Romantic tradition is one of the sources of the originality — indeed, the singularity — of Lefebvre's thought in the historical panorama of French Marxism, marked from the outset by the insidious and permanent presence of positivism. Throughout Lefebvre's entire intellectual itinerary, his reflection continued to be enriched by a confrontation with Romanticism, starting with his work on Schelling in the 1920s, on Nietzsche from the 1930s on, and on Musset and Stendhal after the Second World War.

This perspective even illuminates his reading of Marx: for Lefebvre, Marx's early writings manifest a radical, revolutionary Romanticism for which the mature works provide a practical, nonspeculative foundation.[23] Whence his rejection of the structuralist interpretation of Marxism, which purports to strip Marx's work of its Romantic and humanist dimensions and to dissociate the early writings from the later texts through a so-called epistemological break.

The critique of everyday life, probably one of Lefebvre's most important contributions to the contemporary renewal of Marxist thought, also has its primary source in Romanticism. Examining Lukács's early writings and comparing them with Heidegger's texts from the 1920s, Lefebvre observes: "We have to remember that these themes — the appreciation of everyday reality as trivial, given over to cares, devoid of meaning, the impulse that orients philosophy toward true life, or true life and authenticity — derive from Romanticism. And more precisely from German Romanticism: Hölderlin, Novalis, Hoffmann, and so on."[24]

At the same time, Lefebvre is determined to keep his distance from the problematics of traditional German or French Romanticism and above all from its restitutionist currents, with their total rejection of modernity and their backward-looking illusions. His goal is to transcend the limits of the old Romanticism and establish the foundation for a new Romanticism, a revolutionary Romanticism oriented toward the future.

This aspiration is formulated explicitly and systematically in a programmatic text that Lefebvre published in 1957 in *Nouvelle Revue Française*, at the very moment when, at the heart of the French Communist Party, he was leading the anti-Stalin struggle that would soon lead to his exclusion (or "suspension"). This very interesting text outlines a new interpretation of Marxism and contains the kernel of the worldview that is manifested throughout Lefebvre's philosophic work. Titled *Le romantisme révolutionnaire,* it spells out what distinguishes the new Romanticism, with which he identifies, from the old (Novalis and Hoffmann to Baudelaire). Traditional Romantic irony "judges the present in the name of the historically or ideologically idealized past; it is obsessed with and fascinated by the greatness of the past, its purity." Such is not the case with the new revolution-oriented Romanticism, which rejects nostalgia for the past. Nevertheless, there is an underlying continuity between the two forms: "Every Romanticism is based on dissension, doubling, and tearing apart. In this sense revolutionary Romanticism perpetuates and even deepens the old Romantic doublings. But these doublings take on a new meaning. The gesture of distancing (of setting apart at a safe distance) with respect to the contemporary, the present, the real, the existing, is made in the name of the possible, and not in the name of the past, or of escape."[25]

Nevertheless, Lefebvre's work—like that of all Romantics, even revolutionary Romantics—is not without nostalgia for the past. Thus in "Notes Written One Sunday in the French Countryside," a remarkable chapter of the first version of *Critique of Everyday Life* (initially published in 1947), Lefebvre regrets the loss of "a certain human fulfillment" found in ancient rural communities. Even while criticizing the belated partisans of "the good old days," he cannot help insisting in the subsequent essay, "What is Possible," that "in reply to the naïve theoreticians of complete, continuous progress we must demonstrate in particular the decline of everyday life since the community of Antiquity, and man's growing alienation."[26] In his doctoral thesis on the Campan valley in the Pyrenees, the original version of which was called "Une république pastorale," he describes the dissolution of rural communities under the impact of capitalism, owing to the progressive deterioration of "the delicate equilibrium between populations, resources, and surfaces."[27]

In 1967, on the eve of the May 1968 events, Henry Lefebvre published a book titled *Contre les technocrates,* which may have had a fairly direct impact on some of the individuals behind the student uprising. Referring as much to Fourier as to Marx, he rejects the technocratic mythology—in its reactionary or left-wing form (Soviet authoritarian planning in particular)—and examines the contradictions of technicity from a dialectical viewpoint. He denounces, above all, the danger that cybernetics may lead to the "quantification of the cosmos" and to the "automatic functioning" of society.[28]

We find almost identical formulations in texts from the 1968 student movement, for example in a resolution adopted on the creation of the

March 22 Movement: "These phenomena . . . correspond to an offensive of capitalism eager for the modernization, rationalization, automatization, and cybernetization of our society."[29] In Nanterre and elsewhere, Henri Lefebvre was unquestionably one of the inspirational figures behind the Romantic challenge to society mounted by rebellious youth.

Lefebvre returns to these issues in his essay on the May events. He vigorously attacks those whom he calls the "modernists," whose sole ambition is to respond to the "American challenge" (a rather transparent reference to Jean-Jacques Servan-Schreiber and his disciples) and to "bring France into line with computers, to put an end to the lags"; these are the "recuperators par excellence of the movement," people with "little imagination and a lot of ideology." He contrasts them with those whom he calls the "possibilists," that is, those who go so far as to "proclaim the primacy of the imagination over reason," who explore the possible and want to realize all its potentialities. Among them there are students in revolt against the mercantilization of culture and knowledge, and working-class youth who are "moving toward a revolutionary Romanticism, without theory, but in action."[30]

A characteristic example of this Romanticism in action but without theory in May 1968 is of course the burning of cars, a hated symbol of consumer society and aggressive industrial modernity. In his 1967 book against technocracy, Lefebvre had already written: "In this society in which things are more important than people, there is a king-object, a pilot-object: the automobile. Our so-called industrial or technological society possesses this symbol, a thing endowed with prestige and power. . . . The car is an incomparable and perhaps irremediable instrument, in neocapitalist countries, of deculturation, of the destruction from within of the civilized world."[31] It seems obvious that the young incendiaries had not read the writings of the philosopher from Nanterre, but in his book Lefebvre had given expression to a feeling of revolt that was "in the air."

CONTEMPORARY MASS CULTURE

It may appear highly paradoxical — to the point of calling our conception of Romanticism into question — to claim to find Romanticism in the leading sites of modernity, at the heart of consumer society, in the vital core of that society constituted by the mass media. How can a radically critical vision figure in what the Frankfurt School called the "culture industry," in the phenomenon of reification of culture itself, which, while it unquestionably existed earlier, takes on particular importance in the contemporary period?

But the fact remains that if we look at recent mass-market cultural projects, we cannot fail to find—more or less softened, transformed, manipulated, or even entirely undermined—some of Romanticism's powerful themes. However, the existence of this paradox, troubling at first glance, does not seem to us to invalidate our explanatory framework; quite to the contrary, it tends to shore up our conception of Romanticism.

For the presence of Romanticism at the very heart of the cultural mass production distributed by the consumer society it rejects would reveal instead, as we see it, the extent to which the Romantic thematics corresponds to human aspirations and needs that alienated contemporary society cannot destroy. Indeed, the products of the culture industry get their power of attraction from the fact that they draw on dreams, fantasies, and phantasms to create an emotional charge. In this respect, they have to be based on human desire and imagination as these exist at a given moment.

If a profound feeling of lack and frustration bound up with a sense of loss (that is, the Romantic syndrome) constitutes part of modern subjectivity, the culture industry finds itself accordingly obliged to evoke these—to put them on stage, to find images and narratives that embody them, even if this means, in a second phase, taking them in hand and watering them down, defusing them, domesticating them, manipulating them. Without bringing the concept of Romanticism into play, the American critic Fredric Jameson develops a similar perspective. In an important article, he uses examples from contemporary cinema to analyze mass culture as containing—simultaneously and in an intimately interconnected way—reified moments and utopian moments.[32]

But we must add at once that the relative dosage of utopia and reification, of the power to subvert and co-opt, is highly variable. For the mass impact of Romanticism is in fact manifested in various texts and materials, which stem from different genres, are of unequal aesthetic value, and are aimed at different audiences.

In other words, the culture industry often appropriates certain Romantic clichés for itself—the idyllic life of the countryside, love that proves stronger than barriers of class or money, the incorruptible individual who cannot be bought—and integrates them superficially into a fundamentally apologetic whole that is subject to the dominant values. The Romantic elements are thus neutralized or disfigured by the elimination of their critical thrust; they are distorted and made to serve what is fundamentally a market culture.

The distinction between this pseudo-Romantic culture and an authentically Romantic mass culture is not always easy to make, and we can identify a whole range of intermediate situations; still, the existence or nonexistence of a (not necessarily explicit) rejection of industrial-bourgeois civilization is a criterion that in principle provides a basis for distinguishing between them. As we tried to show in chapter 1, Romanticism cannot be reduced to a list of themes; it is rather a worldview with its own structure and coherence. Looked at in this light, only a segment of the production in question deserves to be called "Romantic" in the fullest sense; that is, these works in which its various themes are organically integrated into a whole whose overall signification tends toward a nostalgic rejection of modern reification and alienation. We propose, then, to take a brief look at selected forms of mass culture from the standpoint of their relation to Romanticism.

Closest to total reification, we find advertising, which constitutes a cultural product in its own right, the most purely industrial and the most directly and wholly reified product of all, since it represents nothing but an unmediated function of exchange value. Now while in all sorts of advertisements (posters, commercials in movie theaters and on television, newspaper and magazine advertisements, and so on) we encounter a great number of modernizing messages, that is, messages that celebrate the technological, industrial, and scientific edge along with the way of life it makes possible, we also find a considerable number of nostalgic, backward-looking discourses that refer to older values.

It may be no accident that this tendency is particularly pronounced in the United States, one of the countries in which technical-industrial-scientific "advances" have gone the furthest, with the most disastrous consequences for the human and natural environment. Indeed, advertising in the United States plays on the deep ambivalence most Americans feel toward their own successes in these areas, and it often expresses a blend of pride and regret.

Moving from the realm of advertising to mass-market fictional narratives, we should perhaps begin by evoking the contemporary "dime" novel, of the Harlequin variety, as a form of literature subjected in its very composition to a process of mass production (the product is standardized and authors are trained to use a set of invariable techniques and formulas). In these novels, intended chiefly for a working-class and lower-middle-class audience, we often find a thematics with Romantic overtones similar to that of advertising, with occasional medieval aspects.

But the imprint of Romanticism on the collective imagination is especially striking in certain highly successful films whose technical virtuosity and inventiveness (at least at first, for each one has given rise to a series of weaker imitations) are undeniable. *Star Wars, The Godfather,* and *ET* are certainly among the films for all audiences (thus crossing all classes and social groups) that have most marked the last two decades. And each in its own way can be called Romantic.

The film *Star Wars* features a struggle between a highly technological empire, the incarnation of evil, led by "paladins," and a "primitive" indigenous people close to nature, supported by "the Force," an invisible spiritual presence that ultimately triumphs over all the most advanced and diabolical technological devices.[33] In *The Godfather,* its critique of the extreme violence of the Mafiosi notwithstanding, we have a warm portrait of Sicilian clan and family ties — primary relations of affection and total commitment — in the cold, dehumanized world of big-city America. As for *ET,* we find the pacifism and goodness of an extraterrestrial identified with the natural environment (ET resembles a vegetable and comes from a pastoral planet) who is persecuted and tortured in the human world of modernity (pursued by the police with the help of the most advanced technological gadgets, then overmedicated at the hospital).

In yet another category, quite different from the others, we encounter works created by serious writers or intellectuals that did not specifically target a mass audience but that nevertheless met with great success and became best-sellers. These works may have aesthetic merits, and some of the best express an undeniable Romantic dimension.

We might mention J. R. Tolkien's *Lord of the Rings,* whose importance has been stressed by Jack Zipes as an index of "the widening gap between a technologically constraining society and its alienated individuals in search of authentic community."[34] Michael Ende's *The Neverending Story* is another example. In an interview with a French journalist, Ende (the son of a surrealist painter) explained his goal in writing the tale of a magical voyage of initiation as follows: "I am not attacking individuals but a system — call it capitalist, if you like — that is leading us — we'll see this ten or fifteen years from now — straight toward the abyss. . . . I do not deny that I tried, in writing *The Neverending Story,* to draw on some of the ideas of German Romanticism. Not to take a step backwards, but because in that aborted movement there are seeds that are still waiting to germinate."[35]

THE NEW SOCIAL MOVEMENTS

The student protest movement of the 1960s gave rise to most of the social movements with a Romantic inspiration that have come to occupy center stage in recent decades: ecology, pacifism, feminism, and so on (and also liberation theology, in a different context).

The neo-Romantic aspect of these movements — especially in Germany — has been noted by a number of observers, often in a polemical and hostile way, for example, in Richard Löwenthal's 1971 book *Der Romantische Rückfall* (The romantic backslide). We also find more objective analyses, such as Uwe Schimank's book on neo-Romantic protest movements in late capitalism (1983); however, the Romantic aspect brought to light in this work remains somewhat vague: Schimank evokes an "aesthetic sensibility" and a "dialogal sociability." The sociologist Johannes Weiss has a more interesting hypothesis: he presents the reenchantment of the world as the central Romantic dimension of the contemporary alternative movements and cultural critiques.[36]

Among all these social movements, ecology is probably the one that has taken the Romantic critique of modernity the furthest, through its questioning of economic and technological progress and through its utopian aspiration to restore the lost harmony between humans and nature. A somewhat naive version of these themes is found in Manon Maren-Grisebach's *Philosophie der Grünen* (Philosophy of the greens, 1982), which denounces the unilateral rationality of technology in the name of a totalizing moral relation of sympathy with nature, inspired by the matrilineal societies of the prehistoric past. This type of past-oriented nostalgia is more common in the fundamentalist strains of the ecology movement, but, as the ecosocialist Jean-Paul Deléage notes, ecological prophecy "often refers to a rural golden age, imagined as a society of free exchange with nature, whose human dimensions please those who dream of an autonomous and convivial community of equals." In any event, the Green movement for the most part shares in the questioning of quantitative productivism (capitalist or bureaucratic) and in denouncing the catastrophic ecological consequences of industrial progress. While ecosocialists such as Werner Hülsenberg turn to the Frankfurt School and its critique of rational-instrumental domination of nature as a source for a new conception of socialism, econarodniks, for example, the Catalan economist Joan Martinez Alier, who draw on John Ruskin and the Russian populists call attention to rural and popular communitarian forms of resistance to capitalist-industrial development, above all in Third World countries.[37]

If it is true that restitutionist illusions predominate among certain fundamentalist ecological groups, whereas among the so-called realist groups (especially in Germany) some seem to believe in the possibility of a reformed Green capitalism, the fact remains that at the turn of the twentieth century the ecology movement constitutes the most important form of renewal of the Romantic critique of modern industrial civilization.

THE NEW RELIGIOUS MOVEMENTS

Another type of social movement with Romantic overtones has appeared on the scene in recent decades: currents of religious renewal. As in the past (in the case of early Romanticism, for example, and again in the late nineteenth century), the "return of the religious" remains one of the most typical forms of Romantic reaction in the face of the disenchantment of the world produced by modernity.

Some of these movements combine an obscurantist religious fundamentalism with the systematic use of the most modern technological means: this is the case with some North American evangelical sects (the televangelists), new religious institutions such as Rev. Sun Myung Moon's Unification Church, some neoorthodox groupings within Judaism (the Lubavitcher sect), and certain currents of Islam. To the extent that these movements are attracted to modern technology (means of communication or military matériel) and do not call the capitalist-industrial system into question, their logic stems more from a reactionary modernism than from Romanticism. In contrast, an authentic Romantic sensibility is present in the numerous more or less traditionalist movements of emotional religious renewal: for example, the Christian charismatic or evangelical renewal, various groups within the mystical-esoteric nebula, the neo-Buddhist cult of Soka Gakkai, some Muslim religious brotherhoods.[38]

Latin American liberation theology constitutes a separate case. We are not dealing here with a phenomenon typical of the entire set of new forms that have appeared in the religious field; we have chosen it as an example because it is the one we know best and because of its considerable political importance.

Liberation theology is the doctrine, or at least the cultural expression, of a vast social movement that arose in the early 1960s within the Christian student movement in Brazil and has spread throughout Latin America. This liberation Christianity became a widespread phenomenon after the meeting of Latin American bishops at Medellin in 1968, with the simultaneous development of church-related communities at its base—groups of believers who met periodically to read the Bible and discuss their social problems—and the writings of liberation theologists (Gustavo Gutierrez, Hugo Asmann, Leonardo Boff, Frei Betto, Pablo Richard, Ignacio Ellacuria, and others); it had a profound impact on the Sandinista revolution in Nicaragua and the popular insurgency in El Salvador.

Liberation theology entails both Romantic and antimodernist aspects—criticism of capitalist modernity, nostalgia for organic communities—and future-oriented utopian aspects: the aspiration to a classless, oppressionless egalitarian society. From this standpoint, it is close to the revolutionary Romantic type. Its critique of capitalism in Latin America articulates the Romantic anticapitalist tradition of Catholicism—moral and religious condemnation of the market economy—with a Marxist analysis of imperialist exploitation. This dual nature, at once progressive and antimodern, is found at all levels of thought among liberation theologists. Partisans of democracy, these people seek the separation of church and state, reject the idea of a Catholic Party, and defend the autonomy of social movements. But they share with the intransigent Catholic current the rejection of privatization of faith and the (typically modern) separation between the spheres of politics and religion.

The liberation theologists' rejection of the privatization of religion is accompanied by a more general critique of modern individualism. For Gustavo Gutierrez, "individualism is the most important note in modern ideology and bourgeois society. For the modern mentality, man is an absolute beginning, an autonomous decision-making center. Individual interest and initiative are the point of departure and the driving force of economic activity." In this context he mentions the work of Lucien Goldmann, who had brought to light the opposition between religion as a system of transindividual values on the one hand and as the strictly individualist problematics of the Enlightenment and the market economy on the other. The conclusion is thus that "the spiritual, to use a contemporary expression, is not opposed to the social. The real opposition is between bourgeois individualism and the spiritual according to the Bible."[39]

The authentic alternative to the self-centered return to the individual is of course community, whose current concrete form is embodied by local church-based groups. Do these correspond to the traditional, premodern, organic community? Yes and no. Given the way modern society produces "a wild atomization of existence and a general anonymity of persons," according to Leonardo Boff, it is appropriate to create "communities in which persons actually know and recognize one another," characterized "by direct relationships, by reciprocity, by a deep communion, by mutual assistance, by commonality of gospel ideals, by equality among members." The integral community, however, is a utopia corresponding to a legitimate and ancient tradition, an authenticity that has long "lain hidden, like live coals covered with ashes."[40] Such communities also rely on popular traditions and customs, primarily rural in origin, that have withstood the process of urbanization and modernization, but they do not merely reproduce premodern social relationships. As Harvey Cox very astutely observes, they entail a dimension of individual choice that is typically modern, giving rise to new forms of solidarity that have nothing to do with archaic tribal or village structures.[41] Owing to this modern dimension, they can be viewed as voluntary utopian groupings, in Jean Seguy's sense: groupings in which the members participate of their own free will and that seek (implicitly or explicitly) to transform the existing global social systems in a way that is at least optatively radical.[42]

In Brazil in recent years the struggle against one of the great "disasters of modernity" of our time, the destruction of the Amazon forest, has brought about a convergence of two social movements that are Romantic in orientation: an ecological current that defends nature and a Christian current, inspired by liberation theology, that seeks to save indigenous communities from ethnocide.

THE CONTEMPORARY ROMANTIC CRITIQUE
OF CIVILIZATION

The debate over modernity and the Romantic critique of capitalist civilization are unquestionably present on the contemporary political scene in

Europe and the United States. At the same time, former leftists are attempting to call Romanticism into question by stressing its dangerous character.

The French political scientist Blandine Barret-Kriegel, a former '68 leftist who has changed her position, is a case in point: she attempts to hold Romanticism responsible for left-wing as well as right-wing totalitarianism. She sees the early German Romantics as the literary equivalent of the Jacobin terrorists. By setting up a disturbing system of correct cultural thinking, "the young romantics were conducting verbal experiments on the guillotine that had only a short time before toppled heads in France." Though she provides no serious analysis in support of her charges, she accuses Schlegel, Novalis, Ludwig Tieck, and their friends of prefiguring the partisan spirit of Communism and the left, both reduced to convenient scarecrows.[43]

The work of the eminent British historian Isaiah Berlin is more interesting. Several of his works are polemics against Romanticism, which he tracks down in all its forms — for example, his book on J. G. Hamann, whom he views as Romanticism's true founder and the most passionate, coherent, implacable, and extreme enemy of the Enlightenment and all forms of rationalism. Despite his eccentric character and his regrettable style — contorted, obscure, allusive, and riddled with digressions, untraceable references, word play, invented words, and cryptograms — Hamann nevertheless inspired Herder, Friedrich Jacobi, Schlegel, Schiller, the young Goethe, Hegel, Kierkegaard, the Romantic revolt, and modern irrationalism.

Fascinated by Hamann as an individual, Berlin recognizes his importance: uttering truths scornfully ignored by the triumphant rationalist schools, Hamann lit the spark that set off the great Romantic revolt. Finally, he struck the first blow to the quantified world of modernity and raised some of the most important questions of our time. But Berlin has a tendency to reduce Hamann's work to a "revelling in darkness," a "blind irrationalism," and a reactionary "obscurantism" that would have suited twentieth-century National Socialism: a highly debatable deduction![44]

Another sort of challenge to the Romantic perspective is represented in the work of Jerome McGann, an American academic. Starting with his celebrated book *The Romantic Ideology,* he developed a form of analysis that has been adopted by others in the United States. The approach seeks to be demystifying: seeing the expression of a bourgeois ideology in the literary, artistic, and philosophic productions of the Romantic period (in the traditional, limited sense), McGann denounces the unacknowledged continuation of that ideology in recent studies of Romanticism and in contemporary intellectual life more generally. Thus while he recognizes that the Romantic spirit has persisted up to our own day, McGann deems it a negative feature. McGann's viewpoint has been quite influential in American academic circles, and it provides the theoretical background for a number of contemporary studies of Romanticism.[45] While the analyses inspired by McGann bring interesting sociohistorical insights in some cases, in our judgment they often miss the crucial point, namely, the power of the Romantic antibourgeois critique and its liberating aspirations.

As far as contemporary Romantic criticism is concerned (and it persists in important ways, in spite of and in opposition to tendencies that are more or less hostile to Romanticism), we shall restrict our discussion here to the situation in France and in England.

In recent French culture, for the most part, one can point to two broad, contradictory tendencies. One of these is the Romantic and the modernizing, the "spirit of '68," that is, the warm, humanistic current valorizing passion and imagination; the other is structuralism, which is followed by poststructuralism (the latter being scarcely differentiated from the former, at least from this standpoint), that is, the cool, antihumanist current valorizing structure and technology. These two tendencies have coexisted since the mid-twentieth century, but the power relations between them have varied. With the waning of the '68 movement around the mid-1970s, the Romantic perspective underwent an eclipse for a time, but we have recently witnessed its resurgence.

While the current debate draws on earlier cultural trends (certain authors in particular have their roots in the spirit of '68), the opposition of Romantics and anti-Romantics now takes the form of an explicit discussion carried out in book-length essays concerning the present state of civilization and future options for social development.

Two key philosophical reference points constitute the intellectual background for the debate in France: Martin Heidegger and Jürgen Habermas. The former represents a fundamental (antimodern) challenge to Western rationality, while the latter represents a continuation of the rationalist project of the Enlightenment and modernity. Nevertheless, the impact of their work is much more ambiguous, not only because of the diversity of interpretations in France but also because these men's relation to modernity is itself ambivalent: let us recall that Heidegger sees in the attempt to master modern technology "the greatness and inner truth" of Nazism, while Habermas incorporates certain aspects of the Frankfurt School's critique of modernity into his own work—especially that school's rejection of the colonization of the world brought about by the instrumental logic of the prevailing systems.

In France in recent years we have observed a persistent thread of Romantic sensibility—a minority position, but one that nevertheless cannot be ignored—that conveys a radical critique of modern civilization. In most of its representatives, significant references to the nineteenth-century Romantic tradition—references that were still very present in the prewar generation—are noteworthy by their absence.[46] There is still considerable literary and cultural interest in Romantic authors of the past, but their works are rarely perceived as a source or point of departure for challenges to industrial society. That role is played by works of certain contemporary thinkers that have been (or are beginning to be) translated in France: philosophers are turning to the authors of the Frankfurt School, or, in contrast, to Heidegger; ecologists are interested in Ivan Illich, while economists have been discovering Karl Polanyi and Immanuel Wallerstein.

Especially after 1983, when *La grande transformation* was published in France, Polanyi's analysis of the fundamental break that the self-regulating market represents in relation to the economy embedded in the social fabric in premodern societies has become a key reference, transcending disciplinary frontiers, for French critics and adversaries of the system.

Some authors make an effort to bring to light the novelty of the current stage of capitalist modernity. According to Jean Chesneaux, for example, we have entered a new period, one not foreseen by Polanyi: owing to a reverse shock, an overturning of the relation between the economic and social realms, the entire tissue of social life has been invaded by the economy and has been torn to shreds. A global system has been established, an omnipresent pancapitalism that covers all the continents and all areas of social life, carrying the Third World and "real socialism" along in its wake. Social disintegration is manifested at the level of space, with the uprooting of populations, the repetitive monopoly of social sites, and the multiplication of ungrounded systems (dissociated from the natural or social environment). It is also translated in a particularly virulent way at the level of temporality. Living solely in the instantaneous and the immediate, modern individuals experience time only in quantitative terms, compressed in the present; thus the sense of duration is obliterated, and people find themselves trapped in "an everlasting present without past and without future" (George Orwell). Time of this sort, Chesneaux observes, is completely unknown in non-Western cultures; it is incomprehensible if not absurd in the eyes of Amerindians and Melanesians, and it is just as foreign to traditional European peasants, who have held onto the art of "taking their time." The frenzy of the instantaneous, the fear of obsolescence, and the obsession with speed have been established with modernization, creating an increasingly intense conflict with the deeper rhythms of the biosphere and the atmosphere.[47]

Other critics, in contrast, stress continuity and the long term, at the risk of submerging modernity within a far broader chronology. In *Adresse aux vivants sur la mort qui les gouverne,* Raoul Vaneigem produces a ringing indictment of market civilization. The situationist philosopher recognizes that over the last two centuries "a frenzied acceleration of the economic process" has taken place, but what he condemns is the entire history of civilization: starting with the Neolithic revolution, "there is no longer any gesture, thought, attitude, or project that is not involved in a quantified relation in which everything has to be paid for by exchange, money, sacrifice, or submission." The predominance of exchange has imposed the structure of the marketplace on behaviors, mores, and modes of thought in society for nine thousand years! The problem with an approach such as Vaneigem's is that it has difficulty accounting for the specificity of capitalist-industrial modernity as a break in terms of history and civilization.[48]

Most of these analyses have a holistic aim: the entire system is at issue, in its structure and its apparently irreversible movement. Among those who have been called the "dissidents of modernity," some, such as Jacques Ellul, Michel Leiris, René Dumont, and Jean Chesneaux, address the phenomenon taken as a whole, seeing its various manifestations as arising from a shared coherence, a single implacable logic. But the authors do not always agree as to how the essential dimension of this capitalist modernity should be defined.

For many, the crucial issue is technology, as a process that has become autonomous, alienated, and reified. These thinkers bring to light the contradiction between technology's liberating potential (especially owing to automation) and its current destructive form. Their critique focuses less on the harm inflicted by industrial society on workers (a theme found in Marx and John Ruskin) than on the broader social consequences of the phenomenon. In a recent philosophic essay, Michel Henry holds what he calls the "techno-scientific barbarity" of modern times responsible for the atrophy of culture, the death of art, and the loss of the sacred. Jean Chesneaux, for his part, draws attention chiefly to the political consequences of modern communications: politics survives today only in simulated television games broadcast to a mass of passive and uninvolved spectators. Citizens give way to televiewers and find themselves cast into powerlessness, indifference, and habituation — conditions that foster a narcissistic focus on private life.[49]

For others, utilitarianism, as a limited instrumental rationality, is the central feature of modern societies, which leads to a unidimensional uniformization and to a flattening of the system of values and reduces everything to the calculation of individual interests. Resulting from the conjunction, starting in the seventeenth century, between the Protestant Reformation, the development of the market, technological progress, and the rise of the middle classes, utilitarianism triumphed with the domination of the self-regulating market (Polanyi). With the enterprise of colonization, it spread across the globe, imposing the paradigms of Western capitalist civilization through deculturation or even ethnocide.[50]

Finally, for the ecologists, "productivism" — production for its own sake, the infinite and irrational accumulation of merchandise as a goal in itself (independent of authentic social needs) — constitutes the original sin of industrial modernity and is the cause of the catastrophic damage inflicted on the equilibrium of nature. Modern ecological disasters (depletion of the ozone layer, air and water pollution, the build-up of waste products, the destruction of forests) are not accidents or mistakes; they follow necessarily from the pseudorationality of productivism. According to the ecosocialists, there is an irreducible contradiction between the modern logic of immediate profitability and the long-term general interest of the human species, between the law of profit and the safeguarding of the environment, between the rules of the market and the survival of nature (and thus of humanity).[51]

These diverse critical analyses of modern civilization — more complementary and convergent than they are contradictory — often return to themes from the Romantic tradition, giving them a new meaning in relation to the specific realities of the late twentieth century. This does not necessarily result from a direct connection or from the intellectual influence exercised by nineteenth-century Romantic thinkers; it is rather the persistence of the essential features of bourgeois-industrial modernity that accounts for the analogy.

The recent Romantic dissidents of modernity share with the earlier Romantics the focus on cultures of the past. It is often a matter of an undifferentiated appeal: the whole set of premodern and precapitalist social formations serves as a reference point, as an example of an alternative mode of life, as a contrast casting into relief the bleak contours of the present, or as the memory of a communitarian universe governed by qualitative values.

Still, we can observe a particular fascination for the so-called primitive cultures, those most remote from modernity — whether in time or space — such as prehistoric civilizations or so-called savage peoples still living today. From this standpoint, one can speak of a "Rousseauist sensibility" in the Romantic thinking of the late twentieth century (already present in the Frankfurt School, in particular with Walter Benjamin). Why do these archaic cultures so often attract contemporary adversaries of modern bourgeois society?

Various hypotheses may be proposed. On the one hand, the more modernity progresses and develops its own implacable logic, the more it arouses, in reaction, the passionate and even sometimes desperate search for a social paradigm that is at the opposite pole from contemporary civilization, one that can represent by its essential nature the antithesis par excellence of modernity. As Piette Clastres has written:

> Humans in primitive societies have always been seized on as the place of absolute difference in relation to those in Western societies, as a strange and unthinkable space of absence — the absence of all that constitutes the sociocultural universe of the observers; a world without hierarchy, people who obey no one, a society indifferent to the possession of wealth, leaders who do not lead, cultures without morality because they are unacquainted with sin, classless societies, stateless societies, and so on.[52]

For earlier generations, the Orient or non-Western societies in general could still play the role of negative mirror, but with the accelerated Westernization and modernization of the Third World by multinational businesses, this sort of mirroring becomes problematic. But the crisis or weakening of the internal challenge to bourgeois society (most notably by the worker movement) also favors looking elsewhere for critical models and an imaginary alterity.

This new Rousseauism (we use the term without any pejorative connotations) goes well beyond the milieu of critical anthropologists (Robert Jaulin, Roger Renaud, and others). Thus, for the antiutilitarians, archaic societies offer proof that self-interested calculation has not always been the dominant feature of social relationships. The great lesson of the so-called savage peoples, among whom exchanges take the form of gifts, is that the community cannot be constituted on the basis of strictly utilitarian criteria, even though it has to satisfy the needs of each member. The logic of disinterest, of gifts, of the nonutilitarian, which governs life in archaic societies, represents the repressed par excellence of modern society.

In this sort of argument we rediscover the old dream of a Golden Age at the dawn of human history. Though he insists that he does not idealize the past, Alain Caillé thinks that "the image of the lost paradise or the golden age is perhaps not as exclusively mythical as is generally supposed": ethnographic studies all concur in showing that in primitive societies the average work time does not exceed four hours a day. "Most of the time is devoted to sleep, play, conversation, or the celebration of rites."[53] Capable of limiting their needs, these societies have no interest in accumulating: if they happen to become more productive, instead of increasing their production they extend the time devoted to leisure.

This critical primitivism is taken to its ultimate consequences by Raoul Vaneigem: for the former situationist leader, it is only in Paleolithic civilization that we find a perfect symbiosis (the "alchemical marriage") between humans and nature — leading to the enjoyment of oneself and others and to solidarity growing spontaneously "from a harmony of the passions fluttering about a passionate love of life." The nonmercantile civilizations based on hunting and gathering that preceded the Neolithic era were to be celebrated for centuries by men of the market economy under names such as Eden, Golden Age, *pays de Cocagne,* and they are described as places where abundance, *gratuité,* and harmony among humans and animals reign. Here is where the collective memory has drawn its nostalgia for a harmonious society, the recollection of an original happiness, which is still a source of inspiration today, despite the market laws of exchange, the "secret exaltation that . . . lends such a sovereign power to love, friendship, hospitality, generosity, affection, the spontaneous impetus of the gift, inexhaustible gratuitousness."[54]

We may criticize the idealization of the archaic in this imaginary and poetic anthropology; we may wonder about the relevance of what are considered savage cultures as paradigms for the transformation of contemporary societies. The fact remains that—as in the case of Marx's or Rosa Luxemburg's writings about primitive communities—this form of detour by way of the past is a powerful and subversive tool for critiquing and relativizing modern Western civilization. While it is risky to see these forms of ancient life as a solution to the catastrophes of modernity, it is nevertheless true that they constitute a reservoir of authentic human values that have lost none of their magic.

For several reasons we have chosen to focus on two authors, Edward Palmer Thompson and Raymond Williams, to illustrate the Romantic current in England. In the first place, their contributions, broad in scope, have played a crucial role not only in their chosen fields but also in English intellectual and political life in general. In the second place, each one embodies the revolutionary form of the Romantic vision in a particularly coherent and fruitful way. Despite some divergences and one or two polemics, we cannot help being struck by the deep affinity between Thompson and Williams, an affinity based on a common effort to revitalize the Romantic tradition for the left. They published pioneering works during the same period: Thompson's *William Morris* in 1955, Williams's *Culture and Society* in 1958.

E. P. Thompson

The critique of civilization runs like a red thread through E. P. Thompson's political, theoretical, and historiographical works. The originality, novelty, subversive power, and coherence of his historical works are intimately connected with his capacity to rediscover, restore, and reformulate in (heterodox) Marxist terms the Romantic tradition of critiquing capitalist-industrial civilization. This is true of *William Morris: From Romantic to Revolutionary* (1955, 1977), *The Making of the English Working Class* (1963), and *Customs in Common* (1991). It is no accident that Thompson's last two books are devoted to Romanticism: *Witness against the Beast: William Blake and the Moral Law* (1993) and *The Romantics: England in a Revolutionary Age* (1997). We shall restrict ourselves here to his great work on the formation of the English working class, a book that has profoundly marked all British historiography over the last thirty years, and to the 1991 collection that does a good job of summing up his undertaking (*Customs in Common*).

Starting with the preface of *The Making of the English Working Class,* Thompson sets the tone, in a statement that will serve as banner flag and sign of recognition for a new tendency in social history: "I am seeking to rescue the poor stockinger, the Luddite cropper, the 'obsolete' hand-loom weaver, the 'utopian' artisan, and even the deluded follower of Joanna Southcott, from the enormous condescension of posterity." The ironic quotation marks around "utopian" and "obsolete" speak volumes: they implicitly call into question the categories of the dominant historiography, imbued from start to finish with the ideology of progress as linear, inevitable, and beneficent. It is a matter not of idealizing these figures of the past in an acritical manner but of accounting for the human and social meaning of their struggle, which was not solely anachronic — far from it:

> Their crafts and traditions may have been dying. Their hostility to the new industrialism may have been backward-looking. Their communitarian ideals may have been fantasies. Their insurrectionary conspiracies may have been foolhardy. But . . . in some of the lost causes of the people of the Industrial Revolution we may discover insights into social evils which we have yet to cure. . . . Causes which were lost in England might, in Asia or Africa, yet be won.[55]

Rejecting the conformist views (the "conventional wisdom") of many economic historians who identify human progress with economic growth, Thompson does not hesitate to evoke "the truly catastrophic nature of the Industrial Revolution." In this context, he seeks to understand (rather than to condemn them out of hand as "regressive") the reaction of the popular strata of society and their nostalgia for a style of work and leisure that preceded the pitiless disciplines of industrialism. A similar sentiment inspired the disappointed Romantic authors who turned toward the past while denouncing the "manufacturing system" in their texts. Refusing to label them reactionaries, Thompson brings to light the subversive potential of their critique: "this current of traditionalist social radicalism, which moves from Wordsworth and Southey through to Carlyle and beyond, seems, in its origin, to contain a dialectic by which it is continually prompting revolutionary conclusions."[56]

Confronted with the merciless doctrine of the earliest ideologues of industrialization, like the famous Dr. Andrew Ure, author of *Philosophy of Manufactures* (1835) — "a book which, with its Satanic advocacy, much influenced Engels and Marx" — the historian takes up a critical viewpoint that draws on two contemporary sources: Romantic culture and popular resistance. He does not hesitate to recognize his debt in this area: "We are helped towards a certain detachment, both by the 'romantic' critique of industrialism . . . and by the record of tenacious resistance by which hand-loom weaver, artisan or village craftsman confronted this experience and held fast to an alternative culture." Thanks to these two dissident voices, "we understand more clearly what was lost, what was driven 'underground,' what is still unresolved."[57] In reality, at the end of the eighteenth century, these two forms (cultural and plebeian) of protest against the new bourgeois industrial society were separate and foreign to each other; it is the historian who retrospectively discovers their invisible solidarity in the face of a common adversary.

Thompson's insolence with respect to the most venerable dogmas is revealed in all its splendor in the chapter on the Luddites: the full generosity of a historian inspired by Romanticism was required to bring those accursed "machine-breakers" out of purgatory. Criticizing the scornful attitude of the orthodox Fabian or academic historians, Thompson does not hesitate to celebrate the heroism of the Luddite directors executed by the authorities (George Mellor, Jeremiah Brandreth). And he shows that Luddism was not merely a revolt against machines but above all a "violent eruption of feeling against unrestrained industrial capitalism" and a quasi-insurrectional popular movement. It is true that the movement was shot through with illusions and backward-looking nostalgia, because it "hark[ed] back to an obsolescent paternalist code, [and was] sanctioned by tradition of the working community." But in certain respects it also announced a future emancipation: "All these demands looked forwards, as much as backwards; and they contained within them a shadowy image, not so much of a paternalist, but of a democratic community, in which industrial growth should be regulated according to ethical priorities and the pursuit of profit be subordinated to human needs." In the two aspects of Luddism, the nostalgic artisanal dimension as well as the one that announces future struggles, we find at work "an alternative political economy and morality to that of *laissez faire.*"[58]

This authentically dialectical analysis of the Luddite movement could also be applied to the contradictions of the Romantic authors mentioned above. In the book's conclusion, Thompson returns to his comparison of the two protest movements, that of the workers and that of the poets, to highlight their common opposition to (capitalist) modernization and especially to regret their historical nonconvergence:

> Such men met Utilitarianism in their daily lives, and they sought to throw it back, not blindly, but with intelligence and moral passion. They fought, not the machine, but the exploitative and oppressive relationships intrinsic to industrial capitalism. In these same years, the great Romantic criticism of Utilitarianism was running its parallel but altogether separate course. After William Blake, no mind was at home in both cultures, nor had the genius to interpret the two traditions to each other. . . . Hence these years appear at times to display, not a revolutionary challenge, but a resistance movement, in which both the Romantics and the Radical craftsmen opposed the annunciation of Acquisitive Man. In the failure of the two traditions to come to a point of junction, something was lost. How much we cannot be sure, for we are among the losers.[59]

We can consider *The Making of the English Working Class* as an attempt to compensate, a century and a half later, for that missed connection.

Customs in Common (1991) is a collection of articles written by Thompson over a period of years. The introduction makes clear what these texts have in common: the analysis of eighteenth-century plebeian culture as a rebellious traditional culture, one that was resisting, in the name of custom, that rationalizations and economic innovations—such as the enclosure movement, industrial discipline, the "free market"—that governments, merchants, and employers were attempting to impose. Rejecting the usual explanations, which view this attitude simply as a retrograde approach in the face of the necessary modernization, Thompson interprets them as legitimate reactions to the transformations that were experienced by the plebeians as an aggravated form of exploitation, the expropriation of their customary rights, and the destruction of valorized work and leisure habits. In Thompson's opinion, the entire history of England in the eighteenth century is the history of the confrontation between the new capitalist market economy and the customary moral economy of the plebeians.

In the historian's eyes, the issue is a problematics that directly concerns today's world. This is true, on the one hand, because what English populations experienced in the eighteenth and nineteenth centuries is being reproduced in different contexts in the countries of the Southern Hemisphere today, and, on the other hand, because the definition of human needs in terms of markets and the submission of all the world's resources to market logic threaten the human race itself—in the north as well as the south—with ecological disaster.

Nostalgia (a critical nostalgia) for the preindustrial life style is present in all the texts of this collection, and in particular in the famous essay on the notion of time, which contrasts the task-oriented work of traditional communities with work regulated by the clock of modern industrial society. Contrary to the natural human work rhythm of premodern societies (of which we recognize vestiges today in the activity of artists, writers, farmers, or parents taking care of their children), time in advanced capitalist societies must always be consumed, utilized, transformed into merchandise. With his healthy-minded irreverent irony, Thompson draws "the moral of the story" of this profound upheaval in the social experience of temporality: "We may be permitted to moralise a little, in the eighteenth-century manner, ourselves. . . . The historical record is not a simple one of neutral and inevitable technological change, but it is also one of exploitation and of resistance to exploitation." Once again, it is a matter not of returning to the past but of trying, in the future, to relearn "some of the arts of living lost in the industrial revolution," by rediscovering "how to break down once more the barriers between work and life."[60]

Raymond Williams

Raymond Williams's work extends from the late 1940s to the late 1980s. It addresses a multiplicity of themes—literature and theater, the media and television in particular, culture in its multiple senses—and it relates these diverse fields to society, history, and politics. While his thinking unquestionably evolved over the years, Williams never renounced its Romantic underpinnings. In the 1970s, like others of the new left and in part under the influence of the group around *New Left Review*, he moved somewhat closer to orthodox Marxism, with structuralist leanings. *Marxism and Literature* (1977) is probably the least Romantic of his works, even though the book shows that the author has not completely abandoned his earlier opinions, as other texts of the late 1970s also indicate.[61] In the 1980s, he reacted more and more energetically against structuralism and poststructuralism and once again put the revolutionary Romantic perspective at the center of his reflection while developing it further.[62]

In *Politics and Letters,* a series of interviews with Williams conducted by several editors of *New Left Review,* one of the topics is *Culture and Society,* a book that made Williams famous and that continues to be viewed as among his greatest. In his interview, Williams explains that the main intention of the book was "oppositional," that he wanted

> to counter the appropriation of a long line of thinking about culture to what were by now decisively reactionary positions . . . , to try to recover the true complexity of the tradition it had confiscated — so that the appropriation could be seen for what it was. . . . The selective version of culture could be historically controverted by the writings of the thinkers who contributed to the formation and the discussion of the idea.[63]

Now the tradition that Williams wanted to save from appropriation by the right (he began the research and reflection that led to *Culture and Society* in 1948, at the beginning of the cold war) was precisely the Romantic tradition (even if he did not always use this term to designate it) in English literature, a tradition that extends from the late eighteenth century to our own day.

As he reviews this tradition, Williams shows the diversity of political options that are found within the same rejection of commercial, industrial, mechanized society. He begins by bringing to light the affinities that existed between conservatives such as Edmund Burke and Robert Southey and radicals or socialists such as William Cobbett and Robert Owen. He goes on to situate the anarcho-communist William Morris in the same tradition, and also T. S. Eliot, with his nostalgia for medieval Christianity. He alludes too (but in a less developed manner) to ideological modifications in certain authors (Thomas Carlyle, D. H. Lawrence, and others) who nevertheless remain Romantic at bottom. While Williams has no sympathy for the conservative or reactionary pole of this tradition, he judges that the veracity of the testimony and the force of the critique at the social level constitute precious contributions even in cases where the author draws regressive conclusions. Moreover, Williams shows that the conservatives' attitudes are not always as simple as one might suppose: in *Colloquies,* for example, Southey (in the voice of Thomas More) stresses that technological progress is by no means to be rejected, "provided that the moral culture of the species keep pace with the increase of its material powers,"[64] a position that Williams himself later developed in different terms.

Williams devotes an important chapter of *Culture and Society* to the connections between the Romantic tradition and Marxism, especially in England (at the time, Williams's cultural horizon was almost exclusively British). According to him, a considerable proportion of English Marxists in the 1930s were continuing the tradition of Matthew Arnold and William Morris in a different form; their attempt to create a Marxist theory of culture constituted "an interaction between Romanticism and Marx, between the idea of culture which is the major English tradition and Marx's brilliant revaluation of it." When Williams adds: "We have to conclude that the interaction is as yet far from complete," he in fact defines the project — perhaps without realizing it — that he himself, and E. P. Thompson as well, will pursue later.[65]

Whereas in the body of the book Williams examines a tradition of thought and art that stems from high culture, analyzing and evaluating them in their own terms, the conclusion introduces for the first time the viewpoint of the working class. For, unlike most Oxford Marxists of the 1930s, Williams had a working-class background (his father worked for the railroad), and in his conclusion he tries to link working-class culture with the Romantic tradition in the elite culture he has just been discussing.

In both cases there is an ethos of community, which is opposed to "the bourgeois idea of society" as an aggregate of competing individuals; but among the Romantics of the "middle classes" who react against the bourgeois spirit, this community is based on an ethic of service, whereas in working-class culture it takes the form of solidarity.[66] Williams does not hide the fact that he deems the latter conception more complete and more fruitful: "The idea of service, ultimately, is no substitute for the idea of active mutual responsibility, which is the other version of community."[67] This statement of an ideal based on working-class culture is an example (we could cite others) of notions already present in *Culture and Society* that are developed more fully later on. For though a shift of emphasis undeniably takes place over the course of Williams's career, his trajectory nonetheless presents considerable continuity.

The Country and the City, written in the early 1970s when Williams had already moved perceptibly closer to Marxism, explores a current in English literature that partially overlaps with the one discussed in *Culture and Society* — the contrast between country and city. He analyzes the often complex relations between literary images and actual history, especially in terms of points of view and class relations. In their interview with Williams on the topic of *The Country and the City,* the *New Left Review* editors welcome this approach as a step forward with respect to *Culture and Society.* However, for them its real importance lies rather in going beyond the usual Marxist problematics; for in general, as they note, the work of Marx and Engels "lacks the idea of a *continuing* tradition of values from the past that informs the struggles of the present."[68] Williams's distinctive contribution, then, would be that he showed the effective presence of precapitalist values, through the historical becoming of the Romantic vision, in the modern emancipatory project.

As he had done on the subject of *Culture and Society,* Williams signals in the interview on *The Country and the City* that that work is a polemical book. But it is interesting that, at two different points in the interview, he claims to have had contradictory goals: on the one hand, he was attacking the time-honored interpretation of poems that praise country houses, an interpretation presenting these poems as "records of the country houses, and so of the organic rural society England had once "been"; on the other hand, however, he was attacking the then-dominant form of thought in the Labour Party, which saw socialism only as "a successful industrial capitalism without the capitalists."[69] In fact, in *The Country and the City,* Williams is fighting in two roles: as a revolutionary, against a mystifying and reactionary Romanticism; as a Romantic, against the perverting of the revolutionary project, its corruption by the modern world.

Williams sees an important modification in rustic literature around the middle of the eighteenth century, a shift away from an idealization of rural retreats toward a melancholy feeling of loss, of degradation of the countryside, which implies a qualitative leap in the development of rural capitalism and already announces the fully Romantic structure of feeling (this is one of Williams's key notions).[70] From here on, this literature will often pine for an era of rural well-being in a recent past, sometimes the author's own youth, which will raise it to the mythical status of a Golden Age. Each generation will relive the illusion of feeling that it has experienced the crisis of the disappearance of Old England and the arrival of a fallen modern world.[71]

In *The Country and the City,* Williams's affinity with the Romantic critical tradition takes on a highly personal inflection. More than in *Culture and Society,* Williams develops his own positions and evokes his own experience. He refers to his youth in a rural region of Wales (his father was a railroad worker, but the family lived in a country village), and to the united character of his community, which had to do in part with its small size (Williams calls it a "knowable community").[72] From his youth he retains a deep attachment to the earth, and the recuperation of that theme by the conservative right makes him angry: "The song of the land, the song of rural labour, the song of delight in . . . the physical world, is too important and too moving to be tamely given up" to the enemies of change.[73]

Williams is also familiar with the alienations of the modern city, and he cites as authentic testimony the narratives offered by William Wordsworth, Carlyle, and Thomas Hardy as well as by Friedrich Engels (in *The Condition of the Working Class in England*) describing their experience of monadization, of social fragmentation, in large cities, something that for Engels becomes the emblem of the fundamental principle of capitalist society as a whole.[74] But Williams also highlights the possibilities for self-development offered by the city, and what he aspires to, finally, is the transcendence of the very opposition between city and country, in a postcapitalist society rooted in precapitalist values. As Williams points out elsewhere in *The Country and the City,* this transcendence of the city-country division, a division that contains all the others, had already been evoked by Blake, when in his famous poem he sought to build "Jerusalem / In England's green and pleasant land."[75]

In the last phase of Williams's career, in the 1980s, up to his death in 1988, his work was more and more oriented toward an attempt to define the form that a new Jerusalem might take and should take, a true transcendence of contemporary society, while he simultaneously continued to draw on authors he had explored earlier. At the same time, too, he summed up his work in sociology and cultural history, by drawing up the outline of a general approach that he called "cultural materialism."[76]

In "Towards Many Socialisms" (1985), as in other essays from the 1980s, Williams tried above all to make a connection between a socialism based on a class analysis and the new social movements.[77] We cannot fail to note that this is part of a larger enterprise, begun long before, aimed at the reconciliation of Marxism and Romanticism. Williams himself shows that he is conscious of this when, in "Towards Many Socialisms," he notes the significant affinity that exists between movements such as ecology, feminism, pacifism, and the Romantic tradition that he had so successfully highlighted.

WHAT FUTURE FOR ROMANTICISM?

While we are determined to defend the contribution of the Romantic cultural tradition against its adversaries, we do not mean to deny that it has limits and weaknesses, and may even present hidden dangers.

On the one hand, the idealization of the past — or its "utopization," one might say — is an integral part of the Romantic vision. Now it is obvious that, when the past that is an object of nostalgia is a real past (prehistory, antiquity, the feudal era, and so on) rather than a purely mythical one, the historical perspective is likely to be distorted to a certain extent.

When "the good old days," whatever they may be, are celebrated without reservation, one can be led, depending on the circumstances, to sweep under the rug or, on the contrary, to include in the celebration the worst moments of those past eras: slavery, servitude, privileges, the subjection of women to men, war, the ravages of illness, and so forth — in short, anything that could make life painful for at least part of humanity. One must doubtless recognize that previous stages of development of human societies have always included important zones of suffering and injustice.

On the other hand, the unease experienced by the Romantics in modern life and their radically critical attitude toward the modern quite often lead them to reject modernity categorically. From the Romantic perspective, everything that is new can easily become hateful. In this case Romanticism produces a blindness as to the positive, or potentially positive, elements in what is conventionally called "progress" — the counterpart of the blindness of positivists, utilitarians, and liberals toward the values of the past. For it is undeniable not only that many of modernity's developments are irreversible, at the individual as well as the social and economic levels but also that certain of these developments represent important acquisitions in the historical process and contributions to the yet-to-be realized flowering of the human race.

Thus it must be acknowledged that not everything in modernity is to be rejected. While it is not a sufficient guarantee against abuses of power, the "state of law" probably constitutes a necessary protection for individuals (who are themselves precious creations of the modern era) as opposed to the arbitrariness of a prince, a party, or "the people" as a whole. Similarly, if contemporary industry and technology imply grave dangers, new forms of modern technology might open a path—by reducing the time devoted to work and the onerousness of much labor, by the unprecedented possibilities of communication and information—to a degree of human self-realization that past societies never achieved.

Finally, in addition to these blind spots, the Romantic vision can be said to entail a danger. We have contested the idea that Romanticism is at the origin of the most pernicious ideologies of the twentieth century, from fascism to fundamentalism, by suggesting that the concept of "reactionary modernism" accounts better for these movements. But we cannot fail to note that the (partial) affinities between the latter and Romanticism make the passage from one to the other relatively easy or to recognize that many alliances have been made between them. Reactionary modernism in both its fascist and its fundamentalist forms has often successfully exploited the Romantic vein in its potential audience and among its intellectual fellow travelers.

In particular, we must admit that a considerable number of artists and thinkers who are inclined toward Romanticism, including some who are first rate (Gottfried Benn, Heidegger, and others), may have played the sorcerer's apprentice by supporting Nazism. While such slippages are far from inevitable (a whole gamut of other Romantic political positions still exists), we cannot deny that they have been produced and could continue to be produced on the basis of the Romantic critique of modernity.

The fact remains that capitalist modernity—and this also holds true for noncapitalist modernity, which is moreover in the process of disappearing—ends in an impasse. On the one hand because of its humanly, socially, and culturally destructive character; on the other, through the threat it poses to the very survival of the species (the danger of nuclear catastrophe or ecological disaster).

Here is where Romanticism has revealed its full critical force and its lucidity, confronting the blindness of the ideologies of progress. The Romantic critics have touched — even if in an intuitive or partial way — on what was the unthought of bourgeois thought; they have seen what was outside the scope of the liberal individualist worldview: reification, quantification, the loss of qualitative human and cultural values, the solitude of individuals, uprootedness, alienation through merchandise, the uncontrollable dynamic of machines and technology, temporality reduced to the instantaneous, the degradation of nature. In short, they have described the *facies hippocratica* of modern civilization. That they have often presented this penetrating diagnosis in the name of an elitist aestheticism, a retrograde religion, or a reactionary political ideology takes nothing away from its acuity and its worth — as a diagnosis. While they have not always been up to the task of proposing solutions to the catastrophes provoked by industrial progress, except for an illusory return to the lost past, they have brought to light the harm done by Western modernization.

Disturbed by the progression of the malady we call modernity, the nineteenth- and early twentieth-century Romantics were often melancholic and pessimistic in their outlook: moved by a tragic sentiment of the world and by terrible premonitions, they presented the future under the darkest possible colors. Still, they fell far short of anticipating the extent to which reality would outstrip their worst nightmares.

The twentieth century in fact experienced a certain number of monstrous events and phenomena: two world wars, fascism, the extermination camps. The force of the ideology of progress is such that one always describes these phenomena as "regressions," instances of "falling back into barbarity." People are astonished that such horrors were still possible "in our time," in the middle of the twentieth century. Yet these events — and other, similar ones, such as the use of the atomic bomb on Hiroshima and Nagasaki or the Vietnam War — are intimately tied in form and content to industrial modernity. We find nothing comparable either in the Middle Ages or among the so-called barbarian tribes, or at any time at all in the past. In reality, such events could not have taken place before the twentieth century, if only because they presupposed a level of technological and industrial development that did not exist until our day. The Romantics — even those of the twentieth century, even those who, like Walter Benjamin, had an intuition of the abyss that was about to open up — could not foresee these catastrophes, but they were alone in perceiving the dangers inherent in the logic of modernity.

This Cassandra role now belongs to the ecologists. If just a few years ago progress-oriented "good sense" and the modernizing consensus believed it was possible to refute their alarming forecasts without difficulty, by labeling them as the imaginings of "incurable Romantics" or "retrograde minds" whose program would take us back to the "age of the cave-dwellers," such is no longer the case today: even if very few concrete measures are taken to protect the environment in a serious way, it is no longer possible for the powers that be to ignore the warnings.

The Romantic perspective could play a particularly fruitful role in the current context, which is characterized among other things by the collapse of "real socialism." For, historically impelled to a great extent by non-Romantic anticapitalism, which misunderstood capitalism's nature as a global civilization, this system took as its goal the surpassing of capitalism by pushing modernity even further rather than by calling its very logic into question. It was thus condemned to reproduce, sometimes in aggravated form, the most basic defects of capitalism.

Is an alternative to "real modernity" possible? Can the desperate recourse to drugs, religious fundamentalism, or xenophobic nationalism be the only response to the social disarray created by the reign of market rationalism? How can we escape from the binary logic that compels us to choose between tradition and modernity, between returning to the past and accepting the present, between obscurantist reaction and devastating progress, authoritarian collectivism and possessive individualism, irrationalism and techno-bureaucratic rationalism?

However, there is a third way, another perspective, to envisage: the dialectical surpassing of these oppositions, toward a new culture, a new oneness with nature, a new community. These new forms are radically different from precapitalist manifestations by virtue of their integration of certain essential moments of modernity.

We cannot yet foresee the concrete modalities that may be adopted by this postcapitalist gemeinschaft, based not on compulsion or on blood ties but on the voluntary commitment of individuals. It will not be the immediate, organic totality, already given, but a mediated totality that operates through the necessary mediation of the modern individual.

Similarly, the new relation to the environment will not entail reinstituting the unscathed, virgin nature of the prehistoric past; it will result from an ecological equilibrium established with the help of new technologies. In other words, it is not a question of turning from the electric-powered mill back to the windmill, but of moving forward toward a new productive system based on the use of renewable energy sources.

Backward-looking Romanticism, in its diverse variants (including a certain type of traditionalist ecology), would have difficulty proposing a realistic and humanly valid alternative to the crimes and devastation provoked by capitalist industrial civilization: its goal of restoring premodern modes of life is completely unrealizable — and moreover completely undesirable.

Reform-oriented Romanticism (which is also present in part of the ecologist movement) is on the contrary perfectly suited to present practical and concrete solutions to the various modern calamities. Its limitation is that it chiefly attacks the symptoms rather than the root of *le mal du siècle*. Moderate and realistic, it comes close to accepting the foundations of the established technological, economic, and social order as an objective given that can no longer be challenged — a position that leads to abandoning the cultural and political universe of Romanticism.

The attitude of utopian-revolutionary Romanticism strikes us as more interesting — or at least we find this true of some of its principal representatives (from William Morris to Herbert Marcuse) and some of its tendencies, of which the contemporary heirs are ecosocialism and various social movements both in industrialized countries and in the Third World. Starting from the historically necessary and humanly legitimate character of certain conquests of the Enlightenment and the French Revolution — democracy, tolerance, individual and collective freedoms — as well as scientific and technological progress, revolutionary Romantics do not seek to restore the premodern past but to institute a new future, in which humanity would rediscover a portion of the qualities and values that it has lost with modernity: community, gratuitousness, gift giving, harmony with nature, work as art, the enchantment of life. But this implies a radical challenge to an economic system that is based on exchange value, profit, and the blind mechanism of the market: capitalism (or its alter ego that is in the process of dislocation, industrial despotism, bureaucratic dictatorship over needs).

It is thus not a matter of finding solutions to certain problems but of aiming at an overall alternative to the existing state of affairs, a new civilization, a different mode of life, which would not be the abstract negation of modernity but its "sublation" or absorption (*Aufhebung*), its insistent negation, the conservation of its best gains, and its transcendence toward a higher form of culture — a form that would restore to society certain human qualities destroyed by bourgeois industrial civilization. That does not mean a return to the past but a detour via the past, toward a new future, a detour that allows the human spirit to become aware of all the cultural richness and all the social vitality that have been sacrificed by the historical process launched by the Industrial Revolution, and to seek ways of bringing them back to life. It is thus a question not of wanting to abolish machinery and technology but of subjecting them to a different social logic—that is, of transforming them, restructuring them, and planning them in terms of criteria that are not those of the circulation of merchandise. The self-governing socialist reflection on economic democracy and that of the ecologists on the new alternative technologies—such as geothermal or solar energy—are first steps in this direction. But these are objectives that require a revolutionary transformation of the entire set of current socioeconomic and political-military structures.[78]

A little more than a century ago, in 1890, the English libertarian socialist William Morris had a waking dream. He imagined a working-class and popular rebellion leading to a great change in England: the advent (after a period of transition) of a free and fraternal society, without classes and without a state, without merchandise or accumulations of capital; a communist world based on the joy of work as an artistic activity and on the gratuitousness of gifts and exchanges; a human community that had succeeded in establishing complementarity between mechanical production and artisanal creativity, between the return to nature and the flowering of a rich culture, between "immensely improved machinery"[79] and an urban architecture inspired by that of the Middle Ages. Despite its limitations and despite certain frankly unacceptable ideas (in particular on the subject of the condition of women!), the communitarian, socialist, and ecological universe of *News from Nowhere* seems strikingly contemporary at the end of the twentieth century.

A utopian dream? No doubt. Provided that we understand the term "utopia" in its original, etymological sense: that which does not yet exist anywhere. Without utopias of this type, the social imaginary would be limited to the narrow horizon of what really exists, and human life would be an oversize reproduction of sameness.

This utopia has powerful roots in the present and in the past: in the present, because it draws on all the potentialities and contradictions of modernity to explode the system, and in the past, because it looks to pre-modern societies for concrete examples and tangible proofs of a qualitatively different mode of life, one distinct from (and in certain respects superior to) capitalist industrial civilization. Without nostalgia for the past there can be no dream of an authentic future. In this sense, *utopia will be Romantic or it will not be.*

Notes

1. REDEFINING ROMANTICISM

Unless otherwise indicated, all translations are my own. — *Trans.*

1 Hans Georg Schenk, *The Mind of the European Romantics: An Essay in Cultural History* (New York: Anchor Books, 1969), p. xxii.

2 Arthur O. Lovejoy, "The Need to Distinguish Romanticisms," in *Romanticism: Problems of Definition, Explanation, and Evaluation,* ed. John B. Halsted (Boston: D. C. Heath, 1965), p. 39. See Stefanos Rozanis, *I Romantiki Exergersi* (The Romantic revolt) (Athens: Ypsilon, 1987), p. 15.

3 Carl Schmitt, *Political Romanticism,* trans. Guy Oakes (Cambridge: MIT Press, 1986), pp. 161–62. See *Politische Romantik,* 2d ed. (Munich: Verlag von Duncker and Humboldt, 1925), pp. 162, 176, 227. We should add that Schmitt, immunized against moral inadequacies, joined the Nazi Party in 1933; in 1934 he published an essay called "Der Führer schützt das Recht" (The Führer protects legality).

4 Benedetto Croce, "A Crisis of Faith" (1934), in Halsted, *Romanticism: Problems of Definition, Explanation, and Evaluation,* p. 54, and Pierre Lasserre, *Le romantisme français* (Paris: Mercure de France, 1907), cited by Christine Planté (along with similar passages from Charles Maurras and August Strindberg) in her fine book *La petite soeur de Balzac: Essai sur la femme auteur* (Paris: Seuil, 1989), pp. 78–79.

5 *Larousse du XXᵉ siècle* (Paris: Librairie Larousse, 1933), 6:30.

6 Fritz Strich, *Deutsche Klassik und Romantik, oder Vollendung und Unendlich; ein Vergleich* (Bern: Francke, 1962).

7 These ideas are developed in detail in M. H. Abrams's two classic works, *The Mirror and the Lamp: Romantic Theory and the Critical Tradition* (Oxford: Oxford University Press, 1971), and *Natural Supernaturalism: Tradition and Revolution in Romantic Literature* (New York: Norton, 1973).

8 René Wellek, "The Concept of Romanticism in Literary History" (1949), in *Romanti-*

cism: Points of View, ed. R. F. Gleckner and G. E. Enscoe (Detroit: Wayne State University Press, 1989), pp. 181–205.

9 Morse Peckham, "Toward a Theory of Romanticism" (1951), in Gleckner and Enscoe, *Romanticism,* pp. 231–57.

10 Morse Peckham, "Reconsiderations" (1961), in Gleckner and Enscoe, *Romanticism,* as sec. 5 of "Toward a Theory," pp. 250–57.

11 Henry Remak, "West European Romanticism: Definition and Scope," in *Comparative Literature: Method and Perspective,* ed. Newton P. Stallknecht and Horst Frenz (Carbondale: Southern Illinois University Press, 1971), pp. 275–311.

12 William McGovern, *From Luther to Hitler* (Cambridge, Mass.: Riverside Press, 1941), pp. 200, 582.

13 Peter Viereck, *Metapolitics: From the Romantics to Hitler* (New York: Alfred A. Knopf, 1941), p. 19.

14 Fritz Stern, *The Politics of Cultural Despair: A Study in the Rise of the German Ideology* (Berkeley: University of California Press, 1961), p. xvii (more generally, see pp. xi–xvii).

15 Jacques Droz, *Le romantisme allemand et l'Etat: Résistance et collaboration en Allemagne napoléonienne* (Paris: Payot, 1966), pp. 50, 295–98; and *Le romantisme politique en Allemagne* (Paris: Armand Colin, 1963), pp. 25, 27, 34–36.

16 Irving Babbitt, *Rousseau and Romanticism* (Boston: Houghton Mifflin, 1919), pp. 377, 378, and John Bowle, *Western Political Thought* (London: University Paperbacks, 1961), p. 438.

17 This analysis is shared both by rationalist critics of Romanticism such as Anna Tumarkin (*Die romantische Weltanschauung* [Bern: Paul Haupt, 1920]) and by German scholars laying claim to the Romantic tradition (see the essays by Hermann August Korff, Gustav Hübener, Walther Linden, and Martin Honecker in *Begriffsbestimmung der Romantik,* ed. Helmut Prang [Darmstadt: Wissenschaftliche Buchgesellschaft, 1968]).

18 Isaiah Berlin, "The Counter-Enlightenment," in *Against the Current: Essays in the History of Ideas* (Oxford: Oxford University Press, 1979), pp. 6–20.

19 Henri Peyre, "Romanticism," *Encyclopaedia Universalis* (Paris: Encyclopaedia Universalis, 1972), 14:368.

20 Albert Joseph George, *The Development of French Romanticism: The Impact of the Industrial Revolution on Literature* (Syracuse, N.Y.: Syracuse University Press, 1955), pp. xi, 192, 193.

21 Christopher Caudwell, "The Bourgeois Illusion and English Romantic Poetry," in Glecker and Enscoe, *Romanticism,* p. 116.

22 Karl Mannheim, *Conservatism: A Contribution to the Sociology of Knowledge,* ed. David Kettler, Volker Meja, and Nico Stehr, trans. David Kettler and Volker Meja (London: Routledge and Kegan Paul, 1986), p. 90, and "Das konservative Denken: Soziologische Beiträge zum Werden des politisch-historischen Denkens in Deutschland" (1927), in *Wissenssoziologie* (Berlin: Luchterhand, 1964), p. 453; see also pp. 491–94, 504. *Conservatism* is a translation of *Konservatismus: Ein Beitrag zur Soziologie des Wissens,* ed. David Kettler, Volker Meja, and Nico Stehr (Frankfurt: Suhrkamp, 1984): this was Mannheim's 1925 *habilitation* thesis, of which the 1927 article is an excerpt. Here Mannheim stresses

that "the romantic experience is a general European phenomenon which emerged at approximately the same time in all European countries. It arose partly as a genuine reaction to identical problems presented by a rationalized capitalist world" (p. 44). The inverse position, namely, the essentially revolutionary character of Romanticism (at least in England), is presented (from a position close to that of Marxism) in the original and interesting work of Paul Rozenberg, *Le romantisme anglais: Le défi des vulnérables* (Paris: Larousse, 1973). Nevertheless, this analysis appears just as one-sided, in that it excludes counterrevolutionary forms of thought (Burke, for example) from Romanticism.

23 György Lukács, "Questions de principe sur une polémique sans principes" (1940?), in *Ecrits de Moscou* (Paris: Editions Sociales, 1974), p. 159. We deal in more detail with the various stands Lukács took toward Romanticism over time in chap. 3.

24 Friedrich Engels, "Letter to Miss Harkness," in *Marx and Engels on Literature and Art: A Selection of Writings,* ed. Lee Baxandall and Stefan Morawski (St. Louis: Telos Press, 1973), p. 116.

25 Jan O. Fischer, *Epoque romantique et réalisme: Problèmes méthodologiques* (Prague: Universita Karlova, 1977), pp. 254–55, 258, 260, 266–67.

26 Pierre Barbéris, "'Mal du siècle,' ou d'un romantisme de droite à un romantisme de gauche," in *Romantisme et politique (1815 1851),* colloquium of the École normale supérieure, Saint-Cloud, 1966 (Paris: Armand Colin, 1969), p. 177.

27 Ernst Fischer, *The Necessity of Art: A Marxist Approach,* trans. Anna Bostock (London: Penguin, 1963), pp. 52, 55, 56–57. During the 1950s, Fischer prepared a book on Romanticism that was not published until several years after his death. This text contains a great wealth of analysis, but it fails to provide a definition of Romanticism — except for a very general and vague "non-concordance with social reality, its negation via criticism and the imagination" (Fischer, *Ursprung und Wesen der Romantik* [Frankfurt: Sendler Verlag, 1986], p. 137). The antibourgeois aspect of some major nineteenth-century artists and writers (suggested but not developed by Fischer) has been remarkably well presented in two recent books (Marxist in inspiration) by Dolf Oehler: *Pariser Bilder 1 (1830–1848)* (Frankfurt: Suhrkamp, 1988), and *Ein Höllensturz der Alten Welt: Zur Selbsforschung der Moderne nach dem Juni 1848* (Frankfurt: Suhrkamp, 1988); in French as *Le spleen contre l'oubli, 1848: Baudelaire, Flaubert, Heine, Herzen,* trans. Guy Petitdemange and Sabine Cornille (Paris: Payot, 1996).

28 Raymond Williams, *Culture and Society, 1780–1950* (New York: Harper and Row, 1958), pp. 30–48; for a reference to William Morris, see p. 153. Similar ideas are put forth by E. P. Thompson in his magnificent biography of Morris, *William Morris: Romantic to Revolutionary* (London: Merlin Press; New York: Pantheon Books, 1977). Finally, and exceptionally, some Eastern European scholars — for example, Jan O. Fischer in Prague and Claus Träger in the German Democratic Republic — escape the straitjacket of dogma to produce highly suggestive studies. In France, Pierre Barbéris is the principal scholar to have examined Romanticism from an openly Marxist perspective.

29 For a descriptive presentation that attributes a similar scope to the phenomenon, see Paul Honigsheim, "Romantik und neuromantische Bewegungen," in *Handwörterbuch der Sozialwissenschaften* (Stuttgart: G. Fischer, 1953).

30 Lucien Goldmann, "La philosophie des Lumières," in *Structures mentales et création culturelle* (Paris: Anthropos, 1970), p. 9. A passage in *The Hidden God,* trans. Philip Thody (New York: Humanities Press, 1964), reveals a Romantic dimension (in the sense we assign to the concept) in Goldmann's own thinking, moreover. In this instance Goldmann maintains that now, more than ever before, the absence of the time-honored old values in the face of modernity — economic individualism and "the technical behavior of rational man" — has revealed "the terrible dangers which it involves" (p. 32).

31 See for example Lucien Goldmann, "Le théâtre de Genet: Essai d'étude sociologique," *Sociologie de la littérature: Recherches récentes et discussions,* 2d ed. (Brussels: Editions de l'Université de Bruxelles, 1973), pp. 9–34; and *Cultural Creation in Modern Society* (1971), trans. Bart Grahl (St. Louis, Mo.: Telos Press, 1976), pp. 87–88.

32 Robert Sayre and Michael Löwy, "Figures du romantisme anticapitaliste," *L'homme et la société* 69–70 (July–December 1983): 99–121; 73–74 (July–December 1984): 147–72. A slightly modified version has appeared in English: "Figures of Romantic Anti-Capitalism," *New German Critique,* no. 32 (1984): 42–92. The English version also appears in an anthology, with a critique by Michael Ferber, in *Spirits of Fire: English Romantic Writers and Contemporary Historical Methods,* ed. G. A. Rosso and Daniel P. Watkins (Rutherford, N.J.: Fairleigh Dickinson University Press, 1990), pp. 23–68, followed by our response to the critique: "The Fire Is Still Burning: An Answer to Michael Ferber," in ibid., pp. 85–91.

33 Concerning the difference between a dialectical concept and an ideal type, we refer to the very pertinent remarks in a recent study by Philippe Raynaud (who acknowledges his own debt to the Weberian method): "The method of ideal types is . . . *antidialectical.* The Hegelian dialectic is in fact based on the idea that thought has to rediscover in itself the rationality that is at work in the real by associating the 'contradictions' found in reality with moments in the developments of a whole; now, since it presupposes that the *meaning* of social phenomena is *constructed* by the scholar starting from a particular point of view . . . , the Weberian method obviously has to reject the claim that reality's 'contradictions' can be integrated into the ideal type. The scholar's goal is thus to construct *noncontradictory* (thus nondialectical) concepts that express only a *partial* view, since the infiniteness of the perceptible world justifies the construction of an infinity of ideal types; the ideal type is thus the result of selection, and it leaves aside reality's 'contradictions,' the study of which belongs not to *sociology* but to *history*" (*Max Weber et les dilemmes de la raison moderne* [Paris: Presses Universitaires de France, 1987], p. 51).

34 Claus Träger, "Des Lumières à 1830: Héritage et innovation dans le romantisme allemand," *Romantisme* 28–29 (1980): 90; H. P. Lund, "Le romantisme et son histoire," *Romantisme* 7 (1974): 113.

35 See Hans Kals, *Die soziale Frage in der Romantik* (Cologne: P. Hanstein, 1974), pp. 7–15.

36 Max Milner, *Le Romantisme (1820–1843)* (Paris: Arthaud, 1973), 1:242.

37 It is interesting that in his *Naissance de la littérature: La théorie esthétique du romantisme allemand* (Paris: Presses de l'Ecole normale supérieure, 1983), Jean-Marie Schaeffer adopts a similar approach. Rejecting Lovejoy's position, as we do, as well as the simple enumeration of themes, Schaeffer undertakes to sketch a definition of Romanticism as

worldview, or as "structure of thought" possessing an "internal logic." The content of his structural definition is entirely different, however, since it is situated solely at the level of the Romantic aesthetic. (See in particular his first chapter.)

38 Jean Chesneaux, *De la modernité* (Paris: La Découverte, 1983); *Brave Modern World: The Prospects for Survival* (1989), trans. Diana Johnstone, Karen Bowie, and Francesca Garvie (London: Thames and Hudson, 1992).

39 *Deutsches Wörterbuch von Jacob Grimm und Wilhelm Grimm* (Leipzig: S. Hirzel, 1893), 8: 1156; François-René de Chateaubriand, *Génie du christianisme,* vol. 2, pt. 3 (Paris: Beauce-Rusand, 1818), p. 9; Alfred de Musset, *The Confession of a Child of the Century* (New York: H. Fertig, 1977), chap. 2.

40 György Lukács, *The Theory of the Novel: A Historico-Philosophical Essay on the Forms of the Great Epic Literature,* trans. Anna Bostock (Cambridge: MIT Press, 1971), p. 112.

41 Hugues Félicité Robert de Lamennais, *Words of a Believer* (New York: Charles de Behr, 1834), pp. 42–45. In Lamennais's eyes, capitalists are far worse than the tyrants of the past; for the man who exploits workers, "Hell alone can furnish a name" (p. 45).

42 György Lukács, *History and Class Consciousness: Studies in Marxist Dialectics,* trans. Rodney Livingstone (Cambridge: MIT Press, 1971); see especially the first section of the fourth essay, "The Phenomenon of Reification," pp. 83–110.

43 The philosopher Gerhard Krüger, cited by Arthur Henkel in "Was ist eigentlich romantisch?" (in *Festschrift für Richard Alewyn,* ed. Herbert Singer and Benno von Wiese [Cologne: Böhlau-Verlag, 1967], p. 296), called Romanticism "the first self-criticism of modernity" (*der erste Selbstkritik der Neuzeit*).

44 Friedrich Schlegel, in *European Romanticism: Self-Definition,* ed. Lilian R. Furst (London: Methuen, 1980), p. 34. The Schlegel section is titled "Classical versus Romantic" (Furst's title, not Schlegel's). The text cited is an excerpt from *Vorlesungen über dramatische Kunst und Literatus, Kritische Schriften,* vol. 5, pp. 25–26.

45 Arnold Hauser, *The Social History of Art,* trans. in collaboration with the author by Stanley Godman (London: Routledge, and Kegan Paul, 1999), 3:163.

46 Walter Benjamin, "Albert Béguin, *L'âme romantique et le rêve,*" review, in *Gesammelte Schriften,* ed. Hella Tiedemann-Bartels (Frankfurt: Suhrkamp, 1978), 3:560.

47 Karl Marx and Friedrich Engels, review of *Latter-Day Pamphlets,* by Thomas Carlyle, in *Über Kunst und Literatur* (Berlin: Verlag Bruno Henschel, 1948), p. 104.

48 Gérard de Nerval, *Aurélia,* trans. Kendall Lapin (Santa Maria, Calif.: Asylum Arts, 1991), pp. 38–42, 53.

49 Schlegel, in Furst, *European Romanticism,* p. 9. Furst titles this section of Schlegel excerpts "Universal Transcendental Poetry." The text cited is from *Gespräch über die Poesie, Kritische Ausgabe,* vol. 2, p. 335.

50 Ibid., p. 3; see Schlegel's discussion of Wordsworth's conception of poetry, pp. 11–12.

51 Dorothea Schlegel cited in *The Literary Absolute,* ed. Philippe Lacoue-Labarthe and Jean-Luc Nancy (1978), trans. Philip Barnard and Cheryl Lester (Albany: State University of New York Press, 1988), p. 6.

52 *From Max Weber: Essays in Sociology,* ed. Hans H. Gerth and C. Wright Mills (Oxford: Oxford University Press; New York: Galaxy, 1958), p. 347.

53 Charles Nodier, *Smarra, Trilby, et autres contes,* ed. Jean-Luc Steinmetz (Paris: Garnier-Flammarion, 1980), pp. 135–36, 144.

54 Jules Michelet, *Le peuple* (Paris: Julliard, 1965), pp. 49–50.

55 *The Complete Poetry and Prose of William Blake,* ed. David Erdman (Berkeley: University of California Press, 1982), pp. 95–96.

56 Georg Simmel, "Das Individuum und die Freiheit," in *Brücke und Tür* (Stuttgart: Kocher Verlag, 1957), pp. 266–69.

57 One notable exception is Alvin Ward Gouldner; see "Romanticism and Classicism: Deep Structures in Social Science," in *For Sociology: Renewal and Critique in Sociology Today* (New York: Basic Books, 1973), pp. 323–66.

58 This concept is developed by Jeffrey Herf in "Reactionary Modernism: Some Ideological Origins of the Primacy of Politics in the Third Reich," *Theory and Society* 10 (1981): 805–32; and in *Reactionary Modernism: Technology, Culture, and Politics in Weimar and the Third Reich* (Cambridge: Cambridge University Press, 1984). At about the same time as Herf, Louis Dupeux analyzed the same phenomenon: see " 'Révolution conservatrice' et modernité," *Revue d'Allemagne* (proceedings of a colloquium held in Strasbourg, 1981) 14 (January–March 1982): 3–34; and " 'Kulturpessimismus,' révolution conservatrice et modernité," in *Weimar ou l'explosion de la modernité,* ed. Gérard Raulet (Paris: Anthropos, 1984), pp. 31–46.

59 *Manifesto of the Communist Party,* in Karl Marx and Friedrich Engels, *Collected Works,* trans. Richard Dixon et al. (New York: International Publishers, 1975), 6:487; Max Weber, "Science as a Vocation," trans. Hans H. Gerth and C. Wright Mills, in *Sociological Writings,* ed. Wolf Heydebrand (New York: Continuum, 1994), p. 302.

60 Hoxie Neale Fairchild, "Romantic Religion" (1949), in Gleckner and Enscoe, *Romanticism,* p. 207; T. E. Hulme, "Romanticism and Classicism," in ibid., p. 58.

61 E. T. A. Hoffmann, "Little Zaches," in *Three Märchen of E. T. A. Hoffman,* trans. Charles E. Passage (Columbia: University of South Carolina Press, 1971), pp. 12–15.

62 Novalis, "Hymn to the Night," 1, in *Hymns to the Night,* trans. Mabel Cotterell (London: Phoenix Press, 1948), p. 27.

63 Bloch cited in Manfred Frank, *Der Kommende Gott: Vorlesungen zur Neuen Mythologie* (Frankfurt: Suhrkam Verlag, 1982), pp. 31–36.

64 Friedrich Wilhelm Joseph von Schelling, *Sämmtliche Werke,* ed. K. F. A. Schelling (Stuttgart: Cotta, 1856–1861), vol. 1, pt. 6, p. 573; and Friedrich Schlegel, "Rede über die Mythologie," in *Romantik* (Stuttgart: Reclam, 1984), 1:240–41. Frank's book *Der Kommende Gott,* which has had considerable impact in Germany, signals a renewal of interest in myth and of the lifting of the taboo that had weighed on this theme; Frank undertakes a utopian rereading of the Romantic vision of a new myth. Let us note nevertheless that when the work was translated into French (*Le Dieu à venir* [Actes Sud, 1990]), the subtitle (*Leçons sur la nouvelle mythologie*) disappeared.

65 Schlegel, "Rede über die Mythologie," pp. 234–35. According to Karl Heinz Bohrer, it is the past-oriented undertaking of "remythification" practiced by the *Spätromantik* that inspires the ideological maneuvers of Fascism. See K. H. Bohrer, "Vorwort," in *Mythos und Moderne* (Frankfurt: Suhrkamp, 1983), pp. 9–10. This collective work (organized by

Bohrer) also bears witness (though in a more prudent and reserved way than Frank's book) to the renewal of the debate about mythology at the end of the twentieth century.

66 Schlegel, "Rede über die Mythologie," pp. 236–37, 240. It is hard to avoid the impression that Schlegel, in these passages, is intuitively designating the realm that Sigmund Freud, a century later, will try to circumscribe with the category of the unconscious.

67 Friedrich Wilhelm Joseph von Schlegel, "Athenäums-Fragmente," in *Kritische Schriften* (Munich: Carl Hanser Verlag, 1964), 48, and "Rede über die Mythologie," 236, 242. On this topic, see Karl Heinz Bohrer's interpretation in "Friedrich Schlegels Rede über die Mythologie," in *Mythos und Moderne,* 62.

68 Schlegel, "Rede über die Mythologie," p. 242. It is only later that Schlegel will renounce his republican and revolutionary convictions to become an ideologue of the Catholic restoration in Vienna.

69 Charles Dickens, *Hard Times* (New York: Harper and Row, 1965), pp. 4, 22–23, 274. Thomas Gradgrind becomes "Member of Parliament for Coketow: one of the respected members for ounce weights and measures, one of the representatives of the multiplication table, one of the deaf honourable gentlemen, dumb honourable gentlemen, blind honourable gentlemen, lame honourable gentlemen, dead honourable gentlemen, to every other consideration" (p. 88).

70 Ibid., pp. 156, 205, 94.

71 Ibid., p. 22.

72 Ibid., pp. 60–61, 158, 157.

73 Edmund Burke, *Reflections on the Revolution in France* (1790), ed. F. G. Selby (London: Macmillan, 1892), p. 84.

74 Dickens, *Hard Times,* p. 22.

75 E. T. A. Hoffmann, "The Sandman," in *Selected Writings of E. T. A. Hoffmann,* ed. and trans. Leonard J. Kent and Elizabeth C. Knight, vol. 1, *The Tales* (Chicago: University of Chicago Press, 1969), p. 161; Walter Benjamin, "E. T. A. Hoffmann und Oskar Panizza," *Gesammelte Schriften* (1977), 2:644.

76 Thomas Carlyle, "Signs of the Times" (1829), in *Critical and Miscellaneous Essays* (London: Chapman and Hall, 1888), 2:233, 235, 245, 243.

77 See the anthology by Jacques Droz, *Le romantisme politique en Europe* (Paris: Armand Colin, 1963), pp. 61, 86, 169. The text attributed to Schelling is found in Manfred Frank and Gerhard Kurz, eds., *Materialen zu Schellings philosophische Anfänge* (Frankfurt: Suhrkamp, 1975), p. 110.

78 Martin Buber, *Gemeinschaft* (Munich: Dreiländerverlag, 1919), p. 17.

79 Mannheim, *Conservatism,* p. 62.

80 Frederick Engels, *The Condition of the Working Class in England in 1844,* in Marx and Engels, *Collected Works,* 4:329.

81 Brentano cited by Träger, "Des Lumières à 1830," p. 99.

82 For a discussion of this concept, its history, and its expression in the novels of Marcel Proust, André Malraux, Georges Bernanos, Albert Camus, and Nathalie Sarraute, see Robert Sayre, *Solitude in Society, A Sociological Study in French Literature* (Cambridge: Harvard University Press, 1978).

83 Nicolas Berdiaev, *Solitude and Society* (London: Centenary Press, 1983), p. 97.

84 See Lilian R. Furst, *Romanticism* (1969; reprint, London: Methuen, 1976), p. 7; and Schlegel excerpt in *European Romanticism*, pp. 4–9.

85 Furst, *Romanticism*, p. 11.

86 Lacoue-Labarthe and Nancy, "Preface," *The Literary Absolute*, p. 4; see also Furst, *Romanticism*, pp. 12–13; and "Romantic," in Raymond Williams, *Keywords: A Vocabulary of Culture and Society* (New York: Oxford University Press, 1976).

87 J. A. H. Murray, ed. *A New English Dictionary on Historical Principles* (Oxford: Clarendon Press, 1914).

88 See for example *Histoire de la littérature anglaise* (Paris: Hachette, 1965), vol. 2, in which the eminently Romantic character of the period starting in 1760 is very well described, but the period continues to be labeled "pre-Romantic" (p. 882). Paul Van Tieghem played the most important role in spreading this notion in France, especially in *Le préromantisme*, 2 vols. (Paris: Rieder-Alcan, 1924–1930).

89 See Northrop Frye, "Towards Defining an Age of Sensibility," in *Eighteenth Century English Literature: Modern Essays in Criticism,* ed. J. L. Clifford (New York: Oxford University Press, 1959).

90 See Jacques Bousquet, *Anthologie du XVIIIᵉ romantique* (Paris: Pauvert, 1972), p. 370.

91 Let us mention some recent titles pertaining to English literature: David Aers, Jonathan Cook, and David Punter, *Romanticism and Ideology: Studies in English Writing, 1765–1830* (London: Routledge and Kegan Paul, 1981); Marilyn Butler, *Romantics, Rebels, and Reactionaries: English Literature and Its Background, 1760–1830* (New York: Oxford University Press, 1982); Timothy Webb, ed., *English Romantic Hellenism, 1700–1824* (Totowa, N.J.: Barnes and Noble, 1982).

92 Bousquet, *Anthologie*, pp. 18, 118. See also Jacques Bousquet's doctoral dissertation, "Définition et valeur de la notion de romantisme comme catégorie de l'histoire culturelle" (supplementary thesis in letters, Sorbonne, 1964). Although Bousquet's approach to Romanticism has much in common with our own, it differs on the essential point: for Bousquet, Romanticism is by its nature a form of individualism, and in this respect it is in harmony with economic individualism (see our discussion of the individualist dimension of Romanticism, above).

93 Pierre Barbéris, *Aux sources du réalisme: Aristocrates et bourgeois* (Paris: UGE, 1978), p. 339; see also pp. 340–50. In "Romantik und neuromantische Bewegungen," Paul Honigsheim sees Fénelon, the Jansenists, and their like as "precursors" of Romanticism (p. 27).

94 See R. H. Tawney, *Religion and the Rise of Capitalism* (New York: Harcourt Brace, 1926), chap. 2, sec. 2.

95 Horace, *Epodes* 2, 1–4, in *The Odes and Epodes,* trans. C. E. Bennett (Cambridge: Harvard University Press, Loeb Classical Library, 1947), p. 365. See the discussion in Sayre, *Solitude in Society,* pp. 21–23. On this theme, see also Raymond Williams, *The Country and the City* (New York: Oxford University Press, 1973), chaps. 3–4.

96 Karl Polanyi, *The Great Transformation* (Boston: Beacon Press, 1957), p. 71; in the French edition, *La grande transformation: Aux origins politiques et économiques de notre temps* (Paris: Gallimard, 1983), see the introduction by Louis Dumont, and pp. 54, 71, 85–86, 106.

97 Jean-Jacques Rousseau, *Lettres écrites de la montagne* (Neuchâtel: Ides et Calendes, 1962), letter 9, p. 284 (emphasis added). And see Marx: "It is not until the eighteenth century . . . that the various forms of the social nexus confront the individual as merely a means towards his private ends, as external necessity" (*Economic Manuscripts of 1857–58* [*Grundrisse*], in Marx and Engels, *Collected Works*, 28:18.

98 Alfred Cobban, *Edmund Burke and the Revolt against the Eighteenth Century* (London: George Allen and Unwin, 1929), p. 202.

99 Eric J. Hobsbawm, *The Age of Revolution, 1789–1848* (1962; reprint, New York: New American Library, 1964), p. 306.

100 Butler, *Romantics, Rebels, and Reactionaries*, p. 16.

101 "Kernel" is the word used by Furst in *European Romanticism*, p. xii.

102 Mannheim, *Conservatism*, p. 45.

103 Bousquet, *Anthologie*, introduction, pp. 129ff.

104 György Lukács, *Georg Lukacs Werke* (Neuwied: Luchterhand, 1964), 7:57.

105 See Träger, "Des Lumières à 1830," p. 95.

106 Henri Brunschwig, *Société et romantisme en Prusse au XVIIIe siècle* (Paris: Flammarion, 1973), p. 56.

107 Ibid., chapter 3, and Berlin, "Counter-Enlightenment," pp. 6–7, and "Hume and the Sources of German Anti-Rationalism," p. 165, both in *Against the Current*.

108 Brunschwig, *Société et romantisme*, p. 206.

109 See Jürgen Kocka, "Bürgertum und Bürgerlichkeit als Probleme der deutschen Geschichte vom späten 18. zum frühen 20. Jahrhundert," in *Bürger und Bürgerlichkeit im 19 Jahrhundert*, ed. Jürgen Kocka (Göttingen: Vandenhoeck and Ruprecht, 1987), p. 43.

110 See E. Fischer, *Ursprung und Wesen der Romantik*, p. 176.

111 Mannheim, *Conservatism*, pp. 47–48, 112–15.

112 For a discussion of the specific aspects of Romanticism in some of these countries, see Zoran Konstantinovic, "Le conditionnement social des structures littéraires chez les peuples du Sud-Est européen à l'époque du romantisme," *Synthesis: Bulletin du Comité national de littérature comparée de Roumanie* (1974, pp. 131–37). And for a discussion of the "national forms of the Romantic movement" in each country where there are manifestations of Romanticism, see Paul Van Tieghem, *Le romantisme dans la littérature européenne* (1948; reprint, Paris: Albin Michel, 1969), bk. 2.

113 See *Histoire de la littérature anglaise*, 2:882.

114 Ibid., and Butler, *Romantics, Rebels, and Reactionaries*, 16–20.

115 Oliver Goldsmith, "The Deserted Village," in *The Poems of Thomas Gray, William Collins; Oliver Goldsmith*, ed. Roger Lonsdale (London: Longmans, 1969). This poem influenced the young Philip Freneau, who was virtually the only representative of Romanticism in the United States in the pre- and postrevolutionary periods. On Freneau's Romanticism, see Robert Sayre, " 'Romantisme anticapitaliste' et révolution chez Freneau," *Revue française d'études américaines* 40:175–86.

116 Auguste Viatte, *Les sources occultes du romantisme: Illuminisme-théosophie*, vol. 1, *Le préromantisme (1770–1820)* (1927; reprint, Paris: Champion, 1979).

117 Bousquet, *Anthologie*, p. 91.

118 Ibid., p. 194; Octavio Paz, *Children of the Mire: Modern Poetry from Romanticism to the Avant-Garde,* trans. Rachel Phillips (Cambridge: Harvard University Press, 1974), p. 33.

119 Other Romantics include Nicolas Bonneville, a friend of Restif and the person who introduced German literature into France (by his translations), and Louis-Sébastien Mercier, mentioned above. Concerning Bernardin and Bonneville, see Robert Sayre and Michael Löwy, "Utopie romantique et Révolution française," in *Dissonances dans la Révolution,* special issue, *L'homme et la société* 94, no. 4 (1989): 71–81; on Restif, see Mark Poster, *The Utopian Thought of Restif de la Bretonne* (New York: New York University Press, 1971).

120 Brunschwig, *Société et romantisme,* p. 171.

121 See Ernst Benz, *The Mystical Sources of German Romantic Philosophy* (Allison Park, Pa.: Pickwick, 1983), esp. pp. 284–85. In Thomas Mann's *The Magic Mountain,* during the discussion between the rationalist Settembrini and the Romantic Naphta, the latter describes these changes at length and defends them.

122 See E. Fischer, *Ursprung und Wesen der Romantik,* pp. 105–6.

123 Karl Mannheim, "Das konservative Denken," pp. 491–92; E. Fischer, *Ursprung und Wesen der Romantik,* p. 103.

2. ROMANTICISM: POLITICAL AND SOCIAL DIVERSITY

1 Novalis, *Werke* (Stuttgart: Hädecke Verlag, 1924), pp. 313–14.

2 For example, in the work of Paul Ernst, György Lukács's childhood friend (see Michael Löwy, *George Lukács — From Romanticism to Bolshevism,* trans. Patrick Camiller [London: NLB, 1979], pp. 45–46); in the work of the Viennese theoretician Othmar Spann; and in that of Stefan George and his circle.

3 Georges Bernanos, *A Diary of My Times,* trans. Pamela Morris (New York: Macmillan, 1938), p. 30.

4 Georges Bernanos, *The Diary of a Country Priest,* trans. Pamela Morris (New York: Macmillan, 1937), pp. 213, 22. On this topic, see the chapter on Bernanos in Robert Sayre, *Solitude in Society: A Sociological Study in French Literature* (Cambridge: Harvard University Press, 1978).

5 Friedrich Schlegel in *Conférences politiques,* cited by Jacques Droz, *Le romantisme politique en Allemagne* (Paris: Armand Colin, 1963), p. 19.

6 Edmund Burke, *Burke's Reflections on the Revolution in France,* ed. F. G. Selby (London: Macmillan, 1892), pp. 84, 86, 112. Anti-Semitic references are common in Burke's writings, as they are in those of many other Romantic authors, socialist (see Pierre-Joseph Proudhon) as well as conservative.

7 Ibid., p. 122.

8 Burke cited by Russell Kirk, *The Conservative Mind* (London: Faber and Faber, 1954), p. 55.

9 *Burke's Reflections,* p. 106.

10 William McGovern, *From Luther to Hitler* (Cambridge, Mass.: Riverside Press, 1941), 111, 112. See also C. W. Parkin, "Burke and the Conservative Tradition," in *Political Ideas,* ed. David Thomson (New York: Basic Books, 1966): "In the era of worldwide Marxism,

Burke's polemic against the revolutionary idea . . . has not lost its relevance or cogency" (p. 131). As for Burke's "democratism," let us simply recall that for this declared enemy of the sovereignty of the people, "a perfect democracy is . . . the most shameless thing in the world" (*Burke's Reflections*, p. 104).

11 Louis Dupeux, "'Kulturpessimismus,' révolution conservatrice et modernité," in *Weimar ou l'explosion de la modernité*, ed. Gérard Raulet (Paris: Anthropos, 1984), pp. 31–46; Gilbert Merlio, "L'audience des idées de Spengler sous la république de Weimar," in ibid., pp. 63–78. See also "Kulturpessimismus, Révolution conservatrice et modernité," ed. Louis Dupeux, special issue, *Revue d'Allemagne* 14 (January–March 1982), especially Dupeux's own articles and those of Gilbert Merlio ("Spengler ou Le dernier des *Kulturkritiker*," pp. 97–112) and Denis Goeldel ("Moeller van den Bruck: une stratégie de modernisation du conservatisme on la modernité de droite," pp. 127–144).

12 See Peter Schwerber, *Nationalsozialismus und Technik: Die Geistigkeit der nationalsozialistische Bewegung* (Munich: F. Eher, 1930), p. 3.

13 Jeffrey Herf, *Reactionary Modernism: Technology, Culture, and Politics in Weimar and the Third Reich* (Cambridge: Cambridge University Press, 1984), p. 220.

14 Gottfried Benn cited by Jean-Michel Palmier, *L'expressionnisme comme révolte* (Paris: Payot, 1978), p. 373.

15 Gottfried Benn, *Essays. Reden. Vorträge* (Wiesbaden: Limes Verlag, 1959), p. 280.

16 Max Weber, *Gesammelte Aufsätze zur Wissenschaftslehre* (Tübingen: Mohr, 1922), p. 159. Among the most prominent academics, let us mention Werner Sombart, Max Scheler, Ernst Troeltsch, Georg Simmel, and Karl Mannheim.

17 See Kurt Lenk "Das tragische Bewusstsein in der deutschen Soziologie," *Kölner Zeitschrift für Soziologie une Sozialpsychologie* 16, no. 2 (1964): 257–87. This tragic dimension is manifested most systematically in Georg Simmel's work, especially in the important essay "Der Begriff und die Tragödie der Kultur" (The concept and the tragedy of Culture), *Logos* 2 (1911–12): 1–25, and in *The Philosophy of Money* (1900), trans. Tom Bottomore and David Frisby (London: Routledge and Kegan Paul, 1978).

18 Ferdinand Tönnies, *Community and Society (Gemeinschaft und Gesellschaft)*, trans. and ed. Charles P. Loomis (New York: Harper and Row, 1957), pp. 35, 232–34.

19 Tönnies responded to his young disciples who were in favor of reestablishing community that one could not fight against aging. See Joseph Leif, *La sociologie de Tönnies* (Paris: Presses Universitaires de France, 1946), p. 71.

20 Victor Hugo, a veritable political Proteus, defined his position after 1830 as simultaneously liberal, socialist, and democratic: see David Owen Evans, *Social Romanticism in France, 1830–1848* (Oxford: Clarendon Press, 1951).

21 Hugues Félicité Robert de Lamennais, "Politique à l'usage du peuple," in *Oeuvres complètes,* ed. Louis Le Guillou (Geneva: Slatkine Reprints, 1980–81), 7:7, 29; and *Words of a Believer* (New York: Charles de Behr, 1834), p. 45.

22 Lamennais, *Words of a Believer,* p. 145: see also pp. 2, 20, 111, 167.

23 Lamennais, "Politique à l'usage du peuple," p. 30.

24 Lamennais, "Le livre du peuple," in *Oeuvres complètes* (Paris: Pagnerre, 1844), 10:189–90; see also p. 123. Cf. "Politique à l'usage du peuple," p. 35.

25 Heinrich Heine, in *Englische Fragmente,* cited in William Rose, "Heine's Political and

Social Attitude," in *Heinrich Heine: Two Studies of His Thought and Feeling* (Oxford: Clarendon Press, 1956), p. 16.

26 From the preface to the French edition of *Lutezia,* cited in ibid., p. 86.

27 The only exception would be the Third World, where because of its delayed development, an authentic Jacobin-democratic Romanticism could persist up to quite recent times, in a José Martí, a Fidel Castro of the first period, and others.

28 György Lukács, "Hölderlin's *Hyperion,*" in *Goethe and His Age,* trans. Robert Anchor (London: Merlin Press, 1968), p. 153.

29 Eleanor Marx Aveling and Edward Aveling, *Shelley's Socialism* (1888; reprint, London: Journeyman Press, 1975).

30 Percy Bysshe Shelley, "Hellas," in *Selected Poetry* (Oxford: Clarendon Press, 1968), p. 292.

31 Ibid., pp. 296, 302, 333, 373 (the citation beginning "Prophetic echoes" is from "Ode to Liberty"; all the others are from "Hellas").

32 A structure that is often found in the major utopico-revolutionary type is analogous to the one Erich Auerbach analyzed in an important essay, "Figura," trans. Ralph Manheim, in *Scenes from the Drama of European Literature* (Gloucester, Mass.: Peter Smith, 1973), pp. 11–76. Auerbach adopts the term "figura" to designate the mode of religious, historical, and textual interpretation, common in antiquity and the Middle Ages, that sees an event, historical figure, or historical moment as a prefiguration of another one, which will be not merely a repetition but also a realization of the earlier phenomenon in its full plenitude.

33 J.-C. S. de Sismondi, *Etudes sur l'économie politique* (Paris: Treuttel et Wurtz, 1837), 1:209.

34 Sismondi, *Nouveaux principes de l'économie politique,* 2d ed. (Paris: Delaunay, 1827), 1: 165–66.

35 Moses Hess, *Die heilige Geschichte der Menschheit, von einer Jünger Spinozas* (Stuttgart: Hallbergersche Verlagshandlung, 1837), p. 249; see also pp. 235–37, 249, 257.

36 Ibid. See also Auguste Cornu, *Karl Marx et Friedrich Engels* (Paris: Presses Universitaires de France, 1955), 1:237–38.

37 Hess, *Die europäische Triarchie* (1841), in *Ausgewählte Schriften* (Cologne: Melzer Verlag, 1962), p. 91.

38 Hess, "Über das Geldwesen" (1845), in *Sozialistische Aufsätze, 1841–1847,* ed. Theodor Zlocisti (Berlin: Welt-Verlag, 1921), pp. 168, 185. It is interesting to note that as an epigraph to his essay Hess cites a long passage from "Queen Mab" in which Shelley expresses his horror of the modern idolatry of money.

39 This is also true for the revolutionary syndicalist circle around the journal *Mouvement socialiste* (Georges Sorel, Hubert Lagardelle, Edouard Berth), for Jean Grave and his symbolist friends, and for the Jewish anarchist Bernard Lazare (a friend of Péguy's). Some writers — Franz Kafka, in particular — may also be linked to this form of the Romantic vision: see Michael Löwy, *"Theologia negativa* and *Utopia negativa:* Franz Kafka," in *Redemption and Utopia: Jewish Libertarian Thought in Central Europe,* trans. Hope Heaney (Stanford: Stanford University Press, 1988), pp. 77–114.

40 Franz Borkenau, *The Spanish Cockpit: An Eye-Witness Account of the Political and Social Conflicts of the Spanish Civil War* (1937; reprint, Ann Arbor: University of Michigan Press,

1963), pp. 20–21. Speaking of his fascination with Spain, Borkenau reveals his own Romantic sensibility: "There, life is not yet efficient; that means that it is not yet mechanized; that beauty is more important for the Spaniard than practical use; sentiment more important than action; honour very often more important than success; love and friendship more important than one's job. In one word, it is the lure of a civilization near to ourselves, closely connected with this historical past of Europe, but which has not participated in our later developments towards mechanism, the adoration of quantity, and of the utilitarian aspect of things" (pp. 299–300).

41 Gustav Landauer, "Volk und Land: Dreissig sozialistische Thesen" (1907), in *Beginnen: Aufsätze über Sozialismus* (Westbevern: Verlag Büchse der Pandora, 1977), p. 8.

42 Landauer, *For Socialism* (1919), trans. David Parent (St. Louis: Telos Press, 1978), pp. 63, 65.

43 Landauer, "Der Bund" (1908–1910), in *Beginnen*, pp. 91–137.

44 William Morris, "How I Became a Socialist" (1894), in *Political Writings of William Morris*, ed. A. L. Morton (London: Lawrence and Wisham, 1979), p. 243.

45 In certain less developed countries we also find thinkers, especially among the founders of the Communist movement in the 1920s, who seek in the precapitalist conditions of their own country a possible sociocultural base for the revolutionary movement: José Carlos Mariategui in Peru, Li-Ta-Chao in China.

46 Arnold Hauser, *The Social History of Art*, trans. in collaboration with the author by Stanley Godman, intro. Jonathan Harris, 4 vols. (London: Routledge, 1999), 3:163.

47 Jacques Droz, *Le romantisme allemand et l'Etat: Résistance et collaboration en Allemagne napoléonienne* (Paris: Payot, 1966), p. 295; see also the anthology by Droz: *Le romantisme politique en Europe*, pp. 28–29.

48 Gerda Heinrich, *Geschichtsphilosophische Positionen der deutschen Frühromantik* (Berlin: Akademie-Verlag, 1976), p. 60; Ernst Fischer, *The Necessity of Art: A Marxist Approach*, trans. Anna Bostock (London: Penguin, 1963), 53.

49 Pierre Barbéris, "'Mal du siècle,' ou d'un romantisme de droite à un romantisme de gauche," in *Romantisme et politique (1815–1851)*, colloquium of the Ecole normale supérieure, Saint-Cloud, 1966 (Paris: Armand Colin, 1969), pp. 175, 171.

50 Karl Mannheim, "Das konservative Denken: Soziologische Beiträge zum Werden des politisch-historischen Denkens in Deutschland" (1927), in *Wissensoziologie* (Berlin: Luchterhand, 1964), pp. 408–508.

51 Honoré de Balzac, *Illusions Perdues* (Paris: Livre de Poche, 1972), p. 199.

52 It is interesting to note that among the characters of Alfred de Vigny's *Chatterton* who are opposed to the capitalist John Bell, in addition to workers we find a poet (Chatterton), a religious figure (the Quaker), and also a woman (Kitty Bell), all of whom thus represent groups that are particularly sensitive to Romanticism.

3. EXCURSUS: MARXISM AND ROMANTICISM

1 Auguste Cornu, *Karl Marx et Friedrich Engels* (Paris: Presses Universitaires de France, 1955), 1:67–69, 75, 93–97, 103. An interesting analysis of the influence of Romanticism

on the poems of the young Marx is offered by Leonard P. Wessell Jr. in *Karl Marx, Romantic Irony, and the Proletariat: The Mythopoetic Origins of Marxism* (Baton Rouge: Louisiana State University Press, 1979). Unfortunately, the bulk of Wessell's book consists in a wholly arbitrary attempt to reduce all Marx's political thought to "mythopoetry."

2   See chap. 25, "The General Law of Capitalist Accumulation," in *Capital* (Marx and Engels, *Collected Works*, 35: 607–703).

3   Frederick Engels, "The Condition of England. *Past and Present* by Thomas Carlyle, London, 1843" (1844), in Karl Marx and Frederick Engels, *Collected Works,* trans. Richard Dixon et al. (New York: International Publishers, 1975), 3:447, 461, 456.

4   Thomas Carlyle, *Chartism* (London: James Fraser, 1840), p. 37, noted by Marx in *Excerpthefte* B35AD89a. This unpublished notebook is in the *Archive Marx-Engels* in the Institute for Social History in Amsterdam, where we were able to consult it.

5   Engels, "Latter-Day *Pamphlets,* edited by Thomas Carlyle," in Marx and Engels, *Collected Works*, 10:301; emphasis added.

6   Engels, "Letter to Miss Harkness" (April 1888), in *Marx and Engels on Literature and Art: A Selection of Writings,* ed. Lee Baxandall and Stefan Morawski (St. Louis: Telos Press, 1973), p. 115.

7   Karl Marx, "The English Middle Class," in Marx and Engels, *Collected Works*, 13:664.

8   Marx and Engels, *Manifesto of the Communist Party* (1848), in ibid., 6:507, 509.

9   Paul Breines, "Marxism, Romanticism, and the Case of Georg Lukács: Notes on Some Recent Sources and Situations," *Studies in Romanticism* 16 (1977): 476.

10 Marx to Engels, Letter 343, 25 March 1868, in Marx and Engels, *Collected Works*, 42:557. On the relation of Marx to Maurer and Morgan, see Lawrence Krader, *Ethnologie und Anthropologie bei Marx* (Frankfurt: Verlag Ullstein, 1976).

11 Engels, "The Mark" (1883), in Marx and Engels, *Collected Works*, 24:456. To be sure, Engels adds: "not in its old, outdated form, but in a rejuvenated form" (ibid.).

12 Engels to Marx, Letter 220, 15 December 1882, ibid., 46:400. A remark in *The Origin of the Family* betrays a nuance in Engels's enthusiasm: "That is the one side. But we must not forget that this organization was doomed" (Engels, *The Origin of the Family, Private Property, and the State,* ed. Eleanor Burke Leacock [New York: International Publishers, 1972], p. 160).

13 Engels, *Origin of the Family,* pp. 159–61.

14 Marx to Zasulich, Letter 44, 8 March 1881, in Marx and Engels, *Collected Works,* 46:72.

15 Marx, "The Future Results of the British Rule in India" (1853), in ibid., 12:222.

16 Marx, third draft of letter to Vera Zasulich, in ibid., 24:365; emphasis added.

17 See Karl Mannheim, "Das konservative Denken: Soziologische Beiträge zum Werden des politisch-historischen Denkens in Deutschland" (1927), in *Wissensoziologie* (Berlin: Luchterhand, 1964), pp. 425, 438, 440, 486, 497, 507–8.

18 See Alvin W. Gouldner, "Romanticism and Classicism: Deep Structures in Social Science," in *For Sociology: Renewal and Critique in Sociology Today* (New York: Basic Books, 1973), p. 339; Ernst Fischer, *Marx in His Own Words* (London: Penguin, 1970), p. 15; Istvan Meszaros, *Marx's Theory of Alienation* (London: Merlin Press, 1970), pp. 48–61; M. H. Abrams, *Natural Supernaturalism: Tradition and Revolution in Romantic Literature*

(New York: Norton, 1973), p. 314; Jürgen Habermas, "What Does Socialism Mean Today? The Rectifying Revolution and the Need for New Thinking on the Left," trans. Ben Morgan, *New Left Review*, no. 183 (1990): 15.

19 The theme is suggested, in connection with the critique of technological instrumentalization, by Gouldner, "Romanticism and Classicism," p. 338.

20 Marx, *Early Writings*, ed. Lucio Colletti (New York: Penguin, 1975), pp. 358–59.

21 Marx, *Capital*, vol. 1, in Marx and Engels, *Collected Works*, 35:370.

22 Ibid., pp. 366, 365, 368, 425–26, 429.

23 Marx, *Grundrisse: Foundations of the Critique of Political Economy*, trans. Martin Nicolaus (New York: Random House, 1973), pp. 704–12.

24 Marx, *Economic and Political Writings of 1844*, in Marx and Engels, *Collected Works*, 3:229–346.

25 Rosa Luxemburg, *The Accumulation of Capital* (London: Routledge and Kegan Paul, 1951), pp. 193, 202, 209, 189.

26 Rosa Luxemburg, *Introduction à l'économie politique* (Paris: Anthropos, 1970). Originally published as *Einführung in die Nationaloekonomie* (Introduction to economics), in *Ausgewählte Reden und Schriften* (Berlin: Dietz Verlag, 1951). Chapter 1 has appeared in English as *What Is Economics?* trans. T. Edwards (New York: Trotsky School, Pioneer Publishers, 1954). The manuscript was drafted in prison, based on notes from her course in political economics at the school of the German Social Democratic Party (1907–1914). The text is doubtless unfinished, but it is astonishing all the same that the chapters devoted to primitive communist society and its dissolution take up more space than those devoted to market production and the capitalist economy together. This unusual way of approaching political economics is probably why this work has been neglected by most of the Marxist economists (Ernst Mandel, the author of the preface to the French edition, is an exception) and even by the biographers of Rosa Luxemburg (except for Paul Frölich). The Marx-Engels-Lenin-Stalin Institute of East Berlin, which was responsible for the reedition of the text in 1951, claims in its preface that the book is a "popular presentation of the fundamental features of the capitalist mode of production," forgetting that almost half the book is in fact devoted to the primitive commune.

27 Luxemburg, *Introduction*, p. 83. As Ernst Mandel notes, "the explanation of the fundamental differences between an economy based on the production of use values, destined to satisfy the needs of production, and an economy based on the production of goods, takes up most of the book" (Preface, *Introduction*, p. xviii).

28 Luxemburg, *Introduction*, pp. 73, 178.

29 Ibid., pp. 141, 155.

30 Ibid., p. 91.

31 Ibid., pp. 133, 180.

32 Ibid., p. 80. This passage seems to suggest an idyllic vision of the traditional structure in India; however, in another chapter of the book, Luxemburg recognizes the existence, beyond the rural communes, of despotic power and a caste of privileged priests, instituting relations of exploitation and social inequality (pp. 157–58).

33 Luxemburg, *Accumulation of Capital*, pp. 376, 380.

34 Luxemburg, *Introduction*, pp. 92, 201.

35 Gilbert Badia, *Rosa Luxemburg, journalist, polémiste, révolutionnaire* (Paris: Editions Sociales, 1975), pp. 498, 501.

36 Luxemburg, *Introduction*, p. 178.

37 Ibid., pp. 142–43.

38 Ibid.: "With the Russian village community, the eventful destiny of primitive agrarian society reached its end; the circle was closed. In the beginning a natural product of social evolution, the best guarantee of a society's economic progress and material and intellectual prosperity, the agrarian community became an instrument of political and economic regression. The Russian peasant being whipped by members of his own community in the service of czarist absolutism is the cruelest historical criticism of the narrow limits of primitive communism and the most striking expression of the fact that the social form itself is also subjected to the dialectical rule: reason becomes nonsense, benefits become afflictions" (p. 170).

39 Ibid., p. 133.

40 For a detailed examination of Lukács's early Romanticism and his path toward Marxism from 1909 to 1918, see Michael Löwy, *George Lukács — From Romanticism to Bolshevism*, trans. Patrick Camiller (London: NLB, 1979).

41 Lukács, "Alte Kultur und neue Kultur" (1919), in *Taktik und Ethik* (Neuwied: Luchterhand, 1975), pp. 136–45.

42 Lukács, "Der Functionswechsel des Historischen Materialismus" (1919), in ibid, pp. 116–22. The version of this essay published in 1923 in *Geschichte und Klass enbewusstein (History and Class Consciousness)* was significantly modified.

43 Lukács, *History and Class Consciousness,* trans. Rodney Livingstone (Cambridge: MIT Press, 1971), pp. 214 n. 47, 190, 91; see also pp. 88–91. The quotation from Breines is from his remarkable essay "Marxism, Romanticism, and Lukács," p. 479.

44 Lukács, *Littérature, philosophie, marxisme, 1922–1923,* ed. Michael Löwy (Paris: Presses Universitaires de France, 1978), pp. 76, 110.

45 Lukács, "Rezensionem 1928: Carl Schmitt, *Politische Romantik*" (1928), in *Geschichte und Klassenbewusstsein* (Neuwied: Luchterhand, 1968), pp. 695–96.

46 Lukács, "Über den Dostojevski Nachlass," *Moskauer Rundschau,* 22 March 1931. Lukács compares Dostoevsky's itinerary, from revolutionary conspiracy to orthodox religion and czarism, to that of Friedrich Schlegel, the republican Romantic who rallied to Klemens Metternich and the Catholic Church.

47 See Michael Löwy, "Interview avec Ernst Bloch," in *Pour une sociologie des intellectuels révolutionnaires* (Paris: Presses Universitaires de France, 1976), p. 295.

48 Lukács, "Über das Schlagwort Liberalismus und Marxismus," *Der Rote Aufbau* 21 (1931).

49 Lukács, *Wie ist die faschistische Philosophie in Deutschland entstanden?* (Budapest: Akadémiai Kiado, 1982), p. 57.

50 Lukács, "Nietzsche als Vorläufer der faschistischen Aesthetik" (1934), in *Friedrich Nietzsche,* ed. Franz Mehring and György Lukács (Berlin: Aufbau Verlag, 1957), pp. 41, 53.

51 Lukács, "Expressionism: Its Significance and Decline" (1934; 1953), in *Essays on Realism,* ed. Rodney Livingstone, trans. David Fernbach (Cambridge: MIT Press, 1980), p. 87.

52 Ibid., p. 113.

53 There is an Italian translation of this unpublished text by Lukács in a collection edited by Vittorio Franco, *Intelletuali e Irrazionalismo* (Pisa: ETS, 1984), pp. 287–308.

54 Lukács, "Es geht um den Realismus," in *Essays über Realismus* (Berlin: Aufbau-Verlag, 1938), pp. 128–70.

55 Lukács, *Ecrits de Moscou* (Paris: Editions Sociales, 1974), pp. 149–50, 159, 167, 235, 243, 257.

56 Lukács, "Dostojewskij," in *Russische Revolution, russische Literatur* (Hamburg: Rohwolt, 1969), pp. 148–49.

57 Lukács, "Vorwort" (1946), in *Der Russische Realismums in der Weltliteratur*, in *Werke* (Neuwied: Luchterhand, 1964), 5:11–12.

58 Lukács, "Die verbannte Poesie," *Internationale Literatur* (Moscow) 5–6 (1942): 86–95.

59 Lukács, "In Search of Bourgeois Man" (1945), in *Essays on Thomas Mann*, trans. Stanley Mitchell (London: Merlin Press, 1964), pp. 33, 35.

60 Lukács, *The Destruction of Reason* (1953), trans. Peter Palmer (Atlantic Highlands, N.J.: Humanities Press, 1981), p. 594; see also pp. 116–18.

61 Lukács, *The Meaning of Contemporary Realism* (1957), trans. John Mander and Necke Mander (London: Merlin Press, 1963), p. 62.

62 Lukács, *History and Class Consciousness*, p. x; Hans Heinz Holz, Leo Kofler, and Wolfgang Abendroth, *Conversations with Lukács* (Cambridge: MIT Press, 1975), p. 100.

63 Lukács, "Mon chemin vers Marx," *Nouvelles études hongroises* 8 (1973): 80–82; "Mein Weg zu Marx" (1933), in *Schriften zur Ideologie und Politik,* ed. P. Ludz (Neuwied: Luchterhand, 1967), pp. 323–29; and "Préface à *Littérature hongroise, culture hongroise,*" *L'homme et la société* 43–44 (1977): 13–14.

4. VISAGES OF ROMANTICISM IN THE NINETEENTH CENTURY

1 The analysis of the French Revolution as an essentially bourgeois event has been widely challenged in recent years. We shall not enter into that debate here; however, it seems beyond question that one of the major historical consequences of the Revolution was the reinforcement of bourgeois power.

2 Let us also cite the founder of the journal *Cercle social,* Nicolas de Bonneville, mentioned by Marx in *The Holy Family* as a precursor of modern socialism. For more about this trend, see Robert Sayre and Michael Löwy, "Utopie romantique et Révolution française," in *Dissonances dans la Révolution,* special issue, *L'homme et la société* 94 (1984): 71–81.

3 It is clear, however, that Coleridge later tried to minimize or dismiss his associations with radicalism and the radicals, especially John Thelwall. See Nicholas Roe, "Coleridge and John Thelwall: The Road to Nether Stowey," in *The Coleridge Connection,* ed. Richard Gravil and Molly Lefebure (New York: St. Martin's Press, 1990), pp. 60–80.

4 Coleridge, "The French Revolution: The First Phase," in *The Political Thought of Samuel Taylor Coleridge,* ed. R. J. White (London: Jonathan Cape, 1938), p. 34 (first published in *The Friend,* Essay 6, sect. 1).

5 Coleridge, *Biographia Literaria* (1817), in *Political Thought,* p. 29.

6 *Biographia Literaria,* p. 35.

7 There were points in common and personal ties, nevertheless, between Coleridge and the radicals. See Nicholas Roe, *Wordsworth and Coleridge: The Radical Years* (Oxford: Clarendon Press, 1988).

8 Burton R. Pollin, "John Thelwall's Marginalia in a Copy of Coleridge's *Biographia Literaria,*" *Bulletin of the New York Public Library* 74 (1970): 81.

9 Coleridge to George Coleridge, 6 November 1794, in *Collected Letters of Samuel Taylor Coleridge,* ed. E. L. Griggs (Oxford: Clarendon Press, 1956), 1:126.

10 Coleridge, "A Moral and Political Lecture," in *The Collected Works of Samuel Taylor Coleridge,* vol. 1, *Lectures 1795 on Politics and Religion,* ed. Lewis Patton and Peter Mann (Princeton: Princeton University Press, 1971), p. 6.

11 Coleridge, "Religious Musings," in *The Complete Poetical Works of Samuel Taylor Coleridge,* ed. E. H. Coleridge (Oxford: Clarendon Press, 1912), 1:121–22.

12 This meaning of Thermidor is emphasized by Charles Cestre in *La Révolution française et les poètes anglais (1789–1809)* (Paris: Champion, 1906), p. 123.

13 Thus Werner Krauss rightly notes with regard to the group of Romantics who ended up abandoning the Revolution: "The other half of the truth is that the Revolution also notoriously abandoned Romanticism during this period" ("Französische Aufklärung und deutsche Romantik," in *Romantikforschung seit 1945,* ed. Klaus Peter (Königstein im Taunus: Athenaüm, 1981), p. 177. From another angle, E. P. Thompson, in an important article on Wordsworth, Coleridge, and the Revolution — "Disenchantment or Default? A Lay Sermon," in *Power and Consciousness,* ed. C. C. O'Brien and W. D. Vanech (London: University of London Press, 1969) — recognizes the difficulty of maintaining one's hopes in the absence of any objective support but sees in the Lake Poets' later denials a moral weakness that would have consequences at the aesthetic level as well.

14 *Collected Letters,* 1:228 (10 March 1798).

15 Coleridge, "France: An Ode," in *Complete Poetical Works,* 1:246.

16 Coleridge, Lecture 6, in *Collected Works,* 1:218.

17 Coleridge, "Introductory Address," in *Collected Works,* 1:39–40.

18 "Religious Musings," p. 114.

19 Coleridge to Southey, 19 January 1795, 13 November 1795, in *Collected Letters,* 1:150, 171.

20 *The Collected Works of Samuel Taylor Coleridge,* vol. 2, *The Watchman,* ed. Lewis Patton (Princeton: Princeton University Press, 1970), p. 269.

21 "Editor's Introduction," Coleridge, *Collected Works,* 1:lxxvii.

22 Coleridge, "Fall of Robespierre," in *Complete Poetical Works,* 2:499–500.

23 "A Moral and Political Lecture," in *Collected Works,* 1:11; see also "Introductory Address," 1:39.

24 Coleridge to Southey, 13 July 1794, in *Collected Letters,* 1:90. Coleridge invented a second name for pantisocracy: *aspheterized,* which means "without property." See Coleridge to Southey, 6 July 1794, in *Collected Letters,* 1:84.

25 Coleridge, "Once a Jacobin Always a Jacobin," 21 October 1802, in *Collected Works,* vol. 3, *Essays on His Times in the Morning Post and The Courier,* ed. David V. Erdman (Princeton: Princeton University Press, 1978), bk. 1, p. 369.

26 "To the Rev. W. J. Hart," in *Complete Poetical Works,* 1:92, and "Religious Musings," 1:122.

27 Coleridge to Southey, 13 July 1794, p. 86.

28 Coleridge to Southey, early August 1795, in *Collected Letters,* 1:158.

29 "Fall of Robespierre," p. 501.

30 Coleridge, "Pantisocracy," in *Complete Poetical Works,* 1:69.

31 Coleridge, "Monody on the Death of Chatterton," in *Complete Poetical Works,* 1:130.

32 Coleridge, "Pantisocracy," *Political Thought,* p. 35.

33 Coleridge, Lecture 6, p. 215. The fable as Coleridge tells it is inspired by the work of an eighteenth-century poet writing in Latin, Benedetto Stay.

34 Ibid., pp. 226, 229.

35 Coleridge, "Religious Musings," p. 123, note (variant).

36 "Ver Perpetuum," in *Complete Poetical Works,* 1:148, note 1.

37 Coleridge, "Remonstrance to the French Legislators," in *Collected Works,* 2:272.

38 See Graham Hough, *The Last Romantics* (1949; reprint, London: Gerald Duckworth, 1978), p. 30.

39 See Nick Shrimpton, "'Rust and Dust': Ruskin's Pivotal Work," in *New Approaches to Ruskin,* ed. Robert Hewison (London: Routledge and Kegan Paul, 1981), p. 52.

40 John Ruskin, *Unto This Last and Other Writings,* ed. C. Wilmer (London: Penguin, 1985), p. 171, note. Still, Ruskin regrets the use of caricature in *Hard Times,* as he does in some of Dickens's other novels; in his eyes, the caricatural aspect of the characters allows some readers to miss the important truths that the novels convey.

41 Ruskin to Charles Eliot Norton, 19 June 1870, in *The Library Edition of the Works of John Ruskin,* ed. E. T. Cook and Alexander Wedderburn (London: George Allen, 1903–1912), 37:7.

42 "Fiction, Fair and Foul," Essay 1, 1880, in *Works,* 34:274.

43 Ruskin, "The Baron's Gate," in *Fors Clavigera,* Letter 10, 1871, *Works,* 27:179.

44 Ruskin, "War," in *The Crown of Wild Olive,* Lecture 3, 1865, *Works,* 17:287; cited in Alan Lee, "Ruskin and Political Economy: Unto This Last," in Hewison, *New Approaches to Ruskin,* p. 75.

45 On the relation between Ruskin and the P.R.B., see Graham Hough, *The Last Romantics,* chap. 2.

46 See Nick Shrimpton, "'Rust and Dust,'" p. 51.

47 Ruskin, *A Joy for Ever (And Its Price in the Market)* (New York: Maynard, Merrill and Co., 1894), intro. Charles Eliot Norton, p. v; cf. "A Joy For Ever," two lectures on the political economy of art, 1857, 1880, in *Works,* 16:1–169.

48 See Gaylord C. Leroy, *Perplexed Prophets: Six Nineteenth-Century British Authors* (Philadelphia: University of Pennsylvania Press, 1953), chap. 4, "John Ruskin," p. 87.

49 Ibid., p. 98.

50 See Hough, *Last Romantics,* pp. 14–15. In this connection, Hough cites R. G. Collingwood, *Ruskin's Philosophy* (Kendal: T. Wilson and Son, 1919).

51 See "Letters on Politics," in *Works,* 12:594–603, and also the introduction to vol. 12, pp. lxxviii–lxxxv, in which several letters are cited at length.

52 In Northrop Frye, *Anatomy of Criticism* (Princeton: Princeton University Press, 1957),

p. 198. See Clive Wilmer's commentary on Ruskin's "King of the Golden River" in *Unto This Last and Other Writings,* pp. 47–48.

53   Alan Lee, "Ruskin and Political Economy," pp. 68–69; and George Bernard Shaw, "Ruskin's Politics" (a lecture delivered at the Ruskin Centenary Exhibition in 1919), in *Platform and Pulpit,* ed. Dan Laurence (New York: Hill and Wang, 1961), pp. 139, 143.

54   Ruskin, "Charitas," from *Fors Clavigera,* Letter 7, in *Works,* 27:115–31, and "The Baron's Gate," pp. 165–80. In a personal letter written in 1886, Ruskin declares himself both a Socialist and a Tory: See Lee, "Ruskin and Political Economy," p. 76.

55   Ruskin to his father, 16 November 1851, in *Works,* 12:lxxix.

56   W. G. Collingwood, *The Life of John Ruskin* (Boston: Houghton Mifflin, 1900), p. 371.

57   Ruskin, "The Baron's Gate," p. 175.

58   Ruskin, "Traffic" (1864), in *The Crown of Wild Olive,* p. 456.

59   Ibid., p. 447; emphasis added.

60   Ruskin, "Ad Valorem," from *Unto This Last,* Essay 4, in *Works,* 17:105.

61   Ruskin, "The King of the Golden River" (1841), in *Works,* 1:347.

62   See Jeffrey L. Spear, *Dreams of an English Eden: Ruskin and His Tradition in Social Criticism* (New York: Columbia University Press, 1984), pp. 14, 15. Spear associates this quotation with a watercolor done by Ruskin himself in 1866, titled *Dawn in Neuchâtel* (p. 15).

63   Ruskin stresses this dual allegiance in *The Two Paths* (1859), in *Works,* 16:325–26.

64   Ruskin, "Work," from *Crown of Wild Olive,* Lecture 1, p. 431.

65   Ruskin, *Two Paths,* p. 340.

66   See Ruskin, "The Nature of Gothic" (1853), from *The Stones of Venice,* vol. 2, in *Works,* 10:180–269.

67   Ruskin, "The Roots of Honour" (1860), from *Unto This Last,* Essay 1, in *Works,* 17:32.

68   Ruskin, "War," p. 473.

69   See, for example, Ruskin, *Two Paths,* pp. 340–43; "The Two Boyhoods," in *Works,* 7:378; "Traffic," p. 444; "Athena Keramitis," in *Works,* 19:365.

70   See, for example, Ruskin, *Two Paths,* pp. 338–39; introduction, *Crown of Wild Olive,* p. 386; and "Fiction, Fair and Foul," p. 268.

71   See the preface to *Two Paths,* especially pp. 253–54, where students of drawing constitute the audience in question, and where, according to Ruskin, the choice between two artistic practices implies an overall existential choice.

72   W. G. Collingwood, *Life of Ruskin,* p. 238.

73   Shaw, "Ruskin's Politics," p. 136. In "Fiction, Fair and Foul," for example, Ruskin expresses astonishment that city-dwellers adore the alienations of their lives and ask for more.

74   "Of Classical Landscape," from *Modern Painters,* vol. 3, in *Works,* 5:231 (see more generally pp. 221–46).

75   Ruskin, "The Storm-Cloud of the Nineteenth Century" (1884), Lecture 1; Ruskin cites a passage that appeared earlier in *Fors Clavigera* (*Works,* 34:33).

76   Cited by Clive Wilmer, introduction, *Unto This Last and Other Writings,* p. 13.

77   Ruskin, "Traffic," p. 448.

78   Ruskin, "Ad Valorem," p. 78.

79   "The Mystery of Life and Its Arts" (a lecture given in 1868), in *Works,* 18:165. See also "Of Kings' Treasuries," where Ruskin condemns the English nation for having despised

literature, science, art, nature, and compassion, "concentrating its soul on Pence" (*Works,* 18:84).

80 Ruskin, "Ad Valorem," p. 88; and "The Advent Collect" (1874), from *Fors Clavigera,* Letter 48, in *Works,* 28:207.

81 See Ruskin, *Two Paths,* p. 402.

82 Ruskin, "Ad Valorem," p. 91.

83 Ibid., p. 89. For an example of the network of bad effects, see Ruskin's discussion of the wrought iron barrier in front of a shop selling alcoholic beverages (introduction, *Crown of Wild Olive,* pp. 387–89).

84 See above, p. 153.

85 Ruskin, "Ad Valorem," p. 79.

86 Ruskin, "Nature of Gothic," pp. 194–96.

87 Ruskin, "Of Kings' Treasuries," p. 89.

88 Ruskin, *Two Paths,* pp. 337–38.

89 See especially Ruskin, "War," pp. 459–93; see also "Charitas," p. 126.

90 Ruskin, "Qui Judicatis Terram," in *Unto This Last,* Essay 3, *Works,* 27:126.

91 Ruskin, "Of Kings' Treasuries," p. 103, and "Traffic," pp. 442–43.

92 Ruskin is of course citing Keats ("A thing of beauty is a joy for ever"); those words were inscribed in gilded letters on the cornice of an art exhibit in Manchester in 1857.

93 Ruskin, "Of Kings' Treasuries," p. 83.

94 Ruskin, "Ad Valorem," p. 105.

95 On these questions, see, for example, Ruskin, *Two Paths,* pp. 47–48; "The Veins of Wealth," from *Unto This Last,* Essay 2, in *Works,* 17:47–48; "Ad Valorem," p. 114; "Charitas," pp. 120–21.

96 Ruskin, "Dictatorship," from *Time and Tide, by Weare and Tyne,* Letter 12, in *Works,* 18:372–73.

97 Ruskin, "Rose-Gardens," from ibid., Letter 20, pp. 420–21.

98 Ruskin, "Mystery of Life," p. 148.

99 See Collingwood, *Life of Ruskin,* pp. 289, 293, 308, 314, 318; and John D. Rosenberg, introduction to section titled "Solitude," in *The Genius of John Ruskin,* p. 320.

100 "The Storm-Cloud of the Nineteenth Century," Lecture 2, in *Works,* 34:78; see also ibid., Lecture 1, pp. 1–41.

101 Cited in Hough, *Last Romantics,* chap. 3, "William Morris," p. 90.

102 Cited in Spear, *Dreams of an English Eden,* p. 200.

103 Marinetti, "Futurist Speech to the English," cited in ibid., p. xi.

104 See John D. Rosenberg, introduction to section titled "Architecture," and introduction to section titled "Society," in *Genius of Ruskin,* pp. 121, 220.

105 Shaw, "Ruskin's Politics," p. 132.

5. VISAGES OF ROMANTICISM IN THE TWENTIETH CENTURY

1 Graham Hough, *The Last Romantics* (1949; reprint, London: Gerald Duckworth, 1978); John Bayley, *The Romantic Survival: A Study in Poetic Evolution* (London: Constable, 1957).

2 R. L. Combs, *Vision of the Voyage: Hart Crane and the Psychology of Romanticism* (Memphis: Memphis State University Press, 1978); Carl Rapp, *William Carlos Williams and Romantic Idealism* (Hanover, N.H.: University Press of New England, 1984); John Bayley, "Contemporary British Poetry: A Romantic Persistence?" *Poetry* 146, no. 4 (1985): 227–36.

3 See for example Gérard Raulet, ed., *Weimar, ou l'explosion de la modernité* (Paris: Anthropos, 1984); Richard Faber, "Frühromantik, Surrealismus, und Studententrevolte oder die Frage nach dem Anarchismus," in *Romantische Utopie, Utopische Romantik,* ed. Richard Faber (Hildesheim: Gerstenberg, 1979), pp. 336–58; R. P. Seifert, *Fortschrittsfeinde? Opposition gegen Technik und Industrie von der Romantik bis zur Gegenwart* (Munich: Beck, 1984). Some British sociologists have also pointed out parallels between the struggles of the 1960s and 1970s and the Romantic movements of the late eighteenth and early nineteenth centuries: see especially Bernice Martin, *A Sociology of Contemporary Cultural Change* (Oxford: Blackwell, 1981).

4 Philippe Lacoue-Labarthe and Jean-Luc Nancy, eds., *The Literary Absolute: The Theory of Literature in German Romanticism* (1978), trans. Philip Barnard and Cheryl Lester (Albany: State University of New York Press, 1988), p. 15.

5 Gérard Klein, "Discontent in American Science Fiction," trans. D. Suvin and Leila Lecorps, *Science Fiction Studies* 4 (March 1977): 3–13, and "Le Guin's 'Aberrant' Opus: Escaping the Trap of Discontent," trans. Richard Astle, ibid. (November 1977): 287–95.

6 Octavio Paz, *Children of the Mire: Modern Poetry from Romanticism to the Avant-Garde,* trans. Rachel Phillips (Cambridge: Harvard University Press, 1974), p. 134.

7 Cecelia Tichi, *Shifting Gears: Technology, Literature, Culture in Modernist America* (Chapel Hill: University of North Carolina Press, 1987).

8 Philippe Jullian, "Le symbolisme," in *Idéalistes et symbolistes: Exposition, 3 octobre–21 décembre 1973* (Paris: Galerie J.-C. Gaubert, 1973), p. 2. See also Hans Helmut Hofstätter, *Symbolismus und der Kunst der Jahrhundertwende* (Cologne: M. DuMont Schauberg, 1965), pp. 23, 58.

9 See Jean-Michel Palmier's fine book, *L'expressionnisme comme révolte* (Paris: Payot, 1978), pp. 115–18.

10 Kurt Pinthus, "Before" (1919), in *Menschheitsdämmerung: Dawn of Humanity: A Document of Expressionism,* trans. Joanna M. Ratych, Ralph Ley, and Robert C. Conard (Columbia, S.C.: Camden House, 1994), pp. 31–32.

11 Jean-Michel Palmier, *L'expressionnisme et les arts,* vol. 1, *Portrait d'une génération* (Paris: Payot, 1979), p. 10.

12 György Lukács, "Expressionism: Its Significance and Decline" (1934), in *Essays on Realism,* ed. Rodney Livingstone, trans. David Fernbach (Cambridge: MIT Press, 1980), p. 92.

13 Let us mention just a few examples of what might be included in a book devoted to the manifestations of the Romantic worldview in the principal realms of twentieth-century cultural life. First, in the plastic arts: from the "organic" forms of art nouveau to expressionism, surrealism, and fantastic art. Second, in music: both the folkloric music of composers such as Béla Bartok and Zoltán Kodaly and the popular pastoral nostalgia of

Igor Stravinski's *Histoire du soldat*. Third, in literature: direct expression in the case of William Faulkner, D. H. Lawrence, and Jorge Luis Borges, less direct (or expressed *en creux*, through its absence) with Franz Kafka and Thomas Mann (on the latter, see Michael Löwy, "Lukács et 'Léon Naphta': L'énigme du *Zauberberg,*" *Etudes germaniques* 41 [July–September 1986]: 318–26). Fourth, in philosophy: countering the utopians and social critics (the young Lukács), a constellation of conservative adversaries of modernity running from Martin Heidegger to Arnold Gehlen. Fifth, in the social sciences: from the historians critical of technology (Lewis Mumford) to the psychologists supporting the antipsychiatry movement (R. L. Laing and D. G. Cooper). The list could be expanded; we can also refer to the examples mentioned in chapter 2, above.

14 Charles Péguy, "Un nouveau théologien, M. Fernand Laudet" (1911), *Oeuvres en prose, 1909–1914* (Paris: Gallimard, La Pléiade, 1957), p. 938 (hereafter *OP* 2).

15 Simone Fraisse, "Péguy entre le nouveau classicisme et l'appel romantique," in *Péguy, un romantique malgré lui,* ed. Simone Fraisse (Paris: Lettres Modernes, Minard, 1985), pp. 28–41.

16 Péguy, "Notes politiques et sociales" (articles from *Revue Blanche,* 1899), in *Cahiers de l'Amitié Charles Péguy* (Paris: L'Amitié Péguy, 1957), pp. 53–86.

17 Péguy, "Toujours de la grippe" (1900), *Oeuvres en prose, 1898–1908* (Paris: Gallimard [La Pléiade], 1959), pp. 192–93 (hereafter *OP* 1). See also "De Jean Coste" (1902), in which Péguy refers to "a very large number of serious young people, [who] gave up the Catholic faith primarily, solely, or especially, because they did not recognize the existence or the persistence of hell" (ibid., p. 508).

18 Péguy, "De Jean Coste," pp. 174, 184–85, 499.

19 Péguy, "Avertissement au Cahier Mangasarian" (1904), *OP* 1:1361, 1377–78.

20 Ibid., pp. 1377–78.

21 Péguy, "Orléans vue de Montargis" (1904), *OP* 1:666. The expression "libertarian socialism" appears in "Avertissement au Cahier Mangasarian," p. 1363. For a careful and nuanced study of Péguy's affinities with anarchism, see Géraldi Leroy, *Péguy entre l'ordre et la révolution* (Paris: Presses de la Fondation nationale des sciences politiques, 1981), pp. 152–56.

22 Péguy, *Oeuvres en prose complètes,* ed. Robert Burac (Paris: Gallimard, La Pléiade, 1988), 2:153, 152.

23 Péguy, "Les suppliants parallèles" (1905), *OP* 1:922.

24 Péguy, "De la situation faite à l'histoire et à la sociologie dans les temps modernes" (1906), *OP* 1:1025 (see also pp. 1016, 1028), and "De la situation faite au parti intellectuel dans le monde moderne (1906)," *OP* 1:1037.

25 Romain Rolland, *Péguy* (Paris: Albin Michel, 1944), p. 213.

26 Péguy, "Memories of Youth," a partial translation of *Notre jeunesse* (1910; reprint, Paris: Gallimard, 1957), in *Temporal and Eternal,* trans. Alexander Dru (New York: Harper and Brothers, 1958), pp. 64–67.

27 See Jean Bastiaire, *Péguy l'insurgé* (Paris: Payot, 1975), pp. 10, 132.

28 Péguy, "De la situation faite au parti intellectuel dans le monde moderne devant les accidents de la gloire temporelle" (1907), *OP* 1:1137–42, 1147, 1158.

29 Péguy, "Memories of Youth," p. 23.

30 Péguy, "Clio: Dialogue de l'histoire et de l'âme païenne" (1909–1912), *OP* 2:178, 129, 125, 128–29, 284, 298.

31 *The Correspondence of Walter Benjamin, 1910–1940,* ed. Gershom Scholem and Theodor W. Adorno (Chicago: University of Chicago Press, 1994), p. 147. See also Benjamin's letter to Scholem dated 23 July 1920: "Do you remember my having spoken to you in Iseltwald about Charles Péguy? . . . Whether I will write an essay expressing my admiration and encouraging approval depends only on whether I finally get to read his most important writings in unabridged versions" (p. 167). See also an interesting study by Hella Tiedemann-Bartels, "La mémoire est toujours de la guerre: Benjamin et Péguy," in *Walter Benjamin et Paris,* ed. Heinz Wismann (Paris: Cerf, 1986), pp. 133–43, and Daniel Bensaïd's remarkable commentaries on the two thinkers in *Moi la Révolution: Remembrances d'un bicentenaire indigne* (Paris: Gallimard, 1989).

32 See G. Leroy, *Péguy entre l'ordre et la révolution,* pp. 199–200.

33 Rolland, *Péguy,* p. 60; Péguy, "L'argent" (1913), *OP* 2:1053–54.

34 Henri Guillemin, "Enfant de lumière ou fils des ténèbres," in *Les critiques de notre temps et Péguy* (Paris: Garnier Frères, 1973), p. 108.

35 Péguy, "Memories of Youth," p. 51.

36 Péguy, *Notre jeunesse, OP* 1:549, 572, 565.

37 Péguy, *Notre jeunesse,* "Memories of Youth," pp. 62–63.

38 Péguy, "Un nouveau théologien," pp. 998, 976.

39 Péguy, "Note conjointe sur M. Descartes et la philosophie cartésienne" (1914), *OP* 2:1446–51.

40 Ibid., p. 1462; Péguy, "L'argent suite" (1913), *OP* 2:1192.

41 Péguy, "L'argent," pp. 1068–69; "L'argent suite," pp. 1204, 1184–85. Nevertheless, the principal basis for Péguy's support of the Commune seems to have been its refusal to capitulate in the war against Prussia.

42 Ernst Bloch, "Wie ist Sozialismus möglich?" (1919) in *Kampf, nicht Krieg: Politische Schriften, 1917–1919,* ed. Martin Korel (Frankfurt: Suhrkamp Verlag, 1985), p. 566.

43 Bloch, *Heritage of Our Times* (1935), trans. Neville Plaice and Stephen Plaice (Berkeley: University of California Press, 1991), pp. 369–70.

44 Arno Münster, ed., *Tagträume vom aufrechten Gang: Sechs Interviews mit Ernst Bloch* (Frankfurt: Suhrkamp, 1978), pp. 21–22; and Rainer Traub and Harald Wieser, *Gespräche mit Ernst Bloch* (Frankfurt: Suhrkamp, 1975), p. 30.

45 Bloch, "Der blühende Spiesser" (1911), in *Politische Messungen, Pestzeit, Vormärz* (Frankfurt: Suhrkamp, 1970), pp. 15–16.

46 Paul Honigsheim, "Der Max Weber Kreis in Heidelberg," *Kölner Vierteljahrshefte fur Soziologie* (1926): 284.

47 Bloch, *Briefe, 1903–1975,* ed. Karola Bloch et al. (Frankfurt: Suhrkamp, 1985), p. 55.

48 Theodor W. Adorno, "Ernst Bloch's *Spuren:* On the Revised Edition of 1959," *Notes to Literature,* ed. Rolf Tiedemann, trans. Shierry Weber Nicholsen (New York: Columbia University Press, 1991), 1:210–11.

49 Bloch, *Geist der Utopie* (1918) (Frankfurt: Suhrkamp, 1985), pp. 20–21; cf. Bloch, *The*

Spirit of Utopia (1923), trans. Anthony A. Nassar (Stanford: Stanford University Press, 2000), pp. 11–12.

50 Bloch, *Spirit of Utopia*, p. 11.

51 Ibid., p. 24; also *Geist der Utopie* (1918), pp. 28–32, 41–42.

52 Bloch, *Spirit of Utopia*, p. 236.

53 Bloch, *Geist der Utopie* (1918), pp. 331–32, 381, 441–42. On the subject of the young Bloch's religiosity, see the remarkable works of Arno Münster, *Utopie, Messianismus, und Apokalypse in Frühwerk von Ernst Bloch* (Frankfurt: Suhrkamp, 1982), and *Messianisme et utopie chez Ernst Bloch* (Paris: Presses Universitaires de France, 1989).

54 Bloch, *Geist der Utopie* (1918), pp. 403, 407, 432.

55 Ibid., pp. 402, 298.

56 Ibid., pp. 9, 444.

57 Ibid., p. 388; John Ely, "Walking Upright: The Dialectics of Natural Right and Social Utopia in the Work of Ernst Bloch and the Problem of a Deficiency of Political Theory in Marxism," June 1988, p. 131. (Ely's unpublished text uses our work as a springboard to study the Romantic anticapitalist dimension in Bloch's work.)

58 The various articles and texts Bloch published in Switzerland during these years have recently been collected (in their original versions, quite different from the form Bloch gave some of them in publishing his complete works) by Martin Korol. See Bloch, *Kampf, nicht Krieg*, pp. 507–17.

59 Michael Löwy, "Interview avec Ernst Bloch" (Tübingen, March 24, 1974), in *Pour une sociologie des intellectuels révolutionnaires: L'évolution politique de G. Lukács, 1909–1929* (Paris: Presses Universitaires de France, 1976), p. 300.

60 Bloch, *Thomas Münzer, théologien de la révolution* (1921), trans. M. de Gandillac (Paris: Julliard, 1964), pp. 81, 227–30. On the libertarian dimension of Bloch's early writings and their relation to Jewish messianism, see Michael Löwy, *Redemption and Utopia: Jewish Libertarian Thought in Central Europe,* trans. Hope Heaney (Stanford: Stanford University Press, 1988), pp. 138–44. Bloch's anarchist interpretation of the peasant war was probably inspired by some passages in Gustav Landauer's book, *Die Revolution* (Frankfurt: Rutten and Loening, 1907), which he "forgets" to cite, however.

61 Bloch, *Thomas Münzer,* p. 177.

62 Ibid., pp. 132, 239.

63 Bloch, *Heritage,* p. 111.

64 Ibid., p. 128.

65 Ibid., pp. 60–62.

66 Ibid., pp. 2, 113–14, 55. Anson Rabinbach offers a very pertinent summary of the book's central ideal: for Bloch, "the fact that it was the Nazis and not the left which gave political form to the utopian substance embedded in the romantic anticapitalism of the German peasantry and *Mittelstand* does not reduce the authentic impulses to be discovered there" ("Ernst Bloch's *Heritage of Our Times* and the Theory of Fascism," *New German Critique,* no. 11 [1977]: 11).

67 Bloch, *Heritage,* p. 4. In Bloch's defense it must be said that in *Heritage of Our Times* he never used the concept of social-fascism.

68 David Gross, "Ernst Bloch, *The Principle of Hope*," *Telos* 75 (spring 1988): 189–90.

69 The passage in question is found in vol. 2, pp. 850–51 of Bloch, *The Principle of Hope* (1959), trans. Neville Plaice, Stephen Plaice, and Paul Knight (Cambridge: MIT Press, 1986).

70 Jack Zipes, review of *The Marxist Philosophy of Ernst Bloch,* by Wayne Hudson, *Telos* 58 (winter 1983–84): 227.

71 Bloch, *Principle of Hope,* 1:8–9. See also Bloch, "Gibt es Zukunft in der Vergangenheit?" (Is there a future in the past? [1969]), in *Tendenz-Latenz-Utopie* (Frankfurt: Suhrkamp, 1978), p. 299; here Bloch calls for a union between "a utopian tradition and a tradition-saturated utopia."

72 Bloch, *Principle of Hope,* 1:136, 3:1368. The Wartburg student festival in 1817 was a movement with an ambiguous ideology blending German nationalism, *völkisch* populism, and democratic aspirations.

73 Ibid., 1:150, 2:735–36, 743, 692, 613–14; see also 2:742–44, 886–87.

74 Ibid., 2:696, 670, 690, 695; see also 2:666–67.

75 Ibid., p. 666; see also 1:9, 2:687–88, 787–88, 3:1330–31, 1341–51; and see Jürgen Habermas, "Un Schelling marxiste," in *Profils philosophiques et politiques* (Paris: Gallimard, 1974), pp. 193–216.

76 Bloch, *Principle of Hope,* 3:1200; see also 3:1195–96, 1290. The theme is developed more fully in Bloch's *Atheism in Christianity: The Religion of the Exodus and the Kingdom,* trans. J. T. Swann (New York: Herder and Herder, 1972).

77 Bloch, *Principle of Hope,* 2:515; see also 2:496–98, 511–15, 3:1233, 1286–93, 1363; and see Friedrich Engels, "Schelling and Revelation," in Karl Marx and Friedrich Engels, *Collected Works,* trans. Richard Dixon et al. (New York: International Publishers, 1975), 6:239. In this context, Bloch also mentions Alexander Blok's famous chiliast-Bolshevik poem, the "March of the Twelve," a remarkable example of "Christo-romanticism" (*Principle of Hope,* p. 514).

78 Bloch, *Principle of Hope,* 3:1359–69.

79 Ibid., 1:198–99, 3:1372. See also Münster, *Tagträume von aufrechten Gang,* p. 96 (interview with José Marchand in 1974) and Bloch, "Recht und Unrecht des Pessimismus" (1965), in *Abschiede von der Utopie? Vorträge,* ed. Hanna Geckle (Frankfurt: Suhrkamp, 1980), pp. 15–19. This is one of the rare passages in Bloch's work in which the significance of Auschwitz for contemporary philosophical reflection is mentioned.

80 Bloch, *Principle of Hope,* 3:1375–76; Adorno, "Ernst Bloch's *Spuren,*" p. 214.

81 Bloch, "A Jubilee for Renegades," *New German Critique,* no. 4 (1975), p. 24.

82 Oskar Negt, "Ernst Bloch — The German Philosopher of the October Revolution," *New German Critique,* no. 4 (1975): 9.

83 On the concept of "elective affinity" in cultural studies, see Michael Löwy, *Redemption and Utopia: Jewish Libertarian Thought in Central Europe: A Study in Elective Affinity,* trans. Hope Healey (Stanford University Press, 1992). This section on Christa Wolf was originally published in *New German Critique.* It was originally written in English and has been edited to conform to Duke Press style.

84 We first presented our interpretation of Romanticism in Sayre and Löwy, "Figures of Romantic Anti-Capitalism," *New German Critique,* no. 32 (1984). This article sparked a

debate that can be followed in the collection of essays, *Spirits of Fire: English Romantic Writers and Contemporary Historical Methods,* ed. G. A. Rosso and Daniel P. Watkins (Rutherford, N.J.: Fairleigh Dickinson University Press, 1990).

85 Anna K. Kuhn, *Christa Wolf's Utopian Vision: From Marxism to Feminism* (New York: Cambridge University Press, 1988), p. 26. The first quoted phrase is the subtitle of the work.

86 Wolf, *Cassandra: A Novel and Four Essays,* trans. Jan van Heurck (New York: Noonday, 1984), p. 278. Hereafter referred to parenthetically within the text as *CNFE.* For a description of her discovery of Marxism, see Wolf, "On That Date" (1971), in *The Author's Dimension: Selected Essays,* trans. Jan van Heurck (New York: Farrar, Strauss, Giroux, 1993), pp. 258–63.

87 Wolf, *The Fourth Dimension: Interviews with Christa Wolf* (London: Verso, 1988), p. 111.

88 Wolf, *Fourth Dimension,* p. 112.

89 Hans Meyer, *Aussenseiter* (Frankfurt: Suhrkamp, 1975). Translated into English as *Outsiders: A Study of Life and Letters,* trans. Denis M. Sweet (Cambridge: MIT Press, 1982).

90 Wolf, *Ansprachen* (Darmstadt: Luchterhand, 1988), p. 42.

91 See Jack Zipes's introduction to Wolf, *Divided Heaven* (New York: Adler's Foreign Books, 1976); see also Andreas Huyssen, "Auf den Spuren Ernst Blochs: Nachdenken über Christa Wolf," in *Christa Wolf Materialienbuch,* ed. Klaus Sauer (Darmstadt: Luchterhand, 1979), pp. 81–87. For a discussion of Bloch's Romantic worldview, see chap. 5, herein.

92 Wolf, "Tuesday, September 27," *What Remains and Other Stories,* trans. Heike Schwarzbauer and Rick Takvorian (London: Virago, 1993), p. 35.

93 Ibid., p. 39.

94 Wolf, *Moskauer Novelle* (Halle: Mitteldeutscher, 1961), p. 21. Unless otherwise indicated, all translations are our own.

95 Ibid., p. 54.

96 A similar point is made by Kuhn, *Wolf's Utopian Vision,* p. 26. Jack Zipes rightly sees in this passage a key to understanding not only *Moskauer Novelle* but all Wolf's later work as well. See Zipes, introduction to *Divided Heaven,* p. 1. The following references to the novel *Divided Heaven,* indicated parenthetically within the text as *DH,* are to Wolf, *Divided Heaven,* trans. Joan Becker (Berlin: Seven Seas Books, 1965).

97 See also Kuhn, *Wolf's Utopian Vision,* p. 46.

98 Wolf, *The Quest for Christa T.,* trans. Christopher Middleton (London: Virago, 1988), pp. 97, 171. Hereafter referred to parenthetically within the text as *QCT.*

99 Wolf, "A June Afternoon," in *What Remains,* pp. 53–54.

100 Myra Love, "Christa Wolf and Feminism: Breaking the Patriarchal Connection," *New German Critique,* no. 16 (1979): 42.

101 Inta Ezergailis, *Woman Writers — The Divided Self* (Bonn: Bouvier, 1982).

102 Wolf, "Reading and Writing," in *The Author's Dimension,* p. 47.

103 On this point, see the interesting (but unsympathetic) essay by Richard Herzinger and Heinz-Peter Preusser "Von Äussersten zum Ersten: DDR-Literatur in der Tradition deutscher Zivilisationskritik" (The GDR Literature in the Tradition of the German Critique of Civilization), in *Text und Kritik: Sonderband: Literatur in der DDR—*

Rückblicke, ed. Heinz Ludwig Arnold and Frauke Meyer-Gosau (Munich: Editions Text and Kritik, 1991), pp. 195–209.

104 Wolf, "The New Life and Opinions of a Tomcat," in *What Remains,* pp. 121–51. Hereafter referred to parenthetically within the text as *NLT.*

105 Wolf, *Fourth Dimension,* p. 36.

106 Wolf, "Self-Experiment: Appendix to a Report," trans. Jeanetts Clausen, *New German Critique,* no. 13 (1978): 113. Hereafter cited parenthetically within the text as SE.

107 Wolf, *Fourth Dimension,* p. 35.

108 Ibid., pp. 34–35.

109 Helen Fehervary and Sarah Lennox, introduction to Christa Wolf, "Self-Experiment," *New German Critique,* no. 13 (1978): 111–12.

110 Wolf, *No Place on Earth,* trans. Jan van Heuck (New York: Farrar, Straus, Giroux, 1982). Hereafter referred to parenthetically within the text as *NPE.*

111 "*No Place on Earth* can be seen as part of an attempt by members of the socialist literary avant-garde to rehabilitate the Romantics" (Kuhn, *Wolf's Utopian Vision,* p. 142). See also Monika Totten, "Zur Aktualität der Romantik in der DDR: Christa Wolf und ihre Vorläufer(innen)," *Zeitschrift für deutsche Philologie* 101, no. 2 (1982): 244–62.

112 Wolf, *Fourth Dimension,* pp. 91–92.

113 Ibid., p. 100.

114 Kuhn, *Wolf's Utopian Vision,* pp. 143, 174.

115 Kuhn notes that "the dialogue between Kleist and Günderrode, the climax of *No Place on Earth,* distinguishes itself from the conversations at Merten's, which both view as empty chatter, in that it is an exchange of intellectual equals who are able to perceive each other as autonomous subjects." See Kuhn, *Wolf's Utopian Vision,* pp. 164–65.

116 The dialogue is constructed in such a way that it is sometimes difficult to know who is speaking, thus emphasizing the spiritual community of the two Romantic writers.

117 "The Shadow of a Dream" is, in translation, also the name of the essay that introduces the book—one of Wolf's most brilliant pieces. To say that it illuminates the novel and brings out its historical context is not enough. It is a literary and critical gem and a decisive contribution to the rediscovery of the life and works of the young Romantic poet who killed herself in 1806 at the age of twenty-six.

118 Wolf, "The Shadow of a Dream: A Sketch of Karoline von Günderrode," in *The Author's Dimension,* p. 133. Hereafter cited parenthetically within the text as *SD.*

119 Wolf, "Your Next Life Begins Today: A Letter about Bettine," in *The Author's Dimension,* pp. 190, 210. Hereafter referred to parenthetically within the text as *YNL.*

120 Wolf, *Fourth Dimension,* p. 118.

121 Wolf, *Cassandra,* p. 142. The English edition comprises all five texts in the same volume, but places the novel first, in spite of the fact that the term applied to the other pieces— "Conditions" (*Voraussetzungen*)—implies precedence. In discussing the work we will therefore restore the original, intended order.

122 For Wolf's discussion of Minoan culture, see Wolf, "The Travel Report Continues, and the Trail Is Followed," in *Cassandra,* pp. 182–224.

123 Kuhn, *Wolf's Utopian Vision,* p. 221.

124   Wolf, *Accident: A Day's News,* trans. Heike Schwarzbauer (London: Virago, 1989), p. 17. Hereafter referred to parenthetically within the text as *A.*

125   Wolf, *Sommerstück* (Frankfurt: Luchterhand, 1989).

126   Wolf wrote the first versions of *Cassandra* in the late seventies and very beginning of the eighties. Revised in 1987, it was not published until 1989.

127   In Wolf, *What Remains.* Originally written in 1979, revised in 1989, and published in 1990 as *Was Bleibt.* Hereafter referred to parenthetically within the text as *WR.*

128   See Todd Gitlin's article on Wolf based on several interviews: "I Did Not Imagine That I Lived in Truth," *New York Times Book Review,* 4 April 1993.

129   See "Sleeping with the Enemy: Stasi and the Literati," *Newsweek,* 8 February 1993; and "Intellectuels est-allemands sur la sellette," *Le monde diplomatique,* April 1993, p. 11.

130   "Intellectuels est-allemands sur la sellette," p. 11.

131   David Bathrick, "Die Intellektuellen und die Macht: Die Repräsentanz des Schrift-stellers in der DDR," in *Der Schriftsteller als Intellektuelle: Politik und Literatur im Katten Krieg,* ed. Sven Hanuschek, Therese Hörnigk, and Christine Malende (Tübingen: Max Niemeyer Verlag, 2000), pp. 235–48.

6. THE FIRE IS STILL BURNING: FROM SURREALISM TO THE PRESENT DAY AND BEYOND

1   Georges Altmann et al., "La révolution d'abord et toujours," *La révolution surréaliste* 5 (1925), pp. 31–32. The text is signed by a large number of artists and intellectuals from the group, including André Breton, Louis Aragon, Paul Eluard, Michel Leiris, Robert Desnos, Benjamin Péret, Philippe Soupault, and Raymond Queneau.

2   André Breton, "Tower of Light" (1951), in *Free Rein* (*La clé des champs*), trans. Michel Parmentier and Jacqueline d'Amboise (Lincoln: University of Nebraska Press, 1995), p. 265.

3   Breton, "Manifesto of Surrealism," in *Manifestoes of Surrealism,* trans. Richard Seaver and Helen R. Lane (Ann Arbor: University of Michigan Press, 1972), pp. 10, 26.

4   Breton, "Second Manifesto of Surrealism," in ibid., p. 153 (the bracketed passages are modifications of the published translation).

5   Breton, "Marvelous versus Mystery" (1936), in *Free Rein,* pp. 1–2, and "Political Position of Surrealism," in *Manifestoes of Surrealism,* p. 217. There is an interesting analysis of the surrealists' relation to German Romanticism in Karl Heinz Bohrer's *Die Kritik der Romantik* (Frankfurt: Suhrkamp, 1989), pp. 48–61. On the connection of surrealism, Romanticism, and the student revolt of the 1960s, see Richard Faber's essay, "Frühromantik, Surrealismus, und Studentenrevolte oder die Frage nach dem Anarchismus," in *Romantische Utopie, Utopische Romantik,* ed. Richard Faber (Hildesheim: Gerstenberg, 1979), pp. 336–58.

6   Breton, "Second Manifesto," p. 128.

7   Breton, "Autodidacts Called 'Naïves'" (1942), in *Surrealism and Painting,* trans. Simon Watson Taylor (New York: Harper and Row, Icon Editions, 1973), p. 293.

8   Breton, cited by Michel Beaujour, "André Breton mythographe: 'Arcane 17,'" in *André Breton,* ed. Marc Eigeldinger (Neuchâtel: Editions de la Baconnière, 1970), p. 225.

9   Breton, "Nonnational Boundaries of Surrealism" (1937), in *Free Rein,* pp. 14–15, 14, 13–14, 17.

10 Breton, "Max Ernst: The Legendary Life of Max Ernst Preceded by a Brief Discussion of the Need for a New Myth" (1942), in *Surrealism and Painting,* p. 159. In general, Breton seems to perceive a mythic dimension above all in the painters known as the "naïves"; this was the idea suggested in the 1942 article on autodidacts as well as in the following remark from 1954: "In modern mythology, the general sense of which remains very obscure still in many respects, the chemist Csontvary is seated between the Douanier Rousseau and the Facteur Cheval, at a good distance from the 'professionals' " ("Judit Riegl" [1954], in *Surrealism and Painting,* p. 238 n. 2).

11 Breton, "Prolegomena to a Third Surrealist Manifesto or Not" (1942), in *Manifestoes of Surrealism,* pp. 287–88.

12 Breton, "Nonnational Boundaries," p. 13.

13 Breton, *Arcanum 17* (1944), trans. Zack Rogow (Los Angeles: Sun and Moon Press, 1994), p. 87.

14 Ibid., pp. 38, 96–97.

15 Daniel Cohn-Bendit et al., "Pourquoi des sociologues?" Nanterre, March 1968; and "Nous sommes en marche," in "Amnistie des yeux crevés" (Censier 453, n.d., mimeographed flyer). For an analysis of the antitechnocratic thematics of the May movement, see an interesting article by Andrew Feenberg, "Remembering the May Events," *Theory and Society* 6 (1978): 29–53.

16 Alain Touraine, *The May Movement: Revolt and Reform* (1968), trans. Leonard F. X. Mayhew (New York: Random House, 1971), p. 279.

17 Vincent Bounoure et al., "Ce n'est qu'un début," *L'Archibras* 4: *Le Surréalisme le 18 juin 1968* (June 1968) — texts written collectively by Vincent Bounoure, Claude Courtot, Annie Le Brun, Gérard Legrand, José Pierre, Jean Schuster, Georges Sebbag, and Jean-Claude Silbermann.

18 Association féderative générale des étudiants de Strasbourg, "De la misère en milieu étudiant, considérée sous ses aspects économique, politique, psychologique, sexuel et notamment intellectuel et de quelques moyens pour y remédier," 1966.

19 Herbert Marcuse, *Eros and Civilization* (New York: Sphere Books, 1969), pp. 151–54, and *Reason and Revolution* (Boston: Beacon Press, 1960), p. x.

20 Marcuse, *One-Dimensional Man* (Boston: Beacon Press, 1964), p. 60.

21 Marcuse, *Counterrevolution and Revolt* (Boston: Beacon Press, 1972), p. 86.

22 Henri Lefebvre, *Lukács 1955* (Paris: Aubier, 1986), pp. 72–73.

23 Lefebvre, *La somme et le reste* (Paris: La Nef, 1958), 2:596.

24 Lefebvre, *Critique de la vie quotidienne* (Paris: L'Arche, 1981), 3:23–24.

25 Lefebvre, *Au-delà du structuralisme* (Paris: Anthropos, 1971), pp. 37, 46.

26 Lefebvre, *Critique of Everyday Life,* trans. John Moore (London: Verso, 1991), 1:209, 229.

27 Lefebvre, *La Vallée de Campan: Etude de sociologie rurale* (Paris: Presses Universitaires de France, 1963), pp. 19–20. See also "Une république pastorale: La vallée de Campan: Organisation, vie, et histoire d'une communauté pyrénéenne. Textes et documents accompagnées d'une étude de sociologie historique" (Ph.D. diss., University of Paris. n.d.). Complementary doctoral dissertation presented to the Faculty of Letters.

28 Lefebvre, *Vers le cybernanthrope* (Paris: Denoël-Gonthier, 1971), pp. 22–23. This is a new edition of *Contre les technocrates,* which was published in 1967.

29 Jacques Baynac, "Le petit 'grand soir' de Nanterre," *Le Monde,* 27–28 March 1988, p. 2.

30 Lefebvre, "L'irruption, de Nanterre au sommet," *L'homme et la société* 8 (June 1968): 65, 79.

31 Lefebvre, *Vers le cybernanthrope,* p. 14.

32 Fredric Jameson, "Reification and Utopia in Mass Culture," *Social Text* 1 (winter 1979): 130–48.

33 While there are numerous direct allusions to the Middle Ages in this film, there are also many indirect ones, for the men struggling against the evil empire closely resemble the cowboys of the classic Westerns, who themselves were modeled on figures from medieval epic poems and romances.

34 Jack Zipes, *Breaking the Magic Spell: Radical Theories of Folk and Fairy Tales* (Austin: University of Texas Press, 1979), pp. 158–59.

35 Michael Ende, interviewed on 16 March 1984.

36 See Uwe Schimank, *Neoromantischer Protest im Spätkapitalismus: Der Widerstand gegen die Stadt- und Landschaftveröderung* (Bielefeld: AJZ Druck und Verlag, 1983), and Johannes Weiss, "Wiederverzauberung der Welt? Bermerkungen zur Wiederkehr der Romantik in der gegenwärtigen Kulturkritik," *Kölner Zeitschrift für Soziologie und Sozialpsychologie,* Sonderheft 27 (Opladen: Westdeutscher Verlag, 1986), pp. 286–301.

37 See Manon Maren-Grisebach, *Philosophie der Grünen* (Munich: G. Olzog 1982); Jean-Paul Deléage, "Le rapport des sociétés à la nature: Une question de vie ou de mort," in *Le rapport à la nature,* special issue of *L'homme et la société* 91–92 (1989): 7; Werner Hülsenberg, *The German Greens: A Social and Political Profile* (London: Verso, 1988); Joan Martínez Alier, "Ecologismo marxista y neo-narodnismo ecologico," *Mientras Tanto* (Barcelona) 39 (1989). An unpublished study brings to light the role of traditionalist or conservative values in the alternative-Green culture in Germany, starting with a detailed analysis of ecological texts and works of authors such as Jean Amery, Erhard Eppler, and others: Thomas Keller, "Les Verts et le conservatisme de gauche: Une nouvelle culture politique en République fédérale d'Allemagne" (Ph.D. diss., University of Strasbourg, 1988).

38 See the work of Françoise Champion, Danièle Hervieu-Léger, Louis Hourmant, Agnès Rochefort-Turquin, and Martine Cohen, in the remarkable collective work *De l'émotion en religion: Renouveaux et traditions* (Paris: Centurion, 1990).

39 Gustavo Gutierrez, *La force historique des pauvres* (Paris: Cerf, 1986), pp. 172–73, 218.

40 Leonardo Boff, *Ecclesiogenesis: The Base Communities Reinvent the Church,* trans. Robert R. Barr (Maryknoll, N.Y.: Orbis Books, 1986), pp. 1, 4, 9.

41 Harvey Cox, *Religion in the Secular City: Toward a Post-Modern Theology* (New York: Simon and Schuster, 1984), p. 127.

42 Jean Seguy, "Protestation socio-religieuse et contre-culture" (seminar at the Ecole pratique des hautes études, 1973–74, mimeograph), p. 11.

43 Blandine Barret-Kriegel, *The State and the Rule of Law,* trans. Marc A. LePain and Jeffrey C. Cohen (Princeton: Princeton University Press, 1995), p. 103. For Barret-Kriegel, Hobbes's doctrine of the "rule of law" is modernity's most fundamental acquisition (pp. 93–94).

44 Isaiah Berlin, *Magus of the North: J. G. Hamann and the Origins of Modern Irrationalism* (New York: Farrar, Straus and Giroux, 1994), p. 121.

45 Jerome McGann, *The Romantic Ideology* (Chicago: University of Chicago Press, 1983).

46 Among the exceptions: in *La raison contradictoire: Sciences et philosophie modernes* (Paris: Albin Michel, 1990), Jean-Jacques Wunenburger insists on the importance of the imaginary as a counterweight to the simplifying codifications of Cartesian rationality, and he rehabilitates the logic of contradiction and paradox that is at work in the Romantic philosophy of nature.

47 Jean Chesneaux, *Brave Modern World: The Prospects for Survival,* trans. Diana Johnstone, Karen Bowie, and Francesca Garviel (London: Thames and Hudson, 1992), pp. 156–57, 166–67 (Orwell citation, p. 167).

48 Raoul Vaneigem, *Adresse aux vivants sur la mort qui les gouverne et l'opportunité de s'en défaire* (Paris: Seghers, 1990), pp. 90–91.

49 See, among others, Jacques Ellul, *The Technological Bluff,* trans. Geoffrey W. Bromiley (Grand Rapids: W. B. Eerdmans, 1990); Michel Henry, *La barbarie* (Paris: Grasset, 1987); Chesneaux, *Brave Modern World;* Armand Mattelart, *La culture contre la démocratie, l'audiovisuel à l'heure transnationale* (Paris: La Découverte, 1984).

50 This theme is developed in particular by the work of MAUSS, the Anti-Utilitarian Movement in the Social Sciences inspired by the work of Marcel Mauss. See especially Alain Caillé, *Critique de la raison utilitaire* (Paris: La Découverte, 1989), a text based on the collective work of that movement. See also Serge Latouche, *The Westernization of the World: The Significance, Scope, and Limits of the Drive towards Global Uniformity,* trans. Rosemary Morris (Cambridge, Mass.: Polity Press, 1996); Latouche, also a member of MAUSS, writes: "One might even say that the unfettered personal self-interest fostered by utilitarianism empties democracy of its essential content by turning men into cogs in the great machine of technology" (p. 34).

51 Chesneaux, *Brave Modern World,* pp. 133–34. See also Michel Serres, *The Natural "Contract,"* trans. Elizabeth MacArthur and William Paulson (Ann Arbor: University of Michigan Press, 1995); René Dumont, *Un monde intolérable, le libéralisme en question* (Paris: Seuil, 1988), and a collection of articles that appeared in *Le Monde diplomatique* and were published in 1990 as *La planète mise à sac* (along with recent works by other students of political ecology, for example André Gorz, Alain Lipietz, and Pierre Juquin).

52 Pierre Clastres, "Archéologie de la violence: La guerre dans les sociétés primitives," in *Libre* (Paris: Payot, 1977), p. 156.

53 Caillé, *Critique de la raison utilitaire,* p. 67.

54 Raoul Vaneigem, *Adresse aux vivants,* pp. 89–90.

55 E. P. Thompson, *The Making of the English Working Class* (New York: Pantheon Books, 1963), pp. 12–13.

56 Ibid., pp. 198, 343.

57 Ibid., pp. 359, 486. See also the following remark, with reference to workers: "The experience of immiseration came upon them in a hundred different forms; for the field labourer, the loss of his common rights and the vestiges of village democracy; for the artisan, the loss of his craftsman's status; for the weaver, the loss of livelihood and of independence; for the child, the loss of work and play in the home; for many groups of

workers whose real earnings improved, the loss of security, leisure and the deterioration of the urban environment" (p. 445).

58 Ibid., pp. 561, 550, 552.

59 Ibid., p. 832.

60 Thompson, *Customs in Common* (London: Merlin Press, 1991), pp. 399, 401.

61 For example, in his review of the English translation of a book by one of the authors of the present volume (Michael Löwy, *Georg Lukács: From Romanticism to Bolshevism* [London: New Left Books, 1979]), Williams refuses to see Bolshevism simply as progress with respect to the diffuse anticapitalist Romanticism of the young Lukács or others. He points out that if the Romantics so vigorously denounced state bureaucracy, the bond between industrialism and the "quantification of thought," as well as the lack of community in modern society, "we can hardly, from the end of the seventies, suppose that they were wasting their time or missing some simple central truth" (*New Society,* 24 January 1980, p. 189).

62 For a monograph on Williams's work as a whole stressing the continuity of its development, see Jan Gorak, *The Alien Mind of Raymond Williams* (Columbia: University of Missouri Press, 1988).

63 Raymond Williams, *Politics and Letters: Interviews with "New Left Review"* (London: NLB and Verso, 1979), pp. 97–98.

64 Robert Southey cited in Williams, *Culture and Society* (New York: Harper and Row, 1958), p. 25.

65 Ibid., p. 280.

66 Ibid., p. 328.

67 Ibid., p. 330.

68 Williams, *Politics and Letters,* p. 314 (italics in the original).

69 Ibid., pp. 304, 314.

70 Williams, *The Country and the City* (New York: Oxford University Press, 1973), pp. 61, 68.

71 On the overall phenomenon, see above, chapter 2.

72 On knowable communities, see especially Williams, *Country and the City,* chap. 16.

73 Ibid., p. 271.

74 Ibid., pp. 150, 215–16.

75 Ibid., p. 149.

76 Williams, "The Uses of Cultural Theory," *New Left Review,* no. 158 (1986): 19–31; this article offers a good summary of his theoretical balance sheet.

77 Reprinted in the posthumous collection, Williams, *Resources of Hope: Culture, Democracy, Socialism,* ed. Robin Gable (London: Verso, 1989), pp. 295–313. Among other texts, this anthology includes reprints of Williams's principal writings and communications from the 1980s. Williams develops his ideas for a socialist future at greater length in *Towards 2000* (London: Chatto and Windus, 1983).

78 See Andrew Feenberg, *Critical Theory of Technology* (New York: Oxford University Press, 1991).

79 William Morris, *News from Nowhere,* in *Three Works by William Morris,* ed. A. L. Morton (London: Lawrence and Wishart, 1968), p. 280.

Works Cited

Abrams, M. H. *The Mirror and the Lamp: Romantic Theory and the Critical Tradition*. Oxford: Oxford University Press, 1971.

———. *Natural Supernaturalism: Tradition and Revolution in Romantic Literature*. New York: Norton Library, 1973.

Adorno, Theodor W. "Ernst Bloch's *Spuren:* On the Revised Edition of 1959." In *Notes to Literature*. Edited by Rolf Tiedemann, translated by Shierry Weber Nicholsen. Vol. 1, pp. 200–215. New York: Columbia University Press, 1991.

Aers, David, Jonathan Cook, and David Punter. *Romanticism and Ideology: Studies in English Writing, 1765–1830*. London: Routledge and Kegan Paul, 1981.

Altmann, Georges, et al. "La révolution d'abord et toujours." *La révolution surréaliste* 5 (1925).

Auerbach, Erich. "Figura." In *Scenes from the Drama of European Literature*. Translated by Ralph Manheim. Pp. 11–76. Gloucester, Mass.: Peter Smith, 1973.

Aveling, Eleanor Marx, and Edward Aveling. *Shelley's Socialism*. 1888. Reprint. London: Journeyman Press, 1975.

Babbitt, Irving. *Rousseau and Romanticism*. Boston: Houghton Mifflin, 1919.

Badia, Gilbert. *Rosa Luxemburg, journaliste, polémiste, révolutionnaire*. Paris: Editions Sociales, 1975.

Bailly, Jean-Christophe. *La légende dispersée: Anthologie du romantisme allemand*. Paris: UGE, 1976.

Balzac, Honoré de. *Illusions Perdues*. Paris: Livre de Poche, 1972.

Barbéris, Pierre. *Aux sources du réalisme: Aristocrates et bourgeois*. Paris: UGE, 1978.

———. "'Mal du siècle,' ou d'un romantisme de droite à un romantisme de gauche." In *Romantisme et politique (1815–1851)*, pp. 164–82. Colloquium of the Ecole normale supérieure, Saint-Cloud, 1966. Paris: Armand Colin, 1969.

Barret-Kriegel, Blandine. *The State and the Rule of Law*. Translated by Marc A. LePain and Jeffrey C. Cohen. Princeton: Princeton University Press, 1995.

Bastiaire, Jean. *Péguy l'insurgé*. Paris: Payot, 1975.

Bathrick, David. "Die Intellektuelle und die Macht: Die Repräsentanz des Schriftstellers in der DDR." In *Der Schriftsteller als Intellektuelle: Politik und Literatur im Kalten Krieg*. Edited by Sven Hanuschek, Therese Hörnigk, and Christine Malende. Tübingen: Niemeyer, 2000.

Bayley, John. "Contemporary British Poetry: A Romantic Persistence?" *Poetry* 146, no. 4 (1985): 227–36.

——. *The Romantic Survival: A Study in Poetic Evolution*. London: Constable, 1957.

Baynac, Jacques. "Le petit 'grand soir' de Nanterre." *Le Monde*, 27–28 March 1988, p. 2.

Beaujour, Michel. "André Breton mythographe: 'Arcane 17.'" In *André Breton*, edited by Marc Eigeldinger, pp. 221–40. Neuchâtel: Editions de la Baconnière, 1970.

Benjamin, Walter. "Albert Béguin, *L'âme romantique et le rêve*." 1939–40. In *Gesammelte Schriften*. Vol. 3, edited by Hella Tiedemann-Bartels. 1978.

——. *The Correspondence of Walter Benjamin, 1910–1940*. Edited by Gershom Scholem and Theodor W. Adorno. Chicago: University of Chicago Press, 1994.

——. "E. T. A. Hoffmann und Oskar Panizza." In *Gesammelte Schriften*. Vol. 2. 1977.

——. *Gesammelte Schriften*. 7 vols. Frankfurt: Suhrkamp, 1972–1989.

Benn, Gottfried. *Essays: Reden: Vorträge*. Wiesbaden: Limes Verlag, 1959.

Bensaïd, Daniel. *Moi la Révolution: Remembrances d'un bicentenaire indigne*. Paris: Gallimard, 1989.

Benz, Ernst. *The Mystical Sources of German Romantic Philosophy*. Allison Park, Pa.: Pickwick, 1983.

Berdiaev, Nicolas. *Solitude and Society*. London: Centenary Press, 1983.

Berlin, Isaiah. *Against the Current: Essays in the History of Ideas*. London: Oxford University Press, 1979.

——. "The Counter-Enlightenment." In *Against the Current: Essays in the History of Ideas*, pp. 6–20.

——. "Hume and the Sources of German Anti-Rationalism." In *Against the Current*, pp. 162–67.

——. *Magus of the North: J. G. Hamann and the Origins of Modern Irrationalism*. New York: Farrar, Straus and Giroux, 1994.

Bernanos, Georges. *The Diary of a Country Priest*. Translated by Pamela Morris. New York: Macmillan, 1937.

——. *A Diary of My Times*. Translated by Pamela Morris. New York: Macmillan, 1939.

Blake, William. *The Complete Poetry and Prose of William Blake*. Edited by David Erdman. Berkeley: University of California Press, 1982.

Bloch, Ernst. *Atheism in Christianity: The Religion of the Exodus and the Kingdom*. Translated by J. T. Swann. New York: Herder and Herder, 1972.

——. "Der blühende Spiesser." 1911. In *Politische Messungen, Pestzeit, Vormärz*, pp. 14–16. Frankfurt: Suhrkamp, 1970.

——. *Briefe, 1903–1975*. Edited by Karola Bloch, Jan Robert Bloch, Anne Frommann, Martin Korol, Inka Mülder, Arno Münster, Uwe Opolka, and Burghart Schmidt. Frankfurt: Suhrkamp, 1985.

——. *Geist der Utopie*. 1918. Frankfurt: Suhrkamp, 1985.

——. *Geist der Utopie.* 1923. Rev. ed. Frankfurt: Suhrkamp, 1973.

——. "Gibt es Zukunft in der Vergangenheit?" 1966. In *Tendenz-Latenz-Utopie,* pp. 286–300. Frankfurt: Suhrkamp, 1978.

——. *Heritage of Our Times.* 1935. Translated by Neville Plaice and Stephen Plaice. Berkeley: University of California Press, 1991.

——. "A Jubilee for Renegades," *New German Critique,* no. 4 (1975): 17–25.

——. *Kampf, nicht Krieg: Politische Schriften, 1917–1919.* Edited by Martin Korel. Frankfurt: Suhrkamp Verlag, 1985.

——. *The Principle of Hope.* 1959. Translated by Neville Plaice, Stephen Plaice, and Paul Knight. 3 vols. Cambridge: MIT Press, 1986.

——. "Recht und Unrecht des Pessimismus." 1965. In *Abschiede von der Utopie? Vorträge.* Edited by Hanna Geckle. Frankfurt: Suhrkamp, 1980.

——. *The Spirit of Utopia.* 1923. Translated by Anthony A. Nassar. Stanford: Stanford University Press, 2000.

——. *Thomas Münzer, théologien de la révolution.* 1921. Translated by M. de Gandillac. Paris: Julliard, 1964.

——. "Wie ist Sozialismus möglich?" (1919). In *Kampf, Nicht Krieg.* Pp. 563–69.

Boff, Leonardo. *Ecclesiogenesis: The Base Communities Reinvent the Church.* Translated by Robert R. Barr. Maryknoll, N.Y.: Orbis Books, 1986.

Bohrer, Karl Heinz. "Friedrich Schlegels Rede über die Mythologie." In *Mythos und Moderne,* pp. 52–82.

——. *Die Kritik der Romantik.* Frankfurt: Suhrkamp, 1989.

——. *Mythos und Moderne.* Frankfurt: Suhrkamp, 1983.

——. "Vorwort." In *Mythos und Moderne,* pp. 9–10.

Borkenau, Franz. *The Spanish Cockpit: An Eye-Witness Account of the Political and Social Conflicts of the Spanish Civil War.* 1937. Reprint, Ann Arbor: University of Michigan Press, 1963.

Bounoure, Vincent, et al. "Ce n'est qu'un début." *L'Archibras 4: Le Surréalisme le 18 juin 1968* (June 1968): 9–10.

Bousquet, Jacques. *Anthologie du XVIIIe romantique.* Paris: Pauvert, 1972.

——. "Définition et valeur de la notion de romantisme comme catégorie de l'histoire culturelle." Ph.D. diss., Sorbonne, 1964.

Bowle, John. *Western Political Thought.* London: University Paperbacks, 1961.

Breines, Paul. "Marxism, Romanticism, and the Case of Georg Lukács: Notes on Some Recent Sources and Situations." *Studies in Romanticism* 16 (1977): 473–89.

Breton, André. *Arcanum 17.* 1944. Translated by Zack Rogow. Los Angeles: Sun and Moon Press, 1994.

——. "Autodidacts Called 'Naïves.'" 1942. In *Surrealism and Painting,* pp. 291–94.

——. *Free Rein (La clé des champs).* Translated by Michel Parmentier and Jacqueline d'Amboise. Lincoln: University of Nebraska Press, 1995.

——. "Judit Riegl." 1954. In *Surrealism and Painting,* p. 238.

——. "Manifesto of Surrealism." 1924. In *Manifestoes of Surrealism.* pp. 1–47.

——. *Manifestoes of Surrealism.* Translated by Richard Seaver and Helen R. Lane. Ann Arbor: University of Michigan Press, 1972.

——. "Marvelous versus Mystery." 1936. In *Free Rein,* pp. 1–6.

——. "Max Ernst: The Legendary Life of Max Ernst Preceded by a Brief Discussion of the Need for a New Myth." 1942. In *Surrealism and Painting,* pp. 155–65.

——. "Nonnational Boundaries of Surrealism." 1937. In *Free Rein,* pp. 7–18.

——. "Political Position of Surrealism." 1935. Excerpts in *Manifestoes of Surrealism,* pp. 205–33.

——. "Prolegomena to a Third Surrealist Manifesto or Not." 1942. In *Manifestoes of Surrealism,* pp. 279–94.

——. "Second Manifesto of Surrealism." 1930. In *Manifestoes of Surrealism,* pp. 117–94.

——. *Surrealism and Painting.* Translated by Simon Watson Taylor. New York: Harper and Row, Icon Editions, 1973.

——. "Tower of Light." 1951. In *Free Rein,* pp. 265–67.

Brunschwig, Henri. *Société et romantisme en Prusse au XVIIIe siècle.* Paris: Flammarion, 1973.

Buber, Martin. *Gemeinschaft.* Munich: Dreiländerverlag, 1919.

Burke, Edmund. *Burke's Reflections on the Revolution in France.* 1790. Edited by F. G. Selby. London: Macmillan, 1892.

Butler, Marilyn. *Romantics, Rebels, and Reactionaries: English Literature and Its Background, 1760–1830.* New York: Oxford University Press, 1982.

Caillé, Alain. *Critique de la raison utilitaire.* Paris: La Découverte, 1989.

Carlyle, Thomas. *Chartism.* London: James Fraser, 1840.

——. "Signs of the Times." 1829. In *Critical and Miscellaneous Essays.* Vol. 2, pp. 230–52. London: Chapman and Hall, 1888.

Caudwell, Christopher. 1936. "The Bourgeois Illusion and English Romantic Poetry." In Glecker and Enscoe, *Romanticism: Points of View,* pp. 108–24.

Cestre, Charles. *La Révolution française et les poètes anglais (1789–1809).* Paris: Champion, 1906.

Champion, Françoise, et al. *De l'émotion en religion: Renouveaux et traditions.* Paris: Centurion, 1990.

Chateaubriand, François-René de. *Génie du christianisme.* Vol. 2. Paris: Beauce-Rusand, 1818.

Chesneaux, Jean. *Brave Modern World: The Prospects for Survival.* 1989. Translated by Diana Johnstone, Karen Bowie, and Francesca Garviel. London: Thames and Hudson, 1992.

——. *De la modernité.* Paris: La Découverte, 1983.

Clastres, Pierre. "Archéologie de la violence: La guerre dans les sociétés primitives." In *Libre,* pp. 137–73. Paris: Payot, 1977.

Cobban, Alfred. *Edmund Burke and the Revolt against the Eighteenth Century.* London: George Allen and Unwin, 1929.

Cohn-Bendit, Daniel. "Pourquoi des sociologues?" Nanterre, March 1968.

Coleridge, Samuel Taylor. *Collected Letters of Samuel Taylor Coleridge.* Edited by E. L. Griggs. Vol. 1. Oxford: Clarendon Press, 1956.

——. *The Collected Works of Samuel Taylor Coleridge.* Vol. 1, *Lectures 1795 on Politics and Religion,* edited by Lewis Patton and Peter Mann, 1971. Vol. 2, *The Watchman,* edited by Lewis Patton, 1970. Vol. 3, *Essays on His Times in the "Morning Post" and "The Courrier,"* edited by David V. Erdman. Princeton: Princeton University Press, 1978.

——. *The Complete Poetical Works of Samuel Taylor Coleridge.* Edited by E. H. Coleridge. Vol. 1. Oxford: Clarendon Press, 1912.

———. "Once a Jacobin Always a Jacobin." 1802. *Collected Works of Samuel Taylor Coleridge*. Vol. 3, pp. 367–73.

———. *The Political Thought of Samuel Taylor Coleridge*. Edited by R. J. White. London: Jonathan Cape, 1938.

Collingwood, R. G. *Ruskin's Philosophy*. Kendal: T. Wilson and Son, 1919.

Collingwood, W. G. *The Life of John Ruskin*. Boston: Houghton Mifflin, 1900.

Combs, R. L. *Vision of the Voyage: Hart Crane and the Psychology of Romanticism*. Memphis: Memphis State University Press, 1978.

Cornu, Auguste. *Karl Marx et Friedrich Engels*. Vol. 1. Paris: Presses Universitaires de France, 1955.

Cox, Harvey. *Religion in the Secular City: Toward a Post-Modern Theology*. New York: Simon and Schuster, 1984.

Croce, Benedetto. "A Crisis of Faith." 1934. In *Romanticism: Problems of Definition, Explanation, and Evaluation*, edited by John B. Halsted, pp. 53–57.

"De la misère en milieu étudiant, considérée sous ses aspects économique, politique, psychologique, sexuel et notamment intellectuel et de quelques moyens pour y remédier." Association fédérative des étudiants de Strasbourg. 1966.

Deléage, Jean-Paul. "Le rapport des sociétés à la nature: Une question de vie ou de mort." *L'homme et la société*, "Le rapport à la nature," 91–92 (1989): 7–11.

Dickens, Charles. *Hard Times*. New York: Harper and Row, 1965.

Droz, Jacques. *Le romantisme allemand et l'Etat: Résistance et collaboration en Allemagne napoléonienne*. Paris: Payot, 1966.

———. ed. *Le romantisme politique en Allemagne*. Paris: Armand Colin, 1963.

Dumont, René. *Un monde intolérable, le libéralisme en question*. Paris: Seuil, 1988.

Dumont, René, et al. *La planète mise à sac*. Paris: Le Monde, 1990.

Dupeux, Louis. "Kulturpessimismus, 'Révolution conservatrice' et modernité." Special issue, *Revue d'Allemagne* 14 (1982): 3–34.

———. "'Kulturpessimismus,' révolution conservatrice et modernité." In Raulet, *Weimar ou l'explosion de la modernité*, pp. 31–46.

Ellul, Jacques. *The Technological Bluff*. Translated by Geoffrey W. Bromiley. Grand Rapids: W. B. Eerdmans, 1990.

Ely, John. "Walking Upright: The Dialectics of Natural Right and Social Utopia in the Work of Ernst Bloch and the Problem of a Deficiency of Political Theory in Marxism." Unpublished. June 1988.

Ende, Michael. Interview. *Le Monde*, 16 March 1984.

Engels, Friedrich. "The Condition of England. *Past and Present* by Thomas Carlyle, London, 1843." 1844. In Marx and Engels, *Collected Works*. Vol. 3, pp. 444–68.

———. *The Condition of the Working Class in England in 1844*. 1845. In Marx and Engels, *Collected Works*. Vol. 4, pp. 295–596.

———. "Latter-Day *Pamphlets*, edited by Thomas Carlyle." 1850. In Marx and Engels, *Collected Works*. Vol. 10, pp. 301–10.

———. "Letter to Miss Harkness." 1888. In *Marx and Engels on Literature and Art: A Selection of Writings*, edited by Lee Baxandall and Stefan Morawski, pp. 114–16. St. Louis: Telos Press, 1973.

——. Letter 220, to Karl Marx. 1882. In Marx and Engels, *Collected Works*. Vol. 46, pp. 399–401.

——. "The Mark." 1882. In Marx and Engels, *Collected Works*. Vol. 24, pp. 441–56.

——. *The Origin of the Family, Private Property, and the State*. 1884. Edited by Eleanor Burke Leacock. New York: International Publishers, 1972.

——. "Schelling and Revelation." In Marx and Engels, *Collected Works*. 1842. Vol. 2, pp. 189–240.

Evans, David Owen. *Social Romanticism in France, 1830–1848*. Oxford: Clarendon Press, 1951.

Ezergailis, Inta. *Women Writers—The Divided Self*. Bonn: Bouvier, 1982.

Faber, Richard. "Frühromantik, Surrealismus, und Studententrevolte, oder die Frage nach dem Anarchismus." In *Romantische Utopie, Utopische Romantik*, edited by Richard Faber, pp. 336–58. Hildesheim: Gerstenberg, 1979.

Fairchild, Hoxie Neale. "Romantic Religion." 1949. In Gleckner and Enscoe, *Romanticism: Points of View*, pp. 206–18.

Feenberg, Andrew. *Critical Theory of Technology*. New York: Oxford University Press, 1991.

——. "Remembering the May Events." *Theory and Society* 6 (1978): 29–53.

Fehervary, Helen, and Sara Lennox. Introduction to "Self-Experiment," by Christa Wolf, pp. 109–12.

Ferber, Michael. "Romantic Anticapitalism: A Response to Sayre and Löwy." In Rosso and Watkins, *Spirits of Fire*, pp. 69–84.

Fischer, Ernst. *Marx in His Own Words*. London: Penguin, 1970.

——. *The Necessity of Art: A Marxist Approach*. Translated by Anna Bostock. London: Penguin, 1963.

——. *Ursprung und Wesen der Romantik*. Frankfurt: Sendler Verlag, 1986.

Fischer, Jan O. *Epoque romantique et réalisme: Problèmes méthodologiques*. Prague: Univerzita Karlova, 1977.

Fraisse, Simone. "Péguy entre le nouveau classicisme et l'appel romantique." In *Péguy, un romantique malgré lui*, edited by Simone Fraisse, pp. 28–41. Paris: Lettres Modernes, Minard, 1985.

Frank, Manfred. *Der Kommende Gott: Vorlesungen zur Neuen Mythologie*. Frankfurt: Suhrkamp Verlag, 1982.

Frank, Manfred, and Gerhard Kurz, eds. *Materialen zu Schellings philosophische Anfänge*. Frankfurt: Suhrkamp, 1975.

Frye, Northrop. *Anatomy of Criticism*. Princeton: Princeton University Press, 1957.

——. "Towards Defining an Age of Sensibility." In *Eighteenth Century English Literature: Modern Essays in Criticism*, edited by J. L. Clifford, pp. 311–18. New York: Oxford University Press, 1959.

Furst, Lilian R. *Romanticism*. 1969. Reprint, London: Methuen, 1976.

——. ed. *European Romanticism: Self-Definition. An Anthology*. London: Methuen, 1980.

George, Albert Joseph. *The Development of French Romanticism: The Impact of the Industrial Revolution on Literature*. Syracuse: Syracuse University Press, 1955.

Gitlin, Todd. "I Did Not Imagine That I Lived in Truth." *New York Times Book Review*, 4 April 1993.

Gleckner, R. F., and G. E. Enscoe, eds. *Romanticism: Points of View*. Detroit: Wayne State University Press, 1989.

Goeldel, Denis. "Moeller van den Bruck: une stratégie de modernisation du conservatisme ou la modernité de droite." Special issue, *Revue d'Allemagne* 14 (January–March 1982): 127–44.

Goldmann, Lucien. *Cultural Creation in Modern Society*. 1971. Translated by Bart Grahl. St. Louis, Mo.: Telos Press, 1976.

——. *The Hidden God: A Study of Tragic Vision in the* Pensées *of Pascal and the Tragedies of Racine*. 1955. Translated by Philip Thody. New York: Humanities Press, 1964.

——. "La philosophie des Lumières." In *Structures mentales et création culturelle*, pp. 1–133. Paris: Anthropos, 1970.

——. "Le théâtre de Genet: Essai d'étude sociologique." In *Sociologie de la littérature: Recherches récentes et discussions*, 2d ed., pp. 9–34. Brussels: Editions de l'Université de Bruxelles, 1973.

Goldsmith, Oliver. "The Deserted Village." In *The Poems of Thomas Gray, William Collins, Oliver Goldsmith*. Edited by Roger Lonsdale. London: Longmans, 1969.

Gorak, Jan. *The Alien Mind of Raymond Williams*. Columbia: University of Missouri Press, 1988.

Gouldner, Alvin Ward. "Romanticism and Classicism: Deep Structures in Social Science." In *For Sociology: Renewal and Critique of Sociology Today*, pp. 323–66. New York: Basic Books, 1973.

Grimm, Jacob, and Wilhelm Grimm. *Deutsches Wörterbuch von Jacob Grimm und Wilhelm Grimm*. Vol. 8. Leipzig: S. Hirzel, 1893.

Gross, David. "Ernst Bloch, *The Principle of Hope*." *Telos* 75 (spring 1988): 189–98.

Guillemin, Henri. "Enfant de lumière ou fils des ténèbres?" In *Les critiques de notre temps et Péguy*, edited by Simone Fraisse, pp. 107–9. Paris: Garnier Frères, 1973.

Gutierrez, Gustavo. *La force historique des pauvres*. Paris: Cerf, 1986.

Habermas, Jürgen. "Un Schelling marxiste." In *Profils philosophiques et politiques*, pp. 193–216. Paris: Gallimard, 1974.

——. "What Does Socialism Mean Today? The Rectifying Revolution and the Need for New Thinking on the Left." Translated by Ben Morgan. *New Left Review*, no. 183 (1990): 3–21.

Halsted, John B., ed. *Romanticism: Problems of Definition, Explanation, and Evaluation*. Boston: D.C. Heath, 1965.

Hauser, Arnold. *The Social History of Art*. 1953. Translated in collaboration with the author by Stanley Godman, introduction by Jonathan Harris. 4 vols. London: Routledge and Kegan Paul, 1999.

Heinrich, Gerda. *Geschichtsphilosophische Positionen der deutschen Frühromantik*. Berlin: Akademi-Verlag, 1976.

Henkel, Arthur. "Was ist eigentlich romantisch?" In *Festschrift für Richard Alewyn*, edited by Herbert Singer and Benno von Wiese. Cologne: Böhlau-Verlag, 1967.

Henry, Michel. *La barbarie*. Paris: Grasset, 1987.

Herf, Jeffrey. "Reactionary Modernism: Some Ideological Origins of the Primacy of Politics in the Third Reich." *Theory and Society* 10 (1981): 805–32.

———. *Reactionary Modernism: Technology, Culture, and Politics in Weimar and the Third Reich.* Cambridge: Cambridge University Press, 1984.

Herzinger, Richard, and Heinz-Peter Preusser. "Vom Äussersten zum Ersten: DDR-Literatur in der Tradition deutscher Zivilisationskritik." In *Literatur in der DDR: Rückblicke,* edited by Heinz Ludwig Arnold and Frauke Meyer-Gosau, pp. 195–209. Munich: Editions Text and Kritik, 1991.

Hess, Moses. *Die europäische Triarchie.* 1841. In *Ausgewählte Schriften.* Cologne: Melzer Verlag, 1962.

———. *Die heilige Geschichte der Menschheit, von einer Jünger Spinozas.* Stuttgart: Hallbergersche Verlagshandlung, 1837.

———. "Über das Geldwesen." 1845. In *Sozialistische Aufsätze 1841–1847.* Edited by Theodor Zlocisti. Berlin: Welt-Verlag, 1921.

Hewison, Robert, ed. *New Approaches to Ruskin.* London: Routledge and Kegan Paul, 1981.

Histoire de la littérature anglaise. Vol. 2. Paris: Hachette, 1965.

Hobsbawm, Eric J. *The Age of Revolution, 1789–1848.* 1962. Reprint, New York: New American Library, 1964.

Hoffmann, E. T. A. "The Life and Opinions of Kater Murr." In *Selected Writings,* vol. 2.

———. "Little Zaches, surnamed Zinnober." In *Three Märchen of E. T. A. Hoffman.* Translated by Charles E. Passage. Pp. 1–108. Columbia: University of South Carolina Press, 1971.

———. "The Sandman." In *Selected Writings,* vol. 1: 137–67.

———. *Selected Writings of E. T. A. Hoffmann.* Edited and translated by Leonard J. Kent and Elizabeth C. Knight. Chicago: University of Chicago Press, 1969.

Hofstätter, Hans Helmut. *Symbolismus und der Kunst der Jahrhundertwende.* Cologne: M. Du-Mont Schauberg, 1965.

Holz, Hans Heinz, Leo Kofler, and Wolfgang Abendroth. *Conversations with Lukács.* Cambridge: MIT Press, 1975.

Honigsheim, Paul. "Der Max-Weber-Kreis in Heidelberg." *Kölner Vierteljahrshefte für Soziologie* (1926), 5. Jrg.

———. "Romantik und neuromantische Bewegungen." In *Handwörterbuch der Sozialwissenschaften.* Stuttgart: G. Fischer, 1953.

Horace. *The Odes and Episodes.* Translated by C. E. Bennett. Cambridge: Harvard University Press, Loeb Classical Library, 1947.

Horkheimer, Max, and Theodor W. Adorno. *Dialectic of Enlightenment.* Translated by John Cumming. New York: Herder and Herder, 1972.

Hough, Graham. *The Last Romantics.* 1949. Reprint, London: Gerald Duckworth, 1978.

Hulme, T. E. "Romanticism and Classicism" 1924. In Gleckner and Enscoe. *Romanticism: Points of View,* pp. 55–65.

Hülsenberg, Werner. *The German Greens: A Social and Political Profile.* London: Verso, 1988.

Huyssen, Andreas. "Auf den Spuren Ernst Blochs: Nachdenken über Christa Wolf." In *Christa Wolf Materialienbuch,* edited by Klaus Sauer, pp. 81–87. Darmstadt: Luchterhand, 1979.

"Intellectuels est-allemands sur la sellette." *Le monde diplomatique,* April 1993, p. 11.

Jameson, Fredric. "Reification and Utopia in Mass Culture." *Social Text* 1 (winter 1979): 130–48.

Jullian, Philippe. "Le symbolisme." In *Idéalistes et symbolistes: Exposition, 3 octobre–21 décembre 1973*. Paris: Galerie J.-C. Gaubert, 1973.

Kals, Hans. *Die soziale Frage in der Romantik*. Cologne: P. Hanstein, 1974.

Keller, Thomas. "Les Verts et le conservatisme de gauche: Une nouvelle culture politique en République fédérale d'Allemagne." Ph.D. diss., University of Strasbourg, 1988.

Kirk, Russell. *The Conservative Mind*. London: Faber and Faber, 1954.

Klein, Gérard. "Discontent in American Science Fiction." Translated by D. Suvin and Leila Lecorps. *Science Fiction Studies* 11 (March 1977): 3–13.

———. "Le Guin's 'Aberrant' Opus: Escaping the Trap of Discontent." Translated by Richard Astle. *Science Fiction Studies* 13 (November 1977): 287–95.

Kocka, Jürgen. "Bürgertum und Bürgerlichkeit als Probleme der deutschen Geschichte vom späten 18. zum frühen 20. Jahrhundert." In *Bürger und Bürgerlichkeit im 19 Jahrhundert*. Edited by Jürgen Kocka. Göttingen: Vandenhoeck and Ruprecht, 1987.

Konstantinovic, Zoran. "Le conditionnement social des structures littéraires chez les peuples du Sud-Est européen à l'époque du romantisme." *Synthesis: Bulletin du Comité national de littérature comparée de Roumanie* (1974): 131–37.

Krader, Lawrence. *Ethnologie und Anthropologie bei Marx*. Frankfurt: Verlag Ullstein, 1976.

Krauss, Werner. "Franzözische Aufklärung und deutsche Romantik." 1962. In *Romantikforschung seit 1945*, edited by Klaus Peter, pp. 168–79. Königstein im Taunus: Athenaüm, 1981.

Kuhn, Anna K. *Christa Wolf's Utopian Vision: From Marxism to Feminism*. New York: Cambridge University Press, 1988.

Lacoue-Labarthe, Philippe, and Jean-Luc Nancy, eds. *The Literary Absolute: The Theory of Literature in German Romanticism*. 1978. Translated by Philip Barnard and Cheryl Lester. Albany: State University of New York Press, 1988.

Lamennais, Hugues Félicité Robert de. "Le livre du peuple." *Oeuvres complètes*. Paris: Pagnerre, 1844. 10: 139–264.

———. *Paroles d'un croyant*. Edited by Louis Le Guillou. Paris: Flammarion, 1973. Translated under the title *Words of a Believer*. New York: Charles de Behr, 1833.

———. "Politique à l'usage du peuple." *Oeuvres complètes*. Edited by Louis Le Guillou. Geneva: Slatkine Reprints, 1980–81.

Landauer, Gustav. *Beginnen: Aufsätze über Sozialismus*. Westbevern: Verlag Büchse der Pandora, 1977.

———. "Der Bund." 1908–1910. In *Beginnen*, pp. 91–137.

———. *For Socialism*. 1919. Translated by David Parent. St. Louis: Telos Press, 1978.

———. *Die Revolution*. Frankfurt: Rutten and Loening, 1907.

———. "Volk und Land: Dreissig sozialistische Thesen." 1907. In *Beginnen*, pp. 3–20.

Larousse du XXᵉ siècle. Paris: Librairie Larousse, 1933.

Lasserre, Pierre. *Le romantisme français*. Paris: Mercure de France, 1907.

Latouche, Serge. *The Westernization of the World: The Significance, Scope, and Limits of the Drive towards Global Uniformity*. Translated by Rosemary Morris. Cambridge, Mass.: Polity Press, 1996.

Lee, Alan. "Ruskin and Political Economy: Unto This Last." In Hewison, *New Approaches to Ruskin,* pp. 68–88.

Lefebvre, Henri. *Au-delà du structuralisme.* Paris: Anthropos, 1971.

———. *Critique de la vie quotidienne.* 3 vols. Paris: L'Arche, 1981. Translated by John Moore. under the title *Critique of Everyday Life.* London: Verso, 1991.

———. "L'irruption, de Nanterre au sommet." *L'homme et la société* 8 (June 1968): 4–99.

———. *Lukács 1955.* Paris: Aubier, 1986.

———. "Une république pastorale: La vallée de Campan. Organisation, vie et histoire d'une communauté pyrénéenne. Textes et documents accompagnés d'une étude de sociologie historique." Ph.D. diss., University of Paris, n.d.

———. *La somme et le reste.* Vol. 2. Paris: La Nef, 1958.

———. *La Vallée de Campan: Etude de sociologie rurale.* Paris: Presses Universitaires de France, 1963.

———. *Vers le cybernanthrope.* Paris: Denoël-Gonthier, 1971.

Leif, Joseph. *La sociologie de Tönnies.* Paris: Presses Universitaires de France, 1946.

Lenk, Kurt. "Das tragische Bewusstsein in der deutschen Soziologie." *Kölner Zeitschrift für Soziologie und Sozialpsychologie* 16, no. 2 (1964): 257–87.

Leroy, Gaylord C. *Perplexed Prophets: Six Nineteenth-Century British Authors.* Philadelphia: University of Pennsylvania Press, 1953.

Leroy, Géraldi. *Péguy entre l'ordre et la révolution.* Paris: Presses de la Fondation nationale des sciences politiques, 1981.

Love, Myra. "Christa Wolf and Feminism: Breaking the Patriarchal Connection." *New German Critique,* no. 16 (1979): 31–53.

Lovejoy, Arthur O. "The Need to Distinguish Romanticisms." 1924. In Halsted, *Romanticism: Problems of Definition, Explanation, and Evaluation,* pp. 37–44.

Löwy, Michael. *George Lukács — From Romanticism to Bolshevism.* Translated by Patrick Camiller. London: NLB, 1979.

———. "Interview avec Ernst Bloch." In *Pour une sociologie des intellectuels révolutionnaires: L'évolution politique de G. Lukács, 1909–1929,* pp. 292–300. Paris: Presses Universitaires de France, 1976.

———. "Lukács et 'Léon Naphta': L'énigme du *Zauberberg.*" *Etudes germaniques* 41 (July–September 1986): 318–26.

———. *Redemption and Utopia: Jewish Libertarian Thought in Central Europe.* Translated by Hope Heaney. Stanford: Stanford University Press, 1988.

Lukács, György. "Alte Kultur und neue Kultur." 1919. In *Taktik und Ethik,* pp. 136–45.

———. *The Destruction of Reason.* 1953. Translated by Peter Palmer. Atlantic Highlands, N.J.: Humanities Press, 1981.

———. "Dostojewskij." 1943. In *Russische Literatur, russische Revolution,* pp. 136–49. Hamburg: Rohwolt, 1969.

———. *Ecrits de Moscou.* Paris: Editions Sociales, 1974.

———. "Es geht um den Realismus." In *Essays über Realismus,* pp. 128–70. Berlin: Aufbau-Verlag, 1938.

———. "Expressionism: Its Significance and Decline." 1934. In *Essays on Realism.* Edited by

Rodney Livingstone, translated by David Fernbach. Pp. 76–113. Cambridge: MIT Press, 1980.

———. "Der Functionswechsel des Historischen Materialismus." 1919. In *Taktik und Ethik*, pp. 116–22.

———. *Georg Lukacs Werke*. 17 vols. Neuwied: Luchterhand, 1962–.

———. *Geschichte und Klassenbewusstein*. Neuwied: Luchterhand, 1968.

———. *History and Class Consciousness: Studies in Marxist Dialectics*. 1923. Translated by Rodney Livingstone. Cambridge: MIT Press, 1971.

———. "Hölderlin's *Hyperion*." 1934. In *Goethe and His Age*. Translated by Robert Anchor. Pp. 136–56. London: Merlin Press, 1968.

———. "In Search of Bourgeois Man." 1945. In *Essays on Thomas Mann*. Translated by Stanley Mitchell. Pp. 13–46. London: Merlin Press, 1964.

———. *Littérature, philosophie, marxisme, 1922–1923*. Edited by Michael Löwy. Paris: Presses Universitaires de France, 1978.

———. *The Meaning of Contemporary Realism*. Translated by Jon Mander and Necke Mander. London: Merlin Press, 1963.

———. "Mein Weg zu Marx." 1933. In *Schriften zur Ideologie und Politik*. Edited by P. Lutz. Pp. 323 29. Neuwig: Luchterhand, 1967.

———. "Mon chemin vers Marx." *Nouvelles études hongroises* 8 (1973): 80–82.

———. "Nietzsche als Vorläufer der faschistischen Aesthetik." 1934. In *Friedrich Nietzsche*, edited by Franz Mehring and György Lukács. Berlin: Aufbau Verlag, 1957.

———. "Préface à *Littérature hongroise, culture hongroise*." *L'homme et la société* 43–44 (1977): 9–25.

———. "Questions de principe sur une polémique sans principes." In *Ecrits de Moscou*, pp. 155–68.

———. Review of *Heritage of Our Times* by Ernst Bloch. In *Intelletuali e Irrazionalismo*, edited by Vittorio Franco, pp. 287–308. Pisa: ETS, 1984.

———. "Rezensionem 1928. Carl Schmitt: *Politische Romantik*." 1928. In *Geschichte und Klassenbewusstein*, pp. 695–96.

———. *Taktik und Ethik*. Neuwied: Luchterhand, 1975.

———. *The Theory of the Novel: A Historico-Philosophical Essay on the Forms of the Great Epic Literature*. 1916. Translated by Anna Bostock. 1963. Reprint, Cambridge: MIT Press, 1971.

———. "Über das Schlagwort Liberalismus und Marxismus." *Der Rote Aufbau* 21 (1931).

———. "Über den Dostojevski Nachlass." *Moskauer Rundschau*, 22 March 1931.

———. "Die verbannte Poesie." *Internationale Literatur* 5–6 (Moscow) 1942: 86–95.

———. "Vorwort." 1946. *Der russische Realismus in der Weltliteratur*. In *Georg Lukacs Werke*, vol. 5.

———. "Vorwort." 1967. *Geschichte und Klassenbewusstein*, pp. 11–41.

———. *Wie ist die faschistische Philosophie in Deutschland entstanden?* Budapest: Akadémiai Kiado, 1982.

Lund, Hans Peter. "Le romantisme et son histoire." *Romantisme* 7 (1974): 107–16.

Luxemburg, Rosa. *The Accumulation of Capital*. London: Routledge and Kegan Paul, 1951.

——. *Introduction à l'économie politique*. With a preface by Ernst Mandel. Paris: Anthropos, 1970. Originally published as *Einführung in die Nationaloekonomie* (Introduction to economics), in *Ausgewählte Reden und Schriften* (Berlin: Dietz Verlag, 1951). Chapter 1 has been published in English as *What Is Economics?* translated by T. Edwards (New York: Trotsky School, Pioneer Publishers, 1954).

Mannheim, Karl. *Conservatism: A Contribution to the Sociology of Knowledge*. Edited by David Kettler, Volker Meja, and Nico Stehr, translated by David Kettler and Volker Meja. London: Routledge and Kegan Paul, 1986. Originally published as *Konservatismus: Ein Beitrag zur Soziologie des Wissens*, edited by David Kettler, Volker Meja, and Nico Stehr. (Frankfurt: Suhrkamp, 1984).

——. "Das konservative Denken: Soziologische Beiträge zum Werden des politisch-historischen Denkens in Deutschland." 1927. In *Wissensoziologie*. pp. 408–508. Berlin: Luchterhand, 1964.

Marcuse, Herbert. *Counterrevolution and Revolt*. Boston: Beacon Press, 1972.

——. *Eros and Civilization*. New York: Sphere Books, 1969.

——. *One-Dimensional Man*. Boston: Beacon Press, 1964.

——. *Reason and Revolution*. Boston: Beacon Press, 1960.

Maren-Grisebach, Manon. *Philosophie der Grünen*. Munich: G. Olzog 1982.

Martin, Bernice. *A Sociology of Contemporary Cultural Change*. Oxford: Blackwell, 1981.

Martínez Alier, Joan. "Ecologismo marxista y neonarodnismo ecologico." *Mientras Tanto* (Barcelona), 39 (1989): 145–52.

Marx, Karl. *Capital*. In Marx and Engels, *Collected Works*. Vols. 35–37.

——. *Communist Manifesto*. In Marx and Engels, *Collected Works*, 6:477–519.

——. *Early Writings*. Edited by Lucio Colletti. New York: Penguin, 1975.

——. *Economic and Political Writings of 1844*. In Marx and Engels, *Collected Works*. Vol. 3, pp. 229–346.

——. *Economic Manuscripts of 1857–58 (Grundrisse)*. In Marx and Engels, *Collected Works*. Vol. 28.

——. "The English Middle Class." 1854. In Marx and Engels, *Collected Works*. Vol. 13, pp. 663–65.

——. *Excerpthefte* B35AD89a. Unpublished notebook. *Archive Marx-Engels*. Amsterdam, Institute for Social History.

——. "The Future Results of the British Rule in India." 1853. In Marx and Engels, *Collected Works*. Vol. 12, pp. 217–22.

——. *Grundrisse*. Edited and translated by David McLellan. New York: Harper and Row, 1971.

——. *Grundrisse: Foundations of the Critique of Political Economy*. Translated by Martin Nicolaus. New York: Random House, 1973.

——. Letter 44, to Vera Zazulich. 8 March 1881. In Marx and Engels, *Collected Works*. Vol. 46, pp. 71–72.

——. Letter 343, to Friedrich Engels. 25 March 1868. In Marx and Engels, *Collected Works*. Vol. 42, pp. 557–59.

——. Letter to Vera Zazulich (draft). February 1881. In Marx and Engels, *Collected Works*. Vol. 24, pp. 364–69.

Marx, Karl, and Friedrich Engels. *Collected Works*. Translated by Richard Dixon et al. 47 vols. New York: International Publishers, 1975.

——. *Manifesto of the Communist Party*. 1848. In Marx and Engels, *Collected Works*. Vol. 6, pp. 477–519.

——. *Sur la littérature et l'art*. Paris: Editions Sociales, 1954.

——. *Über Kunst und Literatur*. Berlin: Verlag Bruno Henschl, 1948.

Mattelart, Armand. *La culture contre la démocratie, l'audiovisuel à l'heure transnationale*. Paris: La Découverte, 1984.

McGann, Jerome. *The Romantic Ideology*. Chicago: University of Chicago Press, 1983.

McGovern, William. *From Luther to Hitler*. Cambridge, Mass.: Riverside Press, 1941.

Merlio, Gilbert. "L'audience des idées de Spengler sous la république de Weimar." In Raulet, *Weimar ou l'explosion de la modernité*, pp. 63–78.

——. "Spengler ou Le dernier des *Kulturkritiker*." Special issue, *Revue d'Allemagne* 14 (January–March 1982): 97–112.

Meszaros, Istvan. *Marx's Theory of Alienation*. London: Merlin Press, 1970.

Meyer, Hans. *Aussenseiter*. Frankfurt: Suhrkamp, 1975. Translated by Denis M. Sweet under the title *Outsiders: A Study of Life and Letters*. (Cambridge: MIT Press, 1982).

Michelet, Jules. *Le peuple*. Paris: Julliard, 1965.

Milner, Max. *Le Romantisme (1820–1843)*. Paris: Arthaud, 1973.

Morris, William. "How I Became a Socialist." 1894. In *Political Writings of William Morris*. Edited by A. L. Morton. London: Lawrence and Wishart, 1979.

——. *News from Nowhere*. In *Three Works by William Morris*. Edited by A. L. Morton. Pp. 179–401. London: Lawrence and Wishart, 1968.

Münster, Arno. *Messianisme et utopie chez Ernst Bloch*. Paris: Presses Universitaires de France, 1989.

——. *Utopie, Messianismus, und Apokalypse in Frühwerk von Ernst Bloch*. Frankfurt: Suhrkamp, 1982.

——. ed. *Tagträume vom aufrechten Gang: Sechs Interviews mit Ernst Bloch*. Frankfurt: Suhrkamp, 1978.

Murray, J. A. H., ed. *A New English Dictionary on Historical Principles*. Oxford: Clarendon Press, 1914.

Musset, Alfred de. *The Confession of a Child of the Century*. New York: H. Fertig, 1977.

Negt, Oskar. "Ernst Bloch — The German Philosopher of the October Revolution." *New German Critique*, no. 4 (1975): 3–16.

Nerval, Gérard de. *Aurélia*. Translated by Kendall Lappin. Santa Maria, Calif.: Asylum Arts, 1991.

Nodier, Charles. *Smarra, Trilby, et autres contes*. Edited by Jean-Luc Steinmetz. Paris: Garnier-Flammarion, 1980.

"Nous sommes en marche." In "Amnistie des yeux crevés." Censier 453, n.d. Mimeographed flyer.

Novalis. *Hymns to the Night*. Translated by Mabel Cotterell. London: Phoenix Press, 1948.

——. *Werke*. Stuttgart: Hädecke Verlag, 1924.

Oehler, Dolf. *Ein Höllensturz der Alten Welt: Zur Selbsforschung der Moderne nach dem Juni 1848*. Frankfurt: Suhrkamp, 1988. Translated into French by Guy Petitdemange and Sabine

Cornille as *Le spleen contre l'oubli, 1848: Baudelaire, Flaubert, Heine, Herzen.* (Paris: Payot, 1996).

——. *Pariser Bilder 1 (1830–1848)*. Frankfurt: Suhrkamp, 1988.

Palmier, Jean-Michel. *L'expressionnisme comme révolte.* Paris: Payot, 1978.

——. *L'expressionnisme et les arts.* Vol. 1, *Portrait d'une génération.* Paris: Payot, 1979.

Parkin, C. W. "Burke and the Conservative Tradition." In *Political Ideas,* edited by David Thompson, pp. 120–33. New York: Basic Books, 1966.

Paz, Octavio. *Children of the Mire: Modern Poetry from Romanticism to the Avant-Garde.* Translated by Rachel Phillips. Cambridge: Harvard University Press, 1974.

Peckham, Morse. "Reconsiderations." 1961. In Gleckner and Enscoe, *Romanticism: Points of View,* pp. 250–57.

——. "Toward a Theory of Romanticism." 1951. In Gleckner and Enscoe, *Romanticism: Points of View,* pp. 231–57.

Péguy, Charles. "L'argent." 1913. In *Œuvres en prose, 1909–1914,* pp. 1043–1106.

——. "L'argent suite." 1913. In *Œuvres en prose, 1909–1914,* pp. 1107–1255.

——. "Avertissement au Cahier Mangasarian." 1904. In *Œuvres en prose, 1898–1908,* pp. 1354–88.

——. "Clio: Dialogue de l'histoire et de l'âme païenne." 1909–1912. in *Œuvres en prose, 1909–1914,* pp. 91–306.

——. "De Jean Coste." 1902. In *Œuvres en prose, 1898–1908,* pp. 487–536.

——. "De la situation faite à l'histoire et à la sociologie dans les temps modernes." 1906. In *Œuvres en prose, 1898–1908,* pp. 991–1030.

——. "De la situation faite au parti intellectuel dans le monde moderne." 1906. In *Œuvres en prose, 1898–1908,* pp. 1031–78.

——. "De la situation faite au parti intellectuel dans le monde moderne devant les accidents de la gloire temporelle." 1907. In *Œuvres en prose, 1898–1908,* pp. 1115–1214.

——. "Memories of Youth." In *Temporal and Eternal,* translated by Alexander Dru, pp. 19–87. New York: Harper and Brothers, 1958. Originally published as part of *Notre jeunesse.* 1910. (Paris: Gallimard, 1957).

——. "Note conjointe sur M. Descartes et la philosophie cartésienne." 1914. In *Œuvres en prose, 1909–1914,* pp. 1301–1496.

——. "Notes politiques et sociales." 1899. In *Cahiers de l'Amitié Charles Péguy,* pp. 53–86. Paris: L'Amitié Péguy, 1957.

——. "Un nouveau théologien, M. Fernand Laudet." 1911. In *Œuvres en prose, 1909–1914,* pp. 841–1041.

——. *Œuvres en prose, 1898–1908.* Paris: Gallimard, La Pléiade, 1959.

——. *Œuvres en prose, 1909–1914.* Paris: Gallimard, La Pléiade, 1957.

——. *Œuvres en prose complètes.* Edited by Robert Burac. Vol. 2. Paris: Gallimard, La Pléiade, 1988.

——. "Orléans vue de Montargis." 1904. In *Œuvres en prose, 1898–1908,* pp. 665–75.

——. "Les suppliants parallèles." 1905. In *Œuvres en prose, 1898–1908,* pp. 869–935.

——. "Toujours de la grippe." In *Œuvres en prose, 1898–1908,* pp. 172–204.

Peyre, Henri. "Romanticism." *Encyclopaedia Universalis.* Vol. 14. Paris: Encyclopaedia Universalis, 1972.

Pinthus, Kurt. "Before." 1919. In *Menschheitsdämmerung: Dawn of Humanity: A Document of Expressionism.* Translated by Joanna M. Ratych, Ralph Ley, and Robert C. Conard. Pp. 27–37. Columbia, S.C.: Camden House, 1994.

La planète mise à sac. Paris: Le Monde, 1990.

Planté, Christine. *La petite soeur de Balzac: Essai sur la femme auteur.* Paris: Seuil, 1989.

Polanyi, Karl. *La grande transformation: Aux origines politiques et économiques de notre temps.* Introduction Louis Dumont. Paris: Gallimard, 1983.

———. *The Great Transformation.* Boston: Beacon Press, 1957.

Pollin, B. R. "John Thelwall's Marginalia in a Copy of Coleridge's *Biographia Literaria.*" *Bulletin of the New York Public Library* 74 (1970): 73–94.

Poster, Mark. *The Utopian Thought of Restif de la Bretonne.* New York: New York University Press, 1971.

Prang, Helmut, ed. *Begriffsbestimmung der Romantik.* Darmstadt: Wissenschaftliche Buchgesellschaft, 1968.

Rabinbach, Anson. "Ernst Bloch's *Heritage of Our Times* and the Theory of Fascism." *New German Critique,* no. 11 (1977): 5–21.

Rapp, Carl. *William Carlos Williams and Romantic Idealism.* Hanover, N.H.: University Press of New England, 1984.

Raulet, Gérard, ed. *Weimar ou l'explosion de la modernité.* Paris: Anthropos, 1984.

Raynaud, Philippe. *Max Weber et les dilemmes de la raison moderne.* Paris: Presses Universitaires de France, 1987.

Remak, Henry. "West European Romanticism: Definition and Scope." In *Comparative Literature: Method and Perspective,* edited by Newton P. Stallknecht and Horst Frenz, pp. 275–311. Carbondale: Southern Illinois University Press, 1971.

Roe, Nicholas. "Coleridge and John Thelwall: The Road to Nether Stowey." In *The Coleridge Connection,* edited by Richard Gravil and Molly Lefebure, pp. 60–80. New York: St. Martin's Press, 1990.

———. *Wordsworth and Coleridge: The Radical Years.* Oxford: Clarendon Press, 1988.

Rolland, Romain. *Péguy.* Paris: Albin Michel, 1944.

Rose, William. "Heine's Political and Social Attitude." In *Heinrich Heine: Two Studies of His Thought and Feeling,* pp. 1–93. Oxford: Clarendon Press, 1956.

Rosso, G. A., and Daniel P. Watkins, eds. *Spirits of Fire: English Romantic Writers and Contemporary Historical Methods.* Rutherford, N.J.: Fairleigh Dickinson University Press; London: Associated University Presses, 1990.

Rousseau, Jean-Jacques. *Lettres écrites de la montagne.* Neuchâtel: Ides et Calendes, 1962.

Rozanis, Stefanos. *I Romantiki Exergersi* (The Romantic revolt). Athens: Ypsilon, 1987.

Rozenberg, Paul. *Le romantisme anglais: Le défi des vulnérables.* Paris: Larousse, 1973.

Ruskin, John. "Ad Valorem." 1860. In *Unto This Last,* Essay 4. In *The Library Edition of the Works of John Ruskin.* Edited by E. T. Cook and Alexander Wedderburn. Vol. 17, pp. 77–114. London: George Allen, 1905–1912.

———. "The Advent Collect." December 1874. In *Fors Clavigera,* Letter 48. In *Works.* Vol. 28, pp. 202–24.

———. "Athena Keramitis." 1869. In *The Queen of the Air,* Lecture 2. In *Works.* Vol. 19, pp. 351–87.

——. "The Baron's Gate." 7 September 1871. In *Fors Clavigera*, Letter 10. In *Works*. Vol. 27, pp. 165–80.

——. *The Crown of Wild Olives*. 1866. In *Works*. Vol. 18, pp. 367–533.

——. "Charitas." 1 July 1871. In *Fors Clavigera*, Letter 7. In *Works*. Vol. 27, pp. 115–31.

——. "Dictatorship." 1867. In *Time and Tide*. In *Works*. Vol. 17, pp. 370–75.

——. "Fiction, Fair and Foul," 1880. Essay 1. In *Works*. Vol. 34, pp. 265–302.

——. *Fors Clavigera*. 1871. In *Works*. Vol. 27–28.

——. *The Genius of John Ruskin: Selections from his Writings*. Edited by J. D. Rosenberg. London: Routledge and Kegan Paul, 1963.

——. *"A Joy for Ever."* 1857, 1880. In *Works*. Vol. 16, pp. 1–169.

——. *A Joy Forever (And Its Price in the Market)*. Introduction by Charles Eliot Norton. New York: Maynard, Merrill and Co., 1894.

——. "The King of the Golden River." 1841. In *Works*. Vol. 1, pp. 305–48.

——. "Letters on Politics." 1852. In *Works*. Vol. 12, pp. 549–603.

——. *The Library Edition of the Works of John Ruskin*. 39 vols. Edited by E. T. Cook and Alexander Wedderburn. London: George Allen, 1905–1912.

——. *Modern Painters*. 1843–1860. In *Works*. Vols. 3–7.

——. "The Mystery of Life and Its Arts." 1868. In *Sesame and Lilies*, in *Works*. Vol. 5, pp. 145–87.

——. "The Nature of Gothic." 1853. In *The Stones of Venice*, col. 2. In *Works*. Vol. 10, pp. 180–269.

——. "Of Classical Landscape." 1856. In *Modern Painters*, vol. 3. In *Works*. Vol. 5, pp. 221–47.

——. "Of Kings' Treasuries." 1865. In *Sesame and Lilies*, Lecture 1. In *Works*. Vol. 18, pp. 1–67.

——. *The Political Economy of Art*. 1857. See *"A Joy For Ever,"* in *Works*. Vol. 16, pp. 1–169.

——. *The Queen of the Air*. 1869. In *Works*. Vol. 19, pp. 279–423.

——. "Qui Judicatis Terram." 1860. In *Unto This Last*, Essay 3. In *Works*. Vol. 17, pp. 57–76.

——. "The Roots of Honour." 1860. In *Unto This Last*, Essay 1. In *Works*. Vol. 17, pp. 25–42.

——. "Rose-Gardens." 1867. In *Time and Tide*. In *Works*. Vol. 17, pp. 417–22.

——. *Sesame and Lilies*. 1871. In *Works*. Vol. 18, pp. 5–187.

——. *The Stones of Venice*. 1851–1853. In *Works*. Vols. 9–11.

——. "The Storm-Cloud of the Nineteenth Century." 1884. In *Works*. Vol. 34, pp. 1–80.

——. *Time and Tide, by Weare and Tyne*. 1867. In *Works*. Vol. 17, pp. 295–482.

——. "Traffic." 1864. In *The Crown of Wild Olive*, Lecture 2. In *Works*. Vol. 18, pp. 433–58.

——. "The Two Boyhoods." 1860. In *Modern Painters*, vol. 5. In *Works*. Vol. 7, pp. 374–88.

——. *The Two Paths*. 1859. In *Works*. Vol. 16, pp. 241–424.

——. *Unto This Last*. 1860. In *Works*. Vol. 17, pp. 1–114.

——. *Unto this Last and Other Writings*. Edited by Clive Wilmer. London: Penguin, 1985.

——. "Utopie romantique et Révolution française." In "Dissonances dans la Révolution." Special issue, *L'homme et la société* 94, no. 4 (1989): 71–81.

——. "The Veins of Wealth." 1860. In *Unto This Last*, Essay 2. In *Works*. Vol. 17, pp. 43–56.

——. "War." 1865. In *The Crown of Wild Olive*, Lecture 3. In *Works*. Vol. 18, pp. 459–93.

——. "Work." 1865. In *The Crown of Wild Olives*, Lecture 1. In *Works*. Vol. 18, pp. 401–32.

Sayre, Robert. "'Romantisme anticapitaliste' et révolution chez Freneau." *Revue française d'études américaines* 40:175–86.

———. *Solitude in Society: A Sociological Study in French Literature.* Cambridge: Harvard University Press, 1978.

Sayre, Robert, and Michael Löwy. "Figures of Romantic Anti-capitalism," *New German Critique,* no. 32 (1984): 42–92. Also published in English as "Romanticism as a Historical Phenomenon," in Rosso and Watkins, *Spirits of Fire,* pp. 23–69. Original published as "Figures du romantisme anticapitaliste." Parts 1 and 2. *L'homme et la société* 69–70 (July–December 1983): 99–121; 73–74 (July-December 1984): 147–72.

———. "The Fire Is Still Burning: An Answer to Michael Ferber." In Rosso and Watkins, *Spirits of Fire,* pp. 85–91.

Schaeffer, Jean-Marie. *Naissance de la littérature: La théorie esthétique du romantisme allemand.* Paris: Presses de l'Ecole normale supérieure, 1983.

Schelling, Friedrich Wilhelm Joseph von. *Sämmtliche Werke.* Edited by K. F. A. Schelling. Stuttgart: Cotta, 1856–1861.

Schenk, Hans Georg. *The Mind of the European Romantics: An Essay in Cultural History.* New York: Anchor Books, 1969.

Schimank, Uwe. *Neoromantischer Protest im Spätkapitalismus: Der Widerstand gegen die Stadt— und Landschaftveröderung.* Bielefeld: A.J.Z. Druck und Verlag, 1983.

Schlegel, Friedrich. "Athenäum's-Fragmente." In *Kritische Schriften.* Munich: Carl Hanser Verlag, 1964.

———. "Rede über die Mythologie." In *Romantik.* Vol. 1, pp. 233–41. Stuttgart: Reclam, 1984.

Schmitt, Carl. *Political Romanticism.* Translated by Guy Oakes. Cambridge: MIT Press, 1986. Originally published as *Politische Romantik.* 2d ed. Munich: Verlag von Duncker and Humboldt, 1925.

Schwerber, Peter. *Nationalsozialismus und Technik: Die Geistigkeit der nationalsozialistische Bewegung.* Munich: F. Eher, 1930.

Seguy, Jean. "Protestation socio-religieuse et contre-culture," p. 11. Seminar at the Ecole pratique des hautes études, 1973–74. Mimeograph.

Seifert, R. P. *Fortschrittsfeinde? Opposition gegen Technik und Industrie von der Romantik bis zur Gegenwart.* Munich: Beck, 1984.

Serres, Michel. *The Natural Contract.* Translated by Elizabeth MacArthur and William Paulson. Ann Arbor: University of Michigan Press, 1995.

Shaw, George Bernard. "Ruskin's Politics." In *Platform and Pulpit.* Edited by Dan Laurence. Pp. 130–44. New York: Hill and Wang, 1961.

Shelley, Percy Bysshe. *Selected Poetry.* Oxford: Clarendon Press, 1968.

Shrimpton, Nick. "'Rust and Dust': Ruskin's Pivotal Work." In Hewison, *New Approaches to Ruskin,* pp. 51–67.

Simmel, Georg. "Der Begriff und die Tragödie der Kultur." *Logos* 2 (1911–12): 1–25.

———. "Das Individuum und die Freiheit." In *Brücke und Tür,* pp. 266–69. Stuttgart: Kocher Verlag, 1957.

———. *Philosophie de la modernité.* Paris: Payot, 1989.

——. *The Philosophy of Money.* 1900. Translated by Tom Bottomore and David Frisby. London: Routledge and Kegan Paul, 1978.

Sismondi, Jean-Charles Léonard Simonde de. *Etudes sur l'économie politique.* Vol. 1. Paris: Treutell et Wurtz, 1837.

——. *Nouveaux principes de l'économie politique.* 2d ed. Paris: Delaunay, 1827.

"Sleeping with the Enemy: Stasi and the Literati." *Newsweek,* 8 February 1993.

Spear, Jeffrey L. *Dreams of an English Eden: Ruskin and His Tradition in Social Criticism.* New York: Columbia University Press, 1984.

Stern, Fritz. *The Politics of Cultural Despair: A Study in the Rise of the Germanic Ideology.* Berkeley: University of California Press, 1961.

Strich, Fritz. *Deutsch Klassik und Romantik, oder Vollendung und Unendlich; ein Vergleich.* Bern: Francke, 1962.

Tawney, R. H. *Religion and the Rise of Capitalism.* New York: Harcourt, Brace, 1926.

Thompson, E. P. *Customs in Common.* London: Merlin Press, 1991.

——. "Disenchantment or Default? A Lay Sermon." In *Power and Consciousness,* edited by C. C. O'Brien and W. D. Vanech. London: University of London Press, 1969.

——. *The Making of the English Working Class.* New York: Pantheon Books, 1963.

——. *William Morris: Romantic to Revolutionary.* London: Merlin Press; New York: Pantheon Books, 1977.

Tichi, Cecelia. *Shifting Gears: Technology, Literature, Culture in Modernist America.* Chapel Hill: University of North Carolina Press, 1987.

Tiedemann-Bartels, Hella. "La mémoire est toujours de la guerre: Benjamin et Péguy." In *Walter Benjamin et Paris,* edited by Heinz Wismann, pp. 133–43. Paris: Cerf, 1986.

Tönnies, Ferdinand. *Community and Society (Gemeinschaft und Gesellschaft).* Translated and edited by Charles P. Loomis. New York: Harper and Row, 1957.

Totten, Monika. "Zur Aktualität der Romantik in der DDR: Christa Wolf und ihre Vorläufer(innen)." *Zeitschrift für Deutsche Philologie* 101, no. 2 (1982): 244–62.

Touraine, Alain. *The May Movement: Revolt and Reform.* 1968. Translated by Leonard F. X. Mayhew. New York: Random House, 1971.

Träger, Claus. "Des Lumières à 1830: Héritage et innovation dans le romantisme allemand." *Romantisme* 28–29 (1980): 87–102.

Traub, Rainer, and Harald Wieser. *Gespräche mit Ernst Bloch.* Frankfurt: Suhrkamp, 1975.

Tumarkin, A. *Die romantische Weltanschauung.* Bern: Paul Haupt, 1920.

Vaneigem, Raoul. *Adresse aux vivants sur la mort qui les gouverne et l'opportunité de s'en défaire.* Paris: Seghers, 1990.

Van Tieghem, Paul. *Le préromantisme.* 2 vols. Paris: Rieder-Alcan, 1924–1930.

——. *Le romantisme dans la littérature européenne.* 1948. Reprint, Paris: Albin Michel, 1969.

Viatte, Auguste. *Les sources occultes du romantisme: Illuminisme-théosophie.* Vol. 1, *Le préromantisme (1770–1820).* 1927. Reprint, Paris: Champion, 1979.

Viereck, Peter. *Metapolitics: From the Romantics to Hitler.* New York: Alfred A. Knopf, 1941.

Webb, Timothy, ed. *English Romantic Hellenism, 1700–1824.* Totowa, N.J.: Barnes and Noble, 1982.

Weber, Max. *From Max Weber: Essays in Sociology.* Edited by Hans H. Gerthe and C. Wright Mills. Oxford: Oxford University Press; New York: Galaxy, 1958.

———. *Gesammelte Aufsätze zur Wissenschaftslehre.* Tübingen: Mohr, 1922.

———. "Science as a Vocation." Translated by Hans H. Gerth and C. Wright Mills. In *Sociological Writings,* edited by Wolf Heydebrand, pp. 276–303. New York: Continuum, 1994.

Weiss, Johannes. "Wiederverzauberung der Welt? Bemerkungen zur Wiederkehr der Romantik in der gegenwärtigen Kulturkritik." *Kölner Zeitschrift für Soziologie und Sozialpsychologie,* Sonderheft 27. pp. 286–301. Opladen: Westdeutscher Verlag, 1986.

Wellek, René. "The Concept of Romanticism in Literary History." 1949. In Gleckner and Enscoe, *Romanticism: Points of View,* pp. 286–301.

Wessell, L. P., Jr. *Karl Marx, Romantic Irony, and the Proletariat: The Mythopoetic Origins of Marxism.* Baton Rouge: Louisiana State University Press, 1979.

Williams, Raymond. *The Country and the City.* New York: Oxford University Press, 1973.

———. *Culture and Society, 1780–1950.* New York: Harper and Row, 1958.

———. *Keywords: A Vocabulary of Culture and Society.* New York: Oxford University Press, 1976.

———. *Politics and Letters: Interviews with "New Left Review."* London: NLB and Verso, 1979.

———. *Resources of Hope: Culture, Democracy, Socialism.* Edited by Robin Gable. London: Verso, 1989.

———. *Towards 2000.* London: Chatto and Windus, 1983.

———. "The Uses of Cultural Theory." *New Left Review,* no. 158 (1986): 19–31.

———. "What Is Anticapitalism?" Review of *Georg Lukács — From Romanticism to Bolshevism,* by Michael Löwy. *New Society,* 24 January 1980, 189–90.

Wolf, Christa. *Accident: A Day's News.* Translated by Heike Schwarzbauer. London: Virago, 1989.

———. *Ansprachen.* Darmstadt: Luchterhand, 1988.

———. *The Author's Dimension: Selected Essays.* Translated by Jan van Heurck. New York: Farrar, Straus and Giroux, 1993.

———. *Cassandra: A Novel and Four Essays.* Translated by Jan Van Heurck. New York: Noonday, 1984.

———. *Divided Heaven.* Translated by Joan Becker. Berlin: Seven Seas Books, 1965. Reprint, with an introduction by Jack Zipes, New York: Adler's Foreign Books, 1976.

———. *The Fourth Dimension: Interviews with Christa Wolf.* London: Verso, 1988.

———. "A June Afternoon." In *What Remains and Other Stories,* pp. 43–65.

———. *Kein Ort: Nirgends.* Neuwied: Luchterhand, 1981.

———. *Moskauer Novelle.* Halle: Mitteldeutscher, 1961.

———. "On That Date." 1971. In *The Author's Dimension,* pp. 258–63.

———. "The New Life and Opinions of a Tomcat" (1981). In Wolf, *What Remains and Other Stories,* pp. 121–51.

———. "Reading and Writing." 1973. In *The Author's Dimension,* pp. 20–57.

———. *The Quest for Christa T.* Translated by Christopher Middleton. London: Virago, 1988.

———. "Der Schatten eines Traumes" (The shadow of a dream). In Karoline von Günderrode, *Der Schatten eines Traumes: Gedichte, Prosa, Briefe, Zeugnisse von Zeitgenossen,* edited by Christa Wolf, pp. 5–52. Darmstadt: Luchterhand, 1981.

———. "Self-Experiment: Appendix to a Report." Translated by Jeanetts Clausen. *New German Critique,* no. 13 (1978): 113–31.

———. "The Shadow of a Dream: A Sketch of Karoline von Günderrode," 1979. In *The Author's Dimension,* pp. 131–75.

———. *Sommerstück.* Frankfurt: Luchterhand, 1989.

———. "The Travel Report Continues, and the Trail is Followed." In *Cassandra,* pp. 182–224.

———. "Tuesday, September 27." In *What Remains and Other Stories,* pp. 23–39.

———. *What Remains and Other Stories.* Translated by Heike Schwarzbauer and Rick Takvorian. London: Virago, 1993.

———. "Your Next Life Begins Today: A Letter about Bettine." 1980. In *The Author's Dimension,* pp. 187–216.

Wunenburger, Jean-Jacques. *La raison contradictoire: Sciences et philosophie modernes.* Paris: Albin Michel, 1990.

Zipes, Jack. *Breaking the Magic Spell: Radical Theories of Folk and Fairy Tales.* Austin: University of Texas Press, 1979.

———. Introduction to *Divided Hearts,* by Christa Wolf. New York: Adler's Foreign Books, 1976.

———. Review of *The Marxist Philosophy of Ernst Bloch,* by Wayne Hudson. *Telos* 58 (winter 1983–84): 227–31.

Index

312

Michael Löwy is Research Director in Sociology at the
National Center for Scientific Research (France). He is the
author of *On Changing the World: Essays in Political
Philosophy, from Karl Marx to Walter Benjamin* (Humanities
Press, 1993); *Redemption and Utopia: Libertarian Judaism in
Central Europe* (Stanford University Press, 1992); *Georg
Lukács: From Romanticism to Bolshevism* (Verso, 1981).

Robert Sayre is Professor of English at the University of
Marne-la-Vallée (France). He is the author of *Solitude in
Society: A Sociological Study in French Literature* (Harvard
University Press, 1978).

Michael Löwy and Robert Sayre jointly edited
*L'insurrection des 'Misérables': Romantisme et révolution en juin
1832* (Minard, 1992), and jointly authored *Révolte et
mélancolie: Le romantisme à contre-courant de la modernité*
(Payot, 1992). This book is a translation of the latter.

Catherine Porter is Professor of French and Chair of the
Department of International Communications and Culture
at the State University of New York, College at Cortland.
Her recent translations include Denis Holier, *Absent without
Leave: French Literature under the Threat of War* (Harvard,
1997); Sarah Kofman, *Socrates: Fictions of a Philosopher*
(Athlone, 1998); Marcel Gauchet and Gladys Swain,
*Madness and Democracy: The Invention of Psychiatric Asylums
in Modern France* (Princeton, 1998); and Louis Marin,
Sublime Poussin (Stanford, 1999). She also directed the
translation of *Greek Thought,* edited by Jacques Brunschwig
and Geoffrey Lloyd (Harvard, 2000).

Library of Congress Cataloging-in-Publication Data
Löwy, Michael
[Révolte et mélancolie. English]
Romanticism against the tide of modernity / Michael Löwy
and Robert Sayre ; translated by Catherine Porter.
p. cm. — (Post-contemporary interventions)
Includes bibliographical references and index.
ISBN 0-8223-2784-8 (alk. paper)
ISBN 0-8223-2794-5 (pbk. : alk. paper)
1. Romanticism — History. I. Sayre, Robert.
II. Title. III. Series.
PN603 .L6813 2001   809'.9145 — dc21   2001037691